1980

W9-CLF-848

GOODBYE

GUTENBERG

GOODBYE
GUTENBERG

The Newspaper Revolution
of the 1980's

Anthony Smith

New York   Oxford
Oxford University Press
1980

Smith, Anthony, 1938-
   Goodbye, Gutenberg.

   Includes bibliographical references and index.
   1.   Newspapers—History.   2.   Communication—
History.   I.   Title.
PN4801.S535   070   79-24263
ISBN 0-19-502709-4
UK ISBN 0-19-215953-4

FOR ROAR

CONTENTS

ACKNOWLEDGEMENTS

I wish to thank Robert Gerald Livingston, President of the German Marshall Fund of the United States, and the Trustees of the Fund for their kindness to me during the two years since this project was born. They have been generous both in funds and in encouragement. I must also thank the previous President of the GMF, Benjamin Read, who originally took up with me the idea of preparing a study of the condition of the newspaper. The entire Washington staff of the GMF have at various times offered friendly help and advice.

I wish also to thank the International Institute of Communication in London for its work on the administrative side of the project. Edward Ploman, Robert Tritt, Joanna Spicer, and John Howkins have all made specific contributions, and Jack Rich and Gerry Jayasuriya have most patiently and efficiently kept the housekeeping side of the project in order. Yvonne Richards provided a splendid manuscript in record time. I wish to thank Pauline Wingate of the Acton Society Press Group in London for her considerable research help and Rex Winsbury of the Financial Times for reading and commenting upon the first draft. The Aspen Institute in Washington kindly allowed me use of its office space and offered a friendly ambiance in which to work for several weeks, and for this my thanks are due to Douglass Cater and Marc Porat.

Thanks are especially due to Sheldon Meyer, Senior Vice President of Oxford University Press, to Susan Rabiner, the editor of this book, and to Shelley Reinhardt, her assistant; they have been an excellent team, always prompt, imaginative, and solicitous.

During the two years of the project, which includes a parallel volume of international studies to be published by the MIT Press, I have visited over a dozen countries and taken up the time of several hundred busy newspaper editors, publishers, executives, engineers, academics, and journalists. It is impossible to thank them all severally, since a mere thicket of names would do little to convey the quality and depth of my gratitude, and a detailed account of their hospitality and helpfulness would add many pages to this volume.

PREFACE

Most books about the newspaper industry—of which there is never a shortage—deal with personalities, money and power. There is nothing wrong with that. However, the newspaper is passing through an era of rapid and accelerating change from one technology to another, and the forces which are generating this transformation are traceable to social trends and technological opportunities far more than to the whims and energies of individuals. This book looks at the newspaper, mainly in America, in the context of its altering circumstances and shows how electronics has been summoned to resolve the internal tensions and crises which face the medium today. The social function of the newspaper is changing, as is the whole culture of journalism and the concept of daily disseminated printed information. For the new electronics offers something quite different from a new production method—it provides for a series of changes in all of the relationships of which the industry is composed. It alters the demarcations between craftsman and organizer, between investor and regulator, between professional and production worker.

Electronic technology is bringing about similar transitions in a large series of human activities, from agriculture to xerography. The newspaper happens to be one crucial information industry which has made substantial progress towards the new era and where some of the kinds of impact, common to many industries undergoing change at the present time, are already clearly visible. What one can see in the newspaper is a microcosm of a new social information system, in which computers help information to be stored and circulated in ways profoundly different from those which have been employed since the Renaissance, when printing first established itself in Western societies. That is why it has been necessary, in a book primarily about the newspaper, to show the parallels between the present transformation in printing methods to certain earlier transformations in human communication systems, in particular to the advent of writing and of printing. The computerization of print is truly a third revolution in communications of similar scale and importance, in that it raises comparably fundamental issues—concerning the social control of information, the nature of the individual creative function, the ways in which information interacts with human memory. In the newspaper one can see certain of the key problems being worked out at the present time as computerization advances: one can see the evolution of the newspaper 'morgue' into an electronic information system, the evolution of the journalist into an information technician.

The computer came in to rescue the newspaper at the end of the 1960s when demographic changes within the newspaper audience had started to undermine the financial nexus through which the medium worked. A naturally competitive industry, founded in the market of the 19th and 20th century city, turned into a naturally monopolistic medium based upon the late 20th century megalopolis. The newspaper, in the course of this changeover (which itself entailed a complete financial and dynastic restructuring of the industry) began to acquire too high a quantity of text for existing technology to cope with. Industrial relations problems, rising newsprint costs, escalating distribution costs all took their toll and computerization—like a deus ex machina—represented an important part of the answer to the newspaper's mounting problems. The computer reduced the setting costs but at the same time introduced the possibility of a further series of changes (which is far from complete) which would, in the long run, change the whole nature of the medium. Thus it was also in the early days of printing, when the Gutenbergian principle was introduced to reduce the labor of copying text but stayed to change the nature of text itself and its role in society.

The computerization of typesetting is, of course, only one aspect of the current transformation of the information industries. Changes are occurring within *all* of the information media—aural, verbal and visual—and it is in the interaction of these that the real revolution will occur. This book tries to set out for a general reader the broad outlines of the next wave of techniques which the semi-conductor industry is now pioneering which may result in completely new relationships between man and knowledge and an emphasis on quite different intellectual skills from those which have seemed to be the key qualities necessary in an age of mechanical industry. That is why I suggest that the information revolution of the 1980s and 1990s offers us a step towards a new kind of Alexandria, i.e., towards an abundance of information of universal availability, but one in which the constraints arise from the modes of storage and cataloguing, rather than from the more traditional constraints of censorship and governmental control. In other words, the librarian or the librarian's computerized successor becomes a more crucial guardian of knowledge than in the past, and the individual researcher/writer is more dependent upon the skill of searching for information than upon the skills of composition. At least, this is one of the main questions which I hope my readers will ponder.

I
THE THIRD REVOLUTION
IN COMMUNICATION

INTRODUCTION

In this era of technological change, the term revolution is often applied with indecent haste to mere innovation. To speak of the computerization of printing as a revolution, therefore, demands justification.

The two previous transformations in human techniques for storing information—writing and printing—promoted a complex transformation of institutions such as education, government, commerce, religion. Each new technique for manipulating knowledge through the use of text also involved changing the prevailing priorities among intellectual capabilities: writing is an artificial extension of memory, but libraries and filing systems are, in a sense, replacements for memory and depend upon mental tracking systems acquired by training. Today the computer, which was developed originally as a device for calculating, has now become a device for handling text in many forms, and this interconnection between computer and text is coming to exercise so transforming an influence upon the human institutions that adapt to it that one may justifiably consider whether a *third* great turning point in information systems has come about.

The computerization of text implies a further set of changes in mental qualities, in the ways in which we train our memories and process the raw material of knowledge. In this book the newspaper industry—because it is one of the first text industries to undergo computerization—is used to exemplify and emphasize the kinds of change associated with the new text techniques. To identify them one has to look into the whole condition of the industry and examine the problems that the computer has been used to solve.

It is easy when looking back at the affairs of the ancient world or of the Renaissance to see the techniques of writing and printing as autonomous phenomena "causing"—as if by their own free will—a series of discrete social effects. But technology is not an autonomous determinant of change. Rather, it is a convenient demarcator of change for the observer attempting to analyze a mass of interconnected events. Thus, in examining the introduction of writing and then printing to earlier societies, it is valuable to move in, as it were, from great heights to see what verdicts were being passed, what changes seemed to be occurring, when the effects of these two previous transformations in communications made themselves felt.

The earliest writing consisted of pictograms, and the skill required to draw them was limited to a small scribal or priestly caste. With the invention of the Phoenician alphabets, quickly copied and adapted by many other societies, writing skills were acquired by nonspecialists. Alphabets, which are not based upon direct connections between sound and sign, are less subtle than pictograms but demonstrably easier to learn. Their coming meant that writing could become a universal and flexible tool of government and business. When papyrus replaced clay, it was possible to form rounded as well as straight-sided letters, and a greater variety of written symbols came into use. Papyrus provided a more suitable storage system than clay or stone because it could be collected and held in a relatively small space, thereby allowing for the categorization of information and the creation of libraries.

With libraries, the process of research through scholarship began in earnest. In the ancient world the great collections of material were very few in number. There was one belonging to Eumenes II, King of Pergamum (in Asia Minor), whose 200,000 volumes were ransacked by Antony and handed over to Cleopatra. Eumenes had developed the art of making vellum, or parchment, when Ptolemy II, the possessor of the rival library at Alexandria, forbade the export of papyrus. Alexandria's collection, together with its subsidiary collection at the temple at Serapeum, was the greatest and most famous in the world. Ptolemy I Soter (305–283 B.C.) had founded it under the inspiration of the Athenian orator Demetrius of Phalerum, and Ptolemy II Philadelphus had had it greatly enlarged. It was the center of the book trade of the ancient world and the first library to develop a cataloging system, which was invented by its librarian, the poet Callimachus. Estimates vary as to the size of the library at Alexandria, ranging from Seneca's guess of 400,000 volumes to Aulus Gellius's of 700,000. In it Eratosthenes, its third librarian, drew up a catalog of the fixed stars and measured the size of the earth to within one percent accuracy. Under his successors Apollonius and Aristophanes it developed into an institution resembling to some extent a university of modern times. It was a place in which knowledge was scanned, absorbed, analyzed, and enhanced.

The destruction of Alexandria entailed the destruction of an irreplaceable treasure felt to belong to the whole world. Symbolically its disappearance left a chasm in man's intellectual sphere; a totality of knowledge had been lost. Thereafter, until the coming of printing, knowledge was perceived to consist of the attempted retrieval, through the close study of worn manuscripts scattered around the world, of that which had been destroyed. Knowledge was thought of as something that had formerly existed. Chronos, the god of time, was the enemy of knowledge, since he continued to destroy the very physical substances—paper, parchment, and papyrus—on which its preservation depended. Human memory, flexible and transportable as it is, was a short-term storage system.

In the Augustan era there was a public library in Rome. By the second century A.D. it had become the fashion for wealthy Romans like Lucullus to keep their own private collections of important works. A thousand years later, however, the libraries of Europe were rare and smaller. Five hundred volumes represented an important holding. A thousand was an exception. The books would be chained to their cases and attached to a reading desk. One of the main functions of the monastic institutions of the Middle Ages was to preserve manuscripts and produce good copies, cleaned of the errors made by weary copyists of the past. These were the exemplars from which later editions would be struck. The Benedictines were particularly conscientious, and their libraries at Monte Cassino, Canterbury, Luxeuil, Wearmouth, and Jarrow bore witness to their sense of obligation towards the task of reamassing the lost treasuries of ancient knowledge. With the arrival in Europe of paper as a generally available commodity in the thirteenth century, students would make copies of important or favorite works as a matter of course. Petrarch, for instance, is known to have kept one hundred manuscripts, which he copied out himself from monastic exemplars.

The coming of writing—by changing the relationship between the two ends of a communication and thereby creating audiences remote in time and space from the speaker—brought about the situation in which knowledge was being transmitted to segments of the society that had not been trained to evaluate and assimilate abstract concepts. Formerly, as

Socrates noted, in describing a preliterate civilization, when communication had been immediate and oral, the dialectician could carefully choose "a soul of the right type" to be planted with the seeds of his wisdom, while the remainder of civilization seemed to have been content "in their simplicity to listen to trees or rocks, provided these told the truth." "Once a thing is put in writing," he mourned, "the composition, whatever it may be, drifts all over the place, getting into the hands not only of those who understand it, but equally of those who have no business with it."[1]

Socrates also made note of the inroads writing had made into the function of human memory. Writing, as printing would later in different ways, created external systems of storage that gradually replaced the mnemotechnics of past civilizations. "The ancient memories were trained by an art which reflected the art and architecture of the ancient world, which could depend on faculties of intense visual memorisation which we have lost,"[2] writes Frances Yates. The ancients impressed "places" and "images" on the mind within which large quantities of information could be indelibly embedded. An examination of the implications of the progressive externalization of information storage through the passage of centuries is extremely important (and will be one of the main themes of this book), for it is a process that has by no means reached its logical limits.

Socrates told his students the story of Thamus, King of Egypt, to whom the god Theuth brought the art of writing (as well as numbers, astronomy, geometry, and the games of draughts and dice). "It is no true wisdom that you offer," said Thamus. ". . . If men learn this, it will implant forgetfulness in their souls; they will cease to exercise memory because they rely on that which is written, calling things to remembrance no longer from within themselves, but by means of external marks."[3] Writing created an external form of information storage, one that distorted the kind of knowledge that formerly could pass only from one tutored mind and memory to another carefully chosen mind. Socrates saw clearly that an important transformation had been wrought not only in the realm of knowledge but also in the whole field of force within which information travels in human society. "For you apparently it makes a difference who the speaker is, and what country he comes from; you don't merely ask whether what he says is true or false. . . ." When the speaker was no longer necessarily in face-to-face contact with listeners, information seemed to exercise an authority of its own and move about spontaneously. After being stored in written form, information could now reach a new kind of audience, remote from the source and uncontrolled by it. Writing transformed knowledge into information.

Likewise, the identity of the communicator was extended by writing. He was obliged to consider himself in relation to a wider range of possible interlocutors. His identity was spread in both time and space, making him an object of thought and imagination in the minds of people out of touch with him or his society. Writing, as Harold Innis pointed out, made individuals apply themselves to ideas rather than things, creating a dualism that required constant reconciliation between objects and thought about objects.[4] The existence of written records enlarged the possibilities of influence and control of social and family systems, enabling larger blocks of humanity to be held together, especially when the sword joined the pen and contributed to the concentration of social power. In Egypt Theuth became the god of magic, "Lord of the creative voice, master of words and books." The scribes who inherited his art became masters of all manner of privilege: "Put writing in your heart that you may protect yourself from hard labor. . . . The scribe is released from manual tasks."[5] The craft of writing was, if not the cause, then the defining instrument of social and psychical transformation in all the societies that it reached.

II

This first revolution in the means of communicating information, therefore, can be seen as having marked a series of fundamental changes in human organization and in conceptions of social order. It also seems to have created several important new divisions of labor, or, rather, given a tangible basis to the evolution of new cliques, classes, and professions in society.

When we turn to printing, which gradually came into widespread use in the fifteenth century, we have the spectacle of another comparable set of alterations. For many centuries the monastic institutions had undertaken, almost exclusively, the business of manuscript copying. They were largely concerned with winning a race against time—to replicate copies of ancient texts faster than the ravages of time wore out existing versions. At the same time, the painful and complicated work of comparing ancient manuscripts stored across a vast landmass had to continue, in the hope of producing better exemplars.[6] As the Renaissance flowered and universities spread, the manuscript-copying institutions, the scriptoria, were unable to meet the increased demand for acceptable texts that had resulted from the development of an educated laity. Printing in Europe developed directly from this unfulfilled requirement for text in scribal society.

Printing evolved from a series of divisions of labor that had been introduced in an effort to speed up the task of manuscript copying. Woodcutting made it possible to reproduce pictures more rapidly than had been possible by hand. Specialist rubricators cut the large flowery capital letters. Illuminists made multiple copies of pictures within a text according to the marginal notes of instruction written by the scribe. The breaking down of text into single letters, each of which could be separately stamped, was a further stage in a natural evolution that consisted of separating out the multitude of tasks entailed in the reproduction of a book; the process began with the preparation of skins, pens, brushes, inks, and ended with the binding and lettering of the covers of the book. The thirteenth and fourteenth centuries saw the progressive refinement and specialization of such tasks. Within the increasingly complicated business of book production, however, the dominant function remained with the holder of the perfect copy, the exemplar, which was the only guarantee of authenticity. It was the institution that employed the copyists and that held a stock of precious exemplars that was the key to the legitimacy of publishing.[7] Printing was at first a backward-looking activity. As a sixteenth-century writer put it: "The invention has greatly aided the advancement of all disciplines. For it seems miraculously to have been discovered in order to bring back to life more easily literature which seemed dead."[8]

The development of "moving letters" as a technology for reproducing information more quickly than was possible under the scribal system depended upon a reasonably large market for its effectiveness. If only ten copies were needed of a given text, then hand copying was probably still much cheaper than a mechanical means of reproduction. But when a hundred or more copies of a given work would be sold—and this depended, in order to locate the potential buyers, upon the existence of a transcontinental book market—it became necessary to invent a new technology for the book production business. With this new system, drawn from metallurgy and already practised by goldsmiths and die stampers, individual letters could be cast in metal and used repeatedly within different arrangements to produce lines and pages of text.

By 1470 the cost of a French printed Bible dropped to one fifth that of a manuscript Bible, but the former was an exact replica of the latter, and great care was taken to ensure that the print letters and ligatures were the same in appearance as manuscript letters and ligatures. Large quantities of letters had to be cast to be put together in the correct combinations to complete a whole work. Small industrial enterprises quickly sprang into existence and acquired their own standards and working practices. In the East, however, there was an interesting contrast, for with languages that necessitated tens of thousands of different signs, printing establishments required a capital and organization so large that only governments had adequate resources. So printing became an ideal industry not only for small-scale private enterprise in Europe but for direct governmental control in the East.

As we have seen, the impetus for printing was the more rapid reproduction of preexisting knowledge, but the technology also made possible a new set of functions. It shifted control of the text away from the keeper of the original and over to the author. Even though authorship, then as now, consisted largely of the assemblage of older pieces of information in a new order to argue a point or reveal a new train of thought, it was the author who began to acquire the *credit*, rather than the collator of the texts from which his knowledge was drawn. New forms of scholarship arose from the traditional task of collation, but they involved the creation of new works rather than the correction of old ones. The guardianship of exemplars—for which we might use the label librarianship—ceased to be the source of informational power, since authority over a text had passed to the new eponymous or "personal" author. With the evolution of authorship came the shifting of the field of social forces within which information was held.[9]

Within a short time printing, i.e., publishing information, was seen as impinging upon the prerogative of Church and State to control what people should know. Printing and government were seen to have overlapping functions, and the problem of how to grant each the purview it needed turned into the interminable conundrum, never resolved, of what forms of censorship were permissible and necessary within given societies. Printing spread knowledge and inspired new thought. Knowledge came to be perceived as being subject to a permanent process of augmentation rather than recovery. Where originality had been considered a danger in medieval society, it now became a need. The idea of authorship paralleled the idea of invention and therefore of research. The scientist, the technologist, the writer, were all adding and accumulating knowledge as a result of individual diligence or genius. This was a major cultural change. The flexibilities that followed from printing were more important than its mere technique. Printing altered the perception of, even the nature of, knowledge.

Printing also created a wholly new form of storage. The book form itself had been an important device for dividing up a text in such a way as to enable the reader to return easily to a given piece of information, to find his way through a train of thought. The Chinese had used "books" that were collections of sheets held together by a single pin through the middle. These were much easier to construct than the book of Western societies but more difficult to store and to refer back to. Only well after the establishment of printing late in the fifteenth century were books stored upright, the front of one touching the back of another, and this simple habit—the result of the growth of large collections of printed books—was the basis of the organization of the new libraries of the Renaissance. The upright book and the library were thus new forms of information storage, and one of their main contributions was the reduction of travel that was previously necessary to anyone who wanted access to information in any quantity. The library with its catalogs was itself a learning system. Printing made it possible for the whole body of classical work to be held simultaneously in many centers. It solved the problems of a millennium but set off a chain reaction of fresh problems and issues in the fields of administration, social control, and education.[10]

After the development of printing, to be well-informed, one would have to spend some hours a day in silence, reading. As a child one would have to be segregated from the normal processes of society for several years in order to be equipped with the necessary apparatus to receive the ever increasing wealth of knowledge—that is to say, with an ability to understand Latin and possibly Greek, as well as one or more vernacular tongues.[11] Printing, like writing, invaded every part of life, and was invoked by every sector of society to resolve its problems. Only temporarily were governments able to prevent the incursions of printing into larger and larger areas. Effective systems of censorship were costly if effective, and the overefficient control of printing, as the Austro-Hungarian Empire came to realize, was a crude weapon that could cut a society off from all the intellectual currents of its time and reduce it to a state of impotence. For several centuries most societies in Europe developed a kind of semicensorship, by which a printing privilege, sometimes covering carefully specified forms of content, was handed out to a guild or to trusted masterprinters, whose productions were thereafter supervised by Church and State authorities.[12] Only the officials of the Church had the necessary skills to determine whether a given work contravened the permitted range of doctrine, but it was the civil authorities who had the ability to search, confiscate, destroy, prosecute. It was against this type of "licensing" that Milton in the seventeenth century penned his *Areopagitica*, which became the great text of the nineteenth century in its fight against later forms of governmental censorship. Licensing was different in its whole scope and "feel" from more modern forms of censorship. It was in essence organized as an enabling mechanism for intervention, rather than an instrument of prevention. It consisted of a series of privileges that could be revoked, rather than a constant interference with text.[13] Printing came into being in a world that was concerned with preventing false doctrines from gaining too wide a credence, rather than one that was concerned with suppressing facts. Indeed, without an institutionalized system for the constant collection of facts, it was impossible to separate the transmission of doctrines and ideas from that of information.

The medieval monasteries and universities of Europe were concerned with the preservation and study of received wisdom, rather than with the seeking out of new knowledge. There was hardly sufficient copying time or material to do much more than preserve the texts they already had. Even if new thought had been welcome, which it was not, it would have been hard to transmit it in any way but orally to small, immediate audiences because of the time and skill needed to create each new book.

After the invention of printing, Europe began to enjoy not only the relative abundance of copies of the old texts, which could now be gathered together, compared, and evaluated, but also the new texts, which could inspire new developments in thought, which in turn demanded fresh information. Institutionalized systems for the perpetual collection of facts now emerged. One of these was the newspaper, the most versatile offspring of the printing press, which has the most varied and numerous relationships throughout society.

A newspaper is an institution for the collection, storage, and dissemination of all kinds of information from hundreds of different microsystems that exist within its sphere. It is, as it were, a library of human activity. More than that, it acts as an information broker to its society, the additional role arising from its ability to sell its primary public to others with commercial messages to send out. These two roles are inextricably entwined. The ways in which the content of a paper is coded for the reader—as news, as comment, or as advertisement—result from the canons (and ethics) of editorial policy. There can be no absolute distinction. In one society the announcement that a ship is arriving or departing is news; in another it is read as an advertisement. The fact that a large corporation is seeking a new top executive is news, whereas its search for a dozen lathe operators would be the subject of a paid advertisement.

In the course of history many kinds of news have turned into advertising, and vice versa. For example, the London newspaper of the eighteenth century would pay theaters for the right to print information concerning the performances, the names of the author, actors, and director. For its part, the theater would pay the newspaper for the right to print comments on the quality of the production (these were the "puffs" that came to earn ridicule and eventually contempt). It was the critic Leigh Hunt, who worked for the *Times* during the editorship of Thomas Barnes, who reversed the system, receiving payment for advertising the performance, but paying independent critics to review the production. James Perry of the *Morning Chronicle* had already begun the new tradition and had written to the manager of one of the main theaters of the town declining to accept puffs any longer and suggesting that the two of them in future pay for admission to each other's premises. With the growth of the number of theaters and the size of the potential theater public, a completely new form of market in theatrical information was required, together with a specialist group of independent, critical judges to maintain an essential brokerage between theater and client. It was the newspaper that took this new function aboard, as it did dozens of similar functions in the field of politics and culture. The two sections of the newspaper—information and advertising—came to occupy equally important roles, separated through tradition and a gradually clarifying ethic. The process of accumulating roles, as we shall see, is far from complete.

Every new section of the society that the newspaper wishes to recruit into its clientele will be brought in generally as a result of the new brokerage function of the newspaper. The newspaper has grown physically in size as it has acquired ever larger audiences. Part of the mid-twentieth-century crisis of the newspaper has arisen from its failure to find more new groups of readers, at least groups that it could profitably add to its collection. With other forms of periodical publication the newspaper came to support a great array of economic activities within industrial societies by providing information and advertising. It also provided a cheap and ready means for assembling large numbers of people in different kinds of meeting places and thus made possible the apparatus of mass sports and entertainment, political meetings, and demonstrations.

Over the three and a half centuries of its existence, the newspaper has wound itself more and more tightly around the lives of its readers, forming or reflecting their ideas and opinions, defining their roles to themselves and to others. It began by addressing itself to citizens wealthy enough to pay a rather large price for a printed newssheet, which brought news of political, financial, and cultural affairs. Then with the invention of newsprint, the amazingly cheap wood pulp paper especially developed for the ephemeral newspaper, it was perceived that great fortunes could be made by publishers who could appeal to the almost universal audience that could now afford the price of a paper. Certain newspapers then became vehicles of mass entertainment, as well as of other forms of information, so successfully that their publishers could guarantee advertisers access to nearly every home. Eventually newspapers came to address and influence their readers in every part of their lives, as citizens and voters, as consumers, sports fans, moviegoers, even as husbands, wives, and children. The newspaper sought to include the basic materials on which all the transactions of an individual life depend.

III

The newspaper as a form has accumulated its different roles throughout history and has seldom abandoned any of them. One speaks of "the newspaper," although it exists in many different forms and in many different stages of development in different societies. However, similar expectations of the medium exist in most societies of the West, Japan, and certain other parts of the Southern Hemisphere. Publishers and editors from each of these countries can meet and discuss their legal, financial and industrial problems with the feeling that those societies that do not share them will come to do so in due course. All newspapers share the headaches and benefits of the basic raw material—newsprint. The great majority of international news is supplied by a small group of international agencies, and this, too, helps to make the newspaper a medium based on an international commonality of interest. Despite the differences between societies, the newspaper's content, role, technology, and cost problems are remarkably similar in each country.

It was in the eighteenth century that journalism first extended into the coverage of debates in national parliaments, and the printing of such material has remained one of the principal duties, albeit fragmentarily discharged, of all national papers. In the nineteenth century it acquired a series of economic functions as trading links multiplied and a general medium of information was required to keep a large merchant community apprised of developments in a wide variety of concerns. As the century wore on, newspapers took on a completely new set of roles arising from recreation, sports, and entertainment as these grew to cater to the new urban populations. It was at this point—with the invention of cheap newsprint as the basic raw material of the press—that it became apparent that great fortunes could be made by turning the medium into a universal one, rather than restricting it to the special groups who needed a regular diet of material drawn from the worlds of politics and finance. These new needs were met by transforming the newspaper, or certain examples of it, into a medium of entertainment and thus attracting so large an audience that publishers could promise the advertiser access to virtually every home. The machinery by which the newspaper industry turned itself into a mass medium was expensive and cumbersome. But by accumulating within the same pages an extremely heterogeneous array of material, most newspapers in industrialized countries could by the second decade of the twentieth century command the attention of the entire consuming public. It was important that every reader be able to recognize in his daily paper all his roles—as citizen, voter, consumer, sports fan, moviegoer.

The whole mechanism of the mass press depended upon industry sensitive to such social factors as the distribution of population between town and country, the structure of the modern family, dominant work, commuting, and vacationing patterns. Though the 1960's saw the newspaper at the height of its circulation in many societies, it was already beginning to suffer from the problem of having fallen slightly out of step with its readers. Social and demographic structures had shifted; various forms of competition and life-style were changing. It was no longer possible or necessary for an individual to take interest in all the areas his newspaper covered. Large sections of the paper consequently came to seem irrelevant to many of the readers and therefore to many of the advertisers, who could see that the other media—television in particular, but also other print media such as the specialist magazine—could reach audiences more easily and more cheaply. The newspaper's readers now seemed to be living in the wrong places, traveling to work at the wrong times to pick up their papers, or destined for workplaces outside the downtown areas, the traditional site for the newspaper kiosk. The paper's manufacturing plant, now vast and ancient, was often situated on valuable pieces of city real estate many miles from the zones in which the newspaper had to be distributed. These zones were now expensive to reach because of traffic blocks and high-priced oil. In the seventies, even newsprint became expensive. Most important, the fact remains that the newspaper is a labor-intensive medium in an era when labor has become highly organized and very expensive.

Electronics and the computer were clearly the instruments to extricate this overexpanded industry from the problems that had grown up around it. Just as the fifteenth-century printing press was constructed to solve the problems of the late medieval copyists, so the computer "revolution" has arrived to help the newspaper perform the role society has come to expect of it and carry out the functions it has taken on but can no longer fulfill. This new computer technology will, of course, be of value to a whole range of printed tasks of modern society, but its impact on the newspaper will be more acute and more multidimensional because of the special nature of the newspaper as a total system of communication. The computer will do more than help newspapers smear a fifth of an ounce of ink across a kilo of newsprint. It has the capacity to store and disseminate information in totally new ways, the capacity to give a person only what he wants and relieve him of the necessity of paying for what he does not.

The mass newspaper cannot store or make available to its public all the vast amount of information that is collected for it daily. It selects only a part and boils this down until it is reduced to a common readership factor, even though some of this undiluted material might be of great interest to some readers. For the computer, there is no advantage in wastage. If the information is collected, and the machinery for distribution and reception available, it can be stored and transmitted to those who want it. Economies of scale achieved by mass replication are balanced by the computer's innate capacity to offer material to the individual.

In some ways the newspaper has become like a telephone directory. Both involve the printing and transportation of a large amount of paper to a large number of homes where only a small proportion of the material will even be consulted (although, conversely, the telephone directory can be a source of irritation because of numbers that are either missing or out-of-date). A computer-based information system could provide each directory subscriber with the numbers he needs, up-to-date, because the computer offers a more malleable form of storage for the material as well as a variety of nonphysical methods for distributing it (via an operator, a TV screen, a printout, etc.). The impact of the computer on the newspaper and other print media is thus potentially very profound and entails a complete reorganization of the concept behind the medium, though it can also be used to help produce the medium in its traditional guise. It is in the nature of the computer, however, to offer society a variety of new ways of collecting, storing, and disseminating information to readers.

IV

One key and most speculative issue is the kind of organization of authority that will arise from the computer revolution and the fundamental changes in terms of power that will emerge. Each previous information revolution has been associated with, has been a fundamental enabling mechanism for, different ways of controlling or dominating human societies. Scribal bureaucracies were different in the nature of their control from typewriter-armed corporate bureaucracies.

The typewriter arrrived at a point in history when there was an abundance of female labor available and when the family business, linked with other family businesses, was ready to give way to the corporation with its own professionalized bureaucracy. The typewriter was a cheap substitute for printing and filled a gap between handwriting, no longer suitable for communication between people unlikely to know one another, and printing, which was already labor-intensive enough to be practical only for large readerships. The typewriter was developed by people who understood the nature of the gap between person-to-person and more general communication and who exploited the need for impersonalized and faster methods of letter writing. We can see in the structures of the modern city center the evidence of the kind of enterprises that the typewriter helped to build—the large corporations whose skyscrapers stand where rows of family businesses, set up in the Victorian and Edwardian years, once stood. From its inception in the 1870's, it was known to be destined to play a role in the emancipation of women. Rudyard Kipling in the 1880's wrote home from America about the "Typewriter Maiden," who earned her own living rather than remain dependent upon her family. Christopher Latham Scholes (1819–1890), producer of the first commercially manufactured typewriter (after decades, if not centuries, of searching for such an aid to writing), said that it would help women "more easily to earn a living . . . it is obviously a blessing to mankind, and especially to womankind." Gilbert Chesterton is reported to have said of the invention, "Twenty million young women rose to their feet and said 'we will not be dictated to' and immediately became shorthand typists." By 1881 classes for female typists were started in America; 60,000 had been trained by 1886.[14] The typewriter was an indispensable device for the new institutions that succeeded the family firm as the basic unit of business life at the end of the nineteenth century. In our culture it has greatly extended the range of forms of discourse. Like all new information technologies it has suggested new genres or specializations within genres. It has cleared an area of social space between printing and handwriting, which it has continued to occupy and expand.[14]

The computerization of information processing makes possible a new set of divisions between ranges of discourse. The media we have belong to specific areas: person-to-person, small audience, mass audience, local, regional, national. Different technologies are associated with specific kinds of content: the telephone did not develop (as some thought it would) as an instrument of entertainment but was used for business and personal message-sending; nor did it develop as an instrument of mass propaganda (as some expected) but as one of conversation.[15] Other tech-

Figure 1

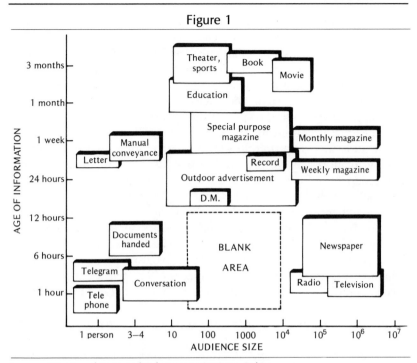

Source: Ministry of Posts and Telecommunications, Tokyo.

nologies took over entertainment and propaganda. Today, however, a reapportionment of roles is possible. The telephone wire will almost certainly become the transmission system for certain categories of public information, perhaps of specialist entertainment as well. Radio and television could be used for dissemination of printed material, and new kinds of optic fiber might provide the basis for a picture telephone or perhaps for some new kind of television-based local communication.

Researchers in Japan have drawn a map of existing systems of information and discourse showing their spread from person-to-person communication on the left to mass media on the right (see figure 1). The vertical measure measures the length of time required between origination and reception of the various media. A blank area clearly emerges for topical information of a moderately specialized (i.e., small audience) kind; it is into this empty terrain that the new electronic information systems will make their appearance during their pioneering period.

There are obvious gaps in the areas in which information media are spread throughout society, gaps that indeed are being partly filled independently of the computer. The enormous growth of specialist magazines in North America, in particular, and the growth of community broadcasting in Europe are both separate manifestations of the same phenomenon. The information and entertainment media are not catering adequately to an important and socially powerful group that requires something between the gossip of a dinner party elite and the watered-down material produced for the mass audience. The material this audience requires and is apparently prepared to pay for (or which advertisers wanting to address it are prepared to pay for) requires a large and diligent group of information collectors and entertainers. The specialist magazines, which have profited from supplying some of the needs of this growing audience, are not supplying the traditional fare of an intellectual elite but highly detailed information necessary for the adherents of a particular life-style. The magazines cater to health freaks and hi-fi enthusiasts; amateur astrologers; amateur psychologists; people interested in technology, science, music, chess. Citizens of late twentieth-century society are prepared to invest a large part of their incomes and their time in hobbies and subsidiary occupations.

The traditional media are not necessarily on the verge of some kind of slump; rather, they find themselves in the position of having helped stimulate a far wider range of tastes than they can now gratify. The reader of the economic pages of a newspaper is less likely to be satisfied today than in the past with the level of information he is receiving, even though the daily provision of financial information is far greater now than a decade ago, even in many third world countries.

The hypothesis implied in the Japanese diagram is that there exists an audience for large quantities of information of a semi- to fully specialist nature to be delivered according to individual choice. Simultaneously, wholly new ways of delivering such information have been discovered, and the question is when and how to put them to use, rather than whether to try. Nearly all of the technical experiments in "new media" at the end of the decade of the 1970's are directed towards this kind of market and are using new telecommunications devices attached to microcomputers or conventional telephone lines or some other new means for distributing information and entertainment material. Britain, France, Germany, Japan, and other countries are advancing rapidly and plurally into the field of teletext, videotex, viewdata—the current names attached to the communication devices that use the common domestic television receiver plus the television antennas or the telephone line (see Part Three). Viewers are being offered much more variety in output as well as a variety of new uses for common domestic equipment. At the heart of these and other experiments and pioneer services lies the computer.

In the 1960's and 1970's surveys of the use of leisure time indicated a gradually increasing proportion of time spent on receiving entertainment and information. Swedish surveys, for example, indicate that between 1970 and 1977 the amount of time the average citizen spent daily with all media (including radio, television, the press, movies, and theater) has grown from three to three and a half hours, an increase of about two and a half percent per year.[16]

In the United States A & C Nielsen Company statistics show that the coming of television produced a sudden doubling of time spent per household per day on radio and TV, from around 4 hours in the 1940's to over 8 in the 1950's. Thereafter, the figure dropped to around 7 hours by 1960, rising gently thereafter to 7 hours 56 minutes in 1965 and 8 hours 48 minutes in 1971. Data collection is fragmentary in this field, collected for different reasons and based on different yardsticks in different societies. However, there is a convergence between many newspaper and broadcasting surveys indicating that increased leisure, in a period when the average household size has been shrinking, coincides with a growth in the use of information media.

An increase, to use the Swedish example, of half an hour over seven years, one sixth of the base figure, offers the media industries a very healthy potential for growth. The incremental audience time, furthermore, suggests more than a corresponding proportion in growth for the output industries, because it is in the extra time dedicated to reading and viewing that an individual indulges his individual tastes, thereby generating a more than proportionate growth in the quantities and diversity of material consumed. It is only when a society is adequately housed, fed, and clothed, that the specialist food, furnishing, and clothing industries find giant markets for a diverse range of their goods. To satisfy the food needs of those who are not hungry requires a much broader spectrum of choice. We have passed a comparable turning point in the development of information: the change from the basic diet of mass entertainment for the work-weary to the profusion of choice required by societies where individual interests can be indulged.

Information technology—applied in industry and the economy—is in any case increasing the availability of leisure. It provides the machinery by which the constant process of rationalization within industry is deepened and accelerated, resulting in the phenomenon of an overall decline in many areas of employment. The essence of the change brought about by computerized information lies in individuation. It is, in a sense, the opposite of industrialization, which is associated with the mass production of cheap goods, for it offers economies of production along with the customizing of each item. Where the industrial revolution was based upon the distribution of energy, the information revolution is based upon the distribution of command, or control. In this present phase of history it is information that provides the infrastructure, and telecommunications is becoming, as it were, the substitute for transport as the focal point of productive activity.

It is hard to visualize the impact of such a change on society; it lies not so much in physical objects as in attitudes and relationships and in the distribution of power. In any case, it remains at present a series of possibilities rather than realities, and a vast area of choice is open to societies: to use the opportunities to reduce centralization, say, or to increase it; to continue to press for economic growth or to stabilize; to increase disparities between developed and nondeveloped societies or to close them.

In some senses the information revolution of the computer age offers a reduction in the regimentation of mass society, in the perception of the public as a mass. Some freedoms that were lost in the age of industrialization and mass production may be regained in the next.

V

The real impact of computerized information, then, began with a shift in the sovereignty over text. We saw how the invention of printing moved to the writer and away from the keeper of the text the power to guarantee the text. This in turn shifted to government the task of controlling and channeling the power of the text within society. The writer's sovereignty became the focal point of centuries of struggles and debate as to the limits of his rights within a society and the most appropriate ways of imposing some other will, some other social or governmental priority, upon them.

At first, in the age of Tudor licensing, the printing press (the technology itself) was the focus of the controls, but later the state found itself presented with the task of controlling the text through manipulation of the content, through bribery and censorship. The French Revolution of 1789 attempted a totally free press and then tried or considered every conceivable substitute, ranging from total repression through licensing stamp taxes and registration to complete editorial domination. Napoleon I, together with other European monarchs, found it necessary to make himself, in effect, editor in chief of the only permitted news periodicals in a desperate attempt to control the flow of information through his domain. The French legislation of 1881, which finally established press freedom, was enacted at a moment when it had finally become possible for government to lay down its burden of censorship in the marketplace. The newspaper and other forms of publishing had become so tightly held within the mechanisms of an industrial economy that governments felt it possible to loosen their grip upon an industry that was already too prolific to be supervised completely. In the succeeding century press freedom was finally established as a norm in Western societies, and derogations of it were felt to be abnormal and anti–social. Power over the text was permitted to rest upon editorial authorities within journalism and individual writers and publishers freedoms of printing supplied the basic ideals and analogies of freedom. However, no society has arrived in the 1980's with all its machinery of information and entertainment supplied with precisely the same kinds of freedoms, or the same degree of freedom.

In computer-controlled information systems the sovereignty over the text moves from the supplier of information to the controller of the technology. Already in the broadcast media we have seen the development of controlling institutions based upon the transmission technology (and justified by a supposed shortage of spectrum capacity) rather than upon the content. Although these institutions—unlike the book-publishing houses, magazines, and newspapers—are statutory bodies or semi-statutory bodies (such as the American networks, whose key stations are federally licensed), they are charged with the task of representing the public, ensuring, in the words of the U.S. Communications Act of 1934, the "public interest, convenience, and necessity." The Federal Communications Commission, which dates back to that act and is the central institution in American electronic communications, was a typical institution of the era of the New Deal. It represented an intervention by the state in a facet of society where private and marketing mechanisms could not be expected to serve the public interest without governmental intervention. They were above the marketplace but designed to mend the tears in a fundamentally market economy.

In the age of the microprocessor this tendency must be carried many steps forward. As more sectors of the economic world become more dependent upon information that passes through the spectrum and through common-carrier transmission methods supervised within the public sector of Western societies, so must the inevitable controls move more firmly into the hands of those who control these technologies. The audience becomes, much more than in the mass-production phase, an audience of individuals or small publics, but the control over information passing into the new media goes into the hands of those supervising the establishment of the technologies, who in the majority of countries (but not the United States) are the PTT's, the postal and telecommunications establishments. As the new media come to play a more powerful role within the existing range of information industries they are bound to influence the development of existing media and will probably encourage them to conform to the needs and attitudes of the newer media.

The new media and information devices that are currently being tried out or discussed around the world are additional evidence of a wholly new stage through which the economies of the West are passing. A great shift is taking place from producer to consumer sovereignty in Western democracies, a shift that is bringing in its train a change in values and in systems of economic management. In the field of information such devices as teletext, viewdata, cassettes, cables, and videodiscs all fit the same emerging pattern: they provide opportunities for individuals to step out of the mass homogenized audiences of newspapers, radio, and television and take a more active role in the process by which knowledge and entertainment are transmitted through society.

So far no new medium has actually become powerful enough to challenge any existing incumbent in its traditional roles. Indeed, despite a host of problems, the newspaper, radio, and television industries are in many countries enjoying historic heights of prosperity, profitability, and circulation. What people are waiting for is the first sign of a traditional medium moving out of a traditional function, abandoning a piece of its territory to new technology. They wait to see whether pay-TV via coaxial cable will replace the movie theater as the means for distributing major films; they wait to see whether the computer-assisted print systems such as viewdata will take over part of the function of selling classified advertising; they wait to see whether community media based on electronic or video technology will replace some of the functions of local newspapers.

This era is a fascinating one in which to observe the way that technology interacts with human society: for each new device that is taken up, several are lost in experiment and in the marketplace. The moment may be more decisive than the method. For it is imagination, ultimately, and not mathematical calculation that creates media; it is the fresh perception of how to fit a potential machine into an actual way of life that really constitutes the act of "invention." Sarnoff's separation of mouthpiece from earpiece helped to turn radio-telephony into radio in the 1920's and turned a person-to-person medium into a means of mass entertainment.

British radio engineers in the 1960's turned a new subtitling device for the deaf in television into the new medium of teletext. Both of these examples developed from a conception of a market, the idea of a possible relationship between a device and an audience.

Invention consists of skillful development plus social insight. We now all know that by the year 2000 or 2010 systems of information will be far more interactive and abundant, based more upon electronic transfer than physical carriage, upon individual selection than generalized transmission. But we don't know which transmission system (coaxial cable, optic fiber waveguide, microwave, or some combination of all) will finally emerge, nor which functions will be served by which set of audience devices (screen, telephone, facsimile, home computer). We cannot sit back to wait and see, for it is precisely the process by which societies "guess" the likely outcome that actually creates the outcome.

A culture grows out of its tools. The hand, the eye, the voice, and the memory were physical functions that gave rise to the arts, crafts, and literatures of mankind. The extension of the limbs into material tools reduced the pain of construction, enabled physical energy to be transferred, increased, stored. Tools separated mind from body, diversified the range of skills and therefore the genres within which human cultures were expressed. The hand-based and mind-based arts and sciences proliferated. New technologies are extensions of old ones. Each mental revolution produced in the era of a new technique (created by the interaction of old needs and new opportunities) is an addition to human experience. The communication revolutions have therefore been cumulative rather than completely substitutive. Each new technology has been summoned into being to cope with an existing and perceived inefficiency or inadequacy and has gradually released its wider potential into society, working out its own peculiar implications. What we have to observe next is the first stage of the journey of computer-based information into our culture, which is taking place more publicly in the newspaper industry than in any other area of society. There it is changing the industrial base of a medium that had already been changing its economic and financial base. It is changing the relationships between all the crafts, professions, and management cadres in what is the basic information industry of Western society.

II
THE NEWSPAPER INDUSTRY
OF THE UNITED STATES

1. THE CONDITION
OF THE NEWSPAPER

The newspaper has always been a medium of the streets. In the seventeenth century the news-hawker with his "relaciouns" was the primary agent of publication, a familiar figure in London, Amsterdam, Cologne, Frankfurt, Budapest. The literate vagabond who undertook the personal risks entailed in distributing seditious material played a key role in the development of the newspaper. It was with him (and frequently her) that the printer had to negotiate the contents, for the authorities would arrest the distribution staff when the writer's identity was concealed.[1] The poet Crabbe a century later leaves us with a picture of the newspaper as the great disturber of the peace in the cities.

> I sing of NEWS, and all those vapid sheets
> The rattling hawkers vend through gaping-streets;
> Whate'er their name, whate'er the time they fly,
> Damp from the press, to charm the reader's eye:
> For, soon as Morning dawns with roseate hue,
> The HERALD of the morn arises too;
> POST after POST succeeds, and, all day long,
> GAZETTES and LEDGERS swarm, a noisy throng.
> When evening comes, she carries with her train
> Of LEDGERS, CHRONICLES, and POSTS again,
> Like bats, appearing, when the sun goes down,
> From holes obscure and corners of the town.[2]

In Paris licensed nouvellistes spoke the news to crowds of illiterates for one sou, and newspaper placards were for many the primary tools of citizenship.[3] Already the newsboys, equipped with horn and cap displaying the title of their papers, disturbed the peace, crying the news on Sundays, when the stagecoach and the printer's shop were at rest.[4] In the nineteenth century the newspaper was the mental highway through which the imagery of the city traveled; it brought people into the city and held them there. Victor Lawson's *Chicago Daily News* built up a complete sales staff from the gamin class, an army of juvenile entrepreneurs who made their living by selling the papers at a profit, when they were not deafening the citizens of Chicago with the brazen music of the Newsboys Band.[5]

The newspaper provided the imagery of the American city; its stories were drawn from the streets, and the city elite heard the same cries as the immigrant masses and fed upon the same gossip. The newspaper created the publicity stunt and sponsored the exhibition, the World's Fair, the school essay prize, the street parade. It was the newspaper that fueled American individualism by creating the stark images of success and failure. The newspaper's readers learned from its text the layers of status and prestige within a newly constructed society; they were daily shown the abyss of disgrace into which the criminal, the drunkard, the bankrupt, could fall.[6] The newspaper proposed the makeshift realities of society, where no other medium of homogeneity existed. It taught the language to the new citizen; it devised headlines comprehensible to those with little command of English. No wonder that to Oswald Spengler the newspaper was the primary intellectual instrument of urban life.[7] No wonder that Walter Bagehot saw the newspaper and the platform as joint supports of what he called the Age of Discussion, in which political change had shifted irreversibly—so he thought—from physical to mental struggle.[8]

The *New York Evening Post* and later the *Tribune* ran the Fresh Air Fund for city children; the *San Francisco Chronicle* established the zoological gardens, and its rival, the *Examiner*, set up the Little Jim Hospital for Incurables. The press created the iconography of public service, of political activity, of citizenship, and these basic images, compounded partly of stuntmanship, partly of sanctimony, merged into the medium itself, and were handed down to later generations of the newspaper's readers.

Editors and publishers of the last century extolled the profession of journalism and the power of publishers as the secular saviours of human society, the creators of the new public values. "For the history of the English press," wrote one British editor, "is the history, if not of

English liberty, of all the popular forces and political franchises which have given strength and solidity to English institutions . . . purified the public service; raised the tone of our public life; made bribery and corruption, in the old sense of the terms, impossible." Charles Pebody, who made this statement went on to acclaim public opinion as "one of the marvels of our time."[9] Certainly the 1880's was the era when the craft of journalism acquired the rhetoric that went with self-confidence. The French press law of 1881 gave tremendous encouragement to other societies: formulated after a solid century of advances towards and retreats from liberal ideals, the French press moved via sedition and insurrection to repression and back again at least a dozen times between the period of the Revolution and the new press law. It began with the glorious words "La Presse est libre . . ." and won the rare compliments of British and American editorial writers, who encouraged the French to go further and remove their remaining shackles and fulfill at last their ultimate duty.[10]

The work of newspapers, in Europe especially, was concentrated around the political news. The esprit de corps in the Press Gallery of the Houses of Parliament was the envy of the nation. Prodigious quantities of ribboned type emerged daily from their cramped quarters, recording verbatim the flowery locutions of proud statesmen who were delighted to be confirmed as such by the mere sight of the columns of their words.

Copy was circulated around the newspaper offices and around the nation by every device that ingenuity could devise to link the telegraphic services to the events covered by reporters. Pigeons, corps of cyclists, special trains, pneumatic tubes, even telephones were quickly harnessed. Every decade brought forth a "new journalism" designed to bring another group of readers into the newspaper's fold. The 1880's also created some of the basic forms of journalism that have survived into the present—the signed dispatch, the professional sports reporter, the interview. "No one is too exalted to be interviewed and none is too humble," wrote the editor of London's *Pall Mall Gazette*.[11] This was the era when the streets of the world's great cities were complete with lighting and drainage, and the political groupings into which their population was to divide solidified. It was the newspaper that held them together and the newspaper that was instrumental in helping politicans fight for the allegiance of the various quarters and neighborhoods of the city. It was through the eyes of reporters and editors that statesmen and politicians saw the world: from Abraham Lincoln, who employed Charles Dana as Assistant Secretary of War to roam the battlefields and report on what he saw, to W. E. Gladstone, who gave advice to John Morley at the

Daily News and read his editorials on Ireland as recirculated expressions of public opinion.

Though our *idea* of the newspaper—and often the idea that newspaper people have of the newspaper—was created a century or so ago, the reality of the medium and the context in which it flourished has greatly changed, especially in the period since the mid-1950's. In Europe the 1940's were a period in which traditional political newspapers proliferated. The years after the Liberation were a last spasm for the old press. Paris had 31 daily papers in 1945; it has 9 today. Germany rebuilt its press up to 255 titles in 1954, though it has only 121 today. Denmark still had 150 papers at the end of the war but has only 45 today.[12] The decline in the number of papers represents a change in the *role* of the newspaper. The medium has come to play a crucial economic role in consumer society and has given up its traditional functions in politics, where it was part of a pluralistic competitive machinery of information. Readers no longer cluster around their newspapers in search of confirmation of their basic opinions and values in contradistinction to those of their neighbors. In Italy, Spain, and Portugal perhaps these roles are still somewhat in evidence, but not in societies that have evolved along the mainstream of consumerism. In Britain the *Westminster Gazette*, which perished before World War II, was the last paper that relied for its circulation on the political guidance it provided for its (25,000) readers.

The newspaper of the second half of the twentieth century is founded upon the perceived need of the reader for facts and entertainment, rather than for an overall ideological explanation of the world from which he can assemble or reassemble his own explanations. As one Anglo-American editor who watched the transition from the old to the new in the 1930's put it: the modern newspaper "provides a daily epitome of world history."[13] Where formerly a scattering of newspapers left the medium open to governmental subsidy and manipulation, the modern newspaper industry tends to reflect the chief concerns of a society, imposing either a mild political coloring (by comparison with the past) or reflecting the values of the society's dominant elite.

The investigative role of the press has loomed larger as its ideological and partisan role has diminished. The term investigative has acquired a special meaning in recent times and has come to imply investigation of official malpractice or political deception or abuse of public interest by private corporations. It is a neutral, moralizing form of journalism that is based upon an adversary notion of the position of the press, a term that embodies a complete internalization of the political and social universe of journalism. The reporter puts himself in the place of a statutory authority or acts as a goad to a statutory authority. There is an assumed permanent relationship between journalism and political bureaucratic power comparable to that between a law-enforcement agency and the criminal classes.

Investigation has become the most highly praised and highly prized form of journalism, taking the place of opinion leadership, the historic purpose of the press. To sustain such a role within a predominately locally-situated press necessitates considerable authority and security within the newspaper industry itself. It is unlikely that the Watergate investigation could have been sustained by the *Washington Post* if it had been competing with half a dozen other daily papers in its main circulation zone. As it was, the Nixon White House consistently attempted to reduce the enthusiasm of the few newspapers that attempted to expose the malpractices of the Administration by threatening the other interests of the newspaper enterprises concerned, i.e., radio and television. Investigative reporting of the 1970's has, of course, plenty of historical precedents dating back to the earliest days of the metropolitan press. But in its modern guise it could only have come about within a newspaper industry that has adopted new journalistic canons as a result of finding itself in entirely difference economic circumstances, i.e., largely in possession of safe local monopoly markets.

It is not at all surprising that throughout Europe and the United States the passing of the old newspaper has been mourned, and its evolution into a new and different kind of medium has failed to be understood. Television has been blamed for the lack of pluralism that now seems to be the fate of the newspaper; trade unions have been blamed for sawing off the branch on which they sat. Publishers have been blamed for the greed with which they amalgamated, absorbed their rivals, and closed down uneconomic properties, and readers blamed for their refusal to buy newspapers in the same quantities as before. But if anyone or anything is to be blamed, it should be the city itself, whose medium the old newspaper was—the city that has disappeared as a basic unit of residence, leaving to its heir, megalopolis, the flotsam and jetsam of the streets that now serve purposes quite different from those for which they were built. Since the end of World War II, the American city has become an interlinked network of town and suburb, its streets turned into islands by the trunk routes along which cars rush their passengers into distant suburbs, which were only empty wilderness or small towns. The new total megalopolitan construct has broken down the social habits on which newspaper circulation depended. City centers are now frightening places after five in the afternoon. Shopping is done in new suburban merchandizing complexes, with ribbons of motels and eating places taking people still further away from the warm comprehensiveness of the town. The very term inner city has become a euphemism for the black population. Nearly 30 percent of the population of America's 50 largest metropolitan areas is black, compared with 5 percent of the suburban regions around them. Downtown is left by the whites after work by car, rather than bus or subway, and much of what remains is derelict—large parking lots empty all night by the places of entertainment, shops, and houses whose denizens have disappeared. In the middle of this area there sits the large building that houses the newspaper, an island of light and activity utterly separated from the streets in which its readers formerly lived and worked.

The elite of the city—political, social, and commercial—have all departed, their loyalty broken. Indifferent to the daily news of the central area, they build their lives in new surroundings and interest themselves in the problems of their school board and town council. Their minds are where their taxes are paid, where their votes are cast, and their children educated. What they value as "news" has shifted its location, and what is left of the city is perceived to be a series of problems, ranging from race and drugs to poverty, homelessness, and mugging. This elite has been cut off intellectually and culturally from the geographical zone whose affairs it once dominated. The newspapers once served these groups with a series of fairly distinct moral perspectives in which all the affairs of the metropolis were unified and valued in terms of a consistent set of images. Even where newspapers had ceased to offer themselves to readers on the basis of their distinct politics, they represented at least in terms of their respective cities the spectrum of available appoaches to a comprehensive reality. Until the great industrial disputes, which removed the majority of New York's newspapers in the 1960's (the *Herald-Tribune*, the *Journal-American*, the *Times*, the *Post*), each seemed to offer the reader a special personality or perspective. Each was committed to the city and spoke for a set of interests that, however much in mutual conflict, were committed to the city, drawing its news values from its connection with a section of the community.

The advertisers were at the mercy of this pluralism. Each store in the downtown area, in setting out its range of goods in one or more of the city's newspapers, knew that the chances of linking with any given group of customers was something of a hit-and-miss affair. Today the downtown store is still there but has had to clone itself into a dozen suburban stores, each of them advertising in the newspapers of its respective suburban zones. For the small advertisers who formerly spent their money on the metropolitan daily, the single monopoly newspaper of today is an expensive proposition. It has grown very large indeed to cater to the vastly expanded market in which it has to function, and its space is concomitantly more expensive. In any case, the small advertiser wants to reach only the inhabitants and workers of his microregion and is unable to benefit from the extra square miles in which his advertisement will have to be distributed.

Demographic statistics help to demonstrate this pattern of change. At the turn of the century roughly one fifth of the American population lived in towns and just over a fifth in suburbs—all the rest were classified as "rural." By the outbreak of World War II 30 percent lived in towns and just under 30 percent in suburbs. The rural dwellers which in sheer numbers had, of course, greatly increased, had sunk from 60 percent to 40 percent of the total. The total population of the country had leapt from 76 million to 132 million, disguising the important changes in location and structure that had occurred. A further thirty-five years on, the population had grown to 220 million, but urban and suburban population, taken together, was now three quarters of the entire figure, and the differences of terrain between the two categories was on the way to obliteration. At the same time, family structure had changed greatly: the population of 1900 was divided into 16 million households with an average of 4.8 members in every household; by 1940 that had fallen to 3.8 and by 1975 to 2.9.[14]

The rate at which population was growing, however, was falling. At the turn of the century population increased at a rate of nearly 10 percent and began a steady decline through the century (apart from a very rapid decline in the Depression years), ending with a rate of 4.8 percent growth in the 1970's. Household growth, however, has followed a different and less smooth pattern, with the seventies representing one of the century's record decades for household increases—now at 11 percent. All media industries, though in different degrees, first require concentrated groups of population to fuel their development, and then, of course, benefit from rapid increases in city population or suburban residences. All the population trends of the century—the new concentrations of population and continuing growth of cities and suburbs at the expense of rural areas—have therefore benefited the information sector of the economy.

However, for the publishers of newspapers the change in population and especially in household formation has brought about a spell of gloom, for though total circulation has held—even, according to some calculations, improved in recent years—it has not kept increasing at the same rate as the formation of households. Even in 1960 there were more newspapers sold than households in the nation—112 newspapers for every 100 households. A dozen years later the crucial figure of one for one was passed, and fewer than 90 papers were sold to every 100 households.[15] Leo Bogart, senior researcher in the American newspaper industry, spelled out the problem in more precise terms in a paper in 1975 and alarmed publishers even further, for he showed that the newspaper seemed to have lost the support of its crucial client group—young adults preparing to start their families and establish their own homes.[16] The babies of the postwar baby boom were by 1960 coming to the end of their teens, 35.6 percent of the population being under the age of 18 at that time. By the mid-1970's the section of the population under 18 was down to 32.4 percent, which represented a small rise in actual numbers. The slightly older age group, those between the ages of 18 and 24, had grown by a larger proportion—over 60 percent in actual numbers—and the study of this group in terms of its newspaper habits showed an alarming phenomenon taking place. In 1960 every 100 young people in the 18 to 24 age group were purchasing between them 365 newspapers. In 1970 the number for the same 100 was 242. This could mean simply that this group was postponing the normal activities of adulthood, producing families later and adopting the traditional habits of adulthood (including the purchase of daily newspapers) at a later stage. However, the evidence for that optimism was hard to locate. If one took the general adult section of the population, those between 25 and 64, newspaper purchase was fairly stable, having dropped from 71 per 100 in 1960 to 68 per 100 in ten years. Newspaper circulation was failing to keep up with the demographic habits of the postwar generation, especially those who were female, poor, little-educated, and nonwhite.

Many newspapers anxiously conducted their own local surveys and found the national trend generally confirmed. One prominent paper in the Midwest, for example, received a report from its consultants that declared that the groups with overall below-average readership were under 35 years of age, that they were blue-collar workers with family incomes under $15,000, and that most of them had spent only a brief time at high school or had not gone to high school at all. However, in the six years from 1970, when the trend seemed to be intensifying, this newspaper found that further declines were taking place among its readership, not merely in this previously identified group but among white-collar workers who had passed through high school and who came from families earning over $10,000 a year. In other words, the readership appeared to be disintegrating, starting with traditionally low-reading sections of the population but now spreading right through the normally high-reading sections. As table 1 indicates, readership between 1971 and 1977 had fallen from 54 percent to 43 percent of all adults but from 47 percent to 32 percent of the important 18-to-34-year-olds. Among those with relatively high family incomes, where readership was once very high (72 percent), it had dropped to less than half of the total.

This and other comparable analyses helped to fuel something of a panic among newspaper firms, which led to the creation of a new and much more detailed readership research project by the American Newspaper Publishers Association (ANPA).[17] It also led to a concerted effort to modernize among publishers, an acceleration of investment in new techniques, new skills, new equipment. The industry was still highly profitable, and its problems seemed still to lie ahead—perhaps it had detected them in time to fight against these demographic pointers and reverse the trends before they turned into a great tidal wave of decline. The anxieties of the American publishers were shared by their counterparts in Europe, where there were similar trends in demographic patterns but even more dramatic changes in newspaper habits.

A great deal of industry-wide development work resulted from these analyses, even though a much more optimistic view became tenable in later years when other data came to light or when new methods of interpretation were applied. One of the many paradoxes of reader surveys is that quite different patterns emerge with different types of surveys and different patterns of questioning. Thus market surveys tend to emphasize the loss of newspaper purchasers among certain age groups, while use-of-time surveys have shown that over the decade between the late 1960's and late 1970's there has been no noticeable decline in newspaper *use* among the same age groups. In fact, one use-of-time survey shows a decline of from 2 to 13 percent among *older* age groups. The Roper surveys have consistently shown over a long period that more people are becoming more reliant on television than on newspaper news, although even in 1971 figures taken from newspaper industry sources used by Ben Bagdikian showed a fundamentally different result— namely, that 78 percent of those surveyed had seen a newspaper the previous day compared with 60 percent who had watched a TV news bulletin and 55 percent who had heard a radio newscast.[18] John Robinson and Philip Converse provided a study a year later showing that less than half of American adults had been exposed to a national TV program the day before, and there have been similar findings when research has been conducted from a newspaper standpoint.[19]

In 1975 and 1976 Robinson attempted another follow-up survey,[20] this time interviewing many hundreds of subjects about their previous day's

Table 1. Percent reading in each group

	January-December 1971	March-December 1972	February-December 1973	March-December 1974	May 1975-January 1976	May 1976-February 1977	March-December 1977
All Adults	54%	51%	52%	51%	48%	43%	43%
Sex							
Male	57	54	57	54	53	49	48
Female	51	49	47	48	43	37	38
Race							
White	55	53	53	52	48	43	43
Nonwhite	47	40	42	41	42	40	41
Age							
18–34	47	37	45	41	39	28	32
35–49	57	60	55	52	49	52	50
50–64	58	60	56	63	52	52	47
65 and older	59	60	53	58	60	53	58
Education							
Some college or more	69	60	66	60	59	51	49
High school graduate	54	60	54	52	47	40	44
Some high school or less	45	39	41	42	38	35	37
Occupation of chief wage earner							
White-collar	70%	64%	**	58%	54%	50%	49%
Blue-collar	47	45	**	46	39	36	36
Other*	53	48	**	49	56	46	46
Income							
Under $10,000	46	43	46	42	44	43	38
$10,000–$15,000	66	62	51	55	41	42	39
15,000 or more	72	66	69	60	58	49	46

*Includes Armed forces, Retired, Student, Unemployed, Not in labor force, etc.
**Occupation of chief wage earner not available for 1973. Occupation tabulated for respondent only.

exposure to news but scattering the interviews across the week in order to reflect a fuller spectrum of publications and editions. He discovered that when people were asked to speak of a "typical" day in their news absorption habits, they refered more often to television, but when asked what they exposed themselves to on the previous day only, the results were more favorable to the written press (see table 2).

His later study went even further, however, and gathered information on overall use of time on the previous day. When news habits and entertainment habits were weighed one against the other, it again appeared that the written press had the upper hand. Roughly 70 percent of those surveyed had read a newspaper compared with just over 50 percent who had watched television. (The audience for news magazines was much lower than many surveys in the past have shown: the three main national news magazines mustered barely more than 5 percent of the total news audience.) The newspaper's lead was maintained throughout the demographic spectrum, although it was more marked in the upper-income and older age groups, wearing down to a very small, even marginal, lead in the lowest-income, least educated, and youngest age groups. Moreover, among the young adults who were thought to have fled from the newspaper, it was discovered that just as high use of newspapers tends to go with high use of television news, so does low newspaper reading go with low television news viewing. Comparing his new survey with the one he conducted in the 1965–66 period, he reveals that the current 15 percent edge of newspaper over television has been cut from a 32 percent edge a decade ago, but that no decline is noticeable in the case of the 18-24-year-olds, and that the greatest decline is with the age group immediately above them, the 25-34-year-olds. Something appears to have happened to the generation born after 1940 to render them more interested in newspapers than the cohort immediately preceding them; something also seems to have gone awry with sections of older cohorts who seem to be less addicted to the medium of print than was formerly believed (see table 3).

Robinson has also attempted to check the amount of time spent each day by the different population age groups on reading their newspapers. He discovered a general falling off in the total time spent, but this decline was far less marked among the group born after 1940 even though the total amount of time they spent with their papers was less than for other age groups. Those who were spending the most time with their newspaper a decade ago, before television news reached its full maturity, had by 1976 reduced their reading time by the largest margin. It would appear that television has won the battle for the upper age

Table 2. Adjusted differences in daily newspaper and TV
news use in 1975–76 (Waves 1 and 3 combined)

	Percent using yesterday	
	Newspaper	TV News
Age		
18–24	51	36
24–29	51	38
30–39	66	45
40–49	67	48
50–59	79	64
60–65	87	68
66 and over	90	73
Education		
Grade school	51	42
Some high school	64	48
High school grad	73	53
Some college	73	52
College grad	74	54
Income		
Under $5,000	53	51
$5,000–9,999	65	51
$10,000–14,999	72	52
$15,000–24,999	74	51
$25,000 and over	75	49
Race		
White	68	51
Black	58	50
Sex		
Male	70	52
of residence		
Population of place of residence		
Over 2 million	68	58
100,000–1,999,999	73	55
10,000–99,999	68	45
2,500–9,999	66	49
Under 2,500	66	49
Total	68	52

Table 3. Relations Between TV News Viewing And Newspaper Reading
(Wave 1 Sample)

	Percent of TV Viewers Reading Newspapers	Percent of Non-Viewers Reading Newspapers	Percent of Persons Using Both
Age			
18–24 (N = 189)	67	49	25
25–34 (349)	66	53	30
35–54 (424)	77	62	35
55 and over (422)	<u>81</u>	<u>70</u>	<u>54</u>
Total (1,404)	75	59	39

Source for Tables: ANPA News Research Center Studies.

groups (see table 4) and lost it to a great extent among the young—a reversal of assumptions that have all but become traditional wisdom.[21]

In March 1977 the Newsprint Information Committee briefed a group of field workers assigned to analyze the news absorption habits of 300 adults in an experiment designed by the Newspaper Advertising Bureau (see table 5). Their findings helped further the process of reversing certain pessimistic asusmptions that had been made since the newspaper "decline" first set in. They found the newspaper continuing to enjoy a leadership among the media.

The news magazines also scored much higher in this survey,[22] which claimed that 21 percent had read a newsweekly in the course of the previous week. (News magazine reading is not a substitute for newspaper reading, however, since the newsweekly readers were the highest newspaper consumers as well.) Only 9 percent had neither seen a daily paper nor a Sunday paper in the previous month, and more than half had read a newspaper on the five previous consecutive weekdays. As many as 61 percent had read a Sunday paper on the four previous Sundays, and only 20 percent had read no Sunday paper for four weeks. This survey attempted to find out what readers would choose to have in their newspapers, if they could have them tailor-made to their own interests, and it was discovered that the most favored categories of information were traditional news topics and tended to be consumer-oriented (best food buys, nutrition, and medical science), with material dealing with the environment and editorials lower on the list. There were also categories to which a majority were actually hostile: some thought that

Table 4. 1965–1975 Differences in Time Spent Reading
for Those Reading Newspapers

	1965–66 (N=1,244) minutes/day	1975–76 (N=786) minutes/day	Differences minutes/day
Age			
18–24	15	10	− 5
25–34	23	16	− 7
35–44	27	22	− 5
45–54	33	22	−11
55–65	40	26	−14
Total	28	21	− 7

Table 5. Daily exposure to news

Newspapers	69%
TV news	62%
Radio news	49%
All sources	25%
Only 1 source	28%

little or no space should be devoted to fashions, personal advice, travel, comics, music and records, and a huge variety of other trivia that seem to attract small clusters of extremely loyal readers and repel those with intense interests in other categories. When each subject was taken through his paper, item by item, and asked to rate each in order of interest and importance, it became clear that there were many categories that commanded a higher degree of reader "interest" than of perceived "importance." International and national news stories scored very high points indeed—more than local news—especially among younger readers. It appeared that the newspaper was used in conjunction with television, which was not perceived as a substitute for newspapers in any age group, and it remained an important medium particularly where it performed its traditional tasks. However, for the marginal and infrequent readers, who were more likely to be attracted into the regular audience—than those who had ceased to read all together,[23] feature material was indeed the most interesting element.

The sense of crisis that hung over the newspaper industry in many industrial societies in the 1960's was a response to a series of changes in society that had thrown the newspaper's internal economy out of gear.

The newspaper was losing a few readers and a small number of titles (especially in Europe), but it began to fear that its techniques of distribution were wrong for the new megalopolitan groupings that had replaced the more homogeneous towns and cities of the previous generation.[24] It began to feel that its production technology was too slow for an age in which television dominated the news business. It began to worry that as a medium of advertising it was losing its grip over important sections of the audience and important groups of clients. As a medium of politics it was losing its links with the 1960's generation because it had become a medium of consensus rather than radical change. Its links with the older generation were also weakening because of a reduction in the adherence to "opinions" or political standpoints. (Newspapers continued to work at the task of opinion moulding, but increasingly a typical newspaper audience possessed no homogeneity of opinion.) The newspaper was passing through a kind of mid-life crisis and, in particular, had started working out the implications of the massive loss of its monopoly over news and advertising delivered to the home to television, which had now arrived at technical maturity and total household coverage.

2. THE NEWSPAPER
IN THE MARKETPLACE

The newspaper industry in the 1960's was subject to various accusations and lamentations: it had become a series of local monopolies, the press was being absorbed into a dozen or so vast chains; within a growing number of communities the ownership of supposedly competing media of newspaper, radio, and television was passing into the same hands; the newspaper was becoming merely a collection of advertisements and a few anodyne syndicated articles.

Within the industry there were fears of a kind of general collapse, comparable to that of the railroad industry when it first realized the extent of the incursions of the automobile and the airplane into its traditional function. The newspaper's share of the advertising market was dropping (it had lost almost the whole of national manufacturers' advertising to television); its readers drove back and forth to work and could no longer read newspapers at this point in their daily lives; television absorbed their spare time when they were at home; the newspaper had lost its grip on the young; it was too expensive to maintain home delivery; the cost of newsprint, the industry's main raw material, was escalating beyond the level at which there was any possibility of profit.

A thorough reappraisal of production and marketing methods and an intense period of self-examination was necessary for the newspaper industry to revive its sense of direction. The new technology (or, rather, technologies) did indeed solve some of the problems, but, more than that, it helped provide a symbol of a new kind of industry that would inevitably spend twenty years or more learning to think of itself no longer as a one-product activity but as an information-collection industry, with a number of new electronic as well as old print outlets developing over time. Only by seeing exactly how the newspaper began to adjust to its new market circumstances can one see how essential this new technology was both to the reestablishment of a clear self-image and to the physical renewal of the medium. The newspaper's rethinking of its nature and role will continue inevitably right through the 1980's as new devices and techniques emerge.

The United States, of course, was not the only country where the press was beset with problems. Rising costs and the appearance of successful rival media caused similar problems in many other societies, although they reached their peak perhaps a year or two later. In some European countries, such as France, the advertising industry did not fully establish itself as a modern social and economic institution until almost 1970. Indeed, one of the reasons the French press had been so susceptible to governmental interference right through the Third and Fourth Republics was precisely the fact that newspapers remained so heavily dependent upon their political friends and the subscriptions of their readers to balance their accounts. Today the full extent of the French government's economic and administrative involvement in the country's major press enterprises is still being unraveled.[1]

But in Europe as a whole the issues were very similar to those manifest in the United States. Vast press empires were being established in Germany (with the Springer and Grüner & Jahr concerns), in Sweden (with the Bonnier family's holdings), in Italy (as a result of the success of Mondadori), and in France (with the rise of the Hersant juggernaut). The United Kingdom had long been familiar with the phenomenon of powerful press empires with extensive extramural interests in television, tourism, oil, fleets of taxis, and there the fears centered on the loss of more of the national titles that give Britain its unique pluralism and a unique corporatism at the same time. Throughout Western Europe the growth of local monopoly was a serious problem, partly for the same reasons as in the United States (lack of competing voices leading to impovishment of service), but partly also because of the important role that the press plays in the political life of European democracies.

In many countries there was alarm because the press was failing to perform its traditional task of sustaining ideological debate in politics. Newspapers found that their political allegiances in many cases repelled rather than attracted new readers and advertisers. During the 1960's

Europeans became tired of the traditional slogans of left and right and, most important, advertisers needed to reach the new nonpolitical mass audience—young couples building their homes for the first time, high-wage earners. The audiences of politics and the audiences of newspapers, hitherto synchronous, now began to be pried apart. The younger, highly political public of the late 1960's found little in the daily newspaper to charm them, only a reaffirmation of their hostility towards the system. As a result, many European countries began to plan or organize governmental subsidy to the press in order to preserve the linkages between daily newspapers and specific blocks of opinion. Sweden started an elaborate subsidy system by which a large annual fund is collected by taxing all forms of advertising: a Press Support Board, endowed by government with an annual sum equal to that which has been collected, then distributes the cash to those newspapers that fail to reach 40 percent of the households in the market in which they circulate. It is a strange Robin Hood device that helps preserve a plurality of politically aligned newspapers in many cities that would otherwise have become subject to newspaper monopolies. In Norway, a less interventionist scheme was started that equalizes the cost of sending national and international news to every newspaper in the country in proportion to the number of readers and that provides help with new investment. Norway has succeeded in maintaining a model newspaper system, in a sense the ideal towards which other similar societies aspire. The country consists of a large series of small newspaper markets, almost every one containing two or three technically advanced, well-constructed newspapers at mutual and permanent ideological loggerheads. Every Norwegian, every day, has access to two or three different papers, all local and all with opposing views.

In France and Italy elaborate manipulative forms of aid were developed, often through the state's paying a large proportion of all telecommunications costs to newspapers or through paying out sums of money on every ton of newsprint consumed, or by adjusting the levels of the universal Value Added Tax (VAT) on advertising to levels at which struggling "opinion" papers were helped at the expense of larger, profitable organs. The Italian government helped to keep its national price index artificially low by holding down the price of newspapers (which had been included after the war in the "basket" of goods on which the index was calculated). It also kept the cost of running newspapers high by restricting entry to the profession through obligatory registration in the Ordine dei Giornalisti, which guarantees journalists extremely high salaries. It also controls the price of newsprint, keeping it at a level above that which the mere operation of the market would permit. Having thus massively entered into the internal economics of the newspaper industry, the Italian state is inevitably obliged to dole out large cash sums to sustain its newspapers through difficult years.

Only Britain, Ireland, and Germany have stood out against overt government subsidy, but in Britain the publishers are permitted by law to hold blocks of shares in commercial radio and television companies and are released from charging VAT on newspaper sales as well as in commercial advertising, a most valuable privilege. In Germany there has been increasing concern about the growth of local newspaper monopolies and about the role of the Springer enterprise, which owns 40 percent of the daily newspaper market and which constantly presses the government to allow it to move into commercial television. There were moments, too, when even Germany was almost persuaded to adopt a subsidy system by the Social Democrats (and some newspaper publishers), who thought this might be the only way to maintain competition and a pluralist flow of news and comment.

The example of Finland is interesting to anyone concerned with Euro-American contrasts. Finland has a press structure that substantially reflects the political evolution of the society, each political grouping that has emerged since the mid-nineteenth century retaining a party office and a newspaper somewhere in the country. Helsinki has 12 publications that call themselves newspapers (although some are only political broadsheets); there is no company operating more than one publication (apart from one group of four Social Democrat papers, which are owned by a nonprofit enterprise). The problems of the Finnish press are caused by the success of some old, independent papers with large circulations that threaten the existence of the party-owned papers. The elaborate program of subsidies initiated in 1966 is directed at supporting the multiparty political structure through the newspaper medium.

In America the newspaper business operates with completely different mental horizons. By 1963 there were only 51 cities with competing newspaper firms, 43 by 1968, 37 by 1973. Fifty years before, the number had been over 500. In half a century the proportion of U.S. cities with competing papers had dropped from 40 percent to 3 percent, and this fact in itself was being treated as if it were a kind of indictment. This charge becomes more dramatic if, instead of analyzing the number and location of competing newspaper firms in the country, one takes the number of copies of competing newspapers actually sold. In 1923 the total number of newspaper sold in multipaper cities was just under 90 percent, i.e., very few Americans were *not* living in towns where newspapers competed; by 1948 the number had dropped to 62 percent, by 1958 to 51 percent, by 1963 to 43 percent, and by 1973 to 32 percent.[2] By 1979 only 2.5 percent, or 34, of the 1600 U.S. communities in which daily newspapers are published had competing publications of any kind. The monopoly newspaper had passed from being the exception to being the rule. Local monopoly, in an era of competing *media*, had become, as it were, the natural state of the newspaper—or so many felt and many feared.

Although Europe was much less inured to the idea of monopoly newspapers than America, it was much more familiar with the phenomenon of the great newspaper chain (if you are against them, you speak of "chains"; if for them, you speak of "groups") and the powerful press baron. France, Germany, and Britain had all seen the evolution of great industrialized information empires since the previous century. Marinoni's popular papers in France had reached circulations of a million and more in the 1880's; Berlin had been rent by the newspaper campaigns of great rival companies before the First World War. Britain's Northcliffe, Beaverbrook, and Kemsley companies grew out of circulations of many millions in the 1920's and 1930's, with political power bases forming around these information empires. But in all these societies, national chains of papers or nationally circulating papers did not in themselves prevent newspaper pluralism: in the really great newspaper cities such as Vienna before the Second World War, there were up to two dozen competing papers. In Paris, Madrid, London, the reader can still choose from eight or nine every morning.

However, in America the phenomena of local monopoly and national groups or chains arrived at the same moment. The newspaper empires of an earlier generation—Hearst's, for example—had leveled off, and a new kind of managerialism which tended to divorce ownership from daily control, was creeping into newspaper publishing. Fears began to be expressed inside as well as outside the industry, especially after the prolonged newspaper strike of 1963 reduced the number of papers in New York—previously considered one of the great newspaper cities of the world—from nine to three. Behind the liberal dislike of monopolies and chains or groups was the specter of Big Journalism, the fear of the rise of another Hearst who would use his papers as stepping stones to political power, the fear of the spread of the kind of propaganda machinery that Upton Sinclair had warned of in his tract *The Brass Check* at the beginning of the century. Political mythology is slow to form and (sometimes fortunately) slow to die.[3]

In terms of total daily circulation, 71 percent of America's newspapers

Table 6.

Year	No. of Dailies	No. of Chains	No. of Chain-owned Dailies
1923	2036	31	153
1930	1942	55	311
1935	1950	59	329
1940	1878	60	319
1945	1749	76	368
1953	1785	95	485
1960	1763	109	552
1966	1754	156	794
1971	1749	157	879
1976	1765	168	1061

SOURCE: Sterling and Haight Table 221-A

were chain-owned by the end of the 1970's, compared with 42 percent at the end of the Second World War and probably 10 percent half a century before that. Yet American chains are and always have been relatively small, with an average of five or six titles. Expressed in graphic or tabulated form, the figures indicate a tripling of the phenomenon since Hearst's heyday in the 1930's—if, indeed, it is the same phenomenon (see table 6).

A very large proportion of the newspapers extant in the United States at the present time were founded in the generation following the Civil War, especially in the eighties and nineties, and many of the families that have inherited them are now looking for the fourth-generation heir willing and able to run them. Such treasures are hard to find. Newspapers consume a great deal of energy. Modern newspaper management requires a range of diverse skills—in technology, economics, typography, labor relations. Local newspapers need publishers familiar with the community concerned. The temptation—or the simple need—for families to sell out to wealthy chains is often overwhelming.

Under the new inheritance tax legislation of 1972, full market value at the time of death has become the legal basis for tax, but the market value of newspaper properties is exaggeratedly high by nature of the current hunger of small chains to become large chains, the phenomenon of chain ownership thereby growing by what it feeds upon.[4] Skilful accountants can multiply the rate of growth of industrial enterprises and the return upon the notional investment. Great economies of scale can be achieved through the merging of facilities, joint bargaining for newsprint and other raw materials, rationalized trading, and corporate career-planning for key personnel. Few of these economies and advantages are visible to the public, and arguably few of them are directly in the public interest, but they are of value to the stockholders who, as the founding families disperse and fourth- and fifth-generation heirs multiply, are in any case increasingly remote from the newspapers they now own and the communities in which they circulate.

Until the early 1960's no American newspaper stock was traded on the Stock Exchange (unlike newspaper stock in Europe); within fifteen years there were thirteen companies being publicly traded, all of them very large concerns with a total daily circulation amounting to 20 percent of the nation's total. The return to stockholders is over 15 percent, and the problem that besets family firms—high taxes and inheritance duties—is automatically avoided. The process of chain growth is further accelerated because the IRS permits newspaper firms to hold over profits at specially low rates of tax if these are being used for further newspaper purchases and thus have become an integral part of the firm's trading activity. A phenomenon that appeals to the American instinct for the rational and the efficient in normal forms of industry tends to arouse alarm when applied to one of the information industries.

One incident that served to confirm the forebodings of those already alarmed occurred at the *New York Times* in 1976. The Times Company owns twenty-seven other enterprises, including a number of sporting magazines, ten newspapers in Florida and three in North Carolina, three publishing houses, and a couple of broadcasting outlets. A few years earlier it had purchased a group of health magazines from Cowles Communications, and when the *New York Times* in 1976 published some articles alleging various forms of medical incompetence and malpractice, a group of medicine-related advertising clients threatened to withdraw half a million dollars' worth of advertising, not from the *Times* but from its innocent medical magazines. The magazines were sold to a publishing house, which may or may not enjoy permanent immunity from similar pressures between its book-publishing and its magazine-publishing wings.

A few of the smaller chains are owned for avowedly ideological purposes, one of the most celebrated of these being the newspapers of John P. McGoff, who owns eight dailies and forty-five weeklies, spread across two distinct corporations. He is very interested in the affairs of South Africa and once attempted to acquire the *Rand Daily Mail*; he also made ineffective attempts to acquire the *Washington Star* before Time Inc. bought it in 1978. His associate Clarence Rhodes has been President of UPITN, a news-film company owned partly by UPI and partly by

Britain's Independent Television News. McGoff acquired 50 percent of this politically sensitive international company. McGoff's beliefs lie very far to the right of the political spectrum, and his ideological position and corporate connections with South Africa as revealed in the "Muldergate" scandal, which brought about the resignation of South African President John Vorster in June, 1979, have been the subject of alarmed discussion in the British Parliament. He makes no secret of the fact that his present and future newspaper properties are subject to a deliberate policy of trying to move political opinion in America and elsewhere further to the right, an extremely rare phenomenon in the American daily press.

Traditional critics of newspaper chains have asserted that the tendency of chain publishers would be to dominate the editorial stances of their possessions, diminish editorial responsibility, and unfairly influence public opinion. In practice, this temptation, if it is such, has not been succumbed to by the publishers. It is obvious that in some of the chains (in particular, Scripps-Howard, Central, Copley, McClatchy, Panax, and Hearst who between them sell 5.5 million copies every day) there are clear editorial lines to which editors normally adhere. Twelve of fifteen of the seventeen Scripps-Howard papers print the editorials sent out to them from the chain's Washington bureau on subjects affecting national and international policy. The Hearst chain sends out several editorials every day to its eight editors, some of which bear the label "must use," although the others are left to discretion of the local editor. Copley editors, with one exception, run without alteration the editorials sent from the *San Diego Union*, the chain's principal organ, which are simultaneously sent to nearly a thousand other newspapers on its syndication list. The McClatchy papers are perhaps in a slightly different category: these are three Californian dailies, including one powerful paper (the *Sacramento Bee*), which dominates the state capital and produces editorials that are used by the Modesto and Fresno *Bees*.

Alarming in some ways are the syndicates that circulate opinion columns and editorials on urgent issues of the day to newspapers that simply print them as if they reflected their own policy. In these cases there is no chain publisher whose well-publicized name carries with it the ideological responsibility for the opinions expressed in dependent newspapers. Thus the Newspaper Enterprise Association controls an activity known as Enterprise Features, whose managing editor pens four columns a week that are printed without the name of the writer in at least a dozen papers with small circulations. Of course, there are scores of syndicates and agencies who send out feature material, but these are normally published with some kind of identifying by-line.

In any case, most of the major chains do not adopt the practice of circulating unsigned editorials, and these include the largest groups such as Gannett, Thomson, Harte-Hanks, Newhouse, Knight-Ridder, Scripps League, Cox and Cowles, as well as the New York Times group.[5]

The most prevalent driving force towards the growth of newspaper chains and media conglomerates in general is the desire to enhance the value of existing assets. The take-over by Samuel Newhouse of the Booth newspapers of Detroit provides an extremely illuminating example of the problems of third-generation inheritors of newspaper properties. The original Booth had been a young Canadian industrialist who acquired the *Detroit Evening News* from his father-in-law's estate. Ninety years later the paper's ownership (together with that of eight other papers in Michigan) was spread among five-score descendants and heirs plus a couple of thousand ordinary stockholders. Some of the descendants were still employed in various parts of the company, and a group of them decided to press the company's managers to adopt a more profit-seeking approach. (The company had developed nearly $200 million in assets without attempting to maintain the overall rate of dividend, which was low for companies of this size in other industries.) The Booth group decided to acquire the highly profitable *Parade* magazine, which is supplied inside a hundred or so American Sunday papers as a special entertainment supplement. The deal took the form of an exchange of shares, and the arrival of new directors after the *Parade* deal (formerly the property of the Whitney empire) increased the pressure upon Booth's management to adopt a more up-to-date trading policy. Newhouse started to acquire stock in Booth partly through the acquisition of some shares that had been in a foundation and partly by buying out the ex-Whitney *Parade* directors for $31 million—but declaring, meanwhile, that he had no intention of moving towards a general take-over. Booth management retaliated by acquiring a group of weekly newspapers in the area of Cleveland in the hope that Newhouse, who owns the powerful *Cleveland Plain Dealer*, would desist from any effort to purchase a company that might land him in antitrust difficulties through the ownership of papers competing with his own.

The Department of Justice declined to intervene, and the internal struggle within Booth intensified. At the heart of it was the presence of a large sum of money—about $50 million—in cash—which the company owned but was not exploiting for further acquisitions or for a general increase in profits. The Detroit paper was itself a valuable prize for any new owner partly because it was and is a technological leader and is operated at relatively low rates of staffing and a high rate of profit per employee. Booth management was unable to adopt the normal expedient of buying out the quarreling members of the family because the sums of cash now necessary for such an operation were excessive. Already the value of the stock had risen, after the Newhouse intervention, by 50 percent from their value of $16 million at the start of 1976. The management decided to try to persuade the Times Mirror Company of Los Angeles (owners of the *Los Angeles Times* and a vast number of other enterprises) to buy into the Booth concern. At this point Newhouse came right out into the open and declared that he would cap any offer made by the Los Angeles Company, which, hampered at that moment with problems arising from other recent purchases, stepped back and allowed him to move in with a $300 million-dollar check, and acquire the paper. The Newhouse chain, despite its enormous size and influence, is not among the publicly quoted comapnies and can afford to go in for dramatic acquisitions, since it has no public shareholders to worry about the temporary repercussions on stock values.[6]

By such processes little groups throughout the United States are swallowing the last privately owned metropolitan papers, and bigger groups are swallowing the little groups. A widely discussed series of articles in the *Washington Post* published in the summer of 1977 began with the prediction that "within two decades, virtually all daily newspapers in America will be owned by perhaps fewer than two dozen major communications conglomerates." The articles sparked off a strong debate, which led to an FTC (Federal Trade Commission) inquiry into the state of press ownership (in which the American Newspaper Publishers' Association declined to participate). What is equally likely to happen, however, is that a very large proportion of newspapers will drift into the arms of less than ten companies, leaving a large number of mainly small enterprises in a large variety of hands. At present, roughly 170 companies own more than one paper (most of them only two or three), but the four largest companies own one fifth of all daily circulation, and nearly all of them are on the lookout for papers to buy or companies wishing to buy them—a sea of sharks and small fishes.[7]

Two factors in newspaper economics will continue to fuel the desire of persons and companies to acquire newspapers. First, according to the research of stock analyst John Morton, posttax profits on the thirteen companies publicly quoted are equivalent to 10 percent of total sales, nearly double the average rate for the *Fortune* 500. Other printing and publishing activity is also a couple of percentage points above the average.[7] Secondly, it is the advertising base and not total circulation

Table 7.

12 Largest Chains in titles		12 Largest Chains in circulation	
Gannett	75	Knight-Ridder	3,481,112
Thomson	55	Newhouse	3,244,182
Knight-Ridder	32	Tribune	3,124,020
Newhouse	29	Gannett	2,866,835
Freedom	24	Scripps-Howard	1,875,877
Harte-Hanks	22	Dow Jones	1,854,418
Scripps-Howard	17	Times Mirror	1,767,798
Cox	15	Hearst	1,411,922
Dow Jones	14	Cox	1,119,261
Copley	10	New York Times	1,048,493
Tribune	8	Thomson	983,717
Hearst	8	Capital Cities Communications	970,239

SOURCE: *New York Times* (4/2/78) and Lane, Colin, Hochstin Co. from ABC (summer, 1977).

that determines the profitability of a newspaper in America (and almost everywhere else) and in a society in which most newspapers have local monopoly distribution zones, which means that a newspaper is able to preside over the total spending power of a whole community without any comparable medium threatening to undercut the rate at which space is sold. The newspaper has competitors in radio and television in respect to editorial content and competition for the reader's time, but a newspaper that can get its advertisements into the vast majority of homes within a given geographical area holds great power over every enterprise attempting to sell goods within that region. If the paper manages its advertising and distribution shrewdly and keeps marginal competitors such as free newspapers or "shoppers" out of the zone, or at least keep them to a manageable minimum of activity, it has a reliable source of income that must steadily expand so long as the economy as a whole continues to grow. Indeed, in periods of sluggish growth the newspaper can decrease its size (if it is a monopoly) and reduce its losses and thus remain profitable through most forms of economic trough. It is therefore a desirable business to get into, although accessible to only a few outside of the existing newspaper publishing houses.

The twelve largest newspaper companies represent a very large proportion of the total industry, whichever measure one uses—titles or circulation (see table 7). "Is it the best thing," asked one well-known American editor at a conference of the American Society of Newspaper

Editors held in Honolulu in May of 1977, "for large numbers of stockholders of most of America's daily newspapers to have a compelling interest in what is in the dividend check, but no interest in what is in the newshole; to have more of a concern about quarterly earnings than editorial positions; not to be able to read daily, or ever, the newspaper which produces their stock earnings? That is the sort of stockholder this movement is creating." The editor (John Seigenthaler of *The Tennesseean*) proceeded to threaten his audience with the specter of large newspaper undertakings being taken over by even larger nonmedia undertakings— oil or banking interests—a decade or two from now. "Will not this trend, if it continues, invite government investigation, government ownership, government encroachment, where in the past, under independent ownership, the interest of government has been minimal?" His audience, the American Society of Newspaper Editors, had already, some months before, seen the first rumblings of Congressional action against the growth of chains, with the announcement by Senator Morris Udall that he would make public demands for an investigation of corporate power concentration among newspapers. Udall's efforts over the years have continued to find a means of stopping dead the bandwagon of chain growth by relaxing inheritance laws in the case of newspapers or by other forms of governmental prohibition. With the seed planted in Congress, it is likely that the concentration issue will attract increasing attention from America's legislators, even though Congress has traditionally been wary of interfering in the internal processes of an industry that is protected under the First Amendment and upon whose goodwill its members depend for electoral support. Allen Neuhart, President and Chief Executive of Gannett, defended the industry on this occasion against Seigenthaler's fears and charges. Sixty-one out of 74 Pulitzer prizes granted between 1970 and 1977 went to journalists employed on chain newspapers. Chain ownership has led to major improvements in newspapers taken over from one-man control—the quality of a newspaper did not depend on the man or company that owned it but whether it was well run.[9]

To such intangibles there can clearly be no irrefutable answers backed by statistics, only the expression of anxieties and counteranxieties. The fact remains that of the 1082 papers owned by commercial groups in America, only 50—half of one percent—have local competition, and only seven of these have competition at the same time of day as their own publication. Among the 50 there are 16 that have agency agreements— by special legal exemption—with their competitors to fix prices and share profits. By 1977 only 677 U.S. papers remained independently owned, and many of these have tiny circulations, of no interest to the chains. Of the rest, 100 had been acquired by chains by the start of 1979, leaving about 300 titles with more than a 5000 daily sale in independent ownership.

Chain ownership is virtually unassailable by American antitrust law, so long as the companies take care to avoid acquiring circulation in overlapping areas; in fact, even the buying of chains by chains remains perfectly legal, despite past efforts of Justice Department officials to devise grounds for challenging it. It would be possible for four skillfully constructed companies to acquire the whole of the daily newspaper circulation of the U.S. without the risk of prosecution *if* great prudence were used in the choice and later development of circulation markets. The Justice Department successfully prevented the *Los Angeles Times* from holding on to the *San Bernadino Sun* in 1968, for example, and the larger paper was obliged to relinquish it; but it proved impossible to prevent Rupert Murdoch's control of the *New York Post* as well as *New York* magazine and the *Village Voice* because the charge that these purchases reduced competition within a "relevant market" could not be substantiated.[10]

The idea of a "relevant market" is the key to antitrust prosecutions in America, and officials tend to regard the advertising market concerned as the basis of definition. The overlapping of circulation areas of two merging newspapers clearly interferes with free competition for readers and advertisers in that area, but the acquisition by one print enterprise of other print enterprises in roughly the same geographical area continues to leave other media competing for the same advertising—in radio, TV, billboards, periodicals, bumper stickers. In any case, many potential sellers of newspapers to other newspapers can claim the "failing company defense" by which an acquisition is justified by proving that the former enterprise was on the brink of collapse and could not have been saved by the entry into the market of a third company. Finally, the cost of entering *ab initio* into an existing newspaper market is considered so costly today that the courts would be hardly likely to demand that a purchaser start a new newspaper as an alternative to purchasing one. The security against prosecution for a moderately prudent chain is thus virtually complete.

The question arises, however, as to whether, in fact, newspaper markets in an area of multimedia advertising and multimedia news are the same as they were when newspapers competed street by street for the allegiance of a city. Antimonopoly feeling is without doubt very high, but it is perhaps tinged with nostalgia for a form of newspaper publishing that is long departed. In 1857 George D. Prentice of the *Louisville Journal* exchanged four pistol shots with Reuben T. Durret of the *Louisville Courier* after an editorial disagreement;[11] the *Louisville Courier-Journal* of today is a powerful local monopoly organizing its circulation and distribution on technically advanced and highly innovative lines.

The newspaper has always existed as a result of considerable economies of scale—perhaps the earliest industry to live by way of minute profit margins on each unit sold. The cost of creating the editorial content is largely independent of the number of copies printed, and therefore the larger the circulation the lower the cost of content per copy. Furthermore, the cost of reproducing a single copy drops with the growth in the number of copies printed, as does the cost of every square inch printed with the growth in the total quantity printed. Perhaps most importantly, the cost of distribution—one of the most rapidly increasing areas of publishing cost—falls with the increased density of sales in a given geographical area. The logic of these equations has taken a century to work itself through the industry into the monopolistic paper of today (and into the vast national circulations of competing papers in Britain and Japan). It does appear to be the case that modern societies can choose—given the nature of the internal economics of the modern newspaper—between local one-paper communities and national or regional competing papers without local information.

Those countries that appear to enjoy competition among newspapers usually have some national characteristic that, when recognized, dampens the envy of the foreign observer. The British press, for example, provides a choice of ten national daily papers for every reader, plus a local morning or afternoon paper in most provincial centers, but in the course of the present century each newspaper has moved into a given segment of the market—normally defined in terms of social class, or as high-brow, middle-brow, and low-brow—and competes with other papers only at the fringes of its circulation. Within the relatively small middle-class market, there are three papers—the *Guardian*, the *Times*, and the *Telegraph*—all attempting to reach roughly the same social class (although the *Telegraph*'s readers are a fairly distinct homogenous group within that class); but all the other papers have a fairly clear idea of a distinct sector of the market for which their content is most carefully designed. Few British readers start their day wondering which paper to buy (very few papers are sold on subscription), for their habits have been created slowly and almost indelibly over the decades. Any group of two or more papers, in Britain or elsewhere, attempting to serve the same market will soon find that one of them will capture a significant scale economy in relation to its rivals that will eventually wipe them out.

Newspaper reading is a habit of populations of industrial societies; that means that newspaper markets are strong because habits are hard to break, but they are delicate, and once lost can seldom by re-created. There have been several prolonged strikes of major metropolitan newspapers in the 1970's that have helped to illustrate this. The *Berlingske Tidninge* of Copenhagen was out of business for six months in 1976 but regained its entire circulation within a few weeks of resuming production. The long New York newspaper strike of 1978 (nearly three months) ended with the *Times* regaining the whole of its circulation, the *Daily News* regaining all but 15 percent, and the *Post* all but 10 percent. On the other hand, the *Long Island Press* (which once dominated the readership in Queens) died after 157 years of existence and many years of gradual attrition of its daily sales (from 440,000 down to 250,000 between 1969 and 1977) as a result of the growth of the New York papers and Long Island's *Newsday*. A paper is almost invincible if it can hold a high level of household coverage in a significant region, but once neighboring papers begin to enter the central circulation heartland, the habits of readers and advertisers can be rapidly shaken. In the thirty-four American newspaper markets that continue to house two or more daily newspapers operated by rival companies, the "losing" papers enjoy a total circulation of 6 million, which is gradually falling.[12]

The larger of two competing papers tends to benefit from the process of mutual reinforcement between circulation and advertising, whereas the smaller of the two is inclined to get caught in a spiral of reverses. That, at least, has been the view traditionally held by experts in newspaper economics. In 1967 the Swedish Press Commission elaborated its subsidy system to aid those papers that were losing the circulation war with their immediate rivals, and its conclusions were based upon research substantiating this classic theory. However, the theory failed to work in instances where a secondary paper in a reasonably sized city (Stockholm, Gothenberg, and Malmö all provided examples) had managed to creep up on its rival and overcome it in a circulation war. This phenomenon has occurred in many countries in the last quarter century. In 1972 the third Swedish Press Commission discovered that a different principle was, in fact, at work: an analysis of 50 different newspaper companies showed that the success of a newspaper depends more upon its establishment of contact with a large number of households within a given area.

Advertisers are attracted not by the total circulation but by the intensity of circulation in the place of issue. Moreover, once a newspaper reaches 50 percent of the households in such an area, it becomes indispensable to most categories of advertiser, and if its rival falls much below that level of household penetration, it begins its inexorable process of decline. There are, however, certain categories of classified advertisement—notably birth, marriage, and death columns—which defy the general rule and are attracted to newspapers for such traditional reasons as the paper's status or its circulation in particular groups of households. Historical analysis of those cities that had apparently defied the previously held theory appear to confirm this substitute hypothesis. With advertising accounting for at least 60 percent of the revenues of papers in Sweden, the power of market penetration over simple sales figures is fairly clear. The Swedish subsidy system has now been amended to take account of the household penetration theory. In the market areas designated by the Press Support Board, subsidies are granted according to the newspapers' levels of household penetration rather than their total circulations.[13]

At one level, the American press and the provincial British press—as well as the newspaper systems in many parts of Germany, Austria, Switzerland, and Norway—all seem to bear out the principle that the level of household penetration determines the survival power of newspapers. In the last decade or so, however, an additional complication has arisen in the U.S. and in a number of countries where advertising is well developed and the economy in constant search of new and effective means of advertising. In fact, within the sphere of newspaper advertising a new form of competitiveness has appeared, replacing the traditional forms of competition but obliging newspaper managers to keep a constant lookout for threats to their income and profitability, even where they appear to be enjoying the easy fruits of local monopoly.

Many major metropolitan newspapers of America—the *Chicago Tribune, New York Times, Los Angeles Times, Washington Post*—began as local papers with a competing city market but as their cities have grown and as the surrounding commuting area has fanned outward from the city center into vast residential regions, these papers (and others like them) have been obliged to undertake the expensive task of distribution over a much larger terrain, within which there exist small cities and populous suburbs with their own daily papers. The metropolitan paper benefits from the continuing reduction of unit costs and tends to invest in developing a package of supplements to appeal to the residents of its new areas of colonization. Its superior home base and general size often enable it to do this better than the home town papers with which it is now competing.

Within this much larger region, newspapers exist in "layers," all inter-acting with the central metropolitan paper, which originally appeared in these new market areas to pursue the city dwellers who had fled to the suburbs, but which has remained to try to develop its circulation over the total area. James Rosse of Stanford University has analyzed in some detail this new layered newspaper market in his own Bay Area, and this account draws heavily on his study.[14]

At the center of the Bay Area newspaper region sits the *San Francisco Chronicle-Examiner*, a pair of newspapers (morning and afternoon) that are technically under rival ownership but that have been given exemption from antitrust prosecution (under the Failing Newspaper Act, 1970) for merging their production, circulation, and advertisement collection. In the central area of the city this twin newspaper circulates very densely, thinning progressively in the surrounding area that covers almost all of northern California. This represents layer one of the regional newspaper system.

The second layer consists of the newspapers whose centers are the satellite cities of Oakland (the *Tribune*, acquired by Combined Communications of Cincinnati, which has itself merger with Gannett) and San José (the *Mercury News*). These papers, like the *Chronicle-Examiner*, circu-late most thickly at their respective city centers and do not overlap with one another even though between them they cover the whole Bay Area with the exception of the section occupied by the *Chronicle-Examiner* at its densest level of circulation.

The third layer consists of sixteen suburban papers, including those of Palo Alto, San Rafael, Hayward, and Berkeley, whose circulation areas are small (in relation to that of the satellite city papers) and do not overlap. There is a fourth layer of weekly, twice- and thrice-weekly papers, shopping papers and free papers, which are distributed at their densest in those areas farthest away from the circulation centers of the three previous layers. Some papers in this category contain a great deal of solid information, and there is one that is circulated in the center of San Francisco itself and owned by the Harte-Hanks group that is a lively paper with a great deal of news, given away free in some areas but for a cover price in others.

First-layer papers have easiest access to the advertising of national and regional advertisers and find it hardest to get advertising from small retail establishments and other highly localized sources. Although their editorial content is generally of a higher standard than that of the other layers, and has evidently cost the publisher a good deal more to obtain (whether from local writers or from syndicates), these papers find it difficult to offer their readers truly local information. The circulation area of the San Francisco paper reaches out towards its nearest neighboring first-layer papers, the *Oregonian* of Portland and the *Times* of Los Angeles, but circulates so thinly at the zones of intersection that their circulation areas scarcely touch at all. Second- and third-layer papers, however, tend to circulate up to the point at which they meet competition from papers of the same layer—the audiences within a single layer being continuous and separate, with no advertising competition among the papers of such a layer. Between all the layers, however, there is vigorous competition for advertisers, since there are groups of advertisers for whom the relative geographical advantages of one layer of papers over another are counteracted by the differences in the cost of advertising in the different layers.

The city and region of Philadelphia provide another example of the problems that population change has brought about for the metropolitan papers that survive—the *Bulletin*, the *Inquirer*, and the *News* (two others have died in recent years). These are now surrounded by twenty-seven suburban dailies, which publish mainly in the afternoon. Even forty years ago there were over twenty of these, but they mustered a circulation of only a quarter of a million between them—they now have over 700,000, 75 percent of which is in the afternoon. Within the eight-county area the population was concentrated in Philadelphia itself, which had 60 percent of all the inhabitants, compared with 35 percent today; it had two thirds of the retail trade of the area, compared with one third today. In addition to these suburban papers, there are a dozen and a half dailies in small towns in the eight counties, many of which are as old as Philadelphia. Over the past forty years their circulation has increased slowly but steadily to just over 1.5 million in aggregate. The fall of a quarter million in the total circulation of the downtown papers is more than accounted for by the gains in surrounding areas, and it leaves the three city papers with a total circulation of just over a million—and a deep desire to recoup their losses through major competitive activities in the suburbs.[15]

It is the size and wealth of the community in which it is distributed that determines the power and potential of a newspaper. Between layers in a vast, segmented market such as the Bay Area in northern California, there is a fierce and tireless search for new advertisers, to whom the commercial effectiveness of a specific newspaper in a specific layer has to be proved. It means that the present structure of the U.S. newspaper market constitutes a pressure towards ever greater investment within each newspaper enterprise in circulation and distribution methods at the cost of editorial development. The task of the newspaper in this stage of its history, competing as it does with the electronic media for the leisure time of its audience, is to maintain the habit of purchase by attracting and holding onto the households that circumstances place at its disposal—to do what is necessary for a "better" paper, but not necessarily "better" in respect to the whole of its content. Despite what has been said, the great majority of American cities do not originate newspapers, even monopoly ones. Of the 7000 urban centers in the United States, only 25 percent are actually the sites of newspaper publishing. Ninety years ago there were only 1348 such population centers but still a larger number of newspapers. As we have seen, metropolitan papers today cover a large number of communities on the same day, offering supplements and special editions of local news. The *Atlanta Constitution* circulates in fifty-five counties, less than half of which have local papers of their own; its area contains up to 1000 public agencies and probably many hundreds of local authorities with the power to levy taxes. It is hard to believe that all of them feel the constant pressure of journalistic scrutiny.

Newspapers have been obliged to follow the logic of demographic and geographic circumstances, as well as their own internal dynastic situation. Los Angeles offers the classic example of a city that despite massive growth found that it could not support competition in the morning field and scarcely any paper at all in the afternoon. The Chandlers and the Hearsts each had a morning paper and an afternoon one, and as the city spread farther and farther outwards, both realized that delivery was impossible. Los Angeles was the television city par excellence, and it was a time when television was eating into the reading time of afternoon papers. With the assent of the Justice Department the Chandlers agreed to drop their afternoon paper (the *Mirror*, which had lost $25 million in thirteen years) if the Hearsts dropped their morning paper, the *Examiner*. In retrospect, it would seem to be an extraordinarily unfair deal. The Hearsts were agreeing to withdraw into a shrinking and increasingly impossible market, strewn with headaches, in exchange for a monopoly within it, while Otis Chandler, third-generation inheritor of his estate, was taking over a vast and growing market, albeit writing off a property the family would have liked to see stay in existence.[16] Since that date, the afternoon paper has struggled to keep an acceptable level of total Los Angeles advertising, and there are many who think it will slide inexorably out of its painful existence in the course of time. The deal was the first triumph of Otis Chandler, newly risen to the publisher's chair. The morning monopoly gave the Chandler family the opportunity to benefit from the economic upsurge of the time: by moving the paper away from its traditionally highly conservative stance, in the fifteen years before 1976 it quintupled the amount spent in the editorial department, doubled its circulation to over a million, and started the valuable joint news service with the *Washington Post*.

A researcher of the future, examining the American dailies of today compared with those of a decade ago, will perhaps be able to confirm what we can now only feel—that flamboyant tabloids bursting with gaudy shopping supplements, trivial local news, and sensational crime news, are all the quintessential offering of the culture of the era, which has sloughed off the strivings and torments of the Vietnam days but absorbed those cultural changes of the sixties that can be turned to profit. The newspaper of the seventies is based upon surveys, its editors more reliant upon the advice of newspaper consultants than of political bosses. Publishers, still weary of defending themselves against those who blamed them for what their newspapers reported, have settled down to the task of making money and consolidating their industry in its new electronic phase, with its monopoly grasp over each reading public. The newspapers have become an industry of publishers and managers more than of editors and journalists.

That, of course, is far from being the whole story. Many of the metropolitan papers that have found a new profitability in local monopoly have opened up new forms of journalism, including the investigative genre, in order to consolidate their public. Several newspapers that were scorned over the last half century by the well-informed and those who wished to be well-informed, have become the editorial leaders of today. Conspicuous among them is the *Los Angeles Times*, which slipped painfully out of its right-wing stance just in time to avoid succumbing to the fashionable John Birchery of the 1960's, which swept up much of the wealthy upper crust of Southern California. This paper has escalated in profits but also in quality. It consistently offers its writers the chance to develop important stories into articles of 2000 and 3000 words, often starting them on the front page. The triviality that disgraced many papers in the sixties has receded from many of the larger metropolitan papers, which are no longer troubled by daily competition for readers. Analysis and imagination are permitted to grace their pages. These papers are still perhaps a minority, if the American press is taken as a whole, but they contain some of the leading titles of the country.

Parallel with and inseparable from the growth of chains and local monopolies is the development of cross-ownership. There are about 60 communities in the United States where newspapers own television stations transmitting in the same area and 200 where newspapers own radio stations.[17] In 1975 the figures were much higher, but they have dropped as a result of a debate launched by the National Citizens Committee for Broadcasting and a series of court rulings obtained by the NCCB. This new turn in public policy towards the press had been developing slowly over the years. The rules of the Federal Communications Commission had long forbidden any company to own more than seven television stations, seven AM radio stations, and seven FM stations; they also forbid any single entrepreneur to hold more than one television station, one AM station, and one FM station in the same market. In 1975 the FCC issued a Report and Order dealing with joint ownership of broadcasting with print outlets in the same market and named sixteen markets, where a newspaper owned the only local TV or radio station, in which such cross-ownership had to cease; it also ordered that all such combinations in future were not to be undertaken, while leaving all existing cross-ownerships intact. Characteristically, the FCC had decided not to indulge in massive acts of forcible divestiture and declared that it would instruct newspaper owners to sell broadcast outlets only if it were demonstrated case-by-case that an abuse of power was occurring. The Appeals Court reversed this judgment, declaring that divestiture was required in all cases except where it could be demonstrated that joint ownership was in the public interest. Even while still awaiting the Supreme Court's view of the inevitable appeal against this ruling, major newspapers, including the *Washington Post*, started a form of divestiture through exhange; several found suitable partners in distant cities with whom to exchange control of their respective broadcasting stations.

The FCC's reluctance to order divestiture was inevitable: only twenty years before, in the 1950's, it was encouraging newspapers in small towns to start up television stations, that being the only way to locate the capital and skills necessary for the new medium. It is difficult even now to find suitable yardsticks of effective stewardship of television in American small towns. "Diversity" is an excellent clarion call and carries meaning in New York City, but in the case of, say, a 30,000-inhabitant town like Watertown in upper New York State, where a single family owns the local paper and television station, it is difficult to find grounds to "prove" that cross-ownership is detrimental.[18] As the owner of the *Watertown Times* himself puts it, "There isn't much diversity to begin with."

What cross-ownership does do, however, is sustain the confidence of local newspaper-owning families that their view of the community they dominate is a valid one, and thus perpetuate the idea that they know what the readers (and viewers) want. When other media in the same community are under dual ownership, the fixedness of view tends to become entrenched, though, like chain-ownership and local monopoly, it can lead to good journalism as well as bad. Very often, as in the Watertown case, which was investigated by the now defunct *More* magazine, the family owning the entire range of locally based news outlets is simultaneously heavily involved in local politics and thus has a deadening influence on any "investigative" urges on the part of its news staff. But divestiture has its own internal contradictions: to sell a television station or a newspaper to a chain with distant headquarters is to remove local control altogether from an important (because scarce) community resource.

Much empirical work has been attempted over the years to establish whether cross-ownership tangibly lowers the quality of available journalism within a community, but "quality" is almost immune to the investigative techniques of social science.[19] There are certain visible practices that cross-ownership engenders: the placement of a radio station in a newspaper building owned by the same firm, the sharing of newspaper carbons with a sister radio or TV station before going to the press, the easy transfer of staff from one unit to the other. A number of studies conducted during successive FCC investigations of the phenomenon were anything but conclusive. One study showed that there were apparent tendencies for cross-owned papers and stations to use less wire service copy and do more public affairs broadcasting,[20] but even this discovery is refuted by evidence from other studies. It is relatively simple to provide *ad hoc* evidence of appalling misjudgment of bias within cross-owned media, and Harvard Professor Stephen R. Barnett, in a study submitted to the FCC, supplied a mountain of such evidence in concrete anecdotal form;[21] but the Appeal Court in declining to use this material expressed nervousness about drawing national and general conclusions from isolated examples. After all, the same quantity of malpractice might well be discovered in any study of any newspaper or radio news operation. Cross-ownership is not a precondition for poor journalism.

There are obvious temptations built into cross-owned media. First, the owner is protected against immediate rebuttal from local rival media, since they share the same employer. Secondly, there is a danger of local news being controlled by an individual or family who is likely to collect over time a series of direct involvements in local organizations and affairs that are themselves subjects of local news. This danger is greatly reduced, of course, when there is an alternative or competitive news source. Thirdly, where different media are jointly owned, inhibitions accumulated in one newsroom as a result of normal day-to-day abrasion can easily be transferred to another.

During the years of this controversy, radio and television have grown financially stronger, and the results of divestiture have become less potentially damaging for any single enterprise. Simultaneously, the argument concerning the burden of proof has shifted from the accusers to the accused. Since the dangers of cross-ownership are permanent and universal, the argument has grown more prevalent that divestiture should occur before rather than after conclusive proof of abuse of privilege. However, even though the divestiture movement in the United States is now firmly under way, further controversy is likely to continue. Public-interest pressure groups are closely observing the journalistic quality of those enterprises that have changed hands as a result of divestiture, and any disappointment with the quality will inevitably cause people to ask whether the hue and cry has been justified. A belief in the virtues of competition runs deep through both liberal and conservative traditions in America, and cross-ownership is bound to remain a vexatious issue—the controversy intensifying with the difficulty in producing convincing proof of where the public interest lies.

One of the principal causes of the jolt felt by publishers in the 1960's was the realization that a new medium, television, was taking a major share of the national advertising budget, including a vast section of the manufacturer-to-consumer advertising on which the mass press of Europe and the metropolitan newspapers of America had been founded. The development of large-space advertising dates back to the early 1880's when so many other elements of the modern newspaper were first introduced. The new department stores that sprang up in the era of financial readjustment, which followed reconstruction, required large blocks of space in the press to advertise their enlarged varieties of goods. An individual store would spend up to $50,000 a year at a single newspaper, transforming the economics of both store and medium. Railroad companies also became major advertisers, taking large areas of paper to describe the scenic beauties of their routes. Competition had broken out between gas and electricity utilities to fight their way into millions of homes. Sewing machines, pianolas, telephones, packaged breakfast foods, all made their first appearance and depended largely upon display advertising to reach the attention of consumers. The newspaper thus became a major vehicle for national advertising as well as classified, local retail, and other kinds of advertising and remained so until the spell was broken by television.

At the beginning of World War II, newspapers took 38.6 percent of total national advertising volume, but this began to fall almost imperceptibly as the war years ended and television began to spread. By 1950 it

Table 8.

	1976	1977	1978
Newspapers	29.4%	29.2%	29.0%
Television	19.9%	20.1%	20.2%
Radio	6.9%	6.8%	6.8%
Magazines	5.3%	5.7%	5.9%
Direct Mail	14.3%	14.1%	13.8%
All other media	24.2%	24.1%	24.3%

SOURCE: Newspaper Advertising Bureau, New York, and McCann Erickson Inc.

was down to 36.3 percent, by 1960 to 30.8 percent, and in 1963 it reached the low point of 29 percent. Since then it has hovered at the 30 percent level.[22]

Once the shock had been absorbed, however, newspapers began to realize that they continued to have a major role in all forms of advertising and as an industry were doing very well against their seemingly invincible competitors. In 1976, for instance, the breakdown of total advertising among media left newspapers with by far the largest single sector and with as much volume of sales as television, radio, and the booming magazine industry put together (see table 8).

Since 1970 the internal divisions within the total volume of newspaper advertising have remained roughly constant, about 60 percent coming from retail, a quarter from classified, and 15 percent from national advertising. However, retail advertising, important as it has now become to newspapers, is largely drawn from four sources: food and drugs, entertainment and hobbies, housing and decoration, clothing and general merchandising. This last sector represents nearly half of the total and leaves the newspaper industry highly vulnerable to any new medium that can provide a large volume of advertising from department and clothing stores.

National advertisers in recent years have increasingly been making straight choices between newspapers and television. Toiletries and toilet goods, medical products, and household supplies contribute a tiny proportion of their advertising (about 4 percent) to newspapers and a large proportion to national television. However, there are six industries that provide two thirds of all national advertising in newspapers: transportation, automobiles, tobacco, publishing, foods, and hotels.[23]

The strategy of the newspaper industry is to keep hold of such national advertising as it can while increasing its local and classified linage, a task that entails considerable internal reorganization, including changes in the editorial format of the newspaper and, most importantly, adoption of methods of production that dovetail the newspaper more and more into the lives of its readers, area by area. Between 1960 and 1970 national advertising fell from 21 percent to 15 percent of the total revenues of newspapers, while local advertising increased from 79 percent to 85 percent, leaving the newspaper pretty well dependent on its own neighborhood for its advertising income.[24] The vast growth of small-town and suburban daily papers (often weeklies turning into dailies) is one aspect of this change in the structure of the newspaper industry. However, as we shall see, much of the technical reform of the industry is in fact directed at the task of improving the ways in which local information and local advertising are collected by metropolitan and other newspapers that have not been trained by history to do this.

One of the most rapidly developing techniques of newspaper advertising has been the preprint, sheets of carefully zoned advertising slotted into the daily or Sunday newspaper just prior to delivery and printed by the newspaper's own plant or by some other local printing house. In the 1970's preprints have boomed, increasing by about 150 percent since 1970, although accurate figures are hard to collect because of the sprawling and sporadic nature of the business. Already the annual preprint market is over $1 billion, its rise spurred on by rapidly rising postal prices (the postman used to carry much of the material that is now finding its way into the preprint medium). The vast proportion of advertisers who use preprints are local (over 90 percent), and new techniques for color printing by roll-fed methods have contributed to the popularity of the medium among local advertisers. Preprints are often worked on by local nonunion printing enterprises, and this has meant that the medium is a cheap, convenient method for encouraging housewives into neighborhood shops and supplying them with up-to-the-minute catalogs of prices for a wide range of goods.

At the end of the 1970's there are many paradoxes in the position of newspaper advertising. The industry continues to shiver with apprehension while raking in a handsome volume of advertising income. Its total dollar income form advertising has more than kept up with the growth of the GNP, even when 1946 is used as the starting base. Newspapers collected $10.2 billion, or 30 percent of the $38 billion spent in 1977 on all forms of advertising. Newspaper advertising has multiplied nearly nine times since 1946, compared with the GNP's growth of eight times in its 1946 figure. Newspapers have outperformed the average industrial rate of growth in almost every sector of their advertising revenue. Even in national advertising, where newspapers have lost a great deal of ground (in percentage points) to television, the newspaper's share of national advertising has multiplied by six (from $250 million to $1.5 billion). In point of fact, the growth, in volume, of newspaper revenue from national advertisers is greater than the entire volume of television advertising, which is supposed to have caused the slippage in the newspaper's hold over that category.[25]

Newspapers have had to spend more, however, to keep their figures in this apparently healthy condition. Their raw materials, especially newsprint, have skyrocketed in price. To expand their size in order to keep the volume of advertising high, they have had to employ more people in almost every section of the business, from editorial to delivery. They reach the end of the 1970's as the third largest employer of labor in the United States, 400,000 people fully employed in the industry, excluding local delivery people (compared with roughly 250,000 at the end of the war; this is equal to one in 230 of the working population, about the same as at the end of the war).[26] Perhaps more significant is the fact that in the late 1970's a higher proportion of the total space in newspapers is occupied by advertising than in previous times. On average, advertising filled 54.5 percent of the space in all sections of the newspaper medium (mornings, evenings, and Sundays together), while today the figure is closer to 64 percent of papers with a much increased pagination.[27]

When an advertiser contemplates the newspaper medium today, comparing it with its modern range of competitors, a number of distinct advantages present themselves. It offers great flexibility in geographical coverage, helping the advertiser select his areas of marketing with great finesse and subtlety. If he is a short-term advertiser, it is an ideal medium, since it involves him in little specialized expertise that he cannot get from the newspaper itself and does not oblige him to commit himself very far ahead. The news basis of the medium gives an aura of immediacy and yet leaves the audience with a permanent, hard-copy record of his information. His access to the audience is a permanent, all-weather daily link—apart from occasional strikes and extremes of climate—yet his market is highly individual and he can direct his messages at specific members of a household be placing them judiciously within the paper. His audience can recognize him if he is a regular local dealer and will record his information as part of the changing information of the neighborhood. And yet with all these advantages he can drop his advertisement at short notice, and start it up again as soon as he feels inclined. Finally, the audience is static and does not have to be built up prior to the advertiser's own campaign.[28]

There are many disadvantages, however, to newspaper advertising. The advertiser cannot select small demographic groups, and if he wants to reach only those readers with children of school age or those who go sailing or smoke pipes, he must pay to reach all the others as well—quite unlike the specialist magazine, for example. If he happens to be a national or regional advertiser, his audience will be relatively expensive, compared with radio or television. If the product concerned depends upon color for its appeal, the newspaper cannot be as effective as television or magazines or billboards, since many newspapers have little or no color possibilities and only indifferent quality reproduction when they do (although this is now subject to rapid technical improvement).

One great advantage of the newspaper's increasing reliance on local advertising is that it is least subject to market fluctuations. Since the 1958 mini-slump, the newspaper industry has been hit less severely by each downturn in the economy than by the previous one. In 1958 it lost 2.8 percent of its total advertising revenue, but in the 1970 recession the revenue held steady, a small increase in local advertising compensating for the drop in national revenue. The 1974 recession saw the newspaper industry achieving a 5 percent rise in revenue, gaining in both sectors as advertisers tried to spend their way through the downturn. The same performance was repeated in the 1975 downturn, which was nearly as serious in parts of the economy as the slump of the 1930's.[29]

Both in profits margins and total earnings the newspaper industry weathered the storms of the last three recessions with hardly a damaged sail. In 1970, for instance, after the wonderful year of 1969 (15.2 percent growth in earnings), publicly quoted newspapers dropped 8.6 percent compared with 12 percent for the *Fortune* 500. In the same year the profits margins of the press after amortization of depreciation and goodwill was 14.7 percent compared with 17.4 percent in the preceding boom year. In the 1974 downturn the operating margins of the quoted companies fell by a tiny amount from 17.5 percent in boom year 1973 to 16.8 percent, while their earnings growth rate dropped to a gain of seven percent from a gain of 22 percent in 1973. If one excludes the losses of the *New York Times* and *Daily News*, the 19 largest U.S. newspaper groups acquired an increase in profits, after-tax, of 31 percent in 1978 over 1977, compared with 16 percent in the rest of U.S. industry.[30]

It seemed that newspapers had learned to ride the storms, were increasingly immune to the cyclical performance of surrounding industry, and could look forward to a long stretch of continuous technical improvement that would reduce operating costs and increase many of the industry's sources of revenue. The causes of the newspaper's gloom of recent years has, therefore, been hardly the result of low profits. It has been the result of the newspaper's finding itself in a changing operating climate. Once, it was the newspaper advertising manager who dominated the relationship with thousands of retail advertisers. Today a series of vast chains have driven tens of thousands of small shops out of business, and their professionalized managers, brandishing charts and graphs, dominate the relationship with the newspaper. A small advertiser would depend on the goodwill of his local newspaper and could possibly choose between one or two of them. Today the chain store examines local advertising media before finally deciding where to place its new outlets. Even the large store that has remained in the city center considers it necessary to have branches in every suburb and to be prominently represented in local print and electronic media.

There have been several leading factors contributing to the weakening of the local power of the newspaper and the undercutting of its rates. The free "shoppers," which offer instant total coverage of all households in a given area, have been extremely popular with advertisers; preprints have become a booming industry since zip-coding was introduced in the 1950's; and mailed advertising is still widely used. The newspaper simply has to work much harder for its living.

The underlying cause of the newspaper's problem with its local (and increasingly important) advertising base goes back to the demographic changes and alterations in the structures of human settlement with which we began. Television has been, in many ways, the ideal medium for the age of megalopolis. The television signal spreads out from a central point and reaches a large circle of the public in suburbs and distant towns, treating them all alike, blotting out subtle historic distinctions between one community and its neighbor, distinctions that were expressed in the structure of newspaper markets but that have nevertheless become worn down in the era of consumer sovereignty. Major retailers have their stores situated in places easy to reach by car across a marketing area that tends to coincide with the patterns of a television transmitter's signal area. Television programming is made to suit appropriate denominators of taste throughout the area of the signal.

In the 1950's Nielsen greatly simplified the task of media planning by creating the Designated Market Areas (DMA's), which cover the whole of the United States contiguously without wasteful overlaps of population, in great contrast to the overlaps and historical subtleties of newspaper readership areas. In fact, the DMA's and the parallel pattern of Areas of Dominant Influence (ADI's), which were drawn up by the American Research Bureau Inc., all contributed to rendering the newspaper readership map of America a hopelessly irrelevant-seeming scheme for reaching the consumer. The "signal" of a newspaper does not cut a finely rounded, geographically simple pattern, and once the television media planners created their own neat systems, the newspaper had to create new arguments for major advertisers to apply themselves to its oddly shaped zones of coverage.

Advertisers thus came to look at newspapers as if they were failed television stations, and a built-in professional bias against the newspaper developed. Using the tools and methods of one dominant medium led media planners to misjudge the advantages of print. Those newspapers whose readership filled the main block of space within a DMA or ADI tended to get the first bite of the advertising cake because their market looked "better," even though other newspapers circulating in overlapping areas and communities might have been able to offer finely differentiated groups of readers suitable for certain approaches or offers. It was if a new human geology was being laid on top of an older set of layers—the new one tending to suppress or overlay traditional civic loyalties and other traditional demarcations. The contributers to the retail revolution and the modern sales manager helped to undermine the confidence of the newspaper as they assisted at the funeral rites of the city.

One further change in the structure of the newspaper industry resulting directly from the change from city to megalopolis was the decline of the afternoon paper in relation to the morning paper. There has been a gentle decline in total circulation of the former since the middle of the 1960's, from 36.5 million, while morning circulation has increased over the same period, from 25 million to 27 million. The decline in the use of streetcars, buses, subways, and trains on which newspapers bought at city kiosks would be read en route home and the corresponding increase in the use of private cars by commuters has led to the death of many afternoon papers and to the decline of street sales in almost all afternoon papers. What has taken the place of kiosk sales is home delivery, which has been much harder to organize in afternoons than mornings. The problem has been to deliver papers before the afternoon television news attracts commuters to their TV sets for the evening. All industry researchers seem to agree that the peak hour for reading afternoon papers is between four and four-thirty, but to get the papers printed for the deadline involves drastic overhaul of editorial and production deadlines; the trucks have to be on the streets ahead of the commuters and the traffic jams that they generate in the late afternoon.

Press times for what were once thought of as evening papers have now changed so widely that the Audit Bureau of Circulations has approved a change of rule that would allow a much broader definition of morning and evening. In the past, morning papers have published between six p.m. on the night before the day whose date they carry to nine a.m. on the day itself; afternoon papers have gone to press at dawn and completed their production at nine a.m. In 1971 the *Detroit Evening News* started to research and plan a morning edition to compete with the *Detroit Free Press*, and it finally came to birth in 1976 with an edition that was delivered in the mornings outside the downtown area and printed just after midnight. A year later it introduced kiosk sales for commuters going in to work, and both maneuvers have proved a success. In the afternoon it changes more than half its editorial content (but not its advertisements) and sells its traditional edition, but this is now almost entirely home-delivered. The *Philadelphia Evening Bulletin* has now started a similar scheme with nighttime printing and a six-thirty kiosk sale in the downtown area. Its aim has been the same as the Detroit paper's—to get back its commuter clients who have moved out to distant suburbs.

One of the most curious situations has arisen in Chicago, where the *Tribune* abandoned its afternoon paper, *Today*, in 1974 and where the *Sun-Times* discontinued its affiliate the *Daily News* in 1978. The *Tribune* started to publish an afternoon edition the day before publication at three-thirty, with a second edition an hour later, both varying the date of the morning edition (which became the last of a series of editions). The *Sun-Times* moved into a parallel cycle of produciton, offering an afternoon edition "the day before" plus three more night-produced editions for delivery during the following morning and afternoon, the last copies of which don't reach the farthest outlying areas until the morning after the date of publication. Early in 1979 the *Tribune* decided to change its labelings of these various editions, and its "Green Streak" edition, which was the name of its very early prepublication-date edition, has now become the last of the cycle of the previous day's publicaton. The *Tribune* has thus created a kind of twenty-four-hour paper going through continuous changes of content, one of the pioneers of a new-style all-day paper that has been predicted for many years as a possible result of modern technology but that has come into existence as a result of the demographic overhaul of industrial and urban life.[31]

Nearly all that has happened to the newspaper industry has resulted from this convulsion within its system of marketing, altering its whole picture of the community in which it circulates information. The death of the city marked the birth of the new technology. "We watched Chicago rot away right up to our loading bays, before we realized what the death of the central city meant to us," says one Chicago publisher.[32] The problem is how to reforge the links between the newspaper and its dispersed readers and to reconnect the newspaper to the altered concept of citizenship. "Only when the city is synonymous with the market can there be an identity between citizenship and the sense of belonging to a place, and thus between the audience and the medium," says Leo Bogart, whose statistical researches since the 1960's have proved the case for rededicating the newspaper to its historic role rather than abandoning it, even though the economic structure of the industry has been considerably altered.[33] Each stage in the creation of the newspaper and its content is being rethought in the seventies and eighties, and at each stage research leads to revision of concepts and to a redesigning of production technology. The computerized newspaper is not one in which simply a large quantity of traditional labor is saved; it is a newspaper that uses the computer to achieve the new purposes of the medium.

It is not necessary to rejoice at these changes in order to see something of their meaning and consequences. To meet its historic problems the American newspaper is redividing its contents, creating new linkages between the newspaper content and the sources of information, new linkages between itself and its readers. The entire form of the newspaper is undergoing one of its periodic remodelings to fit the changes in its entrepreneurial, industrial, and organizational pattern. The newspaper is being sliced into its component parts, it is being "zoned" to fit the areas of residence of its readers, it is being repackaged and redesigned, and this whole operation is dependent upon a series of technologies that arose from the space and missile programs of the last decade and are now infiltrating themselves into a range of industries that have found themselves out of gear with their time.

3. THE NEWSPAPER
& THE COMPUTER

The anxieties of the modern American newspaper publisher are considerable. He may have a local metropolitan "monopoly," with a radio and television station to keep his paper company; he may be comfortingly part of a large publicly quoted chain, with accountants constantly snapping at his heels to keep the share price rising; or he may be simultaneously a cross-owner, a monopolist, a concentrator of ownership. In any event, he is probably permanently scared. Let us work our way through the economic worries of one highly successful publisher/editor in the Midwest with a well-established three-generation family-owned morning and afternoon monopoly.

One major problem for this particular publisher is to arrange delivery of his papers to homes more than a hundred miles from the printing plant. Just to get them all to the local delivery points consumes 450,000 gallons of gasoline. In the outlying areas the cost of delivering the paper is equal to the total revenue collected from the reader. It would be sensible to "sack" these readers, even if they and their families have been traditional readers, but to do so would be an open invitation to various local weeklies to turn themselves into suburban dailies, which, once they established a base for themselves, would expand circulation steadily back towards the city. Were the cost of gasoline to rise above a dollar fifty per gallon, the whole operating profit of the newspaper would disappear.

Another problem with distribution is the fact that the whole system depends upon child labor, and when parents grow more prosperous, they begin to worry about the way their children earn their pocket money. Furthermore, every time a child agent throws a paper in the mud, a subscription may be lost for ever. If Congress were ever to cancel or restrict the newspaper's exemption from child-labor legislation, the newspaper would be sunk. In any case, parents are now complaining about the sheer weight of the papers their children must carry.

Newsprint has more than doubled in price in the years since 1970, from $150 to nearly $350 per ton. In 1957 it was $135, and slightly heavier. Each ton consumes eight barrels of oil, although modern de-inking and recycling techniques have reduced considerably the amount of oil required (to about five barrels per ton). However, if the cover price of the newspaper were to rise much about 25 cents a copy, it would start to become cheaper to distribute news by telecommunications devices than on paper. At 30 cents a copy modern teletext or videotext could become highly attractive substitutes for newspapers in certain sections of the readership, even if they only provide a few headlines and nuggets of information. Some bright entrepreneur with the ear of the wire services could assuredly find a way to send AP and UPI direct into people's homes for a couple of dollars a week.

Of course, new technology is helping to reduce the amount of newsprint used by a newspaper by offering more columns per page and lighter weights of paper. But these materials are really suitable only for papers using modern offset machines. Larger papers with greater print runs still use traditional letterpress equipment purchased a decade or more ago and still to be depreciated, and with these machines paper dust on the lightweight newsprint spoils the pictures. There are problems of linting. If you have to use several thousand plates a week, the likelihood of going over to offset machinery is still fairly small, since offset plates can perform only a limited run before wearing out, and each replating necessitates the loss of a quantity of copies. With 3000 plate changes a week, a paper cancels out the cost savings derived from using a lighter-weight newsprint.

All around the newspaper's central area of distribution a rash of free shoppers and pennysavers has broken out, each of them guaranteeing the advertiser 100 percent household penetration, no annual raising of advertising rates, immunity from risky dependence upon child labor, and freedom from the problem of persuading readers to subscribe. Yet there is little possibility of the newspaper printing its own shoppers because of antitrust laws. Some papers have got round this problem through zoned editions or by starting small suburban weeklies or by distributing copies of their papers free to nonsubscribers. A paper that can manage to acquire and keep a 70 percent household penetration tends to be immune to the depredations of shoppers and throwaways, but this imposes a tremendous pressure upon its circulation department and is leading in some cities to the professionalization of delivery or of the supervision of delivery rounds (thereby raising the cost of circulation). More and more of the traditionally casual part-time labor employed in newspaper delivery is being abandoned and replaced by staff appointees, so great is the pressure today to maintain high levels of household penetration.

Having overcome the vastly increased costs of distributing the newspaper, now enlarged by zoned editions and special supplements, the publisher must deal with the problem of the reader, and the many demands on his or her time. Only about 10 percent of the total information collected every day in the newspaper's newsroom and features desk (all of which is held on-line, i.e., in continuous direct communication with a computer) is actually used in the paper, and yet, according to most surveys, the reader only reads 10 percent of what has gone into his paper. It seems, therefore, that the whole agony of distribution is undergone in order to feed each reader just one percent of the material that has been so expensively collected.

The newspaper now enjoys peace with its work force, who have bravely put up with the havoc wrought upon their careers and risked the massive layoffs that have taken place in the computer era. Several of the presses are forty years old, two are twenty-five years old, and the time is coming for a switchover to the latest generation of offset presses that can take much larger print runs, fairly economically, than their predecessors. Certainly it is much too late now to contemplate replacing existing equipment with anything but offset equipment, although at a cost approaching $40 million, which is difficult to borrow for a paper that has deliberately been running for many years of a lower profit margin than it could have. Yet the moment the new equipment is ordered, it will become apparent that 50 percent of the already depleted work force is not really necesary and ought to be reduced to gain the benefit of the new machines. The paper, therefore, could well be moving slowly towards an era of poor labor relations, perhaps strikes and lockouts. Technology experts from Germany have been touring the country saying that the new offset presses can be run by three men. One machine's accepted manning levels is the next machine's featherbedding make-work scheme.

Our unhappy newspaper publisher must continue, however, to make his paper thicker over the years, as he embraces more and more subtly refined sections of public taste, more "life-styles," as identified by his researchers. The thicker papers still have to be bundled, trucked, and delivered by teenagers or children. He must not increase the price of his paper to defray any of these costs, or he will find himself priced out of the newspaper market by a new or existing suburban daily. A 5-cent rise per copy is equivalent to an extra $10 on a monthly household subscription, high enough to deter a publisher from casually passing on the effects of inflation. Inside the downtown area sales are from heavy vending machines, easy to rifle, even though a significant proportion of the people living there may be unable to read English. ANPA has designed a machine that will permit only one copy to be extracted after insertion of one coin. But efficient though it is, it is no more attractive than the traditional machine, a miniature lubianka of the street corner, utterly lacking in charm. Since 1950 the average American newspaper has increased from thirty-four to sixty pages, and anyone walking along the street with a full attaché case or shopping basket must think twice about adding the weight of a newspaper.

Besides the problems of *today*, publishers live under a cloud of longer-term impending nightmares. What if the environmentalists were ever to get a really tough litter-control bill through Congress, the newspaper equivalent of the recent "Ban-the-Can" attacks on soft-drink manufacturers? The newspaper's readers would be further deterred from buying papers in the street, and publishers might be forced to go through the additional expense of paying for litter collection. What if someone reveals that there are health hazards from ink in the air, especially in and near newspaper production plants? What if someone starts campaigning against noise pollution caused by traditional presses? One day it might become illegal to advertise tobacco in print, as it already is on television, which would impose a serious new pressure on newspaper revenue. Newspapers are energy-intensive industries, and a change in the rate structure of the electricity companies that have hitherto made it cheap to operate plants at night could deal a massive blow to their narrow profit margins. The newspaper publishers of Europe as well as the U.S. benefit greatly from tariff reductions on newsprint importation from Canada and Scandinavia; if these were removed or significantly altered to take account of some switch in national tariff policy, a further disaster would take place. It is highly unlikely that all of these nightmares will become reality at the same time, but any one of them would prove to be a serious blow, and it is very unlikely that none of them will happen.

It is not surprising that America is looking to technology to provide an escape hatch through which the whole newspaper form may perhaps evade its enveloping long-term crisis. Rich though the publishers are for the most part, they sometimes feel themselves shackled with gold. Ever since it was formed by a publisher in the 1950's, ANPA's Research Institute has been working at a program of technical reform, designed to struggle against the encroachments of media as well as the structural problems of the newspaper itself. Its efforts have greatly accelerated the pace of change for the entire press of the developed world, which share many but not all of the problems that have given rise to the anxieties of American publishers. ANPA has cast about for scientific solutions in a wide variety of fields. It has persuaded government departments, universities, and research institutes to turn their attention to the technical problems of the press on a scale unprecedented in this century. There are scientists working on new sources of chemical pulp for newsprint, new inks and bleaches, new de-inking and recycling processes, new vending machines and changes in the mechanical design of delivery vehicles. Above all, there are new ideas for presses, for photocomposition, for newsprint economy, for labor relations, and for exploitation of communication satellites for cheap transmission of print materials.

The whole language of ANPA is a futuristic one, and the publisher is now presented with a profusion of choices in every area of his business—rather like the newspaper publisher of the 1860's who found himself at a similar juncture in newspaper history and could choose from dozens of designs of new presses and composition equipment, only a few of which were destined ultimately to make the grade. The European equivalent, IFRA, in Darmstadt, Germany, finds itself in the wash of waves generated from ANPA's Research Institute in Easton, Pennsylvania, although the problems of its European member publishers are different. The Europeans are concentrating on finding ways to make the best adaptations of new technologies to suit the more varied types of newspaper in Europe, which, on the whole, demand higher standards of printing and design and function in more competitive markets than their American counterparts.

ANPA itself was founded in 1887 as an industry-wide means of rationalizing and collecting the newly developing national advertising for newspapers—and to create a forum in which industry-wide problems could be discussed. In 1926 ANPA established its Mechanical Department, which has held annual Production Conferences and Exhibitions ever since and has made a major and continuing effort to place strong impetus behind technical solutions to organizational and marketing problems. The Department helped newspapers exchange information and helped the industry as a whole exploit new developments and absorb experience and innovations rapidly. In the period after World War II the section was renamed the Mechanical Research Department and thus later merged with the privately founded Research Institute, both dedicated to a more aggressive and deliberate seeking out of innovations to improve the profitability of American (and Canadian) newspapers. The new RI created its own laboratory for piloting and testing new devices, and a Scientific Advisory Committee was set up by the parent ANPA in the early 1960's to assist the operation of penetrating and exploiting America's scientific developments.

The U.S. government was undertaking, in its space and other programs, the largest R & D efforts in human history; new knowledge in many fields was pouring through the hands of government contractees in search of industries to exploit it. ANPA gave commissions from time to time to researchers at MIT in Boston, in particular in the field of computer construction for text work. The aim, according to ANPA President Stanford Smith, was to take advantage "on a continuing basis of spin-offs from massive research projects sponsored by the government and private enterprises."[1] A large range of programs was developed within RI in training personnel and in exploring ways to exploit new electronic equipment. The annual Production Conference has become a massive jamboree celebrating technical achievement and rededicating thousands of participating publishers to pursue through technical advances the salvation of the medium.

There can be no doubt that it was ANPA RI that nudged the industry into the massive transformation that has been taking place in the 1970's. Changes might have occurred without the encouragement and pressure of the Institute, but not as swiftly nor as comprehensively as has been the case. And it is the swiftness and the comprehensiveness of these changes that have reduced unit costs. brought about rapid adoption of innovations and refinements, concentrated the industry on a program of self-help, restored its confidence in its product, and reassured the publishers that the refashioned product was what they really had to produce, despite the demoralizing complaints of nostalgic critics.

There is scarcely a field of modern science into which the newspaper researchers of America have not trodden to find something to help them. Agricultural science has come to their aid with the choice of kenaf, the biennial hibiscus cannabinus (chosen after a search through 500 known species), as the raw material for a newsprint pulp. Lasers, holography, metallurgy, plastics, electronics, photography, chemistry, injection moulding, management science, group psychology—there is virtually no area of modern disquisition and inquiry that has been ignored by the industry's researchers. Today the problem is no longer to "invent" in a primary sense, but to work out and engineer "coincidences" between different areas of existing development—points of convergence of convenience, knowledge, and industrial need—so that produciton breakthroughs can be made. Many areas of the newspaper business have already undergone technical transformation, but the industry is still merely at the beginning of an era of change brought on by shifts in basic conceptions now taking place. To understand how these are coming about, one must look in some detail at how a newspaper is constructed—in human as well as technical terms—for it is today the whole social structure of the newspaper plant that is being altered.

The newspaper should be thought about as something more than a mere set of industrial organizational and mental processes. It is a social system, with unconsciously (though sometimes consciously) inherited practices going back centuries. Eighteenth-century manuals of printing speak of the craft as a set of ancient practices, already made sacrosanct by time. Much of the terminology and craft sentiments of the seventeenth century and earlier remain today. In many parts of Europe the processes of typesetting and presswork are reminiscent of the images of ancient woodcuts. Most of the groupings, craft demarcations, and the "bunker" mentality that goes with the modern newspaper print work date back to the late nineteenth century, when the apparatus of the industry as we know it was being established. The coming of typesetting machines in the 1880's in Europe and America and in the 1890's in Britain (where typesetters had resisted this technical transformation) brought about important and permanent changes in the organization of newspaper work, which is today affected by the impact of the electronic revolution in printing.

It is important to realize that the complex welter of grades, crafts, and professional relationships of which a newspaper is composed are the products of earlier sets of historical changes that were themselves generated by changes in society's flows of information. One can imagine a society as consisting of a vast number of information cycles with the newspaper spanning them, constantly interposing itself into more of them, and adapting its organization to capture the flows of information and reduce them to a form suitable for the medium of the printing press.

The typewriter itself was an innovation of huge importance, conferring new functions on reporters and making the work of typesetters less onerous. At first, typing was thought to be women's work, and it was a generation or more before it became a general tool of journalism. The telephone switchboard was another invention that transformed the nature of reporting (in the 1920's) as had the telephone in the 1880's and

1890's. Until the switchboard arrived, it was almost impossible for a multi-sourced form of information to pass along the telephone, e.g., the results of a large number of football games played simultaneously in different parts of the country or the results of a national election. In many countries pigeons were widely used for such complex stories until about 1930, and many well-organized newspapers kept their own pigeon-lofts. Every fresh system or technology created a new category of workers, proud of their skills and jealous of intrusion from newer crafts.

When Mergenthaler's Linotype machine came to the *New York Tribune* in 1886, it created a sensation. It was by no means the first machine that had been used for setting type. A German named Bessemer had made one in 1842, and an Englishman, Hattersley, made another model that sold quite well in the 1870's. In 1872 the Kastenbein machine was in-stalled at the *London Times*. With all of these the type once used for composing a page had to be taken apart and "redistributed" by hand ready for reuse. In Britain, and elsewhere, the compositors refused to cooperate with unskilled female labor recruited to perform this task, but Mergenthaler's invention, which automatically redistributed the used matrixes, was found acceptable even among the craft-proud compositors on the *London Times*.

The Linotype machine was an invention after its time. It had been urgently needed for years. The speed of printing presses had, in a sense, got out of gear with the speed of typesetting, and newspapers were able to print and sell hundreds of thousands more copies than they had the capacity to print in a single night from a single setting of type. To produce more than a single press run entailed the highly expensive pro-cess of double or treble typesetting, something that had often occurred in the history of the newspaper but that was most inconvenient in the 1890's when papers had increased in size as a result of retail and manu-facturer display advertising. The arrival of Mergenthaler's invention (and its immediate competitors) relieved the congestion of the pressrooms and left many compositors out of work. But an information avalanche was piling up, with a growing public demanding more information through devices that were becoming available to collect it and thread it into the newspaper. The information revolution of the 1890's was the result of a mechanical change designed to catch up with the increase in the demand for reading material. The new information media were built around the new needs of the consumer but had to conform to the standards estab-lished by those workers who already occupied the field.

Many new devices were left lying for years at the side of the road of development, even if they seemed to be potentially useful to the industry.

The printing telegraph, for instance, consisted of a fusion of telegraphy and typesetting and was first proposed by an Australian engineer, Donald Murray, in 1899. It did not take hold until well after the First World War when the Teletype Corporation took it up. On both sides of the Atlantic the newspaper industry could not find a way to use this machine in the actual conditions of plant organization. A similar fate befell offset printing in its early years (the 1930's), when Palo Alto's *Peninsular Mirror* remained the solitary pioneer of the technique. Not for thirty more years did it become a general method for newspaper printing. What appears to determine the rate of adoption of new technologies is a sense of natural historical evolution within an industry itself. Each generation of equipment involves a fresh set of linkages between the medium and the society. The industry's present circumstances, in which it is undergoing a deliberate and rapid transformation, are the result of its frightened perception of the problems it inherited in the age of television.

No two newspapers are the same and no two countries have the same problems or the same priorities. For example, newspapers keep different deadlines, which depend on their sources of news and the size of the area in which they have to distribute or the times of the trains and trucks that carry their papers. Nonetheless, it is possible to express diagramatically the main stages through which the "traditional" old-technology paper has to pass compared with those of the new (see figure 2).

The contents of the traditional newspaper emerge from a variety of news, editorial, and advertising departments and pass to the copy desk in the composing room, which then routes them to the typesetters or to the compositors, sometimes slicing a long article into several sections and distributing the pieces of text to different compositors.

Each compositor sits before a machine to which he pins the copy that has been typed for him by the journalist and marked in pencil by the editor. He uses a keyboard with ninety keys and works through the text causing a stream of matrixes, or metal moulds, to fall into the channels of the Linotype machine before him, one for each key he strikes. The matrixes collect in a "form" into which the operator adds spaces and hyphens to "justify" the lines of text, i.e., fill the column width. As he gets to the end of each line, he moves a control that causes molten lead to be poured into the matrix and form itself into a whole line of type. The matrixes then slip back to their places through the channels of the machine.

A skilled typesetter—working in the English language—can usually manage about five lines of type per minute and normally makes a mistake about once every two minutes. Soon after World War II an important labor-saving development occurred in the United States whereby

Figure 2

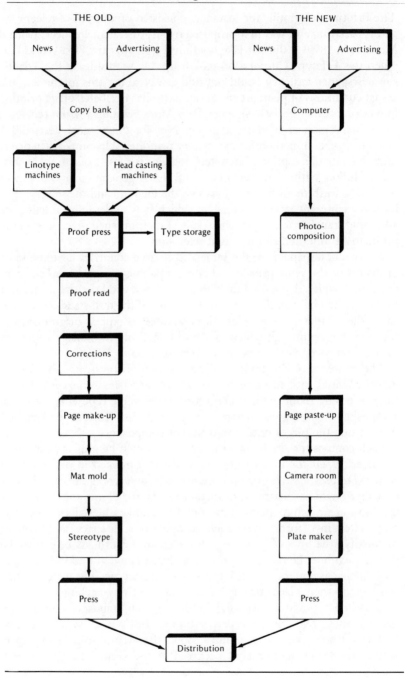

the Linotype machine was driven faultlessly by a punched tape onto which the operator had recorded, as it were, the typesetting instructions. Without the hazards of a human operator working directly upon it, the Linotype machine was able to double and triple its speed and even do the work of hyphenation and justification ("h-and-j") automatically. Tape-setting meant that the average U.S. newspaper saved 40 percent of its setting labor.

Of course, the newspaper's reporters are not the only sources of copy. Wire services pour out millions of words per day, supplied in a variety of "services" from which each newspaper chooses one or more. Agency material has been typed, i.e., keyboarded, therefore, before it reaches the plants. Feature material is often sent to a newspaper in photostatted or mimeographed form. Display advertising arrives in an amateur scribble, on formal layouts, on mats, or increasingly often on complete plates, and all of this has to pass through the hands of a skilled keyboard operator who copies it possibly from a version that has already been keyboarded on a different kind of machine. Most classified advertising reaches the newspaper by telephone and is typed out at least once before it reaches the typesetter for the edition in which it is to appear.

Once the typesetters have finished making a leaden version of the copy, whatever the form it has arrive in, a proof is made and the sheet goes into the correcting process. Each time the copy has been typed out (before or after it reaches the newspaper building), a new possibility of error creeps in. After each page is proofread it goes back to the linecasting process for corrected lines to be extracted, remade, replaced. The whole process may be repeated twice or three times.

It is only at this point that the various strips of text and advertising material are placed in the context of the page in which they will be seen by the reader. The type is assembled in a metal frame, or "chase," on a table equipped with rollers, known as a "turtle." Extensive cutting takes place as the material is made to fit onto the page. All the photographs for editorial and advertising sections have by now been turned into zinc alloy (though increasingly plastic) copies that can be fitted into the chase. At the end of this process there will emerge a metal mirror image of the completed page—perhaps one of sixty for a daily paper or of several hundred for a large Sunday edition.

The turtle is now rolled into the next area, where a moist mat made of papier-mâché is pressed against the type. Great force is needed to press the mat mould, which is trimmed, dried, and curved into the shape that will finally fit around the rollers of the press. Molten lead is now poured over the mat in the stereotype machine, and there emerges an extremely heavy curved version of the page. This is the stereo printing plate, forty pounds in all, which usually moves on a conveyor belt into the press-room, where it is mounted on a cylinder powerful enough to hold a series of such plates. Many copies of the plate will be struck in metal from the same mat mould, depending upon the size of the print run desired. Changes can be made in the text as the hours of printing pass, though all alterations have to be reset, proofread, corrected, made up, and remoulded for a new stereotype, but this process needs to take only a few minutes in a traditionally equipped plant.

The rotary press, on which the stereotype finally performs its labor, is as large and heavy as an old steam engine; it receives a continuous roll of paper and a flow of ink. With a fairly large American paper, about one fifth of one ounce of ink is used for an average newspaper. There is a vivid contrast between the size and energy consumed by the press and the delicacy with which it smears this small quantity of ink across a great surface of paper.

From the presses the newspaper is passed on for folding, cutting, bundling, and stacking and thereafter into the circulation processes for counting, tying, labeling, and trucking.

In the nineteenth century a description of this process would awaken a feeling of astounded wonderment. The newspaper was one of the mira-cles of civilization. Looked at from the standpoint of the era of the computer, it is dirty, labor-intensive, extremely noisy, and repetitive. The material is copied out again and again by different groups of workers. Error after error creeps in and has to be painfully eliminated. All the processes are subject to age-old grievances, pride, jealousies. However, there are many things to be said in the system's favor. First of all, it works. The materials it uses are cheap (papier-mâché), or are constantly recycled (molten lead). It is capable of great speed in the pressroom (70,000 copies per hour). It is responsive to deadlines and to last-minute changes, even though these are awkward and labor-intensive. Many of these advantages are not superseded by the new technology, although most of the disadvantages are eliminated.

Throughout the following description of the "new" technology, which is gradually changing the production system of newspapers, it is impor-tant to keep in mind the nature of the stereotype plate—the cylindrical object that emerges after applying molten lead with great force to the mat mould. The stereotype technology arose from the conception of the newspaper as a miscellaneous form. It is a peculiarly appropriate tech-nology for a medium consisting of pages that act as holdalls for many different pieces of information surrounded by or interspersed with advertising material. The efficiency of the stereotype arises not only from its cheapness, speed, and reliability, but also from the need for different kinds of information to be fused into a single page—display, news, feature, editorial, classified, all the various journalistic forms that had grown up by the middle or late nineteenth century. All the processes of journalism culminate in the creation of the plate, and their deadlines cluster around the need to create it. The presses wait for it before performing their daily act of mass production. The creation of the great pages of a newspaper involves an interface of intellectual, skilled, and semiskilled groups of workers. Much of what is currently happening to the newspaper as an industry is tending towards the rearrangement of the content in a less miscellaneous form, and the computer, with all of its present and future versatility, makes it possible to develop this process much further.

The organization of the technology of the newspaper reveals certain ideas about the nature of the reading public itself, about its assumed attention span, about its preferences for kinds of material, about its homogeneous nature and shared interests. The newspaper has become progressively less like a book in appearance and production method throughout its history—although it began life precisely as a book, a newsbook. Printing from a stereotype plate symbolizes and embodies at once the "massness" of the newspaper and its ephemeral quality. It expresses a special view of the nature of the knowledge appropriate to a newspaper, i.e., that it is culled rapidly from diverse sources and the nuggets thrust into mutual proximity and that the knowledge is interim and discardable. The new system of producing newspapers makes possible a different view of its contents, even though the primary motivation for the new technology arises from the changing circumstances of the newspaper as an industry.

In looking at the various pieces of equipment that go to make up the "new" technology, one must remember that at the back of the minds of all designers of all the present systems, there is the idea of an ultimate system. All of the elements of this system already exist and are used in newspapers in one part of the world or another, but the total system is not yet to be seen. The newspaper in this future system, which will almost certainly be in operation in some places within the lifetime of this book, will start with the newsroom and advertising staffs' feeding copy through video-display units (vdt's) into a computer, where the material, including photographs, will be arranged and edited electronically into newspaper pages with the help of a larger set of vdt's. The computer will then automatically drive a plate maker, which functions with laser beams, to create the necessary printing plates; it simultaneously takes readings off the plates to guarantee the correct setting of the controls on the presses to which the plates pass automatically. The presses are equipped not only to print the copies as required but also insert preprints and advertising throwaway sheets at the same speed as the press run itself. The ultimate system also bundles and wraps the completed newspapers and delivers them, addressed, to the trucks allocated to delivery in each zone.

Between the newsroom and the loading dock very few employees remain. The newspapers that come closest to this vision are all in Japan, but already a very large number of American newspapers, perhaps most of them, possess some of the elements of the complete system. In addition to the use of the computer as a basis for production, typesetting, and circulation, it can be used to store the past contents of the paper, so that it gradually turns into a great general database, making daily additions to its store of information and using the store for its daily output.

II

The essence of the modern "cold type" system as practical today lies in the use of a photographic method for composing the pages and completely eliminating the use of molten lead in the newspaper plant. The images of the pages are created photographically, instead of physically in metal type. At the center of the plant's operation sits the main computer, or central processing unit (CPU), which stores the copy digitally in its memory—where formerly trays of completed metal type covered a large floor area of the composing room. The computer performs the work of h-and-j-ing the text, which used to be done line by line by the fingers of typesetters. The computer also makes the text corrections according to the orders of the editors and proofreaders.

In a fully automated modern newspaper, the text reaches the computer direct from the journalists and editors or through the intermediation of special typists reserved for this purpose. They use vdt's to type their copy with a keyboard resembling that of a standard QWERTY typewriter attached to a cathode ray tube. The text appears on the tube as the keys are struck. The reporter or ad-taker corrects or alters the text as it is composed by moving the "cursor" (a blob of light indicating the point on the screen on which the next keystroke will appear) backward and forward, upward and downward. The reporters and ad-takers are thus composing the text, performing the task of the old typesetter. When the reporter is satisfied, he pushes a button, which sends the text into the CPU from which it can be recalled by editors and subeditors and anyone else in the newspaper whose logging-in code permits him to receive it. (The modern newspaper production system is a great stickler for rank and security, forcing every user to inform the CPU who he or she is before requesting it to project any material onto a screen.) The text can be rolled backward and forward (or "scrolled"), reviewed and altered. It can be made to appear on one half of the screen while another version of the same story is recalled from the CPU to appear on the other half for comparison, or while preliminary notes keyed into the CPU days or weeks before are recalled for review and incorporation. The business of "text manipulation" (editing and transposing, correcting and rearranging the lines of print) grows easier and more flexible with every generation of equipment in the market. Each vdt user has his own small electronic scratch pad, which can hold materials (e.g., notes) that are not yet ready for the main database, or file. The more "intelligent" the terminal is the more dextrous the reporter can be (see figure 3).

In the case of the ad-taker, the vdt permits the operator, while taking down a telephone-dictated classified advertisement, to check the credit worthiness of the customer, plan for future insertions of the advertisement in subsequent editions, inform the customer of the exact cost, and bill him automatically for his order. It has been found also that ad-takers in modern systems are able to sell more space than formerly. For laying out display advertisements, larger vdt's are used that can perform highly complex design and alignment operations (with dozens of different "fonts" of type) manipulating the size and position of every line of the text—functions that would otherwise take many hours of elaborate physical design and layout work, as well as complex procedures of filing and checking.

Another way of placing material into the CPU is through an Optical Character Reader, or OCR, which is sometimes used by newspapers instead of vdt's, sometimes in addition to them. An OCR, or "scanner," takes a reading of a perfect copy of the text typed out on an ordinary electric typewriter. The copy must be near perfect, however, and this often means that a typist must be employed to repeat the keystrokes of the reporter. The OCR creates either an electronic signal, which passes into the CPU's memory, or else creates a punched paper tape, which performs the same task. (Often vdt's can also produce tape versions of the copy while or prior to inputting it to the CPU.) The CPU automatically h-and-j's the copy emerging from the OCR. The OCR is often used for specialist purposes where retyping of material is not necessary, e.g.,

Figure 3

An Editor's Keyboard—in the *Detroit News*

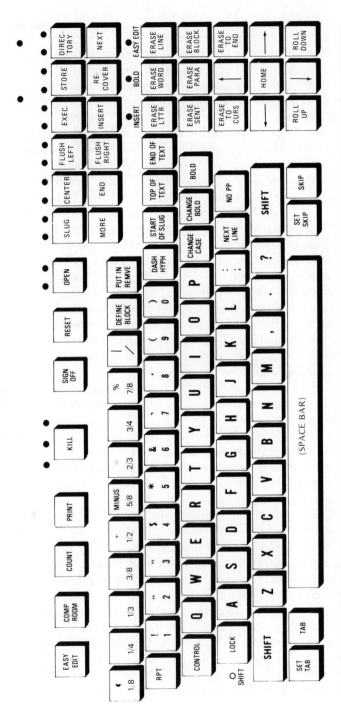

From ANPA R.I. Bulletin 1151 (May 15, 1974).

in handling wire service copy that arrives in scannable form, or material from syndication agencies that are able to supply scannable copy to their client newspapers.

One new and still experimental technology for further improving modern typesetting is based on lasers. "Light amplification by stimulated emission of radiation" (of which "laser" is the acronym) consists of a highly intense, narrow beam of light that does not spread out however far ahead it is projected, nor diverge from the parallel. One of the first typesetters to use lasers was the PTM-1000, which, with the demise of its parent company, Photon Pacesetters, was renamed the DLC-1000 after Dymo Graphic Systems, its adopted parent.[2] This machine will accept a variety of forms of input, magnetic tape, paper tape, or on-line material from a host computer; it converts these into type at a speed of 1000 lines per minute when it is functioning at full capacity. It has a capacity of up to 300 fonts, its versatility ranging from a variety of headlines and point sizes to a considerable number of smaller text type faces. Each font contains up to 128 different characters, and all the characters are stored in digitized form on disc files, from which the CPU extracts the font required and transmits the configuration required in its digitized form to the font memory section of the typesetting machine. In other words, the apparatus does not pull each character when required out of the file but instructs the printer in the design as a whole, making the operation take a matter of nanoseconds. Two beams are generated in the machine, one to "write" the type, the other to locate the position of the character and control its fellow. A set of mirrors directs the beams to a point of convergence through a scan lens, from which a mirror projects the writing onto the film.

It is, of course, possible for the wire services and any other accepted agency to feed copy directly into the CPU of a newspaper, saving all further keyboarding. The newspaper's editors then merely summon the material as desired and edit it to their requirements. This is, in fact, the next stage in the preparation of all copy originated within the newspaper. A second row of vdt's is employed, designed for more complex and specialist operations, at which the editors perform their tasks of selection and rearrangement as well as that of normal proofreading or copy correction. The editor may manipulate the text with more sophistication than the reporter and add all the necessary instructions for size of type, layout of the copy, arrangement of photographs within the copy, etc. (This would have been formerly done by marking the reporter's finished text with pencil marks for the manual typesetter to deal with.) Once the CPU is given the correct instructions, it can perform the work without further error. It has been calculated that the error rate is one in 250,000 lines of type.

It is at this point in the organization of production that the CPU starts to perform its second task (after that of memorizing the copy), which is that of composing the ribbons of text, which it does at a rate seldom less than twenty-five lines per minute and often at a mile of text an hour or several thousand lines per hour. The CPU sends out a stream of text— offering back all the material it has been given—laid out in neat columns on strips of paper and taking into account allof the editing instructions.

It is at this point that the laborious task of laying out trays of type and correcting them would normally have taken place. Instead, the material emerging from the CPU is laid out, cut with paper scissors, and pasted on a life-size copy of the finished page, with spaces left for photographic material. In the case of pages of classified advertisements, several U.S. newspapers now have equipment that automatically lays out the material in whole pages, saving the pasting up of the work by hand. In many newspapers progress towards the creation of complete pages of text within the computer has reached the point at which paste-up is merely a kind of "paste-in," with only a few pieces of material (pictures, special headlines) having to be added to the page after the CPU has done its work.

As computer capacity increases, and as the more sophisticated operations can be incorporated more cheaply, the newspaper is moving towards the total elimination of the pasting process. Instead, the whole of the page can be "laid out" through a highly intelligent editors' terminal. These are now widely used in Japan, where, as will be explained, the nature of the language itself has dictated a different pace of development in the computerization of newspapers.

What we have seen in this account so far is the way in which the functions of the reporter and ad-taker are made to overlap with that of the old compositor, or typesetter. The input end of a newspaper takes on the task of text manipulation and therefore comes to dominate the newspaper plant more effectively than in the past. Historically the newspaper was a printing operation to which specialist groups of information finders and information collectors were added. In other words, the reporter is a later addition to the social system of the newspaper, and his particular skills (shorthand, investigation, interviewing, checking versions of a story, and technologies such as telegraphy and telephony) were grafted onto the operation.

Typesetting and presswork were the heart and lungs of the newspaper. Today the newsroom is finally coming to the fore because it will, more directly than in the past, command the production operation, in conjunction with the advertising department (another input department). Executive roles will also presumably change to take account of this fundamental power shift.

From paste-up the material now goes to the camera room, where a photograph is taken of the paste-up and from the negative a printing plate is made. At this point, two quite divergent systems are used. Traditional letterpress printing, as we have seen, requires a plate with a raised metal surface that is covered with ink and pressed onto the rolls of paper. With those newspapers that continue to use the old or letterpress printing presses, therefore, the photograph of the page with which the modern prepress work ends up has to be turned into such a plate. For this various methods are used. The *Los Angeles Times* has created its own recyclable injection-moulded plate-making system for the 25,000 plates it has to make every week. Hundreds of newspapers use photosensitive plastics, which harden at exposure to the negative of the page, while the area around the actual text (made of polymer or soft plastic material), wears away, leaving the printing surface suitably raised for the presswork. Other plants employ devices using similar materials, which create the same ultimate effect of producing a "shallow relief printing plate" in a material flexible enough to fit around a letterpress cylinder. These are far more expensive to produce than hot-metal stereotype plates, which cost a few cents each. (The metal plates are recycled, while the plastic plates normally have to be thrown away.) The plastic plates take longer to press and dry, but they are still extremely economical, taken in the context of the new process as a whole. Using plates of this kind makes it possible to reduce the total costs of a small-circulation newspaper considerably (because the smaller the circulation the smaller the number of plates used). However, for many years to come, many large-circulation papers will continue to use relief printing methods rather than the alternative "offset" printing or its halfway house, direct lithography.

The most frequently used type of press in the reorganized newspaper is the web-fed "offset" press, which is founded on the basic chemical principle that ink and water are mutually repellent. Those areas of the photosensitive layer that contain type and have been exposed attract the ink, while those that have not attract the water. The offset plate is flat and requires much less pressure than those with a raised surface. It has earned the name offset because the litho plate and the paper never touch each other. A third roller, or "blanket," takes the image from the plate and presses it against a moving roll of paper. One disadvantage of this type of printing is that a certain number of copies are almost invariably lost each time the press is started up, either because it has been fitted with a new plate or with a new roll of paper. The more often this is done the more wasteful and slow the process. It is for this reason that until various recent improvements were added to offset printing, very few newspapers with more than a 50,000 circulation used the method. Today, however, there are 1250 newspapers printed offset in America alone, three with circulations of over a million a day. A useful compromise system was developed in the 1970's whereby an offset plate is fitted to a thickened saddle on the cylinders of a letterpress machine and made to touch the roll of paper directly—hence "di-litho," the name for this method. Because it saves newspapers the high cost of purchasing new presses, it has become very popular as an interim technology, although many newspapers have grown so used to this method that they feel they may stay with it indefinitely.

Offset printing is not a new invention by any means. Lithography had been used for magazines even in the nineteenth century, especially in the form of popular chromolithographs, but the first commercial offset presses came in during the early twentieth century, and a few newspapers (generally weeklies) were using them before World War II. Offset became popular among the new small-circulation suburban papers of the 1950's because of its cleanliness and convenience, and its relative silence. Rapid improvement of web-feeding processes for newsprint took place in the 1960's, and web offset became universal for periodical publications throughout the world.

Some simple statistics help to illustrate the balance of priorities among the different kinds of newspaper for different forms of presswork. Of America's 1786 daily newspapers, 526 use letterpress systems (29.5 percent of the total), but these have 42,249,867 copies between them (68.5 percent of the total 61,836,000). Out of the total, 1260 newspapers are printed offset (70.5 percent), but between them they have only 31.5 percent of total circulation. However, of the papers that continue to use letterpress equipment, 435 use one or another of the direct plate processes (including di-litho), so that 95 percent of all newspapers use photocomposition, whichever form of press they happen to possess—an extraordinarily rapid change, considering it has taken well under twenty years.[3]

Several maverick or unique printing systems have been developed in recent years by the sometimes frenzied search for new techniques among newspaper publishers. The *Los Angeles Times* held out against offset and di-litho plates because of the size of their circulation and the number of pages they print (up to 900 on Sundays). They require more plate changes, more plates, and more copies than any other U.S. newspaper and thus spent a great deal of time searching for a cheap way of exploiting photocomposition and "cold type" without having the problems of wastage and high plate cost associated with offset and di-litho methods. Fundamentally they wished to retain their letterpress equipment and find a plate that could be recycled, and they gradually developed a system that has not been used by any other newspaper as yet. In this new system a full-page engraving is made of every page from which a mould is taken, and this in turn is used to make a plastic plate by an injection-moulding technique. Each plate costs about 35 cents, compared with two to three dollars for other (non-metal) relief printing plates. The capital cost is also surprisingly low, and the basic equipment, after long years of research, cost only $125,000 in 1972, when it was finally built. The *L.A. Times* has thus succeeded in its purpose—of finding a way to reduce the long production deadlines (between page make-up and plate making), which are a feature of most of the offset and di-litho systems.

The *L.A. Times* plate involves a series of new specialized technologies. The film negative is imaged by laser, developed in an automatic film processor, and then exposed to a Mercules-Merigraph plastic master. This is placed in a direct pressure plate covered with plastic mats, which becomes the matrix for the plastic printing plate. It is then placed in the injection die and has polypropylene thrust into it, which forms a plastic printing plate 1/100 inch thick. The die is mounted in a Cincinnati 375-ton injection-moulding press, and the finished plate is trimmed and placed on the saddles that surround the cylinders of the press. In the early 1980's, however, the *L.A. Times* will abandon its unique and revolutionary plate-making system: offset technology is catching up in cost and in the durability of plates to the extent that it is becoming economical even for papers with eighty pages and a million copies a day.

There were many celebrated battles on the way to cold-type technology and photocomposition. One of the key events that spurred American publishers in their task of replacing the costly and labor-intensive traditions of page make-up was a twenty-two month strike in Chicago in 1947, when the International Typographical Union was pressing its case against the Taft-Hartley Act. The Chicago publishers operated a joint system by which the typesetters were evaded altogether: copy was written on an ordinary typewriter, then photoengraved before being cast in hot metal. By the time of ANPA's 1950 conference (also in Chicago), a suitable photocomposition machine for normal use had been developed and was demonstrated. The first daily to take the plunge (apart from the Palo Alto experiment before the War) was the pioneering *Quincy Patriot Ledger* in Massachusetts, which historically has often been among the forerunners in technical experiment. It ordered a machine from the Intertype Corporation and was closely observed by many other newspapers.

The American newspaper took to the computer with greater rapidity under the proselytizing influence of ANPA. Until 1960 the computer was restricted in business and commercial work to the role of accountant's aid, although market researchers too were fascinated by the idea of using a computer for performing novel intellectual tasks. In particular, they realized that computers could be employed as storage places for information that could then be extracted in ways different from those in which it was inserted (i.e., in testing the marketability of one piece of merchandise against the information of market reactions to another with comparable characteristics).

However, it was the development of the idea of time-sharing, i.e., permitting a series of users to exploit the capacity of the same computer at the same time, that really opened up the computer to widespread industrial use, and that potential did not become available generally until 1965. At the end of the 1960's it became clear to the newspaper industry that it too would be able to benefit from time-sharing techniques, not merely to save work but to rethink whole functions within the newspaper enterprise. To see how the time-sharing notion was adapted to the task of typesetting one must go back to another, older problem that the industry had already analyzed in some detail.

In the early 1960's ANPA RI had been working on the analysis of the work of hyphenation and justification in typesetting and had shown that this occupation consumed 40 percent of the typesetter's time. Great amounts of labor could be saved if newspapers decided either not to bother with perfect columns (perhaps by doubling column width and then not justifying) and abandoning an ancient ritual of the craft, or else to devise a mechanical means for performing the task. It was obvious that readers did not really mind if right-hand margins were not perfect, but it was equally clear that the problem was one of mathematics rather than craft. One solution was to use a slightly larger piece of type to fill the empty space instead of a hyphen, but some of the research into this problem ended up by creating basic dictionaries of regular or frequent hyphenations.

It was in this storage of information for h-and-j functions that computers were first used in newspaper offices and wire services. The *Los Angeles Times* managed to run a perforated tape machine with the help of a computer that had learned an early dictionary. Within four years many scores of newspapers acquired computers for this purpose and were then finding other functions within the enterprise that could be helped by the computer. According to an ANPA survey published in 1967, the *Washington Evening Star* was using a Honeywell and an IBM computer for twelve different tasks in the mailroom, in the circulation room, and in various hot-metal and cold-type processes, as well as in office jobs such as accounting and record storage. It was assumed that in time to come editors would use computer as planning aids in their work as well. The first use of the computer in the newspaper industry was thus an interesting example of a phenomenon common in technological history and especially in printing history—the employment of a new technology to relieve old inefficiencies rather than perform new tasks.

The arrival of the time-sharing notion in the mid-sixties revolutionized possibilities for the use of computers in newspapers, and it coincided with the realization of publishers throughout the country that major efforts at labor saving would have to take place in order to keep the industry profitable. As with the Teletypesetters of the 1920's, new technology seemed at first to threaten the sovereignty of editors; it performed functions behind their backs, as it were, and thwarted the lines of discipline and control that held the fabric of the newspaper's social organization together. Gradually they came to see the new techniques with different eyes.

The real problem in applying computer science to the newspaper industry was that of breaking down habitual attitudes and methods within the newspaper organization itself. To alter, for example, the method for collecting, billing, credit checking, and setting classified advertising meant that an entirely fresh view had to be taken of the industry, one that in itself necessitated outside expertise of a kind that most newspapers didn't realize they needed. The history of the very corporations that are now among the most successful in making and selling newspaper equipment illustrates the point. The Harris Corporation, which put the first electronic editor's terminal on the market in 1973, had been founded in 1895 as the Harris Automatic Press Company, which made printing equipment. In recent years it merged with the Intertype Corporation—Mergenthaler's great competitor—and in the 1960's it started acquiring a number of companies operating in space communications that provided the conceptual expertise as well as the knowledge of computers themselves. Raytheon came into newspapers from microwave ovens and guided missiles.

It was hardly surprising that many firms made hopelessly optimistic promises about the time scale of development, some even promising full computerized pagination in the early years without fully realizing the problems involved in building memories of adequate size. The essence of time sharing is reorganization of relationships, and it takes a long time to look at a one-hundred-year-old activity and understand what all the relationships are, which is necessary before they can be rerouted and rebuilt around the information storage and distribution of a computer. In a formal sense, time-sharing merely enables many hands to draw aid from and place information in a computer at the same moment; in fact, "sharing" is hardly the right word, since the parties concerned are not giving up a facility to one another at all, but rather adding to their collective and individual efficiency. At the heart of the activity is the computer's own exclusive function assigning its own time and talents to the many simultaneous users and interpreting their commands. This core memory supervises a variety of smaller distributed storage systems and switching devices and ensures that no user erases or interferes with the activity of another.

Time-sharing is essentially an encoding of a social organization into computer hardware. It took several years of deliberate and often wasted research for companies to discover ways to redefine the relationships of the newspaper production schedule into time-sharing concepts. The computer had to facilitate continuities of existing relationships as well as modify them. It could turn ad-takers into bill senders, it could turn reporters into typesetters, but to explore the relationships undergoing such transformation involved bringing the connections into the open and exploring them from the standpoints of the people concerned. The most effective among the experimenters were those who employed democratic or highly consultative processes of planning. There were plenty of mistakes made between 1968 and 1975 (the year in which the bandwagon of computerization really got going), and some of them were very expensive indeed. By 1975 there were nearly thirty firms offering computers to the newspaper industry and about 1000 computers gathering experience in the field.

Newspapers started acquiring clusters of processing facilities meant to perform different tasks at different stages in the evolution of the art. There were advanced newspapers that were using them for payroll work but were nervous at the idea of acquiring machines that would alter the basic structures of the plant. Photocomposition became a must in order to move from hot-metal to offset printing, and that suggested the acquisition of computers and optical scanners to input the material and set the type.

Editors then observed the time-wasting nature of OCR's when used for the entire output (i.e., the expensive creation of perfect typed text before scanning); the first vdt's arrived on the scene for editorial use only. The creation of editorial "front end" systems (for reporters' direct input of text to the computer) depends entirely upon the acceptance by reporters of the use of vdt's for normal work. Many older reporters preferred to retire rather than learn the new skills—which are greater than those necessary for typing. The vdt had to pass from an outlandish and experimental tool to a glamorous modern necessity before front-end systems could be brought in to the average newspaper. Reporters and editors had to be trained and made to feel that the instrument added to, rather than detracted from, their professionalism. Journalist training schools tended to be given equipment several years old on which to instruct new recruits to the profession. By the time the schools had trained large numbers of young reporters in the use of vdt's, several more years had passed. It took some time, therefore, for the front end bandwagon to roll and for the new technology to extend itself into the newsrooms of the nation.

III

The newspaper with probably the most extensive repertoire of computer-aided functions in the United States is the *Los Angeles Times*. Since 1962 it has been building through steady accretion, adaptation, private research, and innovation an Information System that spans the business and circulation as well as editorial side of publishing. The progressive interlinking and redesigning of functions aptly illustrates the way in which modern newspapers are reconstructing their products and prefigures the new forms of social organization likely to emerge in the mature age of the computer. The *Los Angeles Times* has the largest circulation, the largest payroll, the largest profits, of any newspaper in the country. It originally required computers to cope with its own increase in scale, and its history in the computer business illustrates the way in which "outside" technologies gradually work their way into new industries first to solve real problems, then to transform.

In 1962 the *LA Times* worked with RCA to develop one of the early h-and-j computer programs on an RCA 301. Unjustified text was taken from paper tape and turned into justified text, also on paper tape, which then drove a hot-metal linecasting machine, which created neat rows of text. The system worked for classified advertising and for most news; any type of less than standard size was assembled manually.

Within three years the experience gathered from computer work was sufficient to set up a Data Processing Department to take on both the business operational and production functions, and a pair of IBM 360/30 computers were bought to replace the old equipment. The Typesetting System was made to work with the new computer by the *Times'* own personnel, but now the machine could take many tapes simultaneously, and "sluglines" for news stories could be processed on a typewriter terminal that also operated other business functions performed on the same computer.

Three more years of development brought about a further expansion (in 1968), which permitted storage of news stories on discs that were then retrieved to produce paper tape or hard copy. The IBM 360/30 was upgraded through modificaiton, and additional processors were brought in to perform the work of checking the credit of customers buying classified space. At the same time, a Research and Development Committee was set up to coordinate the new projects that were springing up in various parts of the organization, most of which were clearly moving towards massive and more general use of computers in publishing work. At this point the plan for the New Publishing System of today was born, and within a year parts of it started to emerge.

The changes that came about in 1969–70 were complex but brought the newspaper's computerization to a new level. A new system was planned to handle photocomposition and full page makeup of classified advertising, news, and display advertising. (News and classified were still being justified by the 1962 hot-metal system, while display was handled manually by hot-metal linecasters.) While this was being planned, IBM 4506 vdt's with big screens and upper- as well as lower-case fonts came in to do the credit-checking work, and the Typesetting System was equipped with new terminals permitting the recall of news text for correction work. OCR's came in to replace paper-tape readers in the Production Department. In this period DAL 1 was born, the Display-ad Layout System that took unformatted text, which had been entered and been corrected by the Typesetting System, and then employed magnetic tape to drive the photocomposition equipment and lay out the advertisement. It was a slightly cumbersome system, but it made use of equipment that was already there, and it took on more than half of all the display-ad work. This meant that the paper was at last starting to abolish hot metal.

Within a year (in 1971) design started for a replacement for DAL 1 to provide more sophistication in manipulating display ads, and an Environ/1 computer was acquired as a control system but which would also form the basis of a new system for processing classified advertising on-line (after the ads were taken through vdt's). It took two years to install DAL II, which like its predecessor composed one ad at a time but took on virtually all display-ad composition in the paper. Meanwhile, in the Production Department Compstar 191's were brought in; these were photocomposers that were fed through the Typesetting System, so that part of the news output was now passing out of the era of hot metal. The classified system also arrived and it provided for paper tape to drive hot-metal linecasters. All three sections were now moved to a new large IBM 370/145, but plans were laid for a DAL III, which would use the Environ/1 with vdt's.

Until this moment the paper's management was still thinking in terms of one very large computer that would eventually take on every task in the organization. Its ultimate task would be to achieve the system that the R & D Committee of 1968 had set out to discover—photocomposition of full pages direct from a computer. By 1974 this still seemed to be something of a dream, achievable in theory but still some years away. It was decided to buy an IBM 370/158 to do all the publishing work, and all the classified advertising was now quickly removed to photocomposition with the ads collected on vdt's and fed through Environ/1. More and more news was turned over to photocomposition and to DAL III (which also used Environ/1 for its display-ad work).

At this point the newspaper's management was preparing to make various urgent changes in style of page makeup, in style of type, and in the roll width employed for newsprint. The year 1974 was a time of crisis for newsprint, and the LA Times decided to hold back escalating costs by adopting a program of measures that would be better performed from the start if the paper were wholly photocomposed. The whole pace of change was made to increase, and within a few months the entire paper was converted. Hot metal was finally eliminated. A News Publishing System was hastily put together using the large Environ/1, although vdt's capable of performing the new graphics came only in 1975.

DAL III was completed with its graphic vdt's, and in 1975 the News System was improved to allow for the retirement of the 1960's Typesetting System. Now the entire paper was controlled through Environ/1, and new sophistication (e.g., logo generation with the text) was added to the photocomposition system. By 1977 it was possible to generate whole pages of classified advertisements without paste-up. The Associated Press Digital Stock Information System—with its high-speed transmission of prices—was installed and the New York Stock Exchange and Amex stock tables were typeset and paginated without human intervention within the newspaper. Only at this point were plans made to install a massive editing system with 400 terminals to permit the creation of a front-end system for one of the largest newspaper editorial staffs in history.

The Computerized Publishing System is capable of handling the very high capacity of the *LA Times* for its many supplements, editions, and zonings and is of course capable of handling this volume in accordance with the peaks and troughs of newspaper work. In an average week the system processes between 30,000 and 40,000 classified advertisements, between 3000 and 5000 display advertisements (or alterations of old ones), and between 4000 and 5000 news stories (and any revisions). Between 1000 and 1500 pages of newspaper are prepared per week.

The *LA Times* is not the most advanced newspaper in the United States in terms of the range of applications of its computers, but the systems it employs have a greater capacity than systems elsewhere in all their many fields. The News Publishing System, for example, provides complete processing now of news copy passing through the Editorial Department. Most copy goes through to Composing, where the text is entered by OCR, the rest by editors using vdt's. The text, including headlines, is justified, and a hard-copy proof results, with corrections to be made by vdt. Updating and new headlines are also possible through the use of vdt's. As each story goes through to Photocomposition, a corrected proof appears in the Editorial Department, while the paste-up or paste-in work proceeds.

In the classified section of the paper the Ad Entry and Publishing System prepares the material in a similar manner to the News Publishing System but also captures the billing information and checks the customer's credit. A pagination subsystem plans the budget for each page, reserves space for display ads, banners, and other art work, and then sprays the classified material onto the page according to the rules of layout drawn up by the Classified Department. At the end of each day all the information accumulated is processed off-line (i.e., without being connected "live" to the central computer) by a billing subsystem. Reports are produced for all the various departments concerned analyzing the day's output. A variety of weekly, monthly, and quarterly reports are also produced as part of business routine.

The Display Ad Entry System has a similar repertoire of subsystems; it also has the special graphic vdt's for displaying and reviewing work before release to the photocomposers. In display the text of each advertisement is prepared on vdt's and then stored on disc in the IBM 370 computer. The *LA Times* Page Layout System (which is a plotting board with vdt) then manipulates the text to lay it out according to instructions, this additional data being then transmitted to the 370. The layout data and text data are combined to form the advertisement, which is then input to the photocomposition units where a choice of 80 typefaces and 300 fonts is available. The final stage of making the display ad—the positioning of the artwork—is done through paste-up. From Photocomposition the material passes into the *LA Times*' special injection-moulding plate-making machinery.

While the *LA Times* has been constructing this chain of computerization over the course of nearly two decades, it has also been engaging in a giant "cloning" of itself in its new Orange County plant where the EOCOM Corporation has constructed a facsimile plate-making network using lasers. There are two transmitter-receivers at both plants, and each send images of full pages by laser to the other, which go into the injection-moulding procedure. This large-scale expansion of the *Times* is more than a piece of "zoning"; it multiplies the possible area of home delivery by a large factor and enables the paper to compete effectively in the outer suburban and exurban areas with second- and third-layer papers. Of course, other newspapers would find so gigantic a response to the problem of suburbanization a costly waste, but in the context of the Los Angeles region such vast remedies are the only cures for the disease of deurbanization. The fate of the *Herald-Examiner*, the Hearst paper that functions as the *Times*' daily competitor, illustrates the fate of those who fail to grasp all the technological possibilities of self-preservation. Today the paper has roughly eight percent of the sales of its competitor.

After the installation of cold type and especially after a heavy program of computerization, the whole atmosphere of the newspaper changes. It passes from being a mechanical industry to an electronic one. Much of its older equipment, otherwise still serviceable, becomes out-of-date simply because it reminds staff and management of the age that has passed. Wage bargaining takes place in a different atmosphere among people whose standards have changed. Staff have to be found to show parties of local schoolchildren around the new equipment. Complaints are made about humidity and dust, when for eighty years scarcely anyone complained about the heat, noise, and smell of molten lead.

The *LA Times*' history indicates how fashion has changed even since 1975 in regard to the establishment of large central computer stores.[4] The trend is towards the multiplication of storage units and the creation of "intelligent" terminals at which work can proceed if the central processor goes down or is temporarily overloaded. It is possible to have a backup system that performs less essential organizational and accounting work when it is not needed for generating the text of the day's edition, but even this arrangement still makes for a rather brittle organizational structure in which the plans of one department are suddenly found to be dependent upon those of another. Even where companies such as Harris continue to offer large central systems (often for small papers), they allow for the development and addition of subsystems with their own processing capacity.

Newspapers have also found that centralized systems require extremely expert computer maintenance and management. These systems were often designed without the help of composing-room personnel. Sometimes reporters were left to perform too large a range of tasks on their vdt's (they had to add the codes and command information to their copy—tasks too complex for the computer laity). Early vdt's were too crude in design, not subtly tailored enough to the reporter's craft. The growth of ever cheaper memories, small enough to place in terminals, has helped to minimize the impact of clerical error, because it reduces the total number of operations that go into and out of the central processor.

The use of a central unit has, however, a number of residual advantages, especially in the way it makes the total store of available information accessible to all departments involved, and all at the same time. It prevents inefficiencies resulting from the presence of many departments working separately, and it permits at the same time much more stringent security, cutting down the risk of reporters or administrators losing files or of deliberate or accidental acts of sabotage. In terms of cost the centralized system is often superior and almost certainly reduces the cost per item handled over that of a highly distributed system. Nonetheless, the trend is away from the integrated system, and the advantages seem to be accumulating as the overall cost of computer functions in general falls.

At the same time as this change in basic technology is going forward, terminal equipment is becoming both simpler to operate and more sophisticated in design. The more memory contained within the terminal the more ways in which the equipment can be used. Some vdt's are "stand alone" units, which function separately from the central system until they are ready to pass their "file," or story, into the central unit for editing or composition. Reporters can now do all the work of collecting material for a story by telephone and then keying their notes directly into their private electronic file. They can return to the material accumulated for a series of stories on which they may be working simultaneously and recall on the screen any sections of text they wish to compare as they go along. And they may do this in the knowledge that the material is safer than it would be if simply left in a card index, since access to their material is restricted to the person who holds a unique personal pass number.

Editors' terminals are also growing more versatile. They have long been able to give certain words a brighter prominence within the lines of text, experiment with the removal or displacement of groups of words, and try out new layouts or new sentence structures. The vdt offers them the opportunity to escape from the traditional newspaper routine of cutting stories "from the bottom" (it is just as easy to delete text in the middle). It does not hold up busy human typesetters, the composition equipment being quite content to set the story according to any set of instructions. Like the reporter's terminal the editor's can access and review any of the contents of the common database to which his code entitles him. In some newspapers, as we shall see, the same vdt can summon up the contents of the newspaper's morgue, if this is held on-line.

The *Washington Post*'s Raytheon equipment will provide every reporter with a storage system for his own material and will signal when it has messages waiting. The *Post*'s system, in which there will be 250 terminals, requires a production manager (in addition to the rows of editors) whose job it is to act as a kind of traffic controller, keeping track of the priority on various items, prodding editors and reporters to be cognisant of their place in the routine of the day. The *Post*'s new newsroom took two years to design and was created to overcome some of the same problems of scale as the *Los Angeles Times*. It has 300 reporters on its lists, with 200 liable to be at work at any given moment. It has nineteen remote bureaus in Washington, five more in major U.S. cities—all of which must eventually be integrated into the new system—plus thirteen bureaus outside the United States. Of its daily 66 pages (174 on Sundays), reporters on staff at the *Post* file a larger proportion of the material than at nearly any other paper; it relies proportionately less upon wire services and other agencies than other papers and has a characteristic house custom of handing material around to a series of editors before finally settling on a judgment. This makes the editing processes of the *Post*, which had to be built into the new newsroom facility, rather more complicated than in other papers. A computer system must always be a mirror of a social structure, and in most newspaper systems the hierarchy is fairly simple. In the case of the *Post* the simple tier-upon-tier system would not operate, except for the material it gets from the fifteen wire services (which forms a relatively small proportion of the final content of the paper). Raytheon has therefore created a system designed to be more easily interactive within the newsroom and editing area.

Each newspaper chooses its computer system with the same degree of subtlety as one might choose the furnishings of a house. The materials required depend upon the relationships between the inhabitants and the way they lead their external lives, i.e., the house style of the paper and its circulation methods will help or should help determine the range of equipment it acquires. There is no absolute separation between integrated and distributed systems, since each retains elements of the other; but the differences in costs and function trade-offs between them can only be calculated in the light of the circumstances of a particular paper (see figures 4 and 5). This is why most newspapers today adopt a modular approach, acquiring their systems step by step and bringing about in this way a series of gradual changes in the human system to take account of the stages of the mechanical structures.

There are still newspapers that have rejected front-end systems for reasons of their own (quite apart from trade union problems in the composing room) and will probably never relent. Yet they remain, in their own terms, efficient and indeed "modernized." Sometimes a newspaper begins by purchasing a couple of vdt's and some processing equipment, then places a phototypesetter in the composition area so that the newspaper acquaints itself with a whole string of processes—but on a small scale, no function being completely transformed. Other newspapers have converted their entire newsrooms at a stroke and have then waited to see the results before starting on classified or display advertising. Sometimes they have just computerized the circulation and business systems, on the principle of getting the newspaper's feet wet before plunging in.

Introducing computers to newspapers is no longer "experimental" in the sense of the supplying company being nervous about whether it will work. It is experimental in regard to the organization that receives the equipment. What is common today is the sight of a newspaper that invested the whole of its effort in a given system that has either never materialized or has become obsolete within a year or two of installation. Although in most such cases modification and progressive conversion to newer equipment have been possible, often the newspaper is left with an electronic farrago that pleases nobody completely but that has taken the newspaper too far along the road of development to go back. The literature of ANPA provides its members with a large number of cogent warnings and recommendations as to how to proceed from this point. At hundreds of tiny newspapers in America, some geographically far from centers of discussion and information sharing, lonely publishers survey the problem-strewn floors of their newsrooms and composing room,

Figure 4

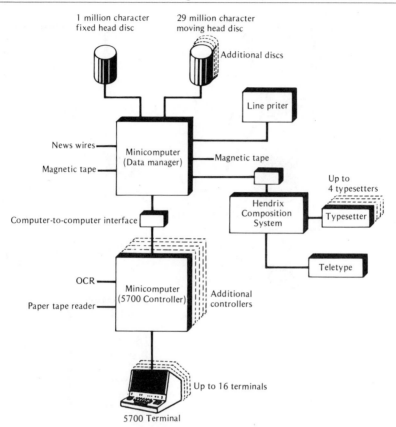

SOURCE: Dineh Moghdam: Computers in Newspaper Publishing—user-oriented systems (Marcel Dekker Inc., New York) p. 55.

having jumped too far or too fast or both. The lessons acquired by hindsight are: one, don't buy systems "off the peg" and, two, get the whole staff into the right frame of mind for the adventure before it begins.

There are several entirely free bonuses that come with the modern newsroom that are more valuable the smaller the paper. When the wire service material goes directly into the computer, a great deal of subsidiary equipment is no longer needed, and the setting of agency material is entirely eliminated. There is no longer a need for extra staff to carry

Figure 5   The Harris 2500 System, with its integrated processing

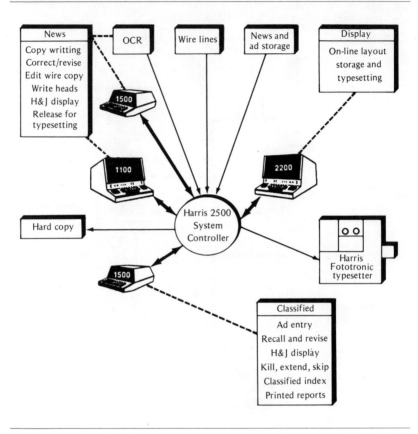

pieces of paper from copy desk to reporter and back again, nor for the proofreaders, whose function no longer exists as a separate personnel category. There is often a visible savings in small things such as scrap paper and other, more expensive office supplies. But when the larger issue of manpower is set aside, it is very difficult to produce a precise balance sheet of the extras and savings entailed in the transfer.

However, there is a long and well-known list of human problems that are easier to identify and impossible to cost. Nearly all of them relate to the tension and anxiety of a staff about to undergo a major shift in work habits, even if direct loss of employment has been eliminated through negotiation. The whole motivational system of the staff is altered. Departments disappear and others are merged. Many simple functions disappear and other (simple) functions appear in their place. All the changes reveal hidden functions that were present in the old system. Relations of trust and dependence between supervisors and employees are often drastically altered.

IV

It took several years for the computer to reach through the news and production departments of American newspapers to circulation. Only in 1977 and 1978 did it start to annex this new territory and continue its long march through the industry. This is proving to be a difficult part of the journey, for every circulation department reflects more conspicuously than other departments the points of individuality of a given newspaper: its degree of emphasis on single-copy sales versus mail and home delivery; its position as a competitor or monopolist in its morning or afternoon market; its Sunday habits; its preprints, zoning, and supplements; its style of promotion and delivery; whether it uses independent merchants, children or adults, employees or shared agents. The circulation department reflects the growth or decline consciousness of the paper, the urbanness or suburbanness of the market, the reliance on telephone or direct mail for promotion, the strategy towards total market coverage, and the custom of subscription collection. It is difficult to find two newspapers with so close a similarity in their circulation habits as to make possible identical systems of computerization.

An enormous variety is required in the kind of data that needs to be collected, held, and used to run a circulation department. One thousand characters of data are stored by one newspaper for every carrier account (of which there are 8000), but the overall impact of bringing the new technology into this area of the business is to provide that air of mechanized assurance that a well-run airline provides for its customers.

The *Indianapolis Star and News* has constructed a line of vdt's to handle customer complaints and subscription starts and stops. The intention is to deal with every call while the caller is still on the line or in the office. The caller is now handled not by a mere message-taker, unable to do anything but pass on information, but by a kind of host, or steward—an instantly knowledgeable human being who gives and receives information. This paper uses six separate files for the service: one listing all the streets with beginning and end numbers for all houses in them, one that contains all customer start and stop information for a period of thirty days, one listing all complaint histories sorted by customer address, one that holds all the complaints of a particular day to check on customers who call back a second time, one that lists all information concerning complaints according to the routes concerned (with appropriate carrier data), and, finally, one with a file of technical information. The system is designed to produce regular management reports, and it also identifies automatically those customers who make frequent calls so that persistent fault-finders are duly noted.[5]

Computerization of circulation departments is now practical and considered financially sound for relatively small papers. The *Oakland Press* in Pontiac, Michigan, for instance, is a six-day paper with a daily sale of 75,000 copies. It has always known the names of its 1400 carriers, but not of its subscribers. The acquisition of a Digital PDP-11/40 has led to the registration of the entire subscription list, each name attached to its carrier route number. At the same time, it is able to improve its opportunities of profiting from direct mailing, and from sampling and solicitation. The paperwork of circulation organization before computerization was complicated by the problems of recording starts and stops, as well as billing and dealing with complaints. Management estimates that computerization has saved nine tenths of the hours of work previously entailed in these processes. It has also improved the reliability and predictability of delivery.

There are now eight people who are employed at the paper's computer terminals to deal with new and existing subscribers and who can gain instant access to the caller's file or start a new file. The equipment automatically sends a message to the relevant district manager. It also automatically prints a new label for the carrier's bundle (which draws attention to the complaint or the start or stop of subscription), alters the accounting information, and calculates the appropriate sum. It then prepares daily, weekly, monthly, and annual reports of circulation information.[6]

The basic information with which the service was compiled was bought from a local mailing company, which had a list of all addresses in the circulation area. Every address was given its own computer file. The newspaper added to this list the delivery history of every subscriber, which automatically provided it with two large groups within the store—subscribers and nonsubscribers. The database was then linked to the carrier information system—bundle drop locations, carrier account files, zip codings, left-hand or right-hand of street data. All door-to-door subscription sellers are given an up-to-date list of nonsubscribers to save unnecessary and troublesome calls on existing subscribers. The nonsubscribers are automatically mailed in direct-mail campaigns with a regular weekly shopper, which guarantees for the paper's advertisers complete household penetration whenever they buy space in the regular newspaper. An added advantage is the automatic weekly billing operation, which eliminates the task of stuffing envelopes. In the future this database will be further exploited for opinion sampling and other editorial uses. The computer has locked the entire newspaper enterprise firmly inside the distribution area, enabling it to benefit from its position within its clearly delineated market.

The *Detroit Free Press*, owned by the Knight-Ridder group, is constructing a mailroom device particularly suited to the needs of a very large metropolitan daily with a penchant for localizing its material. On Sundays the 700,000 print run can include up to 250 different zoned inserts, all of which are to be handled under computer command from the presses to the loading bays. The paper decided that in switching finally to offset printing, it would require a reliable device for identifying and preferably preventing lost copies (presses frequently have to stop and restart for complex zoning, and when a paper prints offset the cost of these losses is much greater).

The *Press* decided to invest heavily in a device that would synchronize mailroom activities (bundling, tying, addressing, loading) with the printing presses themselves; this had previously been tried out by the U.S. Postal Service for bulk postage work and by Sears Roebuck for processing orders. With this system a series of trays move along a never ending track, passing the fourteen truck-loading positions as they do so and emptying tied bundles into the appropriate trucks. A row of nine tying lines is meanwhile monitoring the variations of the product for each bundle and the numbers of copies required for each district. The mailroom will also take over the task of monitoring all wasted papers, which will be automatically marked and then eliminated by the monitoring system.

Among American newspapers the *LA Times* has also gone the farthest in the exploitation of the computer for circulation functions, from billing subscribers to loading delivery trucks. There are 800,000 daily subscribers (840,000 on Sundays) whose names and addresses are all held on-line. Information about the length, positioning, and timing of delivery routes is collected, and all subscriber complaints to dealers and delivery agents are recorded and held. Starts and stops are analyzed. Every temporary stop by a subscriber during holiday periods is noted, and if possible the paper is rerouted. Information about late payment or nonpayment of invoices is quickly available. The paper also runs an accident insurance policy for its readers off the same system. A quarter million street sales of the paper are made on weekdays and 420,000 on Sundays through sixteen street sales centers operated by direct employees. The paper holds on-line all information relating to delivery from the centers to news racks, shops, and street vending machines. All billing and invoicing for this whole range of functions is run from a parallel subsystem. All telephone calls from readers are automatically routed through a call distributor system to any of the 120 phone stations in the Circulation Service Center.

The possession of computing capacity of the size and sophistication required by the *LA Times* and the acquisition by its personnel of intensive experience in such a variety of functions makes possible a further range of income-attracting activities. The *LA Times* (and many other U.S. newspapers) has embarked upon its own program of consumer-trend analysis. To inform the advertisers about their potential customers, it sends out and processes 500 very detailed questionnaires every month and analyses the marketplaces of the region for individual products. The Editorial Department uses the same service to learn more about its readers and to conduct opinion surveys for the feature pages. More and more departments are thus being supplied with vdt's and made to operate the computer on-line.

All of the blessings and potential blessings that flow from computerization of the ancillary departments of a newspaper help to confirm the newspaper as a medium of local monopolies. It is only when a single newspaper takes total command over its universe of households that it can establish the full range of extra functions and services within a community. When the additional energy of an enterprise is saved from the labor of parallel titles, it can invest in those kinds of expansion that consolidate the relationship between paper and reader. Of course, there is a tension between the public dislike of monopoly (which is shared by many embarrassed publishers) and the growing technical and economic convenience of monopoly.

V

Whenever a newspaper has succeeded in transferring the bulk of its daily input of information to a computer, it starts to look for additional services that can be run with the same information. It also looks for other economies or areas or expansion within its overall organization, and among the first of these, ripe for the computer, is the "morgue," or files of back copies and clippings. A variety of newspaper library and morgue retrieval systems have been developed, and from a review of these it is possible to see how a local newspaper with a backlog of stored information can develop an unusual new community service, a kind of central store of local information, which can be sold to paying customers. (This service is made easier if it joins forces with other local information sources such as the local public reference library.) It represents a wonderful way of capitalizing on a wasted and previously wasting asset—the backlog of past editions.

Many newspapers have morgues going back to the days before reporters used typewriters—treasuries of unusable material mouldering in ancient filing cabinets. Transferred to microfiche or to on-line systems, this decaying store of knowledge can become a living asset, available to schools, universities, and other researchers. Since the 1930's many newspapers have added photographs to their filing systems, and with the transmission of images by laser and facsimile in recent years, their storage systems have become hopelessly overloaded, the library staff unable to cope with traditional methods of storage and retrieval.[7]

Newspaper librarianship has become a new kind of specialism, and one university even provides a course in the subject. What has transformed the position of the newspaper library as a social unit is the great increase in the number of graduate journalists and reporters who think in terms of research much more than previous generations of reporters. They tend to place far greater pressure on the existing librarians, hitherto the drudges of the newspaper staff, who are now being hastily professionalized as a possible source of future additional revenue.

One of the most interesting current systems is at the *Los Angeles Times*, which combines microfiche with computer—the former for storage of the clippings themselves, the latter for keeping the index. There are 15 million clippings in the paper's existing library, which dates back to the 1930's. Until the installation of the Zytron Data Systems Library Information System, it was possible to scan the library's information only in a very crude and superficial way. The researcher had to guess which files to ask for. The new system has a core memory used for processing with disc memories the material itself. Thirty-two people can draw material simultaneously. The microfiche sheets are six inches by four, each with 192 frames, with three clippings per frame. Five complete years of the paper are stored at any given moment. Every indexed story is abstracted and registered with date of issue, edition, geographical place names, headlines, personal names, and subjects referred to, and all these represent routes through which the information can be retrieved. The first search, using a keyword, results in the computer's giving the number of stories under the heading concerned within ten seconds. The searcher then refines his demands, suggesting categories such as editorial, interview, obituary, op-ed, biographical, photograph, etc., and when he makes his final choice, the resulting material can be printed at high speed or viewed on the screen. The microfiche is subject to the computer, and both abstract and clipping can be displayed at the same moment (after a wait of less than three seconds).

This system also has the capacity to change the titles of categories of material over the course of time. For instance, everything formerly filed under "segregation" is now filed under "integration," but the two collections are linked. Delicate separations of files can be achieved: if you ask for beef export prices under "beef," you will be protected against cooking columns. The whole system has cost $250,000, but it saves a number of filing clerks, while permitting greatly increased sophistication in editorial research. The disc memory started with a 40-megabyte capacity adequate for holding indexing information but could be expanded to 2000 megabytes, sufficient to hold five years of storage of the *full text* of the clippings if the paper decides to abandon microfiche storage.

The *Boston Globe* has entered into the new age of information storage in a rather different spirit. Its libraries go back to the 1880's and, to take but one category, hold 226,000 obituaries of past Boston residents, a gold mine for genealogists. It holds 800,000 photographic prints, and all of these are now cataloged on-line. Its 9 million clippings have been held in 700,000 folders, and these are now all being turned to microfiche through the use of a system called A.B. Dick/Scott System 200. The problem is to persuade reporters to use microfiche rather than actual clippings, and this has been done by having them transfer their own personal desk-clippings files to microfiche. Details of all the other files are entered into the cold-type system of the newspaper through an optical scanner.

Meanwhile, the Mead Corporation laboratories have designed a system for holding the whole text of the *Globe*'s daily editions in computer storage. To retrieve information a Keyword in Context (kwic) is employed, which flashes on the screen twelve words before and after each keyword requested. Requests are first answered with the number of corresponding clippings and then refined down to the desired information. A variety of colors are used to indicate keyword, search term, text, etc.; the search terms will either blink or indicate with arrows, according to preference. The Mead system can also be used to link the morgues of several newspapers and can be adapted for time-sharing by individual non-newspaper clients. In the first year it succeeded in saving the *Globe* seven members of the thirty-person morgue staff.

The *Toronto Globe and Mail* has constructed a filing system (with QL

Systems of Kingston, Ontario) out of a legal-text-retrieval system of the early 1970's. The whole text of news stories is kept in storage and can be retrieved through keying any word at all in the text, or by using a number of other routes. The *Chicago Sun-Times* is going over to a similar system and abandoning the microfiche-plus-computer systems that were used by the pioneering newspaper morgues. The stories are held as soon as they are registered in the typesetting computers for the day's run and are accessible thereafter under thirteen headings, or "fields," including accession number of the story, date of publication, dateline, type of story, by-line or author, page/column, illustration, wire service, number of words, special pecularities of story, search categories added by the librarian, and other notes, including correction of printed errors. The computer will supply the researcher only with the text, minus all the typesetting commands that originally accompanied the story into the computer.

The QL system has certain other statistical facilities, including the ability to reveal how much copy has been filed by any single reporter, how much material has been printed on a given subject or from a given location. Like the Mead system it will highlight the search terms themselves while revealing the text and will also provide information even where the terms have been truncated or the wrong spelling used. The searcher may choose to work chronologically or backwards in time, and a printer can be attached for hard copies. A reporter in a hurry may, while working at his input terminal in the newsroom, use one half of his screen for his own story and the other half for material taken from library storage. About seven people have been saved on the library staff, equal to about fifty person-hours, but some extra time is required for checking and "enhancing" the stories (i.e., adding necessary search terms to each file).

No one has yet discovered the perfect answer to the problem of newspaper information storage, but certain principles are becoming clear. First, it is inherently inefficient for a newspaper that produces all of its material in scannable form to keep a hard-copy morgue constantly bursting the seams of the file space allocated to it. Discarding the electronic version is in itself a wasteful absurdity. Secondly, it is equally inefficient to force information users into adopting technical devices that are simply inconvenient in partly unconscious human terms; to do that merely encourages the secret hoarding of hard-copy material in various parts of an organization, a kind of underground bureaucratic reaction. Failure to adopt any kind of electronic system, however, in the long run deprives the newspaper of a useful ancillary source of income. A compromise has to be found within the available and imperfect technology.

Even from a brief overview of some of the pioneering electronic systems for information storage, it is clear that something beyond a mere reporter's aid is being born within the newspaper morgue. A new kind of generally available store of knowledge is being created in a series of communities, something that goes beyond the traditional function of the newspaper. Several of the metropolitan newspapers are aware that their files, if well tended, could become a new kind of information resource, useful in education, business, and other fields. Indeed, these forms of database, not previously available to the wider public, could be of tremendous value in an era in which the computer had become a household item.

The best-known and oldest of the existing systems is the New York Times Information Bank, which dates back to 1966 in conception and to 1973 in reality. It is a newspaper morgue that also contains abstracts and citations from a variety of other newspapers and journals. By means of a vdt the user gains access to the database by keying through personal names, organization names (including names of newspapers filed), geographic areas, and a variety of subject headings identified in the system's own dictionary. A further series of "modifiers" must then be employed to refine down the list of possible files, e.g., by providing dates, specific publications, sources such as wire services, or other special categories (i.e., advertisement, letter, obituary, review, editorial). The searcher uses various "Boolean" formal linking terms, such as "and," "or," "not," which help to narrow down the nature of the inquiry. The final result is a bibliographic list, including a microfiche reference number and an abstract of desired articles.

Personnel inside the New York Times Information Bank and outsiders renting usage on a time basis have to have recourse to microfiche or microfilm for any material more detailed than the abstract. One major problem in opening up a newspaper morgue to nonjournalistic use is the fact that great divergences exist between the kinds of information required by nonprofessional users. The New York Times Information Bank was basically designed for selling information to outside corporations. It is one thing to design a system that enables reporters to quickly check the ages and birth dates of Congressmen and another thing to help businessmen learn the details of the policies or market research activity of rival companies. But in the longer run the newspaper's electronic morgue could develop as a new kind of public service, interacting with the domestic user and playing an important role within the "information society."

There are still many advantages to keeping the basic collection of clippings on some kind of microfilm storage rather than putting the whole text on-line. (There are many techniques for doing this of which the much-used microfiche, with its time-consuming creation of neat rows of frames, is only one.) With microfilm, articles can be read exactly as they appeared originally in the correct layout; the full text of a long article can be seen at a glance by "scrolling" through many screenfuls of text; charts, maps, and photographs can be seen at the same time; memory capacity is saved; distant (paying) customers who don't have fully computerized access can select the piece they want, have it displayed on their screen, then disconnect and continue to read it; microfilm will stay in its original form and is safe from being accidentally tampered with during search. This, at least, is the case made by the Info-Ky system at the twin *Louisville* newspapers, the *Courier-Journal* and *Times*, which continue to find that microfilm is faster, cheaper, and easier for noncomputer experts to handle. It too can provide hard copy at the push of a button and can be searched in less than five seconds—its capacity is technically unlimited.

The great advantage of computer-assisted search for information, whether microfilm or disc storage is used for full text, is that the searcher can locate information that cuts across the categories in which paper storage imprisons it. If we wish to know about Kennedy, defense, and Cuba, we have to use three physical files before we can be certain that we have acquired the knowledge we seek. With computer storage it is possible to stick a pin, as it were, through those slices of information that correspond simultaneously to all of the desired categories. But not even computer memory is immune to overload, and it cannot ultimately save the human brain from having to work through the material it itself has chosen. The greater the amount of material stored the greater the difficulties in searching through it, whatever filing system is employed. Abstracts reduce the apparent problem, but at the expense of missing the subtleties of mood and approach in the original text. The gradually increasing quantity of material available will still tend to creep up on the researcher and entangle him if he lacks skill.

In fact, the whole future prospect for newspaper storage and retrieval will depend upon constantly increasing expertise in the field of librarianship, especially in the more complex "deep classification" techniques. Journalists will have to acquire more and more of these skills, while librarians will need to understand more precisely the daily needs of reporters, if they are to file and index their material effectively. A kind of historical collusion is developing between journalism and librarianship, but in the meantime newspaper libraries are likely to be technologically eclectic, mixing microfilm methods with text—and abstract—storage, while retaining a good deal of traditional paper-filing.

A successful electronic newspaper morgue is one that improves the preexisting hard-copy system, which renders itself attractive to its users by enabling them to do more research more rapidly than the old system. It also needs to be designed in such a way as not to increase the cost of use over that of the old system. (In the New York Times Information Bank the cost of use is so high that very little internal research within the newspaper can be done on it.) The more successful newspapers, while realizing the impossibility of transferring a complete back file to an on-line operation, have refrained from imposing an arbitrary cut off date but have transferred the complete text of selected areas to meet the probable needs of future researchers.

This, however, also means that conventional morgues will need to be kept for an indefinite time ahead. No existing or projected system is yet on a scale large enough for all the hard-copy storage of the past decades to be abolished. The long-term development of the morgue into a general public system must await the development of cheaper memories and more sophisticated technologies of data-store management.

The new facilities and new skills being acquired by internal newspaper libraries should be seen in the light of the more general crisis enveloping traditional library systems. Academic libraries are buying proportionately less and less of the newly arriving literature. New publications are increasing in cost and in volume by a factor larger than the general increase in the economy. At the same time libraries are becoming ever more labor-intensive and space-consuming. There have been several plans for "shared and interconnected" library systems, for library "networking," for "zero-growth" libraries, and for "self-reorganizing" libraries. All of these naturally involve automation and the greater use of computers in library management. But these are very limited horizons for librarianship, since the use of the computer, if restricted merely to cataloging and retrieval and other managerial and organizational work, does little more than provide a palliative, mild relief to the problem. Despite these improvements, the library would remain exactly the same as it has for centuries; rows of books and papers would continue to accumulate on shelves. The question today is whether the basic materials of which libraries have been traditionally composed will remain in print form in the next generations. Some librarians are now of the view that with further advances in electronic storage systems, "libraries would wither away, their historic duty done."[8] A transition to new forms of distribution would be forced by the gradual elimination of paper altogether for certain categories of currently printed material.

The rate of growth of scientific material is now so high that the secondary material (i.e., bibliographic and abstract material) has itself been caught up in the cycle of growth to the point that no individual can leap ahead in any major field. It has been calculated that it took thirty-two years (between 1907 and 1938) for *Chemical Abstracts* to reach its first million scientific papers; in eighteen additional years the second million was reached and the third in eight years. The fourth million took three and three quarters years, the fifth three and a half, and fairly soon this bibliographic journal will be dealing with new acquisitions at the rate of a million a year. There are 1500 journals that publish only abstracts and guides to scientific material and another 2000 dealing with nonscientific subjects. The crucial papers in any given field are scattered through one to two hundred journals of primary literature, too many for any single expert to scan. The secondary literature is too bulky to be easily scanned, and in any case it tends to appear months or even years after the primary literature it deals with. The sheer cost of keeping up with the flow of material is now considerable and a large proportion of bibliographic publications are set at prices that no individual could afford and indeed only a few major institutions. *Chemical Abstracts* cost its subscribers $12 a year in 1940 and $3500 a year in 1979. Between the mid-1960's and the mid-1970's the average price of scientific journals increased from roughly $20 a year to nearly $70.[9]

In the world as a whole there are now more than 50,000 journals pouring through university and academic presses every year. They are increasing in size at a compound rate of 4 percent a year. It is common for journals to double their size every five years. At this rate, it has become clear that the traditional forms of publication and systems of access to published material are defeating their own objective of circulating information to those who need it. All forms of economic and social progress depend on scientific discovery and the circulation of information. Moreover, modern science depends upon knowledge acquired by groups, and it is these groups that are often held together through publications. Print and paper have clearly reached the limits of their efficiency in a large number of specialist areas, and as they do so, a new torrent of patents, dissertations, videotapes, and film material are descending upon communities of experts. If a scientist spends a given proportion of his time catching up with his field and continues dedicating the same proportion for twenty years, he will clearly acquire knowledge over a rapidly decreasing proportion of the necessary and relevant material. If he

increases the proportion of his time dedicated to scanning the outpour-
ings of the field, he will have no time for anything else. There are clear
and painful mathematical constraints that must begin to operate.[10]

Since the 1960's there has been a considerable development of machine-readable databases specializing in scientific abstracts. The National
Library of Medicine has operated its MEDLARS system, for example, since
1964, and 500 other comparable institutions are now in existence, providing retrospective search services. Over the years a large number of
librarians, researchers, and scientists have acquired the expertise necessary to search these databases fruitfully. The number of searches handled by MEDLARS alone rose to 20,000 a year by the end of the 1960's and
to 20,000 a month a decade later. The telecommunications cost of
searching a typical database has dropped from $50 an hour to $3 an hour
via the new Telenet system, everything included. Bibliographic Retrieval Services can now provide a full service for searchers, including the
royalty costs and terminal charges, at an average cost per search of
between $5.75 and $8.50.[9] Distance has greatly decreased in importance
as a factor in retrieval costs, and the relative advantages of working in a
large city over working in a small one have been eliminated as well.

We are rapidly moving towards a stage in the evolution of machine-
read material in which the researcher will function in a wholly different
way from the past. An on-line terminal will be the basic means for not
only acquiring relevant information but also for collecting notes and
personal abstracts, for sending out letters to colleagues and reading
them, for the composition and "publication" of research reports. It will
substitute for visiting libraries and the searching of bibliographic indexes. It might even permit certain kinds of scientific on-line dialogue.
The tools of the scientist requiring very high quantities of sophisticated
information will become similar to those of the journalist working in a
well-equipped modern newspaper institution.

What is happening is a fundamental retransposition of all forms of
intellectual communication and, indeed, intellectual work.[11] An author
can draft his material, send it to colleagues for review and criticism,
automatically transpose into his own work diagrams, charts, and tables
from other works, check his own references automatically, and use a full
range of text-manipulation devices that are being increasingly adopted in
newspaper editorial offices. The gradations of publications between
individuals, groups, and general publics can be achieved essentially
through the same machinery. Even the work of checking the "credit" of a
new contribution to knowledge can be achieved electronically; scientific
papers can be "referred" and admitted to specially attested databases by

electronic means. The newsroom has already laid out the basic techniques for passing a text through an editorial hierarchy for review, alteration, and approval. The processes by which material is now selected for publication in a scientific journal are haphazard by comparison with what could be achieved by this means, since there could be automatic codings attached to referred papers that would bring them to the attention of specialist readers just as selections for publication in high-status periodicals are made. Articles would be brought to the attention of the potential audience through computers containing profiles of the interests of all experts in a given subject.

The distinctions between formal and informal systems of communication might well become much less clear in the age of paperless publishing, and the date when these new information resources become generally available is being pushed up by virtue of the increasing number of specialist fields that have already moved to paperless forms of information circulation. The intelligence community in the United States, and possibly in other societies, has transferred largely to a paperless mode of communication and information storage; banking and business have abandoned the traditional systems to a very great extent, and electronic funds-transfer systems promise to make the personal credit card the basis of a more complex and far-reaching change in the nature of daily transactions. Taken together, one can see how a large central core of public and personal activities is now being transferred to a paperless mode, and more will follow within a decade. "Word-processing" is already replacing traditional typing in many corporations, in legal and business offices, and with the advent of common-carrier systems for business information in the early 1980's, the rate of changeover should again accelerate.

The importance of these developments to the well-managed newspaper business is that they offer a greatly magnified opportunity to exploit the newspaper's traditional asset—its information collected by trained professional reporters. The newspaper can become a localized general-research institute, or at least share this role with local libraries and other "natural" databases. The growing repertoire of techniques and technologies offers the imaginative publisher the chance of a quantum leap in function, with a concomitant increase in profitability, at some future stage.

VI

We can now see how the newspaper industry in America has proceeded through a perception of its own structural changes (competition to monopoly, "political" to "neutral," single medium to cross-ownership, family to group control) into the era of new technology. Of course, those papers that have not been subject to this major change in structure have still had recourse to new techniques and have benefited from the corresponding savings in labor and in increased ability to penetrate the modern consumer market. The main lines of development have nonetheless come from the industry's leading enterprises, which have been able to obtain the pace of change and directions of change suitable to them. Newspaper magnates often feel the pressure towards technical changes as if it were an extraneous force independent of mere mortals; in fact, many techniques have arisen directly from the special needs of individual companies or newspapers, interacting with generally available research drawn from other spheres.

It is interesting to observe the "bias" in the technology of the one other society in the world that has developed new methods of production as dynamic as those of America—Japan. Japanese national newspapers have faced a different range of problems, arising from the national nature of their product and the different character of their written language. They have had recourse to the same theoretical technical possibilities but have pressed for change in different directions and at a different pace.[12]

Perhaps the most important contast as regards the external economy is the Japanese system of "administrative guidance," by which the national bureaucracy, the main political parties, and industrial leaders have worked out a coherent policy and a clear theory in advance of investment and experiment. The notion of the Information Society, which was widely used in Japan before it became a familiar tag in the West, acted as a sort of generalized goal uniting industrial and professional groups within a political framework of action. The "Thursday Club" of the Liberal Democratic Party (LDP) took up the theme in the 1960's and provided the links between newspapers and the computer industry. Government, aware of the likely rise in disposable income, was able to proffer advice as to the pace at which new media should be brought on stream. DENTSU, the powerful information giant that controls half of all commercial broadcasting revenue and 40 percent of all the advertising trade of the country (including 80 percent of the advertising in provincial newspapers) was able to control the relationships between the information sector of the economy and the suppliers of the necessary revenue— the advertisers. It has acted as a coordinating and directing instrument, and its people have kept in close contact with the government.

In 1973, for example, it was DENTSU that explained to the Japanese people the dire importance of oil conservation and persuaded them to accept the measures proposed by government to deal with the energy shortage. It had already started the official government paper and helped to staff it. DENTSU's house custom of paying all advertising revenue without delay enabled it to become a kind of banker to the information media, helping to keep various papers (especially the provincial papers) in circulation through difficult times. There are even many DENTSU officials on loan to government departments, and in conditions when advertising rose to account for one percent of the total Japanese GNP (between 1960 and 1970), it came to provide a comprehensive consultative presence in Japanese public life, greatly influencing governmental policy towards the media. The Ministry of International Trade, in the meantime, came to play an increasing role in the financing of new experimental information services, confident of the connections between the home information industries and the overseas market for equipment.[13]

Through other powerful agencies that galvanize specific sectors of the economy, such as the Newspaper Publishers' Association (NSK), the Japanese have been able to select industry goals and marshall the resources necessary to achieve them. The process of rapid and concentrated modernization of the 1940's and 1950's made virtually second-nature such phenomena as standardization of equipment, the streamlining of the approach to choosing new techniques, and the establishing of technical norms. The Japanese Standards Institute thus fixed such minor matters as the kinds of ink used by Japanese papers and the size of print, while creating nationally agreed upon standards for the length of reels of newsprint and the thickness of metal plates. The fact that it is impossible for Japanese firms, though privately owned, to sack members of their work force has meant that expansion constantly has had to take place alongside rationalization and mechanization.

In terms of newspaper production techniques, Japan had quickly gone through three generations of experimental equipment by the mid-1960's. A Character Teletype began work in 1955 at the *Asahi Shimbun*. It produced a tape that could drive a typesetting machine at a rate of ten characters per minute; this led onto a Computerized Type System (CTS) that transmitted the image of characters by facsimile and cut down very greatly the time spent in sending copy to the newspaper's many regional plants. In the third stage IBM Japan and *Asahi* cooperated to create a computerized system suitable for the 2400 characters normally used in Japanese newspapers—plus roman letters, figures, and ligatures—in addition to thousands of extra characters used only occasionally.

The New Editing and Layout System for Newspapers (NELSON) was ready in 1966, and not long after, the Nikkei organization (which produces the daily financial paper of Japan) produced its Automated Nikkei Newspaper Editing and Composing System (ANNECS), which uses a different IBM computer from its companion system. Both of these are attached to full-page photocomposition, which has meant constructing massive computer systems able to machine-read high-definition pictures as well as text into storage and then output complete pages ready for plate making—the first newspapers in the world to achieve this for large quantities of pages per day. (*Asahi* will produce 150 pages per day by this means in its new downtown production plant, due to open in 1980.) These newspaper have also concentrated on computerization of their circulation rooms, bundling, sorting, and truck-loading operations, with results that are spectacular to behold.

The Japanese press's new technology caters to the special bottlenecks in the Japanese newspaper system that are different from those of the U.S. and Europe. Japan will almost certainly never be able to have direct input by journalists because of the complexity of its written language. The Kyodo News Agency has perfected a method for converting roman text submitted by its foreign reporters directly into "kanji" (or Chinese) characters and the two syllabaries, Katakana and Hiragana, which are the basic elements of the Japanese method of writing. The system works through a complex translating "dictionary," which has been taught to the CPU. But there is no way in which ordinary reporters could be reliably expected to punch their own material directly into a composing system. Japanese newspapers will therefore depend on skilled high-speed (human) typesetters, and the electronic equipment, which has been devised for them, reflects the fact that the number of inputting sources will remain relatively small while the memory capacity required will be extremely high. The composition machines must be able to reproduce several thousand characters, many of which, when written by pen or bruch, involve up to thirty-three movements of the hand. Typewriters have thus remained a specialist implement in Japan, and newspaper reporters have to produce their text by hand on specially squared paper and rely on the typesetters to make the necessary corrections and alignments. Working with a massive keyboard and a light pen, which works by a simple touch on the character pads, a skilled typesetter can set as many as 700 characters per minute.

At the same time, Japanese newspapers have a further basic difference from Western papers, one that is currently the subject of a severe crisis. Every day Japan, with half the population of the U.S., produces roughly the same number of newspaper copies (62 million). More than half of these consist of copies of four national papers that produce two editions per day and subscribers, for the most part, expect to receive the "set" at their homes or offices. Furthermore, each of the major national papers operates its own delivery system, in competition with that of its rival papers. (Ninety-nine percent of all papers are home-delivered.) As newspaper sales and profits have been under pressure in recent years, publishers' efforts to increase circulation have resulted in frenzied publicity campaigns, now the subject of a code of conduct designed to cool the competition, which was agreed upon by publishers through their association, NSK.

Japanese law forbids under-age employment, even by newspapers, and the press has traditionally looked to high-school and college students to deliver copies. The papers sometimes provide university grants for their delivery personnel or even arrange for them to go abroad for study after several years of service. The average wage for a newspaper-deliverer is 60,000 yen per month (or $250). There is also a network of private agents, small businesses run at the behest of the newspapers, but these must reach a daily distribution of 2000 copies to stay in business, and this level is very difficult to maintain without staff. As a result, the newspapers are subsidizing large numbers of agents to enable them to keep their employees at work. Sometimes the total subsidy is equal to the selling price of the paper, although the average for Tokyo is equal to about one fifth of the total reader revenue.

In comparison with the system in the U.S., therefore, Japan has had to reckon with the impossibility of achieving staff reductions through direct newsroom input of text (although papers have saved many scores of employees through computerization of typesetting) and to face the problems of a distribution system that is hopelessly labor-intensive for a high-wage economy. It has thus concentrated on improving the appearance of its papers, adopting cold-type color-printing and di-litho printing (about half of the country's papers by 1978 had started to change over), and speeding up the process of delivery. In particular, it has brought in a number of facsimile devices for transmitting text from central newsrooms to provincial centers where local editions are printed, and is now trying to achieve further economies by extending its pioneering full-page Phototypesetting System (FPPS) into the direct making of printing plates, eliminating the whole manual photographic process. At its most experimental it has even tried out direct home facsimile delivery of complete newspaper pages, although this is still impossibly expensive and obliges the subscriber to keep another large machine in his home. (Japanese homes tend to be much smaller than those in America and other consumer societies.)

Of the national dailies three compete across the Japanese terrain at total circulation levels of between 5 million and 7 million per day. Each prefecture has its own morning and evening papers, and these, as a general rule, tend to have a greater grip over their respective markets the farther they are from the center of production of the national papers. The latter, therefore, as they increase the intensity of competition for readers (which they have done successfully despite the difficult conditions since 1973), have to go farther afield for new subscriptions, and this in turn puts additional pressure upon their production costs.

The three national papers, *Asahi*, *Mainichi*, and *Yomiuri*, average twenty-four pages in the mornings and twelve in the evenings but are obliged to insert a large quantity of local pages, which means that the total number of plates employed by each edition can be very high indeed (running into thousands per week at times). These papers have therefore moved relatively cautiously into offset printing, where plates tend to be more expensive to make (400 yen per plate as compared to 100 yen for a recyclable traditional metal plate). Offset has now arrived at most of the smaller-circulation papers (200,000 to 400,000) but has reached the big three nationals only in the 1977–79 period. *Asahi's* new plant, opening in 1980, will take the whole of that paper's daily 7 million copies into offset. The price has been paid by the editorial departments, which have had their deadlines lengthened to cope with the introduction of new technology: reporters have to present their copy anywhere up to half an hour earlier for the complete electronic production system to be able to handle it. On the other hand, mechanization of the circulation departments has helped the papers through some of the increasingly vexing problems of distribution.

Until the mid-1960's Japan was able to develop its newspaper industry by benefiting from successive improvements in imported European and American printing equipment. In the 1890's it imported Marinoni's printing press powered by steam, which had been developed in France only a dozen years before. No fewer than sixty-five of these were brought into Japan to found the press of the Meiji era. At the end of this period, the *Mainichi Shimbun* brought electric high-speed presses from Europe able to print 72,000 copies an hour (three times as fast as Marinoni's). With the new scientific management of the 1930's in America and the arrival of the production line and conveyor belt (which had its effect on the American newspaper industry by encouraging the creation of the Sunday *New York Times* and *Time* magazine), the Japanese press brought in Hoe and Gosse machines, which could reach speeds of 180,000 copies an hour, although they normally cruised at lower rates.

Japan imported the entire range of machinery and copied it, and the habit of import-and-imitate lasted until the 1950's, when the Japanese economy adopted an industrial logic of its own.

At this point Japan's print runs were so large that it had to make its own basic innovations; for example, the machinery of the 1950–60 era required very high skills in start-up to get the balance of plate, ink, and paper roll exactly right. (Every time the machine had to restart meant a loss of copies and time.) The Japanese, concentrating on their special problems of long print runs, had developed devices for automatically joining rolls of paper without having to stop printing, together with transistorized monitoring equipment to control the operation. Speeds of 140,000 papers an hour became common, and techniques for preventing paper-breaks, more important in Japan than in other societies, were developed. Technocrats took the place of the foremen and mechanics, and the character of newspaper production began to change.

In an industry in which the actual selling price is capable of little variation (since all economies made possible by mass production have already been made), competition creates pressure for further increases in productivity and reductions in the cost of production. But the limits of circulation growth were being reached, certainly the limits possible for national newspapers with high distribution costs and a technology that tended to inhibit market segmentation. Paradoxically, the only area of expansion available for Japanese national papers was precisely to create more and more regional and subregional editions to segment markets and to compete with the prefectural or provincial papers more effectively in the latter's advertising markets. Hence, the tremendous emphasis put on improved printing plates, di-litho printing, and facsimile techniques for sending out the made-up pages from the national edition to the regions. One Japanese national daily has no fewer than 143 separate daily editions. The problem was to move from market homogenization to a strategy of market separation without losing any of the economies of scale—a typical dilemma of postindustrial society.

Within Japan's newspaper hierarchy, even more than that of the United States, consultants and technocrats have come to wield great influence relative to that of editors and journalists. The great national newspaper enterprises have become powerful information empires, flanked by electronic media, films, and other subsidiary activities. The internal finances of the Japanese papers have remained fairly secret, in comparison with other industries, because they are family-owned and subsidized where necessary by other investments held by the same family. *Mainichi* went bankrupt in 1976 as a result of mounting problems of management but has recovered as a result of intervention by the banks, who have acquired considerable power within the paper's executive (mitigated to some extent by the introduction of measures of internal democracy and reader accountability). The extraordinary technological feats of the industry, achieved with the help of American computer expertise, have to be seen in the light of the special crisis of the Japanese press, a small group of vast landed whales who have consumed all the plankton available and are wondering where to turn next.

Japan already has the highest level of newspapers to population in the world (if one counts each "set" of national papers as two separate titles). There is one paper sold for every 2.63 members of the population, or 1.25 for every household, a level that would make American publishers deeply envious.

The industry's problems have greatly increased as a result of the downturn in general economic growth (especially advertising), which has afflicted Japan since the 1973 oil crisis. The Japanese press has escalated its approach to the new computerized techniques in an attempt to decrease its level of employment at a rate faster than the increasing proportion of its total costs that go to wages and salaries. Thus, between 1967 and 1977 personnel have come to represent 41.3 percent of total expenditure as opposed to 36 percent at the start of that period, while total employment has been dropping at a rate of about 4 percent a year for several years. In 1975, there were 71,216 workers employed by the Japanese press (spread over 101 separate companies), while the 1977 figure stood at 66,238 (for 106 companies).[14] Virtually all of this drop has been achieved by natural attrition and by finding displaced workers in the large national papers jobs in other branches of the same enterprise. The real problem facing the industry, which is confronted with the classic problems of rising costs, difficult delivery customs, and market saturation, is that it is unable to provide its own funds for major efforts in modernization: the average ratio of company funds to total operating capital is only 6.8 percent, compared with 16.7 percent at the start of the decade. Hence the need for the press to borrow even more to modernize and therefore the increased tendency towards dependency on noninformation activites. Thus new technology has arrived alongside an increased emphasis on financial management and "corporatism" in general.

The difficulties of Japanese papers are therefore directly linked to the style of their investment in new technology and the need to construct their own systems. Their approach is increasingly distinct from that of the United States. Of course, much of Japanese gadgetry can be traced back to the Apollo mission, as can that of the U.S. and Western Europe, but the intensity with which it has been pushed in the specific directions required by Japanese newspapers illustrates aptly how individualized modern newspaper technology has become. The age of directly importing off-the-peg machinery constructed by some other society is over, and when this occurs, disaster may follow, or at least a failure to achieve the intended result. The Japanese have benefited greatly from their totalistic approach to the Information Society, a factor that has had a great deal to do with the very circulation of the phrase itself, which has, in turn, helped to clarify goals and intentions. Increasingly, the Japanese newspapers think of themselves as interconnected but diverse information conglomerates, in which the information-collection function is in constant search of new outlets and new forms of commercialization.

In the U.S. some of the larger newspaper corporations have turned themselves into "communications complexes": a brace or two of metropolitan and suburban papers, with appropriately situated radio and television stations and further investments in newsprint, microfilm libraries, computer terminals, or book publishing. Some companies, such as Gannett, have gone heavily into newspapers and have remained predominately in that single medium, with only minor diversification into electronic and other fields. Other companies have sought to diversify more solidly to the point at which their news-gathering function has become subordinate to other concerns. The *Los Angeles Times* has invested very heavily in newsprint and now supplies two thirds of its own needs; but it has moved equally heavily into other outlets of information and owns New American Library, one of the country's largest paperback publishers. Today many papers are forming alliances with the manufacturers of the new production equipment and forming companies to market what they have pioneered. On the other hand, Time Inc., which now owns the *Washington Star*, is swamped by the size of its newsprint offshoot, to the extent that it is listed in the stock quotations under "forestry."

However, the most important line of development for those newspapers anxious to reduce dependence upon one traditional medium with all its attendant vexations is to find new outlets for the material that its journalists have collected. This is another field in which Japan foresees a line of escape for newspapers. Once material has been put into machine-readable form and is held on-line or stored off-line, it is extremely cheap to reprocess it for uses other than newspaper publication. In London the *Financial Times* and the *Economist*, its stable partner, both run their own "information" businesses, and both have taken the first substantial steps towards computerization. The two newspapers derive significant revenue from selling the contents of their libraries, which are full of business data covering the entire world and, in the case of the *Economist*, of political information too. Subscribers pay an annual fee plus an hourly rate, but they cannot, as yet, acquire the information by electronic means. In both cases, though, the start of the Prestel public service (see Part Three) has enabled them to start offering selections of their daily business information through the Post Office-owned network to anyone who dials their respective numbers on a Prestel receiver.

Perhaps the one company that is most intently making use of modern newspaper technology for direct selling of information is the *Nihon Keizai Shimbun* (familiarly known as Nikkei) of Japan, which now offers the world its "total Economic Information System," a method of increasing the ways through which the input of their 1000 correspondents around the world is made available to a paying public. The entire contents are stored in a computerized databank and fed into 4 newspapers, 7 magazines, and 300 other publications, as well as telephone and computerized information services and radio and television news.

The Nikkei Economic Electronic Databank Services (NEEDS) and the Total Research System for Enterprises Data (TREND) are analytic information services functioning in business and general political affairs and, in addition, receiving material from the general spectrum of national and international agencies. This very large organization feeds the daily flow of articles and reports necessary for the newspaper but also supplies, via electronic techniques, two research centers with private and institutional members and an advertising research institute. NEEDS has thus changed from a newspaper morgue and daily storage device to a semi-independent unit, constantly fed through the accumulation of material by the reporters on Nikkei and its companion daily papers, the *Nikkei Industrial Daily* and the *Nikkei Marketing Journal*. This multi-outlet use of a single storage system (in fact, divided into two separate systems) makes possible a paying system of telephone inquiry, quick market reports, and a range of printed media owned directly by the company as well. NEEDS will supply material to its clients on magnetic tape as well as on hard copy.

The greater the complexity of the techniques employed directly in newspaper production the more sophisticated are the information services that can be provided through other companion structures. Thus the main Nikkei paper has been fully converted to full-page computer composition, a total of thirty-two to thirty-four pages a day in roughly 130 separate local editions. (Its total circulation amounts to 1,800,000 in the mornings and 1,200,000 in the evenings.) The paper uses fifty-three video terminals, which is very high for a paper in which there is no direct reporter-inputting of material. Seventeen of these are used for laying out the pages and are highly sophisticated machines at which the operator "daubs" the columns of material he wishes to lay on the page by means of a light pen. With the complete exploitation of ANNECS, the paper stores its entire input on magnetic tapes for use in its multidimensional output, which is still far from complete. As Japan's "new media" come into existence in the 1980's and 1990's, Nikkei's total information resources and accumulating expertise should start to become highly profitable assets—that is, if the Information Society theories on which Japan is banking turn out to be accurate assessments of future social patterns.

VII

Most publishers are keenly aware of the amount that the new system costs them. They are more hazy about how much it saves them. There are plenty of out-of-context figures available for the number of typesetters removed from the composition room, the number of pressmen "saved" in the pressroom. Several overall calculations end up with figures around 15 percent as the amount of reduction in total costs effected by the introduction of a modern front-end system with full photocomposition in an existing hot-metal newspaper. Most analysts claim that the necessary investment can be paid for within two years from the savings in the wage bill, although that figure, too, is unconfirmable, as an examination of the dozens of variables that must be entered into the ledger will show. Not all staff savings result from the new technology—often not all the staff should have been there in the first place if the previous operation had been operating efficiently. All the changes in organization can be phased in and out, making firm calculations almost impossible.

However, if one takes the experience of a single small daily, the *Allentown* (Pa.) *Morning Call*, as recounted by its former managing editor, the reductions appear to be appreciable. In 1974 there were 150 employees, in 1979 only 103. The total hours worked in production went down to 64 percent after the new technology was fully in operation. The total number of pages has increased by 12 percent on weekdays and 18 percent on Sundays, 15,000 in 1974 and 17,000 in 1977, on Sundays up from 6000 to 7000. The cost savings were $800,000 in the first full year, after a capital expenditure of $770,000—and that included replacing the hot-metal system with full photocomposition, computers, vdt's, advertising terminals, and photopolymer plates. A couple of years later another $180,000 was spent on an extra computer and more vdt's. Not a bad bargain in the eyes of accountants examining the books over a four-year period.

However, before the end of the decade the paper will be in the market for more equipment, the second-generation system, which will require dozens more terminals, especially the remote units for all the papers' bureaus. In the future, the suburban editors will produce their own local sections completely separately from the main paper. The paper moved quickly into the electronic morgue phase and will go in search of computerized indexing, microfiche, and therefore a much larger computer memory. The Info-Ky system, which was chosen, plus the necessary ancillary units (microfilm lab, photo filing system, etc.) cost a further $350,000. There was also the additional cost of more highly trained and specialized staff, although the number remains the same. The paper is now planning to connect its library to a local library network in order to join up with the storage systems of local industry, colleges, and public libraries. Entering the new age of printing technology is like stepping on an escalator. The savings are earned in the earliest stage of the journey, then quickly absorbed and forgotten as further and perhaps heavier investment begins.[15]

A similar tale emerges from the *Seattle Times*, where after three successful years with a Hendrix 3400 system, work has started on a new-generation plan that would enable the paper to scrap the scanning equipment for reporters' copy (which necessitates the reporter's preparing a perfect text for the OCR), to introduce more complex editing systems and improved vdt's, and to expand the overall storage system. This paper, like many, began with a building-blocks approach to new technology, having three different systems for editorial, classified, and display. The process of setting them up and reorganizing around them has turned out to be the preparation work for the installation of a future system. They need not hurry, for the system works, but it points the way to a series of future needs not all of which are met by existing equipment on the market—despite the promises of vendors.

Some smaller, pioneering newspapers have put together much cheaper systems by cannibalizing pieces of hardware from different manufacturers, acquiring the best piece at the best price, and then joining them with system interface equipment that translates the languages of the two manufacturers to each other's machines. The *Scotsbluff* (Nebr.) *Star-Herald* is one such pioneer that has progressively created since the late 1960's a completely computerized photocomposed newspaper with a front-end system purchased from Computype and Hendrix Electronics at a total cost of $171,347. In 1979 prices that would still be under

$300,000. The composing-room man-hours of this small paper were 10.13 per page in 1971 with 25 full-time employees; a year later it was 5.96 man-hours per page with 16 employees. By late 1977 it was down to 2.44 man-hours with 9 employees. The whole system was paid for in 1.89 years, and if acquired at the end of the period rather than at the start, it could still be paid off in two and a half years, taking into account investment tax credit, depreciation, supply savings, and the capacity of costless additional capacity. The paper used its savings on nine extra reporters and advertising personnel, extra wire service material, and laser photo equipment. It claimed an increased circulation of 3000 as a result of the improvements.

The major U.S. newspapers have not rushed forward with publication of the cost benefits of transfer to the new technology. In the case of the *Washington Post,* however, it is known that the new electronic newsroom and composition plant is costing around $7.5 million, although there remain a large number of ancillary and developmental costs that could increase this figure considerably. The paper's management estimates that the staff savings will enable this capital sum to be recovered in little over two years, although here again, in a large work force, there are always several other factors operating at any given moment on the overall level of employment.

Foreign newspaper publishers are sometimes puzzled by the rapidity of technical change in the American press; U.S. newspapers have been, by European and even American standards, dazzlingly quick to cast out one generation of equipment and pack new, often barely perfected gadgetry into their buildings. Newspapers have been building completely new production areas in which to house gleaming new presses and rows of flickering new screens. Part of the secret of the endless adaptability and experimentation lies in the rules of the Internal Revenue Service.

The IRS requires that newspapers replace equipment as fast as they amortize it in order to qualify for tax relief. The publisher has thus always been equally tempted to depreciate quickly and replace quickly, or go through the process slowly. When equipment designs scarcely changed from one decade to the next, which was the case for almost the whole of this century, there seemed little point in going through the upheaval of installing a gleaming new version of virtually existing machinery. There was no significant added commercial gain from having new machines for their own sake.

In the new equipment that started arriving in the 1960's (offset press, photocomposition, then computerized typesetting), publishers rapidly realized that, function for function, new equipment was cheaper than old, and more flexible, more labor-saving, more efficient. There was now a *reason* to go in for regular replacement, to amortize equipment as quickly as possible, to write off as much as possible every year against tax and then buy the next generation of machinery. Newspapers used to keep most of their equipment for twenty years or more; in the case of presses, which scarcely show serious wear and tear if well taken care of, for up to sixty years. New computerized equipment, however, is written off in seven, five, even three years. The pace of change that the computer industry is accustomed to has spread to their customers, the newspapers. With five years' depreciation, a publisher can write off a third of his capital expenditure in the first year's accounts. Some even lease their equipment and treat the whole leasing cost as a deductible expense. Little wonder that the rate of innovation adoption has become so much faster.

There have been many other factors at work encouraging the U.S. newspaper industry to move very quickly into the new era of electronic production. In a nation with as many separate newspapers as the United States, it is much easier for equipment manufacturers to produce a kind of bandwagon effect, trying out a device or technique in one or two papers (and getting their staffs to help design it to their maximum convenience) and then marketing it to scores of other papers of comparable size, operating in comparable conditions. The American press, once it had moved massively into offset printing systems, had become a natural market for computerized typesetting: the two technologies are perfect allies, and once the industry had been drawn into the fascinations of new technology, there were perhaps thousands of employees now trained to take an interest in innovation and rationalization through technology (see table 9). The United States enjoys an inbuilt national predilection for new technology, partly fostered by newspapers and journalism. It was hardly surprising that the industry was attracted to its own mythology.

There have been other, perhaps less attractive strains evident within the U.S. newspaper industry that helped push it into the new era: there is a deep bias in America against trade unions and organized labor which is clearly in evidence at any large meeting of newspaper publishers—and in this respect they are very different from their European counterparts. The computer was seen by many publishers as a weapon for breaking union power, and one that paid quickly for itself. It was at one time the cheapest way of raising the rate of profit against revenue, and a way of reducing total personnel costs. There was a different atmosphere at a newspaper that had gone over to a full set of computerized front-end production methods—the power of the typesetters was broken.

Table 9. Table Use of Electronic Equipment
and Decline of Hot Metal Linecasting

Type of Equipment	Number of Machines Operating in the United States									
	1963	1966	1969	1971	1973	1975	1976	1977	1978
Hot metal linecasters	11,175	12,264	11,557	9,465	6,690	3,451	1,877	1,399	1,158
Computers	11	138	529	632	719	971	1,206	1,472	1,982
Video display terminals				155	685	3,896	7,038	9,876	15,841
Optical character recognition readers				16	186	543	671	708	713
Photocomposition machines	265	595	903	1,452	2,395	2,898	3,076	—	3,090

SOURCE: ANPA RI Bulletin. Annual Issues on "Specification Data."

In the last decade, as we have seen, there has been an upsurge in classified advertising on a scale that made it difficult for the work to be performed by the old methods. The typesetters would have multiplied in number and begun to exercise an even more powerful grip than in the past over the whole newspaper production enterprise. It could easily have happened that the newspaper would have lost this valuable new adjunct to its revenue to some other medium, if a means had not been discovered for setting large quantities of text at great speed and at lower cost than was possible with the Linotype machine. What the American newspaper publisher has provided for himself, therefore, albeit after some expense and much risk, is a production system that has transformed the long-term viability of the medium—bringing in important categories of new revenue, solving old internal tensions and conflicts, revitalizing old plants cheaply, and raising the whole horizon of what might otherwise have become, by the 1980's, a moribund industry.

4. MARKET SEGMENTATION

The Newspaper

Turns into the Magazine

History provides few examples of the connection between new technology and new media and new audiences as clear as that of *Life* magazine. The idea for the magazine and its market existed in its publisher's mind well before the technique for producing it was available. As soon as the final piece of printing equipment was in place, the stupendous and unparalleled success of *Life* was set in motion. The plan for the magazine was drawn up at the end of 1935 by Henry Luce and the Donnelly Company of Chicago, the printers of *Time* magazine. The problem with a mass-circulation photo magazine carrying pictures of high quality is that a type of paper is required that can take the imprint of the plates at a high enough quality and yet not smudge the ink as the paper is rushed through the presses at very high speed. The printing company found a method for coating an ordinary paper with a slick during its passage through the machine. At the same time, they came up with a fast-drying ink made from petroleum, rather than linseed oil, which would respond instantly to the heat supplied by a burner placed within the printing press.

Almost from the first week, *Life's* audience astonished its publishers. They had planned an edition of 400,000 but were forced to print 1 million a week and plan an immediate increase of an extra 500,000 as soon as the machinery could be built. It was the kind of success that knocks a publisher off his feet. demanding enormous quantities of capital outlay and costing its publishers large sums of money, since advertisers in the early stages were having their wares exposed to many more people than those for whom they had paid.[1] *Life* rapidly overcame the problems of its own size and turned the *Time* empire from a kingdom into an empire. *Life* became the epitome of the general-audience magazine, appealing to a wide and varied set of public tastes, fulfilling the desires of readers to see the news as vividly as an eye witness.

In the 1950s television arrived and swamped *Life* with its own, superior power to do the same thing and project its pictures all day directly into the homes of millions. The first response of *Life* to the crisis provoked by the spread of television was to try to beat television at its own audience game and offer advertisers a vastly increased readership, one that rivaled the audience of television itself. By dint of an energetic sales campaign, the circulation was pushed up to 8 million, and introductory offers were made to the millions of newcomers that enabled them to buy the magazine at $12 for eighteen months—15 cents per copy for a magazine that cost its publishers nearly $2 to manufacture. Advertising rates were pushed so high to cover these costs that advertisers became progressively harder to find, and the publishers desperately attempted to save the magazine by "sacking" large sections of the readership they had so painfully acquired.

All the other major general-audience picture magazines were in the same position, and one by one they bit the dust—*Colliers, Saturday Evening Post, Look. Life* adopted a policy of gradually reducing its readership to 3 million, but the spiral of decline had set in irrevocably. After sustaining $30 million in losses, the magazine folded in 1972, which was only a few years before the same company started up *People* magazine, this time benefiting from the excitement of television rather than competing with the new medium. *People* magazine is cheaply produced, relatively speaking, and has been placed deliberately outside the normal magazine-selling and distribution mechanism (most of its sales are acquired in supermarkets, and its readers are people who want to know more about the people they see on television). Thus, the *Life*-to-*People* saga illuminates the process of the reversal of roles that television induced in those print media that attempted to beat television at its own special audience game.

The story of the demise of the mass magazine is a story of the decline of undifferentiated marketing. The magazine in the age of television has either to act as a leech upon the side of television or to construct an audience for itself. Indeed, modern success stories within the magazine field bear witness to changes in the very structure of American audiences and American society, which are today having their impact on the newspaper medium.

At the end of a generation of economic progress and educational advance, America's 200 million market is losing the homogeneity it spent so many decades in acquiring and nurturing. The growth of specialization in jobs has contributed to the creation of thousands of tiny subgroups, which may cohabit within the same suburb or the same corporation but take widely different views of the world and spend their time pursuing quite different interests. Biologists seem to have less and less to say to businessmen, corporate executives to investment analysts. Part of the heritage of the 1960's is a general and increased expectation of personal freedoms throughout the Western democracies, making possible wholly new brands of journalism dedicated to the various new life-styles and human relationships—sexual, psychological, sociological.

The growth in education first led to the diversification of courses and curricula, in the wake of which has arisen a seemingly infinite segmentation of publics. Out of the tens of millions who have passed through colleges and universities in the U.S. since 1960, very few have had precisely the same education. The mass-production industries that first established themselves by offering a narrow range of goods at falling prices (the Model-T formula) now hold onto their markets by offering a far greater range of models: General Motors can sometimes display three dozen different cars in a single advertisement, each one helping to bring out the subtle distinctions between the subgroups of the mass market. Meanwhile, the spread of forty- and thirty-five-hour weeks has provided the time as well as the means to pursue each subgroup identification to its furthest limits. While the general-interest magazines—*Life, Look, Saturday Evening Post*—went the way of the Model-T Ford, a new generation of magazine publishers has successfully translated this process of social differentiation into the print medium. *Life* and *Look* have reappeared in the late 1970's partly as a result of a further upsurge in advertising too specialist for television but too general for specialist journals, partly as a reflection of a mood of disenchantment with television—but both are at much lower circulations than in the past. At the end of the 1950's all the national magazines had discovered that it was too expensive for their advertisers to have to buy pages in all the copies printed. *Time, Newsweek,* and others were producing different editions for different areas (and different editions in various European countries as well) which concentrated the advertising and gave advertisers a variety of cost-cutting alternatives. National advertising, however, still remained the main source of revenue for such magazines—each regional edition bringing in, per page, perhaps less than a quarter of what would be paid for a page in the national edition. The really big magazines such as *Time* have readerships so large that even when segmented they contain a higher proportion of specialist audiences than many specialist magazines; thus *Time* found it had more businessmen among its readers than *Business Week* and started a "businessmen's edition."

In general, however, the specialized press, which can focus its content as well as its advertising on a narrow group of topics, is able to hold sway over the general-interest magazine, and publishers in the field have pursued every new fad and fashion that might help to deliver some new group and render it available for specialist advertising and additional products that can be associated with the publication. Among the earliest publishers to identify the new phenomenon were the publishers of *Saturday Evening Post*, who had learned bitter lessons in modern sociology by enduring the anguish of their magazine's slow demise. John Veronis went into partnership with a just qualified psychologist, Nicholas Charney, and started *Psychology Today*, which they rapidly turned into a publishing success and sold to a conglomerate for $20 million. Their whole marketing approach was different. They sought out only those who might be interested in the product and did not attempt to broaden their sales beyond this particular audience.

The birth of the zip code helped to identify locality as a possible market base. The growth of professional associations within every specialism meant that lists of members could be used for mailing. The computerization of membership lists of churches and other organizations, as well as other magazines, helps publishers to identify and concentrate on targeted audiences. Nearly 3000 business and professional magazines now exist; more than a dozen in electronics, 20 in computers, and approaching 400 in the medical field. There can be as many magazines as it is possible for publishers to single out audiences. If it were possible to acquire a subscription list with the names of one-legged Catholic candy manufacturers—it is sometimes said—advertisers could be found to support a magazine for them.

The problem for publishers of successful specialist magazines was precisely to confine the audience and not permit it to grow beyond the financially profitable level, i.e., beyond the point at which advertisers would have to be charged so much for distribution as to price the space out of their reach. *New York* magazine at first charged a much higher price for subscribers outside the New York area and even now refuses to advertise beyond its profitably narrow borders (which covers a population of 10 million who look to New York for entertainment and shopping). *Scientific American* became wealthy and popular by selling advertising to manufacturers of scientific instruments who could not possibly afford to advertise in a magazine enjoying a much larger audience. When the magazine finally did acquire such an audience, it saw its founding advertisers slip away in pursuit of publications that reached laboratory technicians, scientific researchers, and others who do business with small manufacturers of highly specialized equipment. With its hundreds of thousands of readers, *Scientific American* tried to explain to a new group of advertisers that it reached decision makers, top executives, and other senior corporate personnel; it tried to carve a market out of the same terrain as *Fortune* magazine. In a sense, the magazine compromised itself through its own editorial brilliance in interesting too wide a public in its area of specialization.

Some magazines have even tried to remove sections of their readership. Often, after filling out an application for a subscription to a financial magazine, the applicant will find himself turned down because dentists or lawyers or candy manufacturers are not required. The headaches of marketing specialist magazines can sometimes be avoided by sending the magazine free to a guaranteed specialized subscription list. Rather than try to persuade one segment of a profession to buy a magazine directed solely at that profession, it is often better to send the publication free to the entire list. The catch here is that in the major fields (engineers, for example) so many free magazines are sent out that the publishers have to prove to the advertisers that their magazine is read as well as received by members of the target group, and to do this entails spending a great deal on improving the editorial quality—to the point where the benefits of mass distribution within the specialist public concerned begin to evaporate. Fortunately, the laws of supply and demand do sometimes work in the interests of the publisher who tries to give something of real value to his public. What we have now to examine is the way in which the same processes are working their way into the newspaper industry and offering advertisers and publishers different visions of their shared public. New techniques of marketing and market analysis, allied with new technology of production, are helping to maintain the economies of scale of mass production while acquiring the additional advantages of market segmentation.

"Take your pick of the readers of the special-interest sections in the *Star* and the *Tribune*," urges the joint morning/afternoon paper of Minneapolis in a special brochure aimed at its advertisers. "In addition to choosing your audience by editorial content, you can choose your customers by geographic market. The state is yours with full-run editions; the metropolitan area with zone editions. You can even choose a slice of the metro area with Mini-zones or a hunk of the state with Maxi-zones. The choice is yours." A large proportion of America's pace-setting newspapers now offer their advertisers a similar set of opportunities to define their audiences much more minutely than in the past and much more precisely than is possible in rival media. The desire to help advertisers reach sections of the public either in terms of geography or of life-style or special interest is the key to the restructuring of the newspaper, which is now well underway. The major metropolitan papers now separate their editions for quite small zones within their distribution area and often break this down further into tiny segments of their public—a few hundred or a few thousand homes. They also have come to group their feature material dealing with a specific hobby, subject, or activity (sports, cooking, business affairs, political analysis) and place it within a special, often physically separate supplement. Often the material provided is new to the paper; often it is merely a matter of reorganization. The practice is nonetheless exercising an important influence over the whole relationship between the newspaper and its public.[2]

The breaking up of the miscellaneous newspaper into a series of sections is, however, but one stage in the evolution of the newspaper. A few papers are now experimenting with "tailoring," i.e., the provision of some sections *only* for those demographic groups among the subscribers whom given advertisers wish to reach. All of the new zoning and supplements benefit from the new technologies, but tailoring depends completely upon new equipment to sort out specific readers or streets, label them automatically, and select the sections of the paper, or additional material, that is to be sent to them. These readers then have to pay extra for their subscription, and this information, too, has to be held on-line. The arrival of plateless printing will make such developments in personalizing the newspaper relatively simple, provided that methods of circulation and delivery can by adjusted—at appropriate cost—to the tailoring of newspapers. This whole avenue of development began historically with the "supplement" and "special-interest section," which is where our survey begins.

The original intention in developing supplements was to identify the single "specialist" audience required by advertisers and convenient for editors. Gradually the more adventurous metropolitan papers have moved towards a complete compartmentalization of the paper, dividing into a series of detachable supplements spanning the whole week. In the *Minneapolis Tribune*, for example, the "Flavor" section on Thursdays ("Brimming over with news on nutrition, food-shopping forecasts, kitchen planning, the right pots and pans . . . " according to the bro-chure, which defines the range of topics to appeal to a middle-upper-income consumer) replaces the previous *Tribune* supplement simply called "Thursday," which had been designed partly to suit the needs of national food advertisers. The new section hones in more firmly on its target, knits together material and advertising that used to appear in other parts of the paper, and adds a number of new features.

The *Tribune's* sister paper, the *Star*, carries a similar section on Wednesdays called "Taste," designed for the subscriber earning $15,000 a year or more. Tuesdays and Thursdays are publication days for the paper's "Variety" section, which concentrates on travel on Tuesdays and fashion on Thursdays. This supplement also encompasses material on "life-style and community interests" to attract a high level of male (75 percent) as well as female (95 percent) attention. On Fridays the *Star* publishes a section called "Preview," while the *Tribune* publishes "Friday Special," both aimed at the weekend's entertainment audiences. These offer listings for restaurants, nightclubs, and other outside activities. On Mondays the "YOU" section covers the reader's "everyday decisions" (health, personal relationships, buying choices, and how to make and do things).

The Saturday papers offer a greater variety of special sections. The *Tribune* carries "Neighbors" (dedicated entirely to readers' views, includ-ing letters and a community billboard), while the *Star* offers "Shelter" (buying, selling, renting, investing in homes, "a one-stop marketplace for advertisers of real estate"). Saturday's *Star* also offers a tabloid magazine, providing "high impact and flexibility for advertisers" and offering the reader material on health, public and private personalities, family and consumer issues, life-styles, opinions, child-raising and education. The Sunday set of sections includes "Outdoors/Leisure/Travel" in the *Tribune* as well as "Family," "Super Sunday," and a photogravure magazine called "Picture."

Some of the larger newspapers have used the special supplement to overcome the loss of readers in the 18 to 34 age group, the demographic Achilles heel of the newspaper industry. During the football season the *Chicago Tribune* offers "Kickoff," a guide to the whole range of local and national, professional and college football. On Thursdays the deceased *Chicago Daily News* (now merged with its companion paper the *Sun-Times*) used to bring out "Sidetracks," designed deliberately as the "alternative magazine for young Chicago," to counteract the attractiveness of the underground papers of the city. Other newspapers try to induce the newspaper-reading habit in the preteenage market: *Newsday* on Long

Island offers "Kidsay" for the 7 to 12-year-olds, while the *Minneapolis Star* offers "Smile Factory."

Local competition for advertisers or readers is often the spur to starting the new sections, and many of the papers in the forefront of this development are in competitive markets. David Lipman of the *St. Louis Post-Dispatch* has said he would not be surprised "to see papers of the future evolve into a multitude of specialty packages aimed at particular segments of the audience. . . . I believe technology will eventually make such products feasible for delivery either in printed form or on a television-type unit." In this line of thinking, which is a rather extreme view among American editors, the newspaper will become a more and more closely targeted medium, ending up with a sports paper for sports fans, a business paper for the businessman, a local-news paper for those interested only in community affairs, etc. The newspaper as a miscellaneous form would thus come to the end of this long phase of its development.

Others see the change in more modest terms, simply as a way of keeping the metropolitan papers alive through the next few decades when the problem will be to prevent the circulation drop among 18 to 34-year-olds from spreading throughout the readership. Supplements can keep the newspaper habit going among the backsliding sections of the audience—but perhaps only at the expense of changing the essence of the newspaper habit and encouraging the splitting of the newspaper audience into tiny interest groups. Market research and editorial development that has led to the widespread growth of special supplements in the United States (and Canada) involves an altered view of the nature of the modern newspaper reader; it also presupposes a change of attitude toward news and the newspaper within the mind of the typical reader.

Frank McCullough of the *Sacramento Bee* lists three tasks confronting the American newspaper in this phase of its life: to summarize the news more attractively, to add the kind of hard news that will last the reader until the evening, and to entertain. The growth of supplements is part of what he calls "the struggle to learn to entertain," something that, the newspaper until the era of television was not constrained to do and a skill that it has still not acquired. All three tasks have brought about reforms in internal management in leading newspapers, cutting across existing demarcations of authority.

The *New York Times* is perhaps the only paper in which one can see all three tasks in the process of being achieved. It has tried to lose something of its ancient "elitist" image without losing its elite audience. It is an example of a paper assailed by everyone of the current demographic constraints but obliged to live up to the most tenaciously held expectations on the part of its traditional readership. Yet the paper, for all its prestige, reaches only about 10 percent of the audience within the geographical area in which it circulates and where it must be expensively distributed, an area in which 18 million people reside. The *Times* has found it economical to offer material designed for audiences as small as 60,000, while its management claims that the main body of the paper lacks nothing that was formerly offered its readers. All the new paraphernalia of zones and supplements involve additional material, though this assurance is clearly not accepted at its face value by all sections of the traditional audience.

Until the new supplements came, the *Times'* circulation had been static and even falling in places. Surveys gradually taught its management that its readership consisted of "five percent pockets," little groups that took the paper for one particular part of its information—"scanners and searchers," as the paper calls them. The restructuring of the paper has led to the creation of four new supplements, each under the editorship of a former magazine editor, and each designed to hook the overall circulation onto a larger segment of one of the groups of "specialists" already locked into the paper.

The *Times* now has sports, home, food, and weekend sections on different days of the week. The business-news section has been repackaged with revamped graphics, a daily news summary, and an increase in specialist articles, in the hope of starting a useful form of competition with the *Wall Street Journal*. In this case the special-interest supplement is moving into a very plush demographic grouping in which the *Wall Street Journal* already has a subscription list half of whom enjoy average earnings of $52,000. Supplements for the *New York Times* are therefore part of an attempt to hold onto a high-spending audience, a tactic that necessitates breaking into the extremely lucrative readership of the *Journal*—a hard nut to crack.

Of all the experiments in what might be called the restructuring of the newspaper that are currently underway in the United States, the most conspicuous and furthest developed is zoning, the provision for special sections within a newspaper that are addressed to only one area of a city or suburb. It is an important aspect of the process of reducing costs through segmenting the market and the content, and provides a good illustration of the way in which the newspaper medium is "negating" the very idea of the newspaper in its effort to solve a variety of modern problems.

Sometimes zoned segments of a newspaper carry the same advertising as the principal paper, while completely changing the copy. Sometimes the reverse is the case and readers get the same information, while the advertisements apply only to the retail outlets in a specific area of residence. Sometimes a zoned edition means offering a completely separate supplement dealing with the news of a particular area, in effect placing a local newspaper inside the main one. The *Sacramento Bee's* localized editions have generated a "furious demand" for space by local minority groups who have at last found a means of gaining easy access to the community, according to Managing Editor Frank McCullough. At the opposite end is the *San Francisco Chronicle* whose zoning consists of collecting local advertising for a special "Briefing" supplement, which deals with international affairs only. This strange reversal of the normal pattern of zoning is undertaken in seven areas because local papers such as the *San Leandro Tribune* and the *Oakland Tribune* supply suburban and exurban readers with a full range of local news.

The idea of zoning began as a means to circumvent the demographic shifts of the 1960's. The newspaper wanted to beat its readers, so to speak, to the suburbs before other newspapers started up in business there; it wanted its advertising to take account of the more centralized ownership of shops and their relocation in suburbs; it needed to redress the balance of its overall finances as a result of the newly weakened economy in the downtown areas; it wanted to overcome the loss of sales when the population of the city began to fall; it wanted to sell copies to the new suburbanites while keeping out competition from free shoppers and mailed advertising. The problems were the usual ones, but the design of each area of zoning is very specific—and not all attempts have been successful.

The zoned editions do not always look as if they are part of the main newspaper. The *Chicago Tribune*, for example, in its widely discussed string of nine suburban zoned editions, uses a different technology altogether: the separate localized sections are printed offset and tabloid in a different plant, while the main newspaper is printed letterpress and in broadsheet size. In Orlando, Florida, the *Sentinel* started a broadsheet zoned section, then switched to tabloid, while in St. Petersburg the *Times* experimented with a tabloid that later went broadsheet. There are also no rules for the number of pages in a zoned section, though there are seldom less than two or three, and zoning at this relatively low level can be achieved simply by replating while production of the normal newspaper is underway.

The readership of some American metropolitan papers has become so widespread geographically that the publishers actually try to hide the city's name from their customers. Joseph Elliott, business manager of the

Philadelphia Bulletin, told ANPA, "Most of our readers today live in areas which disassociate themselves from Philadelphia, so that the Philadelphia connotation has become a liability."[3] Many of the new suburban dwellers are no longer even ex-residents of the city and do not travel to work there. The idea of regionalizing and zoning the *Bulletin* arose, in fact, from a desire to prevent the suburbs becoming "hooked" on locally spawned newspapers conveying a greater sense of local identity.

At first, between 1962 and 1964, the *Bulletin* offered inserted supplements of local news twice a week and then started adding local advertising in a daily zoned news page, which gradually grew over the years into a full-fledged detachable section. But the problem was still not being cracked, and in 1971 professional market consultants were summoned who concentrated attention on the important (80,000 copies per day) New Jersey section of the readership, a community that enjoyed a more complete cultural separation by living in a separate state altogether. The results stimulated a complete remake of the paper for the New Jersey area with all reference to Philadelphia or Pennsylvania conscientiously deleted. Three further sections of the readership were similarly treated, with all classified advertising henceforth applying strictly to the region concerned. On Sundays a further edition is produced for the state of Delaware.

Before the new organization of the paper, 56 pages would be produced on an average day with 60 "edition lifts." After the change, 111 pages had to be prepared every day, with 72 lifts—a very considerable increase in the work load of the newsroom, necessitating a complete subdivisioning and overhaul of the news collection operation. To justify the expenditure, the delivery and circulation system has had to be greatly intensified, as well as the collection of advertising. The changes were feasible only because computerization was taking place at the same time, and the complex task of differentiating the classified advertising was taken on by the computer from the start. Certain machine redundancies have necessarily crept into the system, however, the most significant being the need for dedicated (or exclusive) presses for the four papers-within-the-paper, creating a certain amount of idle press time. One great boon of the reorganization of all the delivery routes has been a much more lucrative and efficient selling of inserts, with each of the four zones neatly subdivided into "Select-a-Markets."

If you take a city like Dayton, Ohio, where population has fallen from 250,000 to 200,000 since 1972, the case for suburban editions is overwhelming. The *Times* has lost over 8 percent of its former 160,000 circulation and has tried to recapture its readers by sending out three times a week a special supplement of suburban news in addition to the main paper. In Philadelphia the position is more serious still, since the *Bulletin* is in the rare position of competing with four daily papers in the city center while twenty suburban dailies lurk on the outskirts of the city, blocking the spread of the downtown dailies. Yet total circulation of the metropolitan papers has fallen from 1,643,000 in 1960 to 1,233,000 in fifteen years, as central-city population dropped dramatically (down from 60 percent of the total at the outbreak of World War II to 35 percent). The suburban dailies, however, are doing very well, their circulation leaping upwards from less than a half million to three quarters of a million in the 1960's and 1970's.

Around the Minneapolis/St. Paul region there are no fewer than twenty-six weeklies and monthlies with local news and information. Many of them are nonprofit. Many are put out by the local government itself to report its own activities. In a city like Minneapolis, with a great deal of spare printing capacity, there is no problem in printing 10,000 copies and distributing them within a small radius. And any of these papers could decide anytime to increase its frequency of publication and encroach upon the metropolitan papers' preserves.

Sometimes zoning is used by major papers to keep up their circulation at the peripheries. Such is the case with the *Daily News* in New York City, which has been struggling in Brooklyn, Queens, and Long Island against the encroachments of *Newsday*, once a suburban paper but now a giant able to confront the New York papers with its high-quality coverage of national, international, and metropolitan news and cultural affairs. The *Daily News*, before the long 1978 strike of the New York papers, found that its zoning in Queens and Long Island was producing good returns; its sales in those areas climbed back healthily. Only months after the strike, however, it found itself down 10 percent or more and it has been hard put to get its circulation back ever since.

Sometimes the results of zoning in areas of increasing employment can be startling. Robert Marbut of the Harte-Hanks group claims that one of his papers in Massachusetts (the *South Middlesex Daily News*) achieved a gain of 60 percent in circulation purely as a result of skilled zoning in a matter of four years. Spread over six zones and a few more years, the circulation has doubled (to 50,000) between 1971 and 1977.

A zoned edition can be anything from a mere replating once a week to a completely new enterprise involving its own newsroom and editorial and production staff, but since no extra charge is made to readers, the whole unit must be paid for out of the increment in local advertising plus any extra general sales that can be obtained from subscriptions to the paper as a whole. So far no newspaper has tried to charge extra for zoning nor to distribute only the local zoned section to readers who have expressed lack of interest in the main paper, but there exists a great deal of discussion about the possibility of permitting readers to make a selection from a range of new supplements, including the local zoned news supplement.

The complexities of zoning multiply by a factor greater than the number of different units produced. For example, the *Philadelphia Bulletin*'s geographically zoned editions and multiple-time editions within each zone involve changing up to twelve pages for each section, equivalent to creating half the newspaper over again for each pocket of readers. The sheer volume of copy required becomes something of a burden, especially when many stories will be needed in more than one zone where reader interest overlaps. Reader research by the city editor of the *Milwaukee Journal* indicates that not all readers are satisfied, often complaining that a story appearing in a zoned edition should have appeared in the main paper or in the edition of another zone. The larger the newspaper the greater the problem, because its editorial staff is less geared to the lives of readers in a series of distant suburbs. The able suburban editor can often serve his suburb's readers with local news better than the large metropolitan paper, which is now trying to squeeze its way into the business of local news collector. Some of the more successful ventures by metropolitan dailies into zoning have been founded upon completely separate newsrooms with each zoned edition having its own editor. The greater the authority of the local editor the more successful the zoned edition is likely to be, but then the question of sovereignty arises between zoned and central editor, especially when a major story occurs in a small suburb. Moreover, reporters in a zoned newspaper feel they are doing better in their careers when their stories are published in the main metropolitan edition. A story by a metropolitan reporter sent out only to a zoned edition is often seen as a sign of demotion.

One newspaper where zoning has not produced the gains expected has been the otherwise successful *Louisville Courier-Journal*, which functions alongside its afternoon paper the *Times*. Both papers have run special zoned editions for their distant readership in Indiana and were encouraged to try a similar edition for the *Times* alone in part of Louisville itself, where readers were complaining that delivery was late. The new zoned edition however, was produced from an earlier edition of the main paper, and teenagers (on school holiday at the time the edition was introduced) were used to deliver the *Times* at one p.m. The early delivery produced the opposite effect from that intended: the paper now seemed to be a slightly improved version of the morning news, and though it carried local news, readers found themselves annoyingly deprived of material from their main paper. The school busing crisis was at its height at the time and they wanted to know all the day's developments in this main metropolitan story as well as have local news. The recipients of the zoned edition now felt cut off from the main flow of Louisville events, and this zoned edition was shortly afterwards abandoned.

Some of the most technically and administratively advanced papers have become sceptical of the value of zoning. *Newsday*, for instance, has worked out the cost implications of a meticulous process of microzoning in some of the hundred communities that it currently covers. The editorial costs would not have been met by the additional advertising, the editor concluded. The paper already reaches 60 percent of the potential clients in these areas, and when a monopoly paper reaches household penetration levels of that density, the potential gains in zoning further down to tiny pockets of readers are quickly overcome by the additional costs. In conditions of this kind it is more economic for newspapers to start a few extra weekly papers at their peripheries or, as *Newsday* does, to distribute a special supplement containing all the advertisements of the week to the homes of all nonsubscribers in the readership area. This enables the paper to offer the advertiser complete household coverage while constantly advertising the paper itself to nonsubscribers who might want to join the list. It also helps to keep unwanted free shoppers out of the area.

Another city in which zoning has low priority in the publisher's mind is Washington, where the main suburban stores tend to have important main branches in the downtown area. Washington, in any case, is a city with an active downtown life, where formerly rundown sectors of the inner city are being rapidly refurbished. The *Washington Post* came to the conclusion that little extra advertising would be generated by zoning and that the readers were all interested mainly in the principal events of the region. However, the paper noticed that it was in danger of losing advertising to direct-mail schemes and decided to create a number of inserts and direct-mail supplements of its own, importing new equipment for the in-house part of the process.

In 1977 it started a very limited experiment in zoning in one of the plushest sections of its Sunday edition, the "Magazine," in order to take extra advertising material designed for readers with incomes over $25,000. The typical advertiser would be the seller of a luxury item for a small pocket of consumers but one who could afford to advertise only at a rate far below that of the *Post* generally, and well below the rate charged by the Washington editions of national magazines. The advertiser, in the zoned Sunday *Post* Magazine, can reach only 20 percent of the paper's readers but at one third of the normal space cost. The *Post* recruited a total of eighty-eight pages of advertising per Magazine that it would not otherwise have acquired—75,000 lines or 5,300 inches. Little wonder that the six editions were rapidly expanded to twenty-six, in what the paper labeled its Select Saturation Program.

There are important legal reasons why newspapers are going over to zoning rather than, say, to free shoppers or local throwaway shopping supplements. Nothing can render a party safe from being sued in America, and antitrust suits are frequently brought against metropolitan or small-city papers that undertake any form of printed suburban advertising. Editions or supplements of local news that are clearly part of the main newspaper are *relatively* free from actions for restraint of trade and certainly much safer than going into the free throwaway business.

By strange paradox a newspaper becomes liable to being sued if it starts to publish shoppers in an area in which such a publication already exists, that is to say if it *does* compete, even if the rival is a weekly paper. If the newspaper tries to get around this by making some kind of treaty with the existing publication (for instance, to agree upon rates or upon areas of activity), it renders itself liable to criminal prosecution as well as civil action. The newspaper may in some circumstances be able to buy up any competing publications, but this is an extremely dangerous mode of action for it renders the newspaper liable to prosecution by the Justice Department: if it buys a single competitor it may be thought to be guilty of lessening competition. The decision by a large newspaper to start an entirely new publication in an area where its former readers may have moved is also rather hazardous, for the paper may be accused of attempting to drive a local competitor out of business. This is a particularly serious misdemeanour, and triple damages plus costs may be demanded by a private litigant.[4]

A zoned edition, however, if it is serving the changing needs of a community and has clear editorial purposes behind it as well as those of fulfilling commercial needs, is fairly safe legally, but it must clearly be run at a profit and not as a loss leader. Newspaper accountants must ensure that the cost of the main presses of the paper are being partly amortized against the zoned editions' production costs, and editors must be careful to see that the supplement does provide feature and news material that adds to the total sum of local information. The newspaper also has to be careful about the details of its advertising rate structure, especially to ensure that a favorable position is not given in the zoned edition to advertisers who agree to take space in the main paper—discounts are safe, but not if they appear to "tie" one publication to another.

The siting of offices and plants for zoning is another crucial problem that has been greatly helped by the development of telecommunications-assisted technology. Sometimes the editor of a zoned edition will work in his respective suburb; occasionally, as with the *Chicago Tribune*'s nine zones, all of the editorial staff are housed together, but in a separate building from the main paper. By keeping the whole localized activity out of the city center and close to peripheral lines of transport, the zoned editions can be whisked quickly away to local agents, who then are paid a little extra for stuffing the papers into the main edition. Sometimes, as in St. Petersburg, Florida, where there are four zoned editions, the stuffing is performed by computer-assisted equipment in the main plant. All manner of devices are employed to bring the copy into the main office, where this is relevant. Facsimile, special lines, microwave, and similar devices send material from the main office to the zoned editions. In Los Angeles, a vast facsimile "cloning" of the main paper takes place in Orange County, saving the transportation of enormous amounts of printed newsprint around the Los Angeles region.

The success of the *Los Angeles Times* has led to the closure of no fewer than nine community papers that clustered around the greater Los Angeles Area. Three other local weeklies, however, have succeeded in building themselves up out of new suburbanite readerships into viable daily papers. The struggle between metropolitan giants and tiny suburban papers is a struggle for life on the part of the giants: however rich and powerful they appear to be, they live in constant fear of the sling of David, with its five small smooth stones aimed at their vital parts.

The St. Petersburg paper's zoned editions are much discussed in the newspaper industry. They were started when the paper found itself growing so large in pages and distribution area that it found local news difficult to cover at all, so it decided to add a special northern edition. Later, in 1973, it went over to offset printing in a new plant where the task of making small local changes in content was extremely difficult—partly because the offset printing machinery wasted a large amount of newsprint with every plate change (a problem that many papers have when starting new offset plants, although the latest offset equipment is claimed to be almost loss-proof).

The St. Petersburg paper started three local supplements each covering a single county and each with its own front page; editorial and letters pages; columns dealing with clubs, women's affairs, school sports, trailer park notes, visitors to town, obituaries ("Nothing is too small to cover," says Andrew Barnes, the managing editor), and soon it was found that readers identified with these new sections. Saturday and Monday zoning was stopped, and the paper has settled down to four zones, each with five supplements per week, each with a circulation of between 25,000 and 30,000. The central area has now been split into two, each with its local supplement—the "city plus" editions, which cover events in the central area's twenty-four municipalities, at eighteen to twenty-two pages each time. Twenty-five full-time reporters are employed on this additional activity. The paper can cover a local meeting in a localized edition and have the completed text and page paste-up ready twenty minutes after the end of the meeting.

One of the roots of zoning is the modern management feeling that "you have to give the reader more." The reader expects more of his paper than he used to, and the material has to draw his attention; the mere fact of its being local is not enough. The new material must not appear to be mere filler. It has to bear witness to the same kind of editorial judgment as the main edition, and the problem of planning both geographically and editorially is a very considerable one. Many papers, including successful "zoners" like the *St. Petersburg Times*, have had to drop occasional zoned editions, or realign the boundaries of others. A bad piece of zoning can make the whole newspaper look cheap.

The *Chicago Tribune*'s elaborate venture into zoning has been an extremely expensive operation aimed at strengthening itself in the whole of the area surrounding downtown Chicago, leaving the only competing daily, the *Sun–Times*, to wrestle with the problems of making a tabloid profitable in the decaying downtown area. Its nine surburban editions effectively imprison the *Sun-Times*, which has already closed down its companion paper, the aged *Daily News*, in an effort to streamline its entire internal economy. The "Suburban Tribs" have offices to collect copy and advertising in each area, and the zones have been designed not to cut across blue-collar and upper-middle-class neighborhoods. The supplements are to reflect the homogeneity of communities, and part of their attractiveness in the present mood of American society is that they create a feeling of "hometownness" among people wishing to escape from the class, minority, and race issues of American society.

Sophisticated consumer and reader research is the key to effective use of zoning to improve the profitability of a paper. Robert Marbut remarks that the systems approach has to be used to establish the correct in-depth data concerning "who the subscribers are and aren't and knowing the characteristics of the community so as to meet its needs." He stresses that in doing this the newspaper, especially the metropolitan paper, may end up discovering that it ought to be divided into four separate papers altogether. Richard Warschauer of the *New York Daily News* says that the metropolitan paper suffers from a constitutional difficulty in responding to microzones, though it is here that sales effort has to be concentrated to improve the level of household penetration.

A string of legal problems and some revealing lawsuits have followed in the wake of zoning. As has been indicated, some newspapers started zoning in the first place as an alternative to buying up suburban rivals, which they were inhibited from doing on antitrust grounds. In 1976 a number of local publications sued the Chicago Suburban Tribs for publishing legal notices, which, they asserted, had to be published in juridically separate papers, which—in a legal sense—the Suburban Tribs were not. Such notices had to be *published* in the areas in which they circulated. The response of the Tribs was to claim that the state statute under which the case was brought is in itself an infringement of the First Amendment. In Minneapolis and St. Paul the two main groups of papers are being sued for charging excessively low advertising rates in their zoned editions, thereby obtaining 90 percent of the local newspaper advertising market. A dispute broke out also in Chicago when the *Sun-Times* introduced a zoned real-estate section, which was accused by a local television station of operating a policy of racial residential segregation by making real-estate vacancies known only in areas with an overwhelming majority of white population. Other papers have been attacked in the courts when their zoned editions were distributed on a door-to-door basis, thereby allegedly interfering with the legitimate trade of the local shoppers. The path of zoning is thus strewn with unexpected problems.

There are also certain problems of journalistic ethics and principle, which have inhibited some papers from moving into the business of zoning. The managing editor of the *Detroit Free Press*, Neil Shine, claims that an emphasis on zoning undermines the work of a quality newspaper: it fragments the readership and gives each suburb a negative view of the others. His rival the *Detroit News* has shifted recently in its policy of zoning the front page of the paper and now merely provides local divisions with news of lower priority. To certain cynics in the industry some zoned editions are in fact the creation of a separate newspaper to satisy the whims of a single advertiser and are built around a single suburban shopping center often dominated by one manager of one chain store. Yet newspapers exist that are zoning *within* their zones, in an effort to penetrate deeper and deeper into their circulation community and its advertisers. Very often it becomes easier to create a new mini-edition, especially if tabloid facilities exist, rather than go in for the expensive and often wasteful business of replating within an edition.

At the other end of the spectrum sits the *Wall Street Journal*, which now zones nationally (and, in a sense, globally, if one includes the case of the Asian edition). Every day it produces a string of editions with local news and local advertising, but with substantial sections of material from its main editions via the Westar 1 communications satellite. On the West Coast the *Journal* is set in Palo Alto, then sent by satellite to three centers within the western part of the country: Seattle, Riverside, California, and Denver, where lasers and film re-create the text in metal for readers in the Pacific Northwest, Southern California, and the Rocky Mountain area. One large factor in the construction of this adventurous method of newspaper publishing is that advertising rates in expensive business-oriented papers such as the *Journal* have risen to the point at which advertisers can be lost altogether unless they are "helped" into the paper. In the case of the *Journal*, major advertisers wanting to address one section of the American business community are able to do so at greatly reduced cost per reader by paying for space in just one of the *Journal's* setting centers. It is expected that one major metropolitan paper in the States (probably the *New York Times*) will eventually be tempted into a similar form of publication. Several of the major papers have had schemes on paper for doing this for some years.

At the level of the microzone the whole business of zoning begins to overlap with the process of tailoring the distribution of special packets of information to specific demographic groups or, indeed, to individuals. It overlaps also with the development of forms of ink-jet printing specially designed to assist newspapers in reconstructing their content for each reader. The *Louisville Courier-Journal* is the best-known pioneer of tailoring. It began by pinpointing those of its readers who wanted *Time* magazine and delivering copies of *Time* along with the newspaper. The carriers now deliver the magazine to a quarter of all *Courier-Journal* subscribers who have elected to have it. The demographic profile of every subscriber is held on-line, and *Time* magazine offers four separate editions to cater to four different class and economic groupings. The *Courier-Journal* gets the right copy to the right reader.

The paper has also experimented with the delivery of a "Consumer Extra" to 7500 readers in a test-market area. The intention was to gain experience in identifying the content appropriate for future acts of information tailoring. It has become expensive to deliver new supplements to all readers but relatively easy to use computer programs to design the delivery rounds and print the additional information actually desired by given readers or groups of readers. The procedures are clearly enough known to make many newspaper publishers feel that a new era of selectivity is beginning. The Consumer Extra was a 12-page tabloid delivered with the *Courier-Journal* and containing no advertising at all, with an easy-to-detach center spread, printed in two extra colors, with an index. It offered a host of local information on home-oriented material, as well as data on clothing, personal finance, and travel. This test publication was designed in 1977 to establish whether 12 percent of readers would be willing to pay an extra 25 cents per week for a consumer supplement, which is the level at which the publication would break even. A previous experiment had established a pocket of readers willing to pay one dollar for a special supplement that simply compiled the week's otherwise unused but detailed material on international affairs. Without any special promotional effort hundreds of readers came forward, demonstrating the willingness of many sectors of an audience to make greater use of a local newspaper's now vast database—and pay for the privilege.

Among future plans for the evolving forms of tailored newspapers, there is a first stage in which the reader would choose two out of, say, a dozen possible special-interest supplements; these he would receive free of charge but could receive more of them in return for a small increase in the subscription. Only at a later stage would there be newspapers in which the interests of each reader were recorded and held on-line in the circulation department. The core of the newspaper would remain a matter of the editor's daily judgments, but the rest of each edition would be selected by the reader, produced by a plateless printing press labeled automatically with the reader's address, and delivered to the door.

One economic argument for this line of development, as soon as it becomes technologically possible, arises from the rate at which newsprint prices have been increasing since 1973. Research at the *Courier-Journal* indicates that only 30 percent of its readers ever read the business pages, which use 1851 tons of newsprint a year at a cost of well over $500,000. The *Courier-Journal* also examined the total quantities of information, drawn from a variety of sources, that pass into the newspaper's newsroom but are never used and thrown away; almost a million words a week are simply destroyed, including 120,000 words of business material, 135,000 of international news, 100,000 on the arts—all of which could have been typeset and printed with extreme ease. A few very simple marketing experiments indicated that hundreds of people were willing to pay additional sums to acquire this material—if it could be distributed to the people who wanted it and not wasted on those who didn't.[5]

One further reason why this line of newspaper evolution is not an immediate one, even though the conditions within society as a whole seem ripe for it, is that the equipment for putting the different parts of a newspaper together on a differentiated basis are not yet available. There is a real need for machinery that will insert supplements and separate publications at the same speed as that at which the newspaper is printed. Some papers have started installing the first generation of on-line insertion equipment, which in time could solve some of the bottlenecks and bring closer the date when the newspaper delivery round will turn into a profitable business activity in itself.

One current problem is that on-line inserting ties pressroom and mail-room activity together; the inserting machine is closely related to the presswork itself, and if it jams, the whole press has to close down. The *Washington Star*, in its first months of use of such equipment, found that it produced an additional mail room wastage of 2000 copies every day on which the on-line inserter was used (out of a 360,000 run). A large amount of electrical and mechanical apparatus has to be constructed between the conveyor device and the loading bays, and this in itself can be a nuisance to service and maintain. The equipment also imposes a certain discipline, not to say inflexibility, upon the timing of the presses: in the past it was possible to run the press faster if a later start had occurred (late news set in type), but now that is extremely difficult if the on-line inserter is itself controlling the speed of the press and cannot move at the required extra pace. The on-line system works on the principle of introducing a gap-maker, which separates the oncoming stream of newspapers into batches that are directed through a trapdoor, stuffed with the preprinted material, and moved onwards to a hopper. In normal circumstances the method actually helps to increase the press capacity by having sections of the newspaper printed in off-duty periods. The problem of mislaying separate sections on delivery trucks or delivering them to local agents too soon is thus avoided. It has also made possible a new kind of business activity for mail-order houses, which are able to organize a mail drop to nonsubscribers to the newspaper on the same day as the identical material is delivered to all the homes of actual subscribers.

One of the new stuffing machines, manufactured in Switzerland (the Muller-Martini 275), will operate at speeds of 22,000 papers per hour with each of its two delivery systems. It takes one newspaper into each of its twelve pockets in turn and drops the preprinted sections into place; it can take a newspaper of 96 pages or one with as little as 4 and stuff into it a preprint as small as 2 pages or as large as 48. One American newspaper that has been using it, the *Bangor* (Maine) *Daily News*, calculates that it will pay for itself in four years, partly by helping the paper take on additional business but mainly through the reduction of the staff required on a "preprint night" from between 31 and 34 to between 20 and 24; all overtime will be eliminated when the machine is fully operational. But so far this branch of technology is only suitable for newspapers with relatively small circulations.[6]

The tailoring and customizing of the newspaper raises again the problems entailed in relying on young people to deliver copies, a practice historically connected with the rise of the cheap newspaper of the last few generations but now liable to jeopardise the delicate arrangements of modern technicalized circulation techniques. Successful tailoring would be impossible without an effective and skilled household delivery force. The employment of children to carry newspapers to readers' homes is one of the most firmly rooted traditions of the medium. It has survived efforts in the last quarter century to curtail door-to-door selling and the more serious assault of protectors of child labor against exploitation; it has even survived the youth cult of the last decade when teenagers enjoyed a period of relative economic independence. One and a half million American children haul tens of millions of papers through the towns and suburbs of the country, taking home $22 million every week as they do so. Many larger newspapers (in Chicago, for example), have found it necessary in the vexed conditions of the inner city to use only directly employed newspaper staff for delivery work. But in general the employment of children means earlier delivery than would be possible with old people or direct employees and makes it easier to provide for collection of subscriptions while pleasing individual readers who want their papers left behind the storm door or put through the milk chute— or not through the milk chute.

Under 18's are exempt from the Social Security Act, the Fair Labor Standards Act, and the enforced withholding of tax under the Internal Revenue Code. They can be used for delivering advertising leaflets, for inserting preprints into bundles of paper before delivery, and for folding local and special supplements into their delivery bundles. But more and more there is feeling among publishers that children are no longer the answer, despite an impressive series of advantages. Children cannot be expected to be wholly reliable in the increasingly important business of starting and stopping subscriptions when readers go away; they cannot be expected to put the paper before homework, sickness, class examinations. Where a few missed deliveries a month would not have mattered twenty years ago, the modern management of newspapers has become a precision business conscious of the importance of image in the eyes of every potential client.

One way in which newspapers have succeeded in overcoming the problems of employing large squads of children is by creating networks of professional or semiprofessionsl district managers on the staff of the newspaper itself. These supervise delivery by children and act as a link between circulation department and subscribers. They have, of course, always existed in one form or another, but today they are beginning to take on more of the complex sorting work involved in zoning, computerized subscription lists, and guaranteed delivery at a specific moment in the day.

Despite a host of difficulties, new techniques of printing and distribution do indeed make feasible a new role for the newspaper as a "holdall" for information products, whether these are offshoots of the main paper or foreign products altogether. As a result the newspaper might be able to make better use of its expensive network of local delivery and cover the costs of keeping such a labor-intensive function up to the standards now necessary. Problems will arise in the future where local delivery personnel themselves are obliged to pack dozens of different individualized products into the main segment of the paper. But ink-jet printing methods already tried out by the Mead Corporation at the *Dayton Daily News* could facilitate the production of individual newspapers with the name of the individual subscriber printed on the front. Tiny droplets of ink are sprayed at the rate of 45,000 lines of digital information or 48,000 characters per minute. It will still be some years before information storage is large and cheap enough and computers able to operate at the same speed as modern presses with plates; but in theory, at least, it is possible now to envisage a completely individualized newspaper, printed platelessly by computer and filled with material corresponding to the interests and orders of a single reader. The computer is not bound by the same limitations as a plate-based printing system.

What we have been examining are the stages by which the newspaper is beginning to recognize within its own evolving form certain changes and tensions within the readership. The mosaic pattern of reality, which the newspaper creates and re-creates every day, is both a reflection of the kind of society that gave rise to the form and the kind of technology that was available to satisfy that society. Market researchers and developers of printing technology are together, step by step, beginning to unravel the complex interconnections between the form and the audience to the point at which a new kind of newspaper could evolve. In the current processes of market segmentation, zoning, supplements, and tailoring we can see in the shape of human organization the shadows of a new kind of information organization that will in time summon into existence the technical instruments necessary to it.

5. CHANGING
JOURNALISM

Every profession, according to George Bernard Shaw, is a conspiracy against the laity. Journalists have always suspected this to be the case and have remained a sort of candidate profession, never quite claiming their activity to be an *echt* profession and never being successfully persuaded by governments, or others, to incorporate themselves into fully self-disciplining organizations. In the 1930's there were moves both within the Newspaper Guild of America and the National Union of Journalists in England and in trade unions elsewhere to move towards some kind of permanent "official" status for journalists.

For a long time, however, there had been two mutually exclusive tendencies among reporters—some wanting to become trade unionists pure and simple and others wanting to remain in organizations of a more "professional" character, such as the British Institute of Journalists, which accepts editors and proprietors as well as working reporters. The American Society of Newspaper Editors is an organization of the same style and vintage. In Italy the Mussolini regime created the Ordine dei Giornalisti, which still survives, in which all Italian journalists are compulsorily enrolled and which guarantees considerable social and financial privileges; the Ordine limits and licenses those admitted to journalism and organizes the holding of qualifying examinations. Attempts have been made by the special commission for communication problems of UNESCO to raise again the question of professional status for journalism internationally, but without evoking great enthusiasm in those countries that permit a free press. Even when quasi-diplomatic status has been proposed as a way of protecting reporters on dangerous missions, the proposal has been treated with extreme scepticism by journalists' organizations, since this would imply a kind of "corporatism" for reporters approaching professional status.

One barrier to full professional status in most countries has been that journalism nearly always involves direct employment in circumstances in which editors, publishers, and proprietors all exercise power that is "moral" as well as entrepreneurial. Journalists, apart from one or two special instances, do not control the policies of their own papers and seldom seek to do so. Very rarely have they sought to exercise the kind of control over entry to their craft or profession or over the conduct of fellow members that would render journalism comparable with, say, law or architecture.

In both America and Britain there have been heated debates over whether unions of journalists are permitted to operate closed shops. On the one hand, as workers organized in the normal way, they require the power to conduct industrial bargaining as effectively as possible; but on the other, the closing of a newspaper's columns to nonprofessionals has always seemed an undue interference in the necessary freedoms of editors to control the content of their papers. Professionalization is very similar in form of organization to a closed shop and is often opposed by journalists and others for the same reasons. Like the closed shop it could be a powerful weapon in wage bargaining as well as a limitation to press freedoms, but professionalization would imply that the journalists, and their societies, had dealt satisfactorily with a complex range of unresolved questions concerning journalistic activity and its proper role in society. The complexities of these questions have increased over time and the age of new technology presents them in more intractable form than ever before.

Journalism has always had a shifting set of ethical principles, complicated by the fact that prevailing catchwords have often been expressed in the same tones and phrases ("separating fact from comment," "objectivity," "accuracy," "impartiality"), which have had widely different meanings at different times and places. Moreover, the whole development of the craft or profession itself has been almost totally conditioned by the changing circumstances of the major newspaper dynasties; these are the powers that have established and reestablished over the decades the moral and intellectual context in which reporting takes place.

The generally accepted ethic of objectivity arose during the course of the present century, though today the changing position of reporters is stretching the possibilities of the doctrine to its limits, and the new forms of work expected of journalists are bringing about important alterations in prevailing codes. It is, in fact, too precise to speak of codes, since the word suggests that reporting can in practice be conducted according to a priori principles. Reporters use the tools available, technical and mental, to perform the tasks that newspapers require. The extent to which reporters, as a group, can lay claim to a set of rules designed to protect society and guarantee "truth" is itself a question that reveals or conceals a number of concentric logical and practical dilemmas. True, it is what the reporter serves up that the reader digests, but it is the situation of the reporter that largely determines what he actually does and with it his view of what he is trying to do. Industrial and organizational circumstances establish the boundaries of the reporter's moral world as much as his practical world.

As the newspaper settled down in the 1880's and 1890's in its modern guise as a popular one-penny medium for presenting and explaining the affairs of the world, a cloud of ethical riddles suddenly appeared to hover above the heads of publishers, editors, and reporters, which has become thicker over the ten decades that have passed since Pulitzer and Hearst first tangled with the moral consciences of their employees. As soon as the function of reporting the world's affairs became a specialized activity—separate from that of editor, printer, owner—it was obvious that some special moral link connected the journalist to his readers, a link that could not—whatever anyone said or did—be either completely free from interference by the publisher or completely subject to his whim as owner of the plant and the capital on which the medium depended. The same dilemmas had cropped up earlier in the newspaper's history, in the eighteenth, even seventeenth, centuries, but the creation of a specialized *reporting* profession complicated the issues and made them appear to center on the actions of a new group of people who were not legally the owners or managers of the press.

The reporter was constantly obliged—as were the other partners in the enterprise—to explain himself, to search repeatedly for suitable philosophical principles in which to cloak or justify his activity of reporting. Many institutions grew up attempting, as they still do, to provide a kind of moral backing to the craft or profession of reporting and editorializing. The Newspaper Guild was founded in 1933 when the American Society of Newspaper Editors was already long in existence; the publishers had created ANPA back in 1887. Each decade has left in American newspaper life some of the debris of the continuing intellectual battle over the social and moral role of journalism.

The newspaper's new technology of the last century was not, of course, the only new communications technology to emerge at that time. In some ways the camera made a more lasting impression on those who asked how an image of the world was and ought to be created. It seemed to offer the opportunity of a kind of realism, something purer than that which had been provided by the professional sketchers who toiled alongside the reporters in battles and at murder scenes and in newsrooms, evoking for readers a mental image of the events reported in the news columns. Kipling devoted a novel to war sketches, *The Light that Failed*, in which he considered the inadequacy of the whole news system, which was based upon popular values and not subject to the more searching tests of relevance and realism: "With the soldiers sweated and toiled the correspondents of the newspapers, and they were almost as ignorant as their companions. . . . The syndicate did not concern itself greatly with criticisms of attack and the like. It supplied the masses, and all it demanded was picturesqueness and abundance of detail; for there is more joy in England over a soldier who insubordinately steps out of square to rescue a comrade than over twenty generals slaving even to baldness at the gross details of transport and commissariat."[1]

In philosophy, science, anthropology, and sociology, Darwin and Spencer were clearing a path, plainly signposted "realism." It invaded industrial management, theology, history, law and, above all, painting and literature. All intellectual effort had now to aspire to the condition of the camera, which seemed to be the long-sought mirror that man at last could hold to nature. Its images were reproducible, its authority unquestionable. It was an instrument of reporting par excellence and one on which the human reporter could model his own technique. The word "objectivity" was not used in journalism, but the word "fact" was increasingly being used, and it was to the world of facts that the reporter was destined to bend his efforts: the gleaning and assembling of facts turned journalism into a camera of reality; the skilled pursuit of facts gave the reporter a status comparable to that of scientists, explorers, and historians. Every society bred a "new journalism," designed to be popular and informative, to which the reporter—armed as he was with the obligatory technique of Pitman's shorthand—contributed a dimension of irrefutable truth.

The shadow that fell between reporter and fact was that of the publisher and occasionally that of the editor. "You furnish the pictures and I'll furnish the war" was Hearst's famous message to his reporters in Cuba,[2] who, excluded from the putative theater of war by the Spanish military authorities, had wired their employer that there was "no trouble here" and that they wished to return home. Fact was but one step from sensation. In England W.T. Stead, founder of the "new journalism" of the *Pall Mall Gazette*, was imprisoned briefly for having purchased a small girl in the streets of London to prove that such deeds regularly occurred under the nose of authorities in the immoral traffic of the white slave trade. "The journalist is the eye of the people," wrote Stead later, "but if . . . you do not feel strongly, you will not, as a rule, be able to write powerfully."[3] The reporter could become an actor in affairs, and the "newer" the journalism, the more popular it was and the more personal the nature of the reporting. Facts could truly horrify, prompt a sense of moral outrage. It was common for reporters to hang on the way their editors' favorite slogans, such as "Who, what, why, when, and where," but an admixture of imagination was also encouraged, one that provided a sparkle to attract the reader, a mood or congenial atmosphere in which he would feel at home.

The training of young journalists gave a clearer idea of the prevailing view of the profession, perhaps, than the actual day-to-day practice. Lincoln Steffens looked back in the 1890's to his youth on the *New York Evening Post*: "Reporters were to report the news as it happened, like machines, without prejudice, color, and without style; all alike. Humor or any sign of personality in our reports was caught, rebuked, and, in time, suppressed."[4] "Newspapering" had adopted its own particular way of *seeing* and its own protective self-discriptions that were in practice progressively relaxed in the course of a reporter's career, but that remained in the formal textbooks of the profession, and were after used by the industry's detractors. The empirical spirit had invaded the age as a tool of radicalism, as a method for proceeding towards the elimination of inherited superstitions and prejudices and as the ultimate weapon of a new elite against an old economic establishment. In the bewildering world of the twentieth century, where the consolidated values of the middle classes on both sides of the Atlantic were burst open by the conflicts of the age, placing the settled craft of reporting once again in strategic danger, it came to be used as a tool *against* the young reporter, as a repressive method of self-protection. The call for facts that had provided the popular journalists of the late nineteenth century with social cover became the raw material for training the next generation of reporters whose world had lost the moral certainties of the Victorian era, which alone had made the ideology of "factualism" intellectually satisfying.[5]

It was Stead's incessant campaigning that had compelled the British government to send an abortive force to relieve Gordon at Khartoum. The reporter and his editor never blamed themselves for the hundreds of dead their impetuous leaders had brought about. They congratulated themselves for the success in their campaign for the "Plimsoll Line" to be painted on all cargo ships, for the Campaign on the Housing of the Poor, for the Criminal Law Amendment Act, and for other successes in popular causes. Their power carried no responsibility. Their activity panicked steady-minded politicians into taking measures that would otherwise have been avoided. Their "empiricism" became an institutionalized interference in administration. They were raking up the "news" in a manner previously unknown.

In much earlier stages of the evolution of newspapers the medium's basic stock-in-trade had been known as "intelligence," i.e., material passed on from one person in the know to another, a term that contained the overtones of diplomatic knowledge garnered in high places and transmitted along reliable routes to the offices of the editor. "Intelligence" was passed from the well-informed to the well-informed. The technical revolution that made the penny newspaper possible and opened up the medium as the chief sustaining instrument of a popular consumer economy brought its own reformulation of the idea of what the newspaper should contain. News and entertainment became parallel and equal duties of the various new journalisms, and both were, in a sense, manufactured products, designed as the software of the new popular press. The reporter and his companion the artist, or later the photographer, were technicians whose judgment, energy, and savoir faire procured and shaped the newspaper's content. The press, like other manufacturers, was already obliged to advertise its own wares: Pulitzer's *World*, and its imitators in England, France, and Germany, was obliged to puff itself with every issue like a fairground operator.

In every society in which a new lurid, prurient popular press was born, newspapers of an older vintage remained, serving a class of reader with more staid—and more mercantile—tastes. The *New York Times*, the *London Times*, and their imitators in the European and colonial worlds moved firmly in a different direction from that of the pushy, brash popularizers. For the former, "information" was the highest pursuit, untainted, unbiased, unarousing. Their readers existed in sufficient numbers. Furthermore, the codes in which they approached them (close type without cross-headings, without banner headlines, nor pictures) confirmed what their readers wanted, which was a pure review of the affairs of the world as they saw it—political and economic questions predominating over scandal, crime, *"faits divers,"* and other material appealing to the emotions rather than the intellect.

There grew up, therefore, two separate sets of standards within the journalist profession itself, one that emphasized the steady market for information and one that went out for the volatile competitive market of the mass reader. In the United States a vast proportion of the population were after first-generation English speakers or not English speakers at all. Pulitzer himself had learned his journalism on a German newspaper in the Midwest, which introduced its immigrant readers to their first words in English. The language of the headlines and the style in which the popular papers described common events were part of the attempt to ease the path of the newspaper form into the hands of the new Americans who formed a large section of the readership. These styles and approaches have in essence survived into modern journalism or, at least, have evolved into the varied styles of the present day. The absence of competition within the cities, however, has acted as a spur towards a growing consensus of language and approach. Metropolitan papers are more aware today of the need for "good writing," for a mode of discourse that unites them with the whole of their variegated audience. As long as the reporter had a number of different possible professional languages—each with its own implied ethic—it was difficult for reporting itself to become a profession. There could be individuals or categories of high status within the profession. However, there could be no *profession* in the strict sense of a group that holds some kind of publicly demonstrable authority over its own standards and practices until a common diction for the journalist evolved; and this, in turn, depended upon a further evolution in the prevailing notion of what a newspaper really is.

The slogan that adorned the *New York Times* under the ownership of Adolph Ochs after 1896, "All the News That's Fit To Print," expressed the short-term solution to a dilemma. The newspaper provided a comprehensive array of information and was able to do so because the techniques of modern news collection—the telegraph, the telephone, the wire services, the teams of correspondents and expert informants—made it possible in appearance at least for the whole world to be scanned for "information" within the compass of a day. However, behind the presentation of news lay the moral sensibilities of those for whom information was the basis of their influence; their attitude towards the categories of material that could only arouse emotion or be described in language that had to be avoided made it necessary for "unfit" news to be omitted. The readership thus precensored its reading material. It protected itself under a code, ostensibly to do with language, from the material that would have undermined its powers of concentration upon pure information.

The word "objectivity" was not used widely in the context of the debate about journalism until after the First World War; until it came into general use, the idea of information depended partly upon the broad gathering of comprehensive material. The purpose of the *Times* was to provide *all* of the news: to limit it only by excluding the material that belonged to other types of newspapers with morally unacceptable methods of attracting readers and to broaden it by including material that suited all political tastes. Adolph Ochs needed to increase his readers and his advertisers by appealing to a nonpartisan sentiment that expressed a single set of values, and he promised all of the readers a share in the "influence" that such information opened up to them. Thus, in the first issue of the *Times* under the new ownership of Ochs, he expressed the paper's purpose in a sentence that could have been printed in a number of comparable newspapers in other countries: "To give the news impartially without fear or favor, regardless of any party, sect or interest involved." News-gathering routines were by then sufficiently developed, nationally and internationally, for a major metropolitan paper to proceed along this path of neutrality and gain readers along the way.

The values of twentieth century journalism were learned in a late nineteenth century intellectual world in which the readership of papers such as the *Times* provided all the moral cover necessary to the craft of reporting—so long as this kept to the technical, institutional, legal, and political routines that had been laid down. In the period following the carnage of World War I, science no longer supported the established canons of journalism, but these were so firmly entrenched in the new journalist-training schools and in the needs and practices of a new, trained, and confident profession (in the broad sense of the term) that the gradual disappearance of "objectivity" from the external sciences did not impinge upon the newspaper.

Freud, Einstein, Heisenberg, and all of the twentieth-century movements in the arts and social sciences could shift and manipulate the term at will without greatly disturbing the newspaper world. Lenin could take it over and apply it to a totally different journalism in which reporting of the external world was subject to the "real" needs of a class and a party. Goebbels could take over the world's most flourishing and intellectually varied newspaper industry and subject its wealth of talent and expertise to the propagandistic requirements of a paramilitary clique. The great press barons of England, one by one, went directly into politics—fishing for honors, position, status, and direct political office without disturbing their employee journalists' sense of due purpose.

At the Peace Conference of 1919 all the major statesmen kept key newspaper publishers and editors as their advisers. Those who had demonstrated during the war that they held power over the popular imagination seemed to hold a key to the principal political problem of the democratic world of the 1920's, which was how to govern in an age when political power was spread across so large a mass of people. The press barons were the technicians of the mass mind, and they had become absorbed into the political and social establishments. Crowd psychology had become a major preoccupation of social science and of politics after 1890; it interested criminologists as much as politicians and political managers.[6] The crowd confronted democratic politicians with the crucial paradox of power—that acquiring it seemed to necessitate different tools and different values from holding it. Electioneering required one kind of statement and government another. Only the press continued its curious form of political power from one administration to the next, and it had the unique ability to remind politician and citizen of the undertakings each had delivered to the other. Perhaps this is part of what Baldwin meant when, in a phrase of Kipling's, he spoke of the press's "power without responsibility, the prerogative of the harlot throughout the ages." There was a new kind of political power abroad after the War: it was revolutionary in Russia, insurrectionary in Europe, based upon the popular franchise in the English-speaking world, but mingled with propaganda everywhere, and everywhere dependent or seemingly dependent upon those who wielded the tools of mass communication.

In the 1920's the insights of Walter Lippmann and Sir Norman Angell were all concentrated upon this problem.[7,8] Representative government was in danger of faltering because of the inadequacies of the public that supported it, "the failure of self-governing people to transcend their casual experience and their prejudice by inventing, creating, and organizing a machinery of knowledge," as Lippmann put it. It was no longer possible for reporting for the mass electorate to operate according to the goals of Adolph Ochs, successful though he was within the confines of a limited but economically powerful audience. The problem lay elsewhere in those regions of society that the newspaper had captured with entertainment and "news," in the context of a highly competitive industry offering rival versions of every story, exaggerations, scares, threats, encouragements to every vice. The news values of the prewar period (which are substantially still those of today) were heavily tinged, as Herbert Gans shows,[9] with the politics of the Progressive Party and its pastoral vision of small-town democracy.

Lippmann in his later work (e.g., *The Phantom Public*, 1925)[10] started to relocate the problem in the growing corporatism of the economy and political world: the private citizen could no longer *see* the world of politics, obscured as it now was by thousands of press agents working within the departments of government and intervening between journalists and their information. Public affairs had disappeared behind a screen of managed publicity: "They are for the most part invisible. They are managed, if they are managed at all, at distant centers, from behind the scenes, by unnamed powers."[11] In the economy share-ownership had spread so far that management had split away from direct possession of capital. The simple confrontation between those who held power of any kind and those who collected information about them had become extraordinarily complicated by the intrusion of professionalized intermediaries.

Even the forms of journalism had failed to catch up with events. The interview, as a form, had seemed in a previous generation to provide the reporter with a new and immense tool of power, to enable him to question the politician, the head of state even, at his own desk and to report the *ipsissima verba* of those who held power, on the same day even, to all those over whom power was held. But now the interview and other journalistic techniques seemed to have become swords of cardboard used against those holding but the mask of authority, not the real commodity itself.

In the intervening period America had started to acquire a machinery of state, a bureaucracy that could juxtapose its own routines and its own insuperable secrecy between reporters and their information. The larger government grew, the more material it spewed forth, and the more difficult was the decoding and interpretation of it. Where reporters could formerly have spoken directly to those in office and their subordinate officials, today an apparatus of press offices (public-relations specialists) occupy the key positions in parties, in political campaigns, in departments of government, in industry. From the 1930's to the 1960's these machines continued to grow, and the real material of popular politics was conveyed by the electronic media, where popular folk heroes, flanked by technical experts, could speak directly to the people way above the heads of editors, reporters, and editorial writers.

The news magazines, not wedded to the ideology of objectivity, reached out towards the first national audience for printed news in the history of America. The press responded with the development of syndicated material that spread across the country, hundreds of newspapers reproducing the favorite columnists of the day for readers in tiny towns and villages. In the 1930's the "column" became the dominant journalistic form, in which an assessment of what mattered in the public sphere was provided under the signature of an individual respected for his insight, his judgment, and for being "in the know." Thus overnight Lippman himself became the archetypical columnist, reprinted in many hundreds of small-town and metropolitan papers. But the column lay outside the canons of objectivity; the columnist was a privileged reporter, with a staff of his own, who had been released from the burden of collecting clearly labeled information. The columnist spoke with his own authority, which was above that of editors or publishers and which was self-legitimizing and mitigated only by other columnists with contradictory views.

The code of objectivity as it emerged in the period before the Second World War was very different from the emphasis on facts that had helped the press through the period of its growth earlier in the century. The techniques of journalism had clearly broken during the First World War. In *Mein Kampf* Hitler blamed the allied popular press for the troubles of Germany. Americans blamed the European press for having dragged it into a useless war. The philosopher Robert E. Park remarked that political thinkers in the past had assumed a degree of intellectuality in mankind that it had never really possessed and pointed out that most journalists had a poor opinion of the public whom they served, dissecting them like children while attempting to do them good.[12] "Dictatorship cannot solve the problem . . . "wrote Norman Angell. "There can be no workable government of any kind fit to face the complexities of modern life unless we make provision to correct the outstanding weaknesses of public judgment."[13] On both sides of the Atlantic the century of democracy was already in tatters, having failed to pass the first real test. The blame was generally laid at the door of the information disseminators and the inadequacy with which they dealt with the popular psychology.

Objectivity was partly a response to the chaos in the international political sphere; it fostered the collection of information on the basis of a special diction, which restricted the definition of a statement to that which could be assented to by all. It was a response, albeit unconscious, to the criticisms of Lenin and Goebbels and led up to the more destructive internal criticisms of the 1960's. Western objectivity meant basing reportage upon the denominator of unexceptionable and verifiable statement. It used the minimum of consensus. It was what was left after the combined scepticisms of the age were stripped away from the reporter's vision of the world. It was the remnant of reality left behind when the reader had been protected from the one-sided truths of the press agent and the double-edged truths of the politician. It was the ideology of an age that had grown to *distrust* democracy, which had seemed to fail both politically and economically in the 1930's. The painful cautiousness, for example, of the BBC in England in building up a news service based upon the reports of the wire services alone bore witness to this phase in the development of journalism. The call for the Hutchins Commission (originally conceived in 1942, although it did not finally report until after the war) to settle some of the doubts and dilemmas of the press industry about itself was an American response to the problem. In the defeated countries of Europe and Japan there was, first of all, a retreat to the politicization of reporting—a return to the ethic of Third Republic, of Weimar Republic, of pre-Mussolini Italy, in which a multiplicity of party papers sprang into existence. These gradually slipped away after a burst of anachronistic vigor, leaving an "information press" (*Le Monde*, *Franfurter Allegmeine Zeitung*, etc.) in each country surrounded by a swarm of popular or partisan journals.

Each country made its own adjustments to the concept of objectivity, but in each the older generation of journalists found it possible, after the bewildering rigors of the 1930's and 1940's, to accept the new credo. The concept was unaffected by the decline of empiricism in science, by the growth of relativisms in various guises in the rapidly expanding social sciences—not at first anyway—because this objectivity was a refuge, not the result of a quest. It helped them through the Cold War until television journalism rose to the bewildering events of the 1960's.

In looking for the causes of the breakdown of objectivity in the 1960's, one must look at the news events that shook the world of the reporter in the postwar period. Objectivity had been a perfect retreat in the period of the Cold War, in that it papered over the cracks in consensual values and enabled a society to slip quickly from the popular front to the ideological partition of the intellectual world at the time of Korea and yet still appear to hold certain commonly accepted standards of reporting. But it laid the whole business of reporting open to the manipulation of a McCarthy who would use the routines and genres of journalism for his own ends. Joe McCarthy understood the procedures of reporting, its deadlines, and its divisions between journalists who collected facts at press conferences and asked plain questions in order to "get it right" and those who wrote columns and assessed situations. The phenomenon of McCarthy was a modern media phenomenon, different from the demagogies of the 1930's, although clearly owing something to them. McCarthy provided good pictures for cameras, good sound for radio, good stories for newsmen. He provided all the media with what their routines and specialist natures required. News was bigger and more powerful than comment and could drown it. Opposition to McCarthy actually did exist and was expressed in some corners of the press, but he concentrated on the points where impact was most easily and most dramatically achievable and, in doing so, showed up the weaknesses of the system. He could give a press conference to announce that he was going to give a press conference, and be duly and correctly reported. The news maker became the center of news and made the work of reporters both morally and practically easy. The processes of news collection had become well enough organized for a value-free factuality to damage the craft of reporting as much as it had saved it in earlier circumstances.

It now seemed that where facts could once be permitted to speak for themselves, there was a danger that they could be manipulated and made to speak for a special interest. Research into the impact and techniques of television journalism demonstrated virtually for the first time that when subject to the competitive requirements of network television, the genre of news was capable of gross distortions. Kurt and Gladys Lang's research into the coverage of MacArthur's procession on returning to America and other great media news events indicated that the cameras moved towards action, towards activity that best symbolized the "meaning" that had been attached in advance to an event.[14] The entire dedication to objectivity was in jeopardy both in the print and electronic media. The structure of the news story was beginning to be perceived as a value-loaded device structuring reality according to preconceptions, not a device for exploring reality according to a professional canon of neutrality. The media had permitted themselves to slither through their own liberalism into a structured conservatism, an institutionalized bias not towards but against the integrity of science. Where Lippman had wanted journalism to become one of the learned professions, and where newspaper magnates such as Vere Harmsworth had argued that it had already done so, the reporter began once again to appear to be a kind of trickster, all the more to be condemned for not realizing the ends to which his very craft lent him.

II

Objectivity arose then out of uncertainty, out of a world where values had ceased to be widely agreed upon or universal but were merely relative. The American newspaper industry has clung in its self-defense to the rules of objectivity despite the attacks that have been made upon it, particularly by the generation of reporters that emerged from the universities and training colleges in the 1960's. Arguably the industry has emerged in the 1980's with a newly adjusted version of the doctrine, liberalized to accommodate some of the most skillful proponents of the subjectivism of the sixties but substantially the same set of occupational ideals. In the universities in the 1960's, it was not merely the objectivity of reporters in Vietnam that had fallen into intellectual disrepute but the whole idea that reporting was a profession at all. All it had to offer as its credentials was an exploded view of its ability to amass objective fact. At the same time, writers in the school of Ivan Illich were casting doubt on the social objectivity and therefore the authority of the other professions (medicine, law, education). In some ways the reversal of values of the 1960's was the response by a new generation of Americans to the discovery of the existence of a full-scale "state" of a classic kind. Successive wars had left America with an apparatus of bureaucracy and secrecy that the mythology of American democracy had never previously admitted. With Watergate American journalism applied a new doctrine that permitted and encouraged certain deliberate forms of confrontation between reporting and the state machine. Apologists and glorifiers of the Watergate reporters spoke as if this form of confrontation were normal and historically sanctioned in journalism, claiming at the same time that objectivity was a myth, a trick that had been played *upon* journalists rather than by them. The reporters stationed at the great demonstrations, battles, and riots of the period found that events themselves were breaking loose from the procedures of journalism, which were no longer able to cope, certainly not on a scale that would enable print journalism to maintain its own against television. The television camera was now able to wander freely in Prague, Saigon, Paris, Chicago—anywhere that news was being made—inducing a kind of instant public theater, with spectacle rather than speech and debate dominating both the event and the reporting of the event. It was not newspaper reporting but television that exhausted the formulas of journalism.

Tom Wolfe, in looking back at the origins of the New Journalism, a term that he traces back to 1966, points out the way in which the early practitioners of the new genres deliberately broke loose from the techniques—and the *status*-rooted processes—that the newspaper medium bequeathed them. Jimmy Breslin "made the discovery that it was feasible for a columnist to actually leave the building, go outside and do reporting on his own, genuine legwork. . . . As obvious as this system may sound, it was unheard of among newspaper columnists, whether local or national."[15] The voice of the reporter started to change from that of outside narrator—speaking as if unmoved and uninvolved, checking on places, names, ages, dates—to that of informed bystander, who now dared to enter the personality of a main character in the story itself. The task of reporting broke loose almost spontaneously from the constraints, but not ultimately from the purpose, of objectivity. It was as if it had stultified within its own rules—the "Geneva conventions of the mind,"

as Orwell had called them—which, in the age of flexible television reporting, were simply holding print journalism back from the truth rather
than helping it to guarantee the truth. "They were moving beyond the
conventional limits of journalism," continued Wolfe, "but not merely in
terms of technique. The kind of reporting they were doing struck them
as far more ambitious, too. It was more intense, more detailed, and
certainly more time-consuming than anything that newspaper or magazine reporters, including investigative reporters, were accustomed to.
They developed the habit of staying with the people they were writing
about for days at a time, weeks in some cases. They had to gather all the
material the conventional journalist was after—and then keep going. It
seemed all-important to be *there* when dramatic scenes took place, to get
the dialogue, the gestures, the facial expressions, the details of the
environment."[16] Here he is discussing primarily the new magazine writing of the late 1960's, but the basic tenets spread far into the world of
newspaper journalism as it attempted to reveal the attractiveness of the
new visual world created by the television film-reporter, that is, created
in the events that television had encouraged to take place in the era of the
politics of spectacle. The reporter found that a greatly increased range of
masks and personalities were now available to him, and many of these—
such as those of participant observer, sampler of experience, interpreter
of roles and emotions—had been handed on from the world of social
science, another emergent reporting profession that advanced into the
same areas of disquisition in the 1960's, armed with purposes as serious,
as professional, and as concerned with truth and objectivity as was journalism itself.

It is interesting to compare Wolfe's account of the origins of the New
Journalism of the 1960's with Mencken's account of the origins of his
own "new journalism" of half a century before. Mencken was looking at
the conditions that had given rise to the new sense of professionalism and
dedication in the journalists of his later years as compared with those of
his youth: "[The journalist] elects representatives and they meet in lugu-
brious conclave to draw up codes of ethics. . . . He changes his old
cynical views of schools of journalism, and is lured, now and then, into
lecturing in them himself. He no longer thinks of his calling as a business, like the haberdasher's or the tallow-chandler's, or as a game, like
the stockbroker's or faro-dealers', but as a profession, like the juriconsul-
tant's or gynaecologist's. His purpose is to set it on its legs as such—to
inject plausible theories into its practice, and rid it of its old casualness
and opportunism. He no longer sees it as a craft to be mastered in four
days, and abandoned at the first sign of a better job. . . . Once he

thought of himself . . . as what Beethoven called a free artist—a gay adventurer careening down the charming highways of the world, the gutter ahead of him but ecstasy in his heart. Now he thinks of himself as a fellow of weight and responsibility, a beginning publicist and public man, sworn to the service of the born and unborn, heavy with duties to the Republic and to his profession."[17] One must make allowance for Mencken's retroactive cynicism and for the fact that examples can be found from other, previous generations of journalists of old reporters looking back at the rising tide of moral improvement sweeping over their craft. Nonetheless, there was a real movement towards professionalism in evidence during his later years. And it was this inherited professionalism that petered out again in the 1960's when it seemed not to match the moral challenges of the day, which were presented to young reporters caught up in national and international student movements; nor did it match the task of purifying political life, which the major mainstream newspaper press set itself to perform in the months of Watergate.

The disrepute of professionalism in the old sense among sixties journalists was due in part, as sociologist Michael Schudson argues, to the general disrepute into which professions in general were falling. The readers of Ivan Illich among journalists were bound to make comparisons between his critique of schooling and of medicine and the business of reporting. The professions—law, medicine, education—appeared to be responsible for the specialized social problems they were set up to deal with. They had vested interest in disease, mental illness, ignorance, injustice, and their "codes" were structurally incompetent to protect the public against the conscious and unconscious depradations of organized practioners in the professions concerned. In journalism there was a perceived collusion between the professional critics of institutions and the institutions themselves, whose existence gave the former their opportunity and provided them with a clear set of guidelines within which the criticism took place. There was therefore persistent conflict between editors and "new" journalists, the latter wanting to take up positions within the press as it was, in the conventional way, and yet join the ranks of their own generation and accept its critique.

The new styles of journalism were, in part, the resultant response to these two pressures: on the one hand, a resistance to the conventions of news that seemed to oblige the reporter to conduct himself compliantly to the point of complicity, and on the other, an opportunity in the New Journalism for self-expression, vividness of style, and political purpose, which cut the reporter from the mainstream of national information. The bias to which reporting unwittingly gave itself stemmed from the very procedures that tied journalism to its sources, forcing it to use methods of validation that left information culled from socially underprivileged sources structurally invalid. Journalism helplessly underpinned a social system that was content with and depended upon a kind of objective truth that that very social system constrained, even crippled.

Within the news pages could be seen the explicit interpretation that was continually going on, clearly traceable to the influence of government upon the outward flow of news on major issues, upon the organized management by government of all knowledge about society—ranging from government-sponsored research contracts in universities to Saigon's Five O'Clock Follies, the daily briefings that confused a decade of reporting on the war in Vietnam. Government could be perceived simply as a system of information management, creating the central "realities" of the society. The institution of press agentry that Lippmann had criticized was but the excrescence of the process of government itself, which had been invading one area after another of society, its arbitrary behavior shrouded in a thicket of structured information. It was this discovery that brought out a theme long present in discussion about the role of the press—that of a deliberate and necessary confrontation between reporter and authority. This idea had loomed large in nineteenth-century newspaper ideology especially in England, where the newspaper had been essentially a tool of the middle class in their struggle against a state machine operated by an older dominant class. It had acquired its mythology in nationalist struggles, but in America, with its relatively thin layer of federal government, the Washington reporters had been a small, privileged group participating in the struggle between factions. Now the Washington correspondents grew in esteem and importance as they found themselves participants in the major battlefield of social history, that between elected government and people, in which they alone wielded the necessary weapons of war.

In the context of a political system that relied heavily upon television, the White House reporter became a kind of gladiator, the "proxy opposition" who linked the issues of the moment to the man responsible for doing something about them. In the days of Nixon the gradual unfolding of the Watergate affair seemed to confirm something the President had known since he first attempted to gain the office, that the *Washington Post* and the White House had become locked in a struggle symbolizing the adversary relationship between White House and media—and that this had been in the process of becoming journalistic orthodoxy over the years.[18] In West Coast papers like the *LA Times*, which had supported Richard Nixon almost all of the way through his political career, the conflict was fought out between their Washington bureaus and the White House. Every newspaper with an office participating in the competitive world of Washington reporting was drawn into the relationship, whatever the political predilections of the owner, editor, or publishing company. The Watergate Pulitzer Prize went not to the reporters who had dug out the story but to the newspaper and its publisher, who had made the task of bringing down a President corporately possible. After all, the President had attempted to undermine the confidence of the newspaper corporations by threatening their peripheral profits centers in the electronic media, over which government held ultimate power. Nixon had attempted to inject anxiety into the *New York Times*, for example, by taking actions that jeopardized the paper's radio stations in Florida. He had manipulated the candidacies for office in the Corporation for Public Broadcasting and had then watched the Public Broadcasting Service take its revenge when it televised the Watergate hearings *in extenso*.

The struggle for media independence from government—an ancient cause—took on new meaning and necessitated new weapons in the age of electronic media and conglomerate ownership of print with electronic media. It meant that there were now two "establishments," with overlapping personnel but when it came to it, clear adversary functions: Executive versus Media. This was a new doctrine for the media, though rooted in the past, and it had resonances throughout the reporting profession— in journalist training schools, in the expectations the readership had of its newspapers, in the attitudes of all reporters to all reporting.

During the Carter Administration, government was spending $1 billion a year on its own information services (the Pentagon alone had 1500 press officers, spending $25 million a year)—and this under a President who had made deliberate efforts on entering office to cut down on unnecessary expenditure.[19] Presidents, and politicians in general, had long depended upon the press for *publicity*. Virtually the entire line of American Presidents from Jefferson onwards had had deliberate policies towards the newspapers—editing them, nudging them, flattering them, depending upon them, learning to read their personalities like books, and studying their techniques until they could be played like a keyboard. No President before Carter, however, had entered office with the understanding that the press had now learned to think of itself as an opposition, almost in the European sense, as a counterpower, part of whose raison d'être consisted in the constant search for ways to dethrone the incumbent in office. Under Carter the bureaucracy started quietly to regroup and reconstruct its blown cover.

During the Carter presidency the courts started to unravel some of the great freedoms and liberal interpretations of traditional freedoms that the courts in the 1960's and early 1970's had granted. Journalists could not expect, in all circumstances, to have their sources' identity concealed with impunity; nor could they get away with concealing their notebooks from the eyes of demanding judges—at least not without a spell in jail. In New Jersey reporter Peter Bridges went to jail for refusing to tell a grand jury about an article he had written for a now defunct paper, the *Newark Evening News*, about local corruption. The state of New Jersey proceeded to pass a powerful "shield law" to prevent such jailings in the future, but within months a similar case started up in the very same state, when *New York Times* reporter Myron Farber was jailed for refusing to hand over his notes in the course of a murder trial. A heavy daily fine was levied upon the *Times* for the duration of its reporter's refusal to hand the papers over.

In all seventeen states that have shield laws people wondered how strong the protection of reporters really was at a time when judicial respect for their privileges was wearing thin. The cases trickled through, some even to the Supreme Court. The *Stanford Daily* lost a case in which it had asserted its right not to have its office files removed by the police in the course of an investigation. Three reporters agreed to a subpoena, in March, 1979, ordering them to give evidence in a marijuana smuggling case. The Reporters' Committee for Freedom of the Press argued that information gathered by a reporter but not used was not the business of the authorities, even if the source was not confidential. The judge in this particular case remarked that lawyers were beginning to abuse their privilege of requiring reporters to produce their notes of stories written and published months before, but the tide of court decisions seemed to be ebbing from the increased protection that had been given the press during the period between Kennedy and Nixon. The Supreme Court, for example, upheld early in 1979 a lower court ruling permitting the Justice Department to acquire telephone bills listing all long-distance calls made from a newspaper when the Department was trying to track down informants of Washington columnist Jack Anderson. The Reporters' Committee, which lost this case, claimed that the Bell Telephone company had made records available on 32,000 separate occasions. In a long series of cases the possession of complete occupational legal protection seemed to slip from the grasp of the newspaper, returning to authority some of the powers it had earlier surrendered.

Until the Watergate revelations the main thrust of the discussion of relations between press and presidency in America had centered on the older issue of government control and official interference in the press. The Hutchins Commission of 1947, for instance, concerned itself largely with the problems that had become important in America before and after World War I, when government had been involved in cajoling reporters and threatening newspapers. The Commission evolved a new theory of the press, the "social responsibility theory," by which newspapers would render themselves more accountable to public opinion; the Commission's report urged that there be a kind of Press Council of the type that was set up voluntarily by the British press shortly afterwards with the participation of trade unions and the general public. The National News Council of the U.S., which emerged in later years, and the local news councils that have proliferated across America have all remained under deep suspicion by the purist among the information newspapers. The *New York Times* in particular fears any intrusion upon the untrammeled liberty of an editor to pursue the truth as he sees it in the ways he thinks best. However, the issue of where and how the power of the press is balanced in society against its public and against authority has never been resolved in the United States and has been further complicated by the arrival of the new formulations of press-government relationships as a result of the upheaval of the 1960's. Government's sheer power to obfuscate and confuse the inquiring reporter made more urgent the development of doctrines that sanctioned the reporter's intrusion into government processes, at least on a scale sufficient to acquire clear answers to issues that government chose to conceal.

The adversary role of the press had been prepared for, in effect, back in the days of the Roosevelt Administration, when a network of press offices was set up in every department of government (many of these had, of course, existed right through the century); the reporter was obliged to *dig* for information, and to do so he embarked upon a police-type role and was therefore inevitably going to find himself, under one Administration or another, in direct conflict with the most basic necessities of power. This represented a substantial change in prevailing doctrine even if, in practice, there was plenty of precedent.

The presidency plus a "national security state" provided American reporting with an inexorable opponent and an unavoidable moral task. With America in the cockpit of world politics, foreign policy became central to American affairs, and political coverage came face-to-face with the problem of official concealment and national security. Here the problem was not one of a conflict of policy between press and government but a conflict over the availability of information. Until the later stages of the Vietnam War the press was nearly always compliant under government when grounds of national security were offered as reason for denying information to the public. The *New York Times* cooperated with Kennedy and witheld information it had acquired relating to the Bay of Pigs invasion in 1962. The press had refrained from drawing attention to the inability of President Eisenhower to conduct affairs of state during his treatment for coronary thrombosis.

There came a point during the Vietnam War when a combination of new doctrines, widespread disbelief in the wisdom of prevailing policies, and dislike of personalities encouraged the press not to cooperate on *principle*, in fact, to demur on principle. Kissinger continued until the end to benefit from the willingness of reporters to cooperate with the presentation of news in the manner desired by a national leader: the rules of what was "background" and what was "off the record" and "on the record" were adhered to by virtually all of those who followed the Secretary of State on his many missions, and his almost obsessive concern with secrecy was indulged by reporters. At the same time, Kissinger was *publicized* by radio, television, magazines, and newspapers to an extent enjoyed by no other previous incumbent in his office. The offer of publicity combined with the voluntary witholding of information meant that Kissinger was able to present himself to the public almost exactly as he wished. The press willingly agreed to represent his statements as those of a "senior official," and when his word was challenged at the Vienna Press Conference of 1974 (he was questioned on his complicity in wiretapping his subordinates), he used to devastating effect (upon the press) the threat to resign, if the attack on his integrity continued. The routines of the reporters and their general willingness to render under Caesar helped perpetuate the favorable image that Kissinger had acquired as a result of general cooperation by all of the media. The spectacle helped create a rift between those reporters who went along with this and those who quietly resolved to try to break through the smokescreens and half-truths when they got the chance. Part of the importance of Watergate was that it seemed to explain to journalists the way in which their role in Washington politics had altered and legitimized in their eyes the occupation of a more forward position in the daily struggle for information.

Increasingly, the issue of the media themselves became one of the major topics of journalists. It had started with the publication of Daniel Boorstin's *The Image*,[20] which spoke of the "thicket of pseudo-events" with which press agentry and public relations and the media had suffused all reality; it was intensified by the popular discussion of Marshall McLuhan's book on college campuses and in the press; it explored its own internal contradictions in the first group of films about Vietnam, in particular *Medium Cool*, which made the question of the reporter's handing himself over to the demands of television into one of personal morality. But it was the work of disclosure, which was pursued in the major newspapers themselves, that clarified the issue of media confrontation in the course of their practice of it. Thus, the publication of the Pentagon Papers shocked at first but then seemed to justify the breaking down of secrecy in the eyes of a wide section of the public, and the publication of the Nixon tapes seemed to go further and confirm the value of publications of all material that came to light. Where the press had continued, in the context of warfare, to give authority its appearance of dignity even in the context of growing scepticism of its policies, power in the final days of the Nixon Administration was stripped of its last formal privileges. The doctrine of the Fourth Estate was temporarily transmuted into a doctrine of permanent opposition. It attracted thousands of students into the journalism training schools in the post-Watergate years and gave journalism a recoating of spurious glamour. However, Watergate did not, in fact, provide journalism with a restored objectivity, nor leave it with a body of intellectual or professional skills of a kind that could turn the newspaper into a tool of knowledge.

The almost total failure of the press to understand the internal politics of Iran before the collapse of the Shah and his army, together with their secret apparatus of repression, helped to bring home to more reporters the need to look outside the routine sources of journalism for reliable information on the affairs of the world. Iran had been a further example of Western journalism following blindly the flow of official handouts and pursuing information only within the general lines of national policy. Ayatollah Khomeini had overthrown a regime on which the Western powers had placed a very large measure of reliance, and almost no one in the press had reckoned with him or treated him as anything but a fringe fanatic.

Where the lessons of confrontation with official policy had been well learned, now another problem in the occupational makeup of reporting seemed to become paramount, one that had profound implications at one level for such matters as journalistic education and on another level for the issue of that reality that journalism accepted as the basis of its work. In ignoring the Ayatollah, the press of the West had acted, in effect, as his opponent. The *Columbia Journalism Review* castigated it for its omissions: "For by and large the American news media routinely have characterized the Iranian conflict as the work of turbanned religious zealots in league with opportunist Marxists, rather than—as they might have—the reaction of people outraged by a repressive regime. By doing so the press has helped to misinform American public opinion and narrow the range of debate on this bellweather foreign-policy crisis."[21] In 1978 the debate over the UNESCO Declaration on Communications had brought out the hostilities harbored in many parts of the Third World against the alleged institutionalized bias against them in the international news agencies and all the other major reporting media of the developed world. With the overthrow of the Shah, at the head of one of the few economically powerful states in the Third World that was wholly within the Western lines of policy, it seemed that the press had failed within its own terms, had failed indeed to confront the policies of its national leaders, had failed to listen to well-informed people within the Third World, had suffered from a structured inability to perceive a reality that it then had quickly to acknowledge. The writers in the *Columbia Journalism Review* emphasized the ideological blockage separating the reporters of America from the very impartiality that would have enabled them to see the events of Iran with greater understanding. "Religion is one of the major cultural barriers for American reporters covering Iran. . . . Would it occur to American reporters covering the Vatican, for example, consistently to refer to priests in their everyday garb as "black-robed?" This descriptive phrase regularly is applied to mullahs. For that matter, would it occur to a North American reporter to refer to Latin American worker-priests as religious extremists or fanatics?"

It was the press—and a very small number of reporters and editors at that—that created the sense of those realities around which the affairs of the world were conducted. The question of responsibility was driven home as it had never been in the days of the publication of the Pentagon Papers. Here was an issue in which the press was acting as a power in its own right but was acting unconsciously and in ignorance. It was no longer enough to blame the CIA for manipulating news or manipulating the internal affairs of foreign countries. Here, the press was responsible.

In a study of the American voter published in 1976,[22] it had been shown that voters had become more personally involved in politics but at the same time ever more distrustful of government (in 1958 24 percent of the population thought that the government could not be trusted to do right, while 57 percent thought so in 1973). Yet here was a case in which the trustworthiness of the press at its fundamental task of providing information was at stake. The movement in the dominant occupational ideal of journalism reflected a more general change of feeling in American society. The student movement was spectacular in its methods and tended to give the impression that the change in mood that it represented was confined to those who participated in the culture of a particular generation. In fact, the change in attitude towards government moved through much larger areas of the society, and Watergate ensured that expressions of disaffection and disillusion with the central political processes were possible in all classes and places. The utopianism that lay at the root of much of the political and journalistic activity of the period was a new strain in American life, and certainly new as a force in journalism. The older strain of progressivism in the early twentieth century, which had influenced journalism through the "muckrackers," had been more overtly patriotic in tone, much more concerned with nailing the holders of power to specific tasks of reform and with forcing change through the comparison of actual conditions and actual behavior to the traditional ideals of American life. Lincoln Steffens and Upton Sinclair, for example, expressed a faith in American purpose as they castigated the powerful and the exploiters of labor. In comparison with the muckrakers, the radicals of the sixties were outsiders, ranting disconnectedly, cut off from their national tradition. But their critique was a powerful one and a moral one, which could not fail to leave its mark on the professional group most intimately concerned with reflecting and creating the changing moods of American society. Even former vice-President Spiro Agnew spoke of a "post-Watergate morality."

One important seedbed of the new approach to reporting was the tradition of the news magazines. *Time* had been born in the 1920's, at a moment when a great deal of the news available on foreign topics was merely bewildering to the reader. What then seemed to be needed was a form of popular writing that placed foreign stories in context, dressed them up as entertainment, above all, interpreted them. From *Time* there spread outwards an important subdoctrine among reporters under the label "interpretative," which fitted into the growing scepticism about the value or the possibility of being objective. Hearst and McCormick and other autocratic and ideologically self-willed publishers were in any case using their newspapers for propagandistic purposes while pretending that they held their reporters to the spirit of objectivity. The Hutchins Commission itself gave a clean bill of health to this new flexibility in reporting, arguing that it was "no longer enough to report the *fact* truthfully. It is now necessary to report the truth about the fact." Where editors had accepted the need for "interpretation" in the context of foreign news, they were now being slowly persuaded by their reporters to permit the pursuit of "truth," which was a stage beyond the objective tradition.[23]

Truman Capote's *In Cold Blood* demonstrated the depths of "truth," which could be extracted from the painstaking collection of facts and interpretative material, if the skills of the fiction writer were added to those of the reporter. Gay Talese and Norman Mailer produced their work after steeping themselves in fact but deploying their material with the versatility of the novelist. A completely new range of possibilities and compulsions were added with the rise of black journalism and other radical brands of reporting from minority groups anxious to make changes rapidly in American society. The women's movement, the Chicago movement, and the black movement broke through the dike, once it had been breached by the new journalism of the novelists. One journalism instructor spoke of a fourth revolution in journalism (after the freeing of the press from government, the growth of objectivity, and the rise of interpretation), which permitted activism in reporting. "The journalist activist believes he has a right (indeed an obligation) to become personally and emotionally involved in the events of the day. He believes he should proclaim his beliefs if he wishes, and that it is not only permissible but desirable for him to cover the news from the viewpoint of his own intellectual commitment. He looks at traditional reporting as being sterile, and he considers reporters who refuse to commit themselves to a point of view as being cynical or hypocritical. . . . "[24]

The influential practitioners of the new journalism of commitment did most of their work outside the newspaper medium—in *Esquire*, in the *National Review*, in *Rolling Stone*, and in a myriad of other underground publications that rose from the waves of the 1960's youthful discontent. (Some of them sank back again when the movement's energy was spent.) The magazines in many cases represented the most pointed and most glamorous forms of journalism of the time, and the new freedoms became a *temptation* to the whole range of print reporting, including the daily press. There were frequent complaints and frequent surveys to the effect that opinion was "creeping into" news columns. What attracted the reporter was perhaps not so much the opportunity to express an "opinion" but the chance to borrow techniques from other kinds of writing and to borrow a new persona altogether, a new mask, with which to perform the function of reporter.

When the passions of the period died away, there was less desire to use the newspaper for purposes of propaganda by reporters but a strong desire to continue developing investigative reporting, especially in local affairs, and to experiment with styles of writing. The changes in the structure of the newspaper form contributed to the opportunities available in many metropolitan and even suburban papers for writing at different levels, for different audiences, in different moods. The sixties left their sediment upon all reporting—indeed, some of the new journals of the time such as *Rolling Stone* continue thriving—and have helped to modify the doctrines of journalism as a whole. In collected Vietnam material, such as that of Michael Herr in *Dispatches*,[25] one can see something of what has endured of the new strains of reporting: a deep commitment to straight facts and background, suffused with the passions of an individual who feels free to use his emotions as a guide to the event while holding back from pressing opinions of a political kind—the reporter offering his experience as part of his material without prejudicing accuracy or objectivity. Though the reporter has been released from a kind of repression of self, he reembraces his craft ethic.

The student reporters of the 1960's have moved through the press gradually shedding the passions of the antiwar movement and civil rights and the demands for open language and open sexuality, but they have kept with them a sense of an enlarged range in journalism and the need for the barrier between reporter and subject to be bridged before the "truth" can be extracted. Where a young reporter in the sixties sent to cover a topic related to his generation felt embarrassed by the sense of his own treachery, of his being made an agency of a rival culture spying upon his own, today he would probably feel more at home in his role, less constrained by the canons of the journalistic tradition, more able to level with his subject.

The reporter faces the 1980's, therefore, with a considerably enriched set of ethical beliefs about his duties and function. He has more freedom within the traditions of his occupation and a wider variety of styles and roles passing through the profession by way of the training schools and journalism departments of universities, which have come to play a larger and more widely accepted part in the newspaper industry. But the whole business of reporting remains under a cloud of scepticism, reinforced internationally by the continuing debate between Third World and developed world (the socialist camp playing little part in the development of the critique although a major part in politically strengthening the Third World position) over what constitutes a "free and balanced flow of information." This moral attack upon the work of Western journalists in the reporting of international affairs and, in particular, the domestic affairs of Third World countries cannot but spill over into the internal professional debate about how reporters should perform their work.

What much of the research of the 1970's has brought out is the way in which the routines of news gathering predetermine the image of reality that reporters purvey. Information is accepted at face value from some quarters and not from others; objectivity is a "strategic ritual" (as the sociologist Gaye Tuchman calls it, in a now popular phrase),[26] designed more to protect the journalist against outside attack than to help him direct his mental faculties in a particular way. Paul Weaver has developed an effective criticism of the idea of the "story" itself, the internally structured narrative formula around which news collecting takes place and which is used as a criterion of newsworthiness as well as a method of news writing. An event becomes a story when it impinges upon an area of agreed and known attitude and prejudice, when it confirms or undermines a preexisting assumption, when it continues rather than unravels, when it is easily extractable from a continuing surrounding circumstance.[27] What places the journalist in a more difficult and pregnable position is the additional criticism that the whole business of journalism takes place on the basis of an accepted body of political beliefs that remain unquestioned throughout the professional life of the individual reporter. Under this view objectivity is little more in substance than rhetoric, since the reporter is bound to accept the basic institutions of his society (the family, private enterprise, the corporations, the political system, etc. and therefore sees society only in terms of them.

Journalism has, in a sense, had its conventions exposed to view in the conditions following Vietnam and Watergate through events that put the whole inherited structure of codes and practices to an extreme test of serviceability. Once displayed, the conventions cannot again become the comfortable and enduring bedrock of occupational confidence that they formerly were. Of course, there are enough examples of professional deviance throughout the long history of American and European journalism to support the argument that nothing new has, in fact, occurred, that we are living through a simple continuity of conduct in which earlier themes—such as the American novel, progressivism, and muckraking—have come to the fore. But what is different today is the fact that the critique has been made and remains upon the table, that the public as well as the reporters have acquired an understanding of the processes of reporting, a demystification, which leaves the forms of journalism as interesting as the content. The movie of *All the President's Men*, the account by Bob Woodward and Carl Bernstein of how they investigated the mysteries of Watergate and how the corporate as well as reportorial response to the scandal developed day by day, has left the newspaper reader with an awareness and indeed a respect for reporting, which raises his expectations of what can be done. Journalism has been seen *through*, but has also been reinforced in its acceptability; it is no longer seen as a threat to the settled order of things but rather as a stabilizer.

Investigative teams now operate in many newspapers. Perhaps rather self-consciously they look for misdeeds in their communities as though society consisted of areas of "correct" behavior (as described by their noninvestigative colleagues) and isolable pockets of deviant antisocial activity, which are the proper province of a separate genre of journalism. Investigative reporting has thus acquired its own built-in world view, which reinforces a belief in solidity of values and the acceptability of the reporter's world as he finds it. But it has left journalism much more individual and personalized and more of a profession.

III

To see how the persona of the reporter is developing, one must examine the changed managerial structure of the newspaper itself, although generalization is even more precarious in this discussion that in that of the reporter. The growing self-consciousness of reporting has occurred alongside a gradual internal democratization of the newsroom, especially in those (few) newspapers that have taken the path of information rather than entertainment. As a general rule, the more a newspaper conforms to the manner of a document of record the more open and internally consultative it becomes. No American paper has gone as far as *Le Monde* in permitting an elective editorship or jointly-decided editorial policies, but the *New York Times* and the *Washington Post* demonstrate in their changing pages the way in which editorial management has become a group or federal rather than individual function. The earlier stages in the evolution of the ethic of journalism were closely connected with the lines of control in the family-owned nineteenth-century newspaper, with its relatively small staff, its single managing editor, and its powerful news editor, who passed on corporate policies and carried out the paper's competitive strategy among the rival titles within a single community.

In a newspaper of record the reporter's task was often to obtain verbal account of events, either detailed eye-witness reports or transcripts of speeches, sermons, political statements, and discussions. The interview was itself a form of discourse created by the reporter for the purpose of transcription interspersed with comment and description of a personality. The news pages were filled with material that had begun life in a verbal form. The techniques of reporting consisted of observing, making notes, obtaining material through digging and questioning. Expertise in a specific subject was rarely required, unlike the twentieth-century newspaper, which has been progressively devoted to a wider range of subjects and demands a large and growing number of specialists. But the specialists have started to be welded into collegiate formation rather than simple line-management, and the more a reporter depends upon his personal stock of knowledge as well as his journalistic technique the more he feels a desire to participate in the ultimate use of his expertise.

The *New York Times* used to contain 24 stories on an average front page in the first years of the century; at the quarter century the average had dropped to 13. Since World War II it has hovered around the dozen mark, with an equal number of "jumps" (which were exceptional at the start of the century).[28] This is a rough piece of evidence, perhaps, but it indicates the extent to which this paper has moved, period by period, further towards a policy of running fewer and longer stories. In 1900 its front page carried 342 stories in an average fortnight, now only 81. The tendency towards detail is a reflection on the increasing tolerance and interest on the part of the generation of readers, but it also points at the way the information newspaper now tries to reach its audience at the level of the subject itself, rather than at a generalized presumed mean acceptability. Of course, at the other end of the newspaper market, the audience is given a more trivialized treatment of news, and the division grows deeper all the time.

Whereas a newspaper would formerly publish *documents* and the official and nonofficial *records* of events, now it more often exploits its reporters' contacts and their ability to interpret events, to perform a kind of brokerage between the makers of the events and the surrounding society. While the *New York Times* used to publish the texts of the sermons delivered by the clergy of the city, it now has a religious-affairs correspondent who reports interpretatively on issues and problems within the various religious communities of the city. The power of brokerage has thus passed from news editor to correspondent and specialist reporter, and as a result the editor cannot wield the same kind of authority he did in previous generations. Many editors report this change in their status and in their growing dependence upon the judgment of the heads of each section of the paper as to what stories to cover and to what extent. Since newspapers are basically political units at this senior level, the editor's power has come to be that of a kind of patron, a *primus inter pares*, a leader of semicollegiate structure in which great power resides among the editors responsible for each desk.

Indeed, the front page of the *Washington Post* bears witness to this change in managerial structure and mood, as do those of other American papers: very seldom does a front page not contain at least one major foreign story, one metro story, one political story, and one home story—and normally two of each. News values are ascribed according to the needs of internal governance, rather than from an attempt to perceive the order of interest in the readers' minds. One could put this another way and say that the newspaper's collective judgment is now trusted by the reader, reducing the need for the newspaper to keep scrambling after him. The editors are themselves leaders of squads of reporters each hungry for promotion and recognition, and their ability to lead is judged in part by their ability to fight their people's stories into prominent positions in the paper. The managing editor sits at the apex of this pyramid of political pressures and over the course of time tends to equalize his patronage across the various desks and departments. Modern news values have to be seen in the context of the newspaper as a social system as much as a manufacturing enterprise; it has started to borrow techniques of management and organization from the research institute and the college as much as from the modern office and plant.

One must balance, therefore, the earlier picture of the reporter as individualist with a picture of the newspaper organization itself, which is increasingly run on bureaucratic lines with firmer divisions of labor than in the past. There are reporters specializing as editors, as assignment reporters, or as permanent reporters on specific topics such as the arts, society, sports, and economics. Large cities are divided into beats covered by reporters who acquire allegiences and specialist expertise relating to the industries, social problems, and planning questions that a particular beat contains. The same issues can come to be seen from different perspectives by reporters working in different sections of the hierarchy and specialist divisions, and conflicts arise between reporters and editors, between overseas bureaus and home bureaus, and between reporters in different beats of the same city. The conflicts between personalities, therefore, often come to symbolize or simply contain conflicts relating to issues and the treatment of issues. At the heart of the modern newspaper lies a complex bargaining process with four dimensions: between news editors and managers within the newspaper, between reporters assigned to different responsibilites, between reporters and the source of their material within society as a whole, and between competing sources of information attempting to gain the attention of, or avoid the attention of, the newspaper. These tensions underlie much of what finally appears in a paper and influences the choices made along the editorial chain. The reporters' routines are dependent on the lines along which information travels within the news business and within the society or community they are reporting on. Former *New York Times* editor Turner Catledge remarks in his autobiography that "the hardest decisions tended to be those within the organization, within the family, decisions regarding policy and people, decisions that demanded a courageous spirit less often than a careful balancing of complex issues."[29]

The tensions within the news gathering process help to accentuate the dependence upon recognized channels and therefore the power of those channels over the shaping of news itself. Competition between reporters of different newspapers working at the same beat will ensure that they will not want to miss press conferences, announcements, or social functions at which principal makers of news or providers of information may be present. Competition will make them dissatisfied with the shared channels but will tend to entrench those channels in their importance. Routines help journalists cope with the hazards of journalism and cause convergences of material passing through different media. It is safe to report what others are reporting, even if one wants to go further than one's rivals. These tensions within the newspaper and between newspapers make it possible for officials and politicians to make tactical use of the press. It helps them control the flow of disclosure and the timing of news, and it forces the paper into acting as a kind of semiauthorized intermediary between authority and public as often as it encourages it to break loose from the bonds of dependence upon sources. In the circumstances of competition, the reporter is constantly looking for material from outside the recognized channels that form the central route for information, but his desire to obtain exclusive information also increases his vulnerability; he can as easily become a carrier of information outside the normal channels for the same officials.[30] One man's scoop is frequently another's carefully camouflaged handout.

In the circumstances of the newspaper as an organized management system, news choices and content emerge far more as a result of the structure of relationships than as the result of a conscious working professional ideology. Where objectivity has failed to survive the test of criticism, it is mainly because news organization has acquired its own imperatives. The newspaper is a series of themes on which can be played minor variations, and occasional major ones. It is a bureaucracy whose end product is essentially itself, with the newspaper as a kind of by-product of the interplay of social and internal organizational forces. Today, however, this complex of forces is in the process of being assailed from another quarter; the new machinery of news gathering and newspaper production is having to come to grips with the formal and informal channels along which the content of the newspaper emerges.

IV

Throughout its history the newspaper has encoded in its organizational and production system its moral outlook, its relationship with its audience, its assessment of its social role. The choice of a technology entails a conscious (though partly unconscious) recapitulation of the nature of *the newspaper* as a medium. The manufacturers of the technology themselves have to conceive the purposes of the medium they are assisting into being. Very often they have themselves been newspaper managers or production engineers. In the transference to computerized methods, many of the principal pioneering newspapers have had to undertake detailed descriptions of themselves as communication and social systems while preparing the specifications for the physical machinery they are ordering. What we will now do is restate some of the issues already explored that relate to the internal structure of news and the newspaper and relate them to the judgments that have been made by one newspaper, the *Washington Post*, in the course of constructing its new production facility.

The creation of a newspaper, then—daily, weekly, or monthly—depends upon the existence of a series of routines, as does any other industrial product. To the reader these routines, taken together, represent an integrated information system, a single "voice" as it were, presenting a daily account of the world that is ordered according to a single judgment, which in turn is based upon a judgment as to the nature of the collective readers' interests. The title of the newspaper is a symbol of that interconnected and assumed unity of judgment, the publisher's and the readership's. The newspaper provides an image of the world and an explanation of the world. Each readership is a unity in the eyes of the editor or publisher, though, like the newspaper itself, it contains many "specialisms." Yet the essential trick of the newspaper is to integrate as many of these as it can within its routines and procedures, to capture a comprehensive enough view of "reality" to create the feeling of providing an overall explanation of the world.

Yet within the organization of the newspaper this information system is not an integrated one but a distributed one. The larger the newspaper the more discrete elements it contains within its information-collecting machine. As a medium, it moves towards a consensus with its readership (whether that readership consists of a social class or a geographical district or the supporters of a single political party), and as an organization, it collects its information from a variety of constituencies within the area inhabited by its readers.

Figure 6 Organization of a Large Newspaper

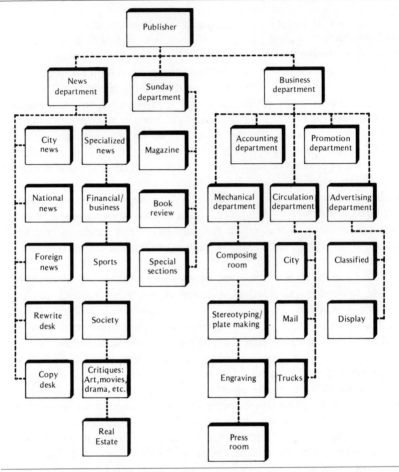

SOURCE: Dineh Moghdam, *Computers in Newspaper Publishing* (New York: Marcel Dehker, 1978), p. 9.

We can understand more about this information system by examining a diagram of the internal of a large newspaper staff (see figure 6). Each of its information inputs is built around a separate activity in the external society: reporters in, say, the sports pages work for a sports editor whose function it is to work within a kind of consensus with his particular group of information creators, the world of sports people. The real-estate editor is doing much the same thing, and readers might suspect him of being biased towards the general position of real-estate dealers or real-estate consumers or of trying to work out a general median position. But the routines of each information sector depend partly upon the routines generated by the actors within that sector, partly upon the needs of the readers, partly upon the needs of the newspaper as an information-producing system. Each editor resolves those interconnecting needs and in so doing necessarily imposes an intellectual structure upon the "deal" made between them all and expressed in the final product—the page he edits.

Some sections of the information found in a newspaper are perceived by the reader to come straight from the information "creator" and to be paid for by him. These we call advertisements. Some information comes in practice from the "creator" (though originating in the form of a handout) but is recoded or sanitized into reporter's copy. Some information arrives *despite* the *reluctance* of the information source. Most information arrives with the neutral cooperation of the source who is aware of the information being collected from him but is not actively involved. Finally, much of the information in the paper arrives from another intermediary, the wire service, which in turn has checked or otherwise legitimated information from sources that are accepted as valid, but that may or may not have directly intervened. Book reviews are another category in that—somewhat like political commentators or business analysts—they come from outside the newspaper from validated sources who are acting as brokers between readers and primary sources (the writers of the books) whose information is being evaluated. The newspaper in organizing the concentrated criticism of literature is supplying integration to a very highly distributed information system.

It is easy to see that the newspaper is a holdall—or a hold*some*. It is more difficult to see through the production technology of the newspaper into the inner system by which it works—the routinizing of the unrouted and the placing of dozens of small information systems, which are essentially of different kinds, within its own technological and distribution systems. The newspaper's categories of information are heterogeneous and often belong to quite different nonoverlapping primary audiences. These audiences agree, in a sense, to share in the newspaper's conception of them as a unity and make countless mutual bargains in order to do so. So does the newspaper in regard to them. It can make compromises that mislead the audience (through the omission, distortion, or delay of information that may in the light of later history have been vital), or it may enrich the development of the audience by making them aware of ranges of knowledge that otherwise would reach only a small segment of the society.

The *Washington Post* was deeply concerned about the maintenance of flexibility when it went over to its new system. Its display and classified advertising as well as its news content remain in flux until the last moment. The paper prints more words than most others in the U.S; its reporters move about more than most; its editors confer among themselves more than editors normally do. It is a highly distributed and highly interactive information system. Even wire service copy goes through more processes at the *Post* than on other papers, according to equipment manufacturers, and much of this material is used in snippets or as odd quotes by reporters writing their own stories on the same topic.

A paper the size of the *Post* has to be foolproof in its production process against all problems created by haphazard external circumstances. There are too many reporters caught in traffic jams, too much material lost accidentally in transmission—just by the actual laws of hazard—for production of the whole journal to be placed at risk by such incidents. It has to be possible for the editors to tear up whole sections of the paper, change major sections of input, break into the flow of typesetting in massive ways, without damaging the presentation of the finished product or making it look in any way out of the ordinary.

There are ten operational departments under the upper triumvirate of executive editor, managing editor, and deputy managing editor: National, Foreign, Metro, Financial, Sports, Style, Weekend/Magazine/TV Channels (all Sunday supplements), Outlook/Book World (also Sunday sections), Photo, and News Desk. Each desk has its own hierarchy of five or six people, including the assignment editors, all of whom constantly check and review one another's operations. The "slot" editor in each department hands out the stories to "rim" editors who edit the final stories, checking back both with the reporter(s) concerned and with the slot editor, and then write the headlines and captions before delivery to Composing. The night operation continues the day operation, desk by desk, the staff growing progressively thinner in numbers until one rim editor is left at each.

Editorial workers on the *Post* therefore consider themselves linked in a number of chains and hierarchies. They belong to departments, to the hierarchy of editors running through the whole paper, to times of day, to speciality of subject (real estate, literature, congressional politics, etc.), and to their varieties of function (assignment, copy editors, makeup editor, etc). As the *Post* explained to their equipment manufacturers in its long document of specification, these interactions are too complex to narrate or to display in diagram form. A desk editor may deal with a dozen reporters in different departments to collect or check information or acquire a judgment on a given story—either addressing them verbally or sending a memo. He will deal with the photo desk. He might offer material to the Maryland editor or the Virginia editor, or they might offer material to each other or to him, or offer advice on a vast number of points in connection with dozens of stories scheduled for different days. The new newsroom system had to be designed to take account of all these convolutions and crosscurrents if its operations were to be successfully transferred from a paper-bound to an electronic system. Figure 7 shows the path taken by a single story through many of its possible stages between origination outside the paper to page makeup—though this is a considerable simplification.

The system that emerged from the two years of planning was designed to meet the high degree of flexibility and reliability required. It also had to be fully operational and backed up by all necessary fail-safe devices to take account of all known risks. The system was designed to provide for full privacy for each user in regard to his personal material, notes, and unfinished stories through the use of the control data at the head of each "take," or session of work, in the system. A staff member first establishes his right to use the system through a sign–on procedure, which also establishes the "level" of his activity within the editorial or advertising hierarchy. A special password was designed that is never seen on the screen but that induces the system to answer the user's commands and disgorge nothing until the user is recognized.

To describe the full details of the way in which the computerized system interacts with the functions of the reporter is in itself to demonstrate how the complex organization of a newspaper is a halfway house between an integrated and a distributed information system. There is no longer a truly "eponymous" writing function left in it (where the text hangs upon the name of an individual writer); there is no "auteur" in newspaper information. There is only the newspaper *system*, which guarantees certain elements of individuality to the reporter, of personal integrity within the streams of activity generated by a collective (but hierarchical) system.

The *Post's* computer system offers the writer access to his own notes and to all other source material whose path is built into the system, such as wire service reports set aside for him by his assignment editor, notes from other reporters, and their past and current stories. The reporter can create a read-only copy of his work and place it in storage for the assignment editor to retrieve, but not to amend. The reporter can also return the whole story to the database without its being accessible to the

Figure 7

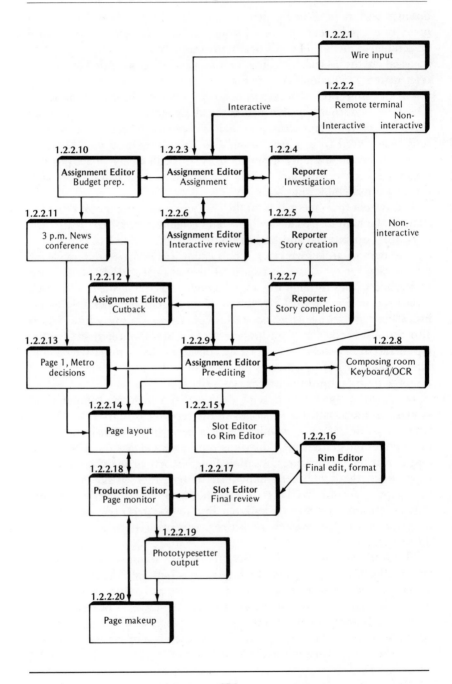

editor, and he can move material from one of his own files to another. At the same time, a reporter whose work has been checked may break up his story to help it into the editing stream, but may then be unable to alter it (at some point in the process it goes out of his control, and control can be regained only by a further negotiating process with the editor). The reporter can send the opening sections of a story in the process of being written to the editor on a read-only basis, but the editor can, on a split screen, start rewriting the story in a new file and send it back to the reporter and/or to other editors for further judgments. Once the reporter sends the finished story to the assignment editor, he can retrieve it only in a read-only mode himself. The assignment editor has much greater flexibility in his vdt in terms of what he can do to alter the content, style, length, and pattern of a story, but his changes will be displayed in such a manner as to indicate where the reorter's version differs from the edited version.

The system is also built to take into account the daily stages of cutback of stories as the editorial conferences proceed and the page budgets for the day are determined. The contents of the first page are a matter of intense and indeed legendary competition. The assistant managing editor at the news desk and the news editor are heavily involved in the judgments and adjudications. At the daily 6:15 p.m. conference, the executive editor, managing editor, and deputy, and assistant managing editors for National, Foreign, and Metro desks decide which stories to keep on the short list and are able to have immediate access to the text (as it stands) of all page one candidate stories. At the same time, a similar and often equally volatile series of decisions are being made in other departments, where priorities between stories are set up and where stories are often swapped between departments (e.g., when a sports story becomes of general news interest). When this happens, the story enters the system with two sets of composition instructions.

Each slot editor and rim editor is also situated at the point of convergence of multiple flows of information. The former receives input from assignment editors (for further editing), from the layout editor (for headline and composition instructions), the production editor (for changes in stories or headlines necessitated by changes in makeup), and rim editors (who send copy for review). The rim editor remains the last port of call for any of his stories—checking for spelling, grammar, inconsistencies, missing facts, but also rewriting and even combining different stories into one. It is he who codes the story for composition and adds typographic instructions. He passes every story back to the slot editor who tends to scan quickly at this stage and then send the whole thing back to the rim editor or on to the production editor.

The figure of the production editor is a new one, which has been thrown up by the sheer complication of the computerized system. He is a traffic expediter, whose duty it is to organize routes and copy flow in such a way as to maximize the amount of time available to the reporter. His work is performed on the telephone rather than through the system, and he tries to spot gaps and holdups by monitoring the status of every developing page; he can build up lists of material on his screen and see if all the components (text, headlines, captions) have been checked off and approved by the responsible hierarchy. In the newsroom the production editor coordinates the output of the Sports, Style, and Financial departments.

At the end of all these processes the material passes into typesetting, where galleys are made. (The versions that reach phototypesetting are saved for the archives until the moment when a general purge of the system memory takes place). The work of pasting up the galleys is done manually according to the pattern laid down earlier in the day on a series of dummies. At this stage there are further requests for alterations and adjustments that are relayed via the production editor to slot editor to rim editor, who sends the alterations back for rephototypesetting.

Another whole category of information emerges from the wire services and passes into the paper on both high- and low-speed wires. There are special wires for stocks, weather, race news, telex copy to and from the paper's own correspondents and its special centers in London and Paris. It has a special Reuters wire, and direct connections exist between the *Post* and the *Los Angeles Times* for their joint news service. The *Post* thus receives (and sends) a very high volume of wire material. However, it also processes wire copy to a greater extent than most other papers—perhaps all other papers—and its problem with regard to wire copy is that of routing it to destinations *within* the newspaper's organization. Each desk must build up files of connected stories, join up different stories and components of different stories, and move sections of wire service material into its own reporters' stories—and this applies to the output of all wire services except stocks and racing. Every urgent incoming story must not only be swiftly and accurately routed to the right desk within the paper but must automatically activate a flash or urgent signal and generate a hard copy of the full text on a printer. The wire room, in all, handles about a million words of copy a day. The vast proportion of this material never finds its way into the paper. In addition, every day nearly 100,000 words pass through the wire room in messages from overseas bureaus and from clients of the Times-Post News Service.

The *Post* developed for the benefit of Raytheon, the equipment manufacturers, a set of detailed analyses of important news stories of the recent past as they were covered at the time (see figure 7, page 194). Each of these is an apt illustration of the ways in which print journalism has been developing during the time it has had to compete with radio and television. It has moved, in fact, more and more into a multisource medium of news information and further away from the "journalism of disclosure" or the reporting and revealing of existing texts or of single eyewitness reports. The nineteenth-century reporter assumed that his main responsibility was to see, take down in shorthand, and reproduce; the nineteenth-century editor saw his job as that of collecting the material of his reporters and correspondents and, having validated the material and given it salience by placing it in the columns of his paper, would in addition proffer his readers intellectual guidance and political observation. He held onto his smaller audiences by satisfying their needs as citizens while entertaining them to encourage their loyalty. The modern newspaper is essentially reaching out towards the *television* audience, a demographically defined audience, paid for by advertisers, which requires the kind of detail that turns into spectacle or reveals the panorama of events lying behind the reports that have already reached the audience in aural and/or visual terms.

One short Foreign Desk report that eventually filled a column of the *Post* with routine information on world events was derived from the equivalent of twenty-seven columns of wire service copy, without any extra material sent in by the *Post's* own reporters. What the reader perceived to be an interesting comparative presentation of foreign events was in reality the product of scores of wire service personnel strung across the globe who had diligently filed mounds of copy in the course of several days. Each reporter involved had been trained to his task over the course of years, each culled his copy from a variety of local sources, many acquired after years of residence and careful nurturing. The processing of the sources and of the product was the summation of an extremely long series of activites. The final result, as far as the reader was concerned, was a column that was readable within ninety seconds and that purported to be the *Post's* summation of the state of the globe. There was no author but an enormous panoply of news technology between events and text.

Another model for a collective news event is a Presidential election, with all its special significance for readers of the *Washington Post*. In a story of this kind the *Post* has to function as a provider of *local* news throughout the country, since the Washington-based staff and the associates of every congressman are anxious to know as many details as possible of the progress of the election in their home districts. The *Post* circulates among a primary audience situated in three different electoral districts—the District of Columbia, Maryland, and Virginia—all of which have dozens of their own local contests. The Presidential election of 1976 necessitated a special rearrangement of the *Post's* routines: the National and Metro Desks operated as normal, with the addition of special Charts, Decision, and News Desks, plus a variety of special additional groups of aides, copy runners, dictationists, wire room attendants, return-takers, accountants, and operators. Altogether, several hundred normal and extra staff were involved across the country, all under instruction to telephone in key pieces of information to "takers," each of whom had a complex distribution list within the newspaper. Information had to go to correspondents, for comment and analysis, but also to chart writers, who collated and compiled information from diverse sources into a highly diversified machinery of internal-copy decision making.

A third and even more potent illustration of the trend towards the collectivization of news writing was the coverage of the Hanafi siege, which broke out on March 9, 1977, on the very doorstep of the *Post* itself, in Washington. It was a local, national, and world story exploding beneath the paper's feet. Small bands of gunmen had invaded three buildings in quick succession, taking a total of one hundred hostages. A radio reporter died and a councilman was wounded. The hostages were ill-treated and threatened with a variety of weapons. The events were spaced over three days and became the major preoccupation of almost the entire newspaper for that time. The importance of the story in terms of the functioning of the process of reporting is that it fitted none of the obvious or predictable categories, nor any of the normal procedures. The information and expertise that it required cut across all departmental divisions and newspaper sections. And yet, in many ways, it was a typical major news story of the era.

The gunmen involved were all members of a black religious sect, the Hanafi Muslims, the family of whose leader had been killed four years before in a well-reported Washington mass murder. Members of a rival black Muslim sect had been convicted for these killings, leaving Khaliss, the Hanafi leader, still unsatisfied and intent upon revenge. The sect's headquarters became an armed camp, and the demands made on March 9, when the gunmen moved into three positions (the District Building near the White House, an Islamic mosque in the embassy district, and the office of the Jewish representative organization, the B'nai B'rith), consisted of handing over the convicted Muslims, the television transmission of a life of Muhammed, the repayment of a fine imposed upon Khaliss for disrupting the previous trial, and the summoning of the Arab ambassadors to a meeting. The siege itself lasted for forty hours and ended when the ambassadors of Egypt, Iran, and Pakistan entered the B'nai B'rith building and persuaded Khaliss to hand over all of the hostages and surrender.

The news reached the newsroom at midday, and the process of dispatching reporters to the various locations involved in the story began. By late afternoon there were twenty-eight reporters at work on the story. Three were at the B'nai B'rith, three at police headquarters and at the special police command center that had been set up, two at the District Building and two at the Islamic center. Almost as soon as the news came in, two were dispatched to find Israeli Prime Minister Itzhak Rabin, who happened to be in Washington at the time. Two were stationed at the Hanafi headquarters, two at the Foundry Methodist Church (where relations of the hostages were gathering); one at the Washington Hospital Center, where an injured councilman had been taken, and one at George Washington University Hospital (near the B'nai B'rith, where shooting had taken place). One was sent to the Gramercy Inn (because he had noticed that Justice Department officials were gathering there and checked himself in as a guest); one to the Superior Court (where special protective precautions were being taken); and one moved around the city on a motorcycle to gather reactions from the public and to observe the effect of the siege on traffic. Meanwhile, seven reporters remained in the newsroom, attempting to gain contact with the sect members by telephoning into the captured buildings, checking on special arrangements being made by government organizations, making contact with Jewish leaders, researching the background of the sect, and collecting details of disruption in city life.

In addition, a writing team within the paper had been hastily recruited to start the task of processing the flood of incoming material. All those working outside the building were under instruction to telephone in every half hour and dictate a report. Three television sets brought in additional information from the local television reporting teams. Twelve people operated as dictationists (some regulars, some snatched from other departments). All the telephoned reports went on six-ply paper to a single editor who sent the material to the various units at work. Five separate stories were designated—the main story, the three siege buildings, and the Hanafi sect—each with two writers who received all relevant incoming reportage. The National reporters settled down to write the main story in a room some distance from the central bustle, with a third of them scanning all memos in search of the main facts they could use and keeping an eye on the television sets. Although extra editors were at work on the story, the basic editing routine followed normal lines, with copy passing through the hands of an assignment editor and the the copy desk, for fine editing and typesetting instructions, headlines, and picture captions. Copies went on to coordinating editors at the Metro Desk, the News Desk, and the executive editor, who were gradually working out the newspaper's policy toward the placing and length of the siege coverage. In addition to the hard news of the story, the Style section of the *Post* produced accounts of the television coverage and of a movie that the sect wanted withdrawn. There were thus 60 people directly involved, including editors and reporters and 8 senior personnel. The grand total of those employed by this one newspaper for collecting material for this one story reached nearly 100: 28 reporters, 21 writers, 35 editors, 12 dictationists.

The stories produced in the first day of coverage reached 350 column inches, or nearly 100,000 characters. Eleven separate stories appeared in the paper. Despite the long hours that the story took, the pieces of copy were all completed during the period between 6:30 and 9:00 p.m. Extensive changes had to be made constantly during the course of writing and editing as fresh material came in. The flow of incoming memoranda itself entailed a large volume of text—fifteen outside reporters filing every thirty minutes for six hours provided ninety full pages, equal to the total volume of text published in the paper in the first edition of the siege. A vast quantity of wire service material came in, as well as public-relations handouts from many of the organizations involved. All memos and handouts went to at least six destinations within the reporting complex and up and down the editorial hierarchy. (This, of course, was not the only story of the day—President Carter gave a press conference, which was only one of several other important simultaneous events).

In the late city edition half of all the stories were altered, although little else changed in the editions that followed. The street reporters were changed before midnight, and editorial staff were kept on throughout the night, in spells. In the morning the reporters in the street locations were changed again and increased in number. By mid-morning ten editors were processing incoming material. Copy continued coming into the paper until 3:30 A.M. the following (i.e., third) day.

The line of decision making at the News Desk followed a different set of routines. It was here that dispositions had to be made for the newspaper as a whole, including the big Carter story and other events. It was obvious at 11 A.M. when the siege story started up that a large amount of space would be required, and before midday the production department was told to provide for six extra columns and three open pages in the main news section. The makeup section was able to persuade advertising to drop a page of paid advertisements. The paper had to be laid out all over again, replacing the pattern that had been prepared the night before for the pre-booked advertising material. It turned out that an increase in the overall size of the paper was not necessary because a proportion of the booked advertising was of a nonurgent nature and could be delayed. However, the news of the siege started growing when the second and third locations were seized, and it was decided to meet the extra requirement by deliberately curtailing non-Hanafi stories and advancing the deadline for all non-Hanafi material one hour to 6:30 P.M. The composing room thus had to be warned that there would be an abnormally high volume of material coming in both rather early and very late. The press-run was also increased by 300,000 to 630,000.

One important bottleneck in this procedure was the dummying process, which took a great deal longer than with a normal edition. The vital decision on which non-Hanafi stories were to appear on page one had to precede the activity of dummying most of the rest of the paper. All the work of headline writing, art work, and the ordering of type had to await this decision, which had to be taken after consultation at high levels of the editorial hierarchy. Each time the Hanafi story grew or altered during the afternoon, the organization of the story within the paper changed considerably, and dummying the various pages had to be deferred.

The composing room managed the crush more easily, although the constant and late redummying of pages caused page composition delays. Although dummying of parts of the paper continued a full two hours later than normal, composing managed to complete its work just after 10, barely a quarter of an hour after the time it was due. An hour before the first edition closed in the composing room, work had started on the second edition, and three columns of type were reprocessed for the Late City. All the inside pages that dealt with the Hanafi had to be redummied, and non-Hanafi material was restricted to a bare minimum of remaking. This edition closed twelve minutes after midnight. In later editions there was a diminishing quantity of alteration. At 12:45 P.M. the last copy reached the composing room for twenty pages to be remade for the first replate. The last copy reached composing at 2:25 A.M. for thirteen pages for the next edition and just two more remakes for the final edition, which reached the composing room at 3:36. The pressrun finished at 4:30, at which point work on the next day's coverage and on planning the shape of the paper was well underway. A conference had been held at 2 A.M. where it was decided to ask for twelve extra columns and two open pages. Hanafi coverage, in fact, eventually filled eight inside pages and forced national and foreign news to fill space vacated by the Metro section.

The second day differed from the first in that the story itself, while generating plenty of material, did not change in nature or extent. Constant revision in the dummies caused a great deal of delay, but this was the result of rewriting, rather than dramatic switches of focus; and relatively little had to be changed between editions. However, it was evident that another night of waiting was in store when the final edition went through the composing room. The edition was finished at 4:30 A.M. again because of the extra 30,000 copies ordered.

However, it was at 2 A.M. when the news came through that the siege had ended, soon after the first replate had passed into the composing room. What had been merely a set of revisions the previous night suddenly turned into a major new edition. All the front page material was suddenly out-of-date. The late news also involved rewriting a number of Hanafi-related stories. The problem was that the pressrun, which was underway, might well be over before all the work of redummying, rewriting, and recomposing was finished. Production agreed to stop the presses to await new plates at 2:42 A.M. The plates arrived at 3:13— enough to convey the news of the collapse of the siege. By 3:23 nine more pages had left the newsroom, the last one clearing composing ten minutes later. The last new plate reached the cylinders at 3:49. An extra replate had to take place to correct a faulty headline, and that reached the press at 4:13. The edition ended at 5:04 in the morning. One quarter of the entire edition—159,000 copies in all—contained the news of the lifting of the siege, and 100,000 copies contained complete sets of altered pages. By the next day the Hanafi siege was down to six extra columns, six inside pages, and five different stories on page one. No abnormalities occurred in the production process at all.

What hardware manufacturers have to do with such descriptive material of the internal operations of a newspaper is to incorporate it within a computer system structure. They must register its overt and implicit flow and ensure that the equipment they supply is able to comprehend the given pattern and adapt to it. In the case of the *Washington Post* that is an extremely difficult thing to do. The users of the new system are apt to say that the pattern of relationships and information flow to which the resulting equipment locks them is the result of the technology, while in fact the technology is a result of an effort to embrace the pattern of their activities.

The Hanafi siege was a local story and an international one; it played upon racial tensions, the Middle East crisis, law and order, public-police relations, the politics of theater. There was considerable interest, no doubt, in the editorials and comment that the event evoked, but the readers' attention could be held with the information alone, which affected them physically (traffic, danger, etc.) as well as intellectually and emotionally. This information had to be culled from countless sources and, in theory at least, the number of reporter-hours that might have been spent on the affair could have been doubled or tripled—with the only cutoff point being the moment at which reader interest would begin to drop off.

The newspaper has always been a collective information system. The anonymity that was an essential part of the journalist's code in many societies in the nineteenth century was part of the newspaper's attempt to assert its own collective validity, its integrity as an information mechanism. Today there is an inevitable tension between our concept of the journalist as a species of *author* (whose identity is a necessary part of the process of validating the newspaper's content) and the diminishing originality of his enterprise. As we have just seen, the "writers" of the finished story at the *Post* were part of an industrial process. If they had been using vdt's for their work, they would have been printers as well as writers. They based their work upon the research of an army of reporters, wire services, memo takers, and interim compilers; they passed their work into an editorial process that functioned bureaucratically, managerially. The newspaper has industrialized the information-gathering process just as the late medieval scriptoria industrialized the business of manuscript copying. Each stage was broken down into its component actions and placed in the hands of a group of specialists. This reorganization of human processes reflected in the mechanical organization of a large reporting project like the Hanafi siege shows how computerization will enhance and develop further the *historic* tendency within the industry for reporting to become collective, hierarchical, and industrialized.

At the end of the process, however, we may well ask ourselves, where has the *author* gone? When reporters scan the contents of their newspaper morgues for the data with which to compile their new material and when they feed into their computers word pictures of the world from the daily flow of wire service and other (collective) information sources, is it any longer right to think of them as *writers?* Should we have thought of them as writers in the first place? Perhaps much of what has been thought to be private single-handed authorship has in reality been the routine reformulation of material gathered from reality by collective processes? In other words, the process of computerization is bringing out various aspects of modern journalism that have long been implicit but not consciously realized.

The work of creating the specifications for some of the larger newspaper systems have helped to demonstrate some general directions that newspaper work is now taking. Above all, the discussion about the preferability of integrated over distributed systems has focused attention on the collective nature of the modern newsroom. The newspaper has had to find new forms of journalism with which to compete with the immediacy of television and with the kind of major stories that have occurred frequently in the era of television—and have even perhaps been brought about partly by television. Terrorism, the large-scale demonstration, modern warfare, have all made a contribution to the development of new techniques in print journalism precisely because they have been so spectacularly covered by electronic journalism and, in a sense, have a special historic relationship with electronic journalism. Television is able to show some of these events live, in color, and in some detail. The politics of the theater has become an essential element in all modern radical activity. Television itself creates a splendid background for such staged traumas as the kidnapping of the Israeli team at the Munich Olympics, the outbreak of street fighting in Beirut, Belfast, Teheran. Newspaper journalism has found new roles for itself after rethinking its whole mode of action in a time when primary events are known to the public long before the newspaper is printed.

Newspaper coverage of a major political spectacle, natural disaster, or war has changed considerably since the year of 1968 when a succession of major news stories of an insurrectionist and military nature forced viewers and also governments to become aware of the new incandescent power of television news. Newspapers now provide far more background to stories, assuming that the facts are known. Moreover, they undertake much more detailed research to create stories on their own initiative, as it were, as a result of "enterprise journalism" and investigative reporting.

One important aspect of the computerization of so many American newspaper operations is that it has altered the relationship between the wire services and the newspapers. In 1975 at the Montreal Olympics UPI made its vdt's available to its Data News subscribers, each subscriber being given a private code to ensure that its material was not readable by others and was being directly transmitted to its own computer. In 1976 UPI repeated the experiment at the political conventions. The AP's DataStream service offered to transmit members' copy on their behalf. The wire services are thus able to use their network and high-speed wires to create new services to link their newspaper clients and members.

The wire services can also now help newspaper editors reduce the overload of incoming material while speeding up the flow of copy overall. No longer dependent on the 66 words per minute of the old machines, UPI and AP can make their copy flow at 1200 words per minute and by attaching different codes to the various items of news, ensure that each story goes to the right editor at the receiving newspaper. With UPI's DemandNews system an editor receives abstracts only, until he signals the information he wants to receive in full; these he can obtain either in his computer direct or on punched tape, or as scannable hard copy.

As we shall see in Part Three, however, new technical developments in the information business will enable the news agencies, far more easily than in the past, to display their material directly before the eyes of the reader—without the mediation of the newspaper and the intercessionary judgments of news editors. The wire service is thus able to play a more directly useful part in the construction of the newspaper as an information system, but it can also branch out on its own, finding its own (admittedly far more specialized) audiences, who may choose to multiply their lines of information and at the same time go directly to primary sources for it.

As newspaper systems become more subtle in their adjustment to the social systems—the newspaper organizations—into which they have been introduced, they begin to alter the whole structure of publishing possibilities. The first generation of newspaper computers tended to straitjacket the whole production process and in so doing drew a certain amount of journalistic hostility, or at least suspicion. The next group of engineers analyzed the operations of the newsroom and production process so minutely that they were able to create, inside the computer architecture, a kind of total duplication of the activities and connections they had observed in operation in "reality." But once the computer was installed in its new home and fitted better into the human organization of the paper, its innate flexibility came into its own and offered the craft of reporting a dramatic expansion of scale and function.

The reporter is now equipped to become a rather different kind of information broker from the past. Many of the routines that necessitated reporters' performing humdrum reprocessing tasks are being or could be technologically eliminated. The newspaper, it is true, has to surrender a certain sovereignty to other intermediaries who have the right of direct input to its computer, but it has more of an opportunity to review incoming materials and choose between the stories offered. The newspaper will probably be able to reduce the number of reporters or editor-hours used on a range of traditional copy-editing tasks and use the time to collect more original material or perform more thorough research. As we saw earlier, the techniques of the newspaper librarian begin to overlap with those of the reporter, whose task becomes increasingly that of a collator and comparer of versions—more of a scribal function, in some ways. The more skilled the reporter the more of a researcher he becomes, a human scanner of data bases, an intermediary between the enormous and ever growing store of available knowledge and the reader.

Older journalists are probably going to be more bewildered than previous generations as they watch a new cohort of reporters emerge in the 1980's. The new journalist will be either a technician of entertainment-news or a specialist with a loyalty to his subject resembling that of an academic rather than a spot-news reporter. A great division seems inevitable between these two groups: the one catering to a kind of information helotry, for whom the right to know has been subtly transmuted into the right to be entertained; the other catering to an enlarged class of well-informed people who have themselves acquired the ability to evaluate and handle sources and compare different versions of the same event. The reader himself is acquiring some of the expertise of the reporter (and editor), which will be necessary in an age in which the reader makes more of the choices as to what knowledge he wishes to receive.

The code of objectivity, with which we began this exploration, is really too slight to take the measure of the qualitative change that seems to be occurring. Historically it was designed to be a kind of guarantee for the reader against being duped. In the context of a news-gathering apparatus that is far more sophisticated than ever before, it is the collective judgment and knowledge and honesty of the gatherers that is the only guarantee, rather than any specific technique or quality of character. Yet with the growth of knowledge comes decreasing certainty. The confidence that went with objectivity must give way to the insecurity that comes from knowing that all is relative.

6. PRINTING UNIONS & TECHNOLOGICAL CHANGE

Printing is the oldest of the industrial processes. It has confronted technical change on a major scale roughly once a century since the Renaissance, when moving type was first introduced in Europe. What makes the computerization of print so thoroughly different from the previous shifts from one set of techniques and machines to the next is that it seems to threaten the very existence of several of the crafts of printing. Of course, not even in newspapers, where the authors themselves (i.e., the journalists) are taking over part of the job of typesetting, will all of the graphical skills disappear. There will always be a need for such skills in newspaper production, but on a drastically smaller scale than in the last century or so. As country after country moves towards the introduction of new technology, we read of more dramatic and often prolonged disputes, strikes, shutdowns, and lockouts. It is easy to gain the impression that the newspaper is engaged in some kind of ultimate showdown, which must end in the disappearance either of whole companies or of their printing staffs.

It is extremely difficult to assess the impact of the new technology upon total employment. Clearly, there is a dwindling requirement for traditional typesetters, and modern offset presses require far fewer operators and machine minders. However, the total number of maintenance workers will inevitably increase with the expanded investment in equipment. The expansion in the roles of the newspaper and in the varieties of advertising and other content will mean, in all probability, an increase in the number of service and distribution workers. As we shall see in later chapters, a completely new set of new media is now being created, which, although they require very few distribution and administrative personnel as paper-bound information systems do, will greatly increase the number of "keyboard" workers, perhaps on a scale sufficient in time to refill the membership ranks of the typesetting unions. All of the new electronic text systems (now generally known by the generic name "videotex") are highly labor-intensive in typesetting. Although much of their text work can be set by journalists, secretaries, and others involved in the process of information collection, there will remain a great deal of specialist work, which would grow over the years, that would really benefit from the traditional skills of typographical work. It is therefore impossible to foresee whether global employment in the newspaper and contiguous industries is declining in the 1980's, or whether a temporary decline, as computerization takes place within the newspaper as such, will be followed by an upward climb thereafter, as the new text media expand. In the short run, nonetheless, the members of an ancient craft are facing an agonizing process of group attrition in many countries of the world.

What is really at issue is whether *all* those engaged in the industry during this period of its total reshaping are collectively capable of the imaginative leap necessary from the temporary securities of the present to the rearrangements of roles and functions of the future. The advent of the computer and the vdt makes possible a wholly new place for print in civilization, but only after a terribly difficult physical transition. The question is first, whether management will merely exploit the situation now arising and grab a once-and-for-all improvement in the return on their capital and second, how print workers and their unions will use their power to control and develop the working environment of the next generation. The "how" of the transition is as crucial as the "where" of the destination—for both sides of the industry. The trouble is that the last major round of technical change, that which took place at the end of the last century, is to a great extent still visible in the daily practices of the newspaper and printing worlds, in the attitudes and in the demarcations in the distribution of status. That is why we must look at some of the implications of the present transformation in the light of the previous one.

On May 2, 1900, the fiftieth anniversary of its founding and the five hundredth birthday of Gutenberg, the New York Typographical Union Local No. 6 arranged the first exhibition of printing equipment in the

United States. By joint resolution of both houses of Congress the original printing press of Benjamin Franklin had been removed from the Smithsonian and transported to New York. The chief manufacturers of printing equipment, as well as book and newspaper publishers, led the list of thirteen full pages of exhibitors. The union local (known throughout its history as Big Six) published its own daily newspaper to mark the occasion. Crowds swarmed over the 40,000 square feet of exhibition space rented at the junction of the Lexington Avenue and Forty-third Street, examining the very newest labor-saving devices of the industry—gleaming Mergenthalers and Intertypes, whose introduction only a decade before had been responsible for the displacement of 36,000 skilled compositors.[1] For every machine that the employers had purchased, two compositors had been thrown out of work. But the power of the International Typographical Union, and in particular that of Big Six (founded in 1850, two years before the union itself), had ensured that an eight-hour day was imposed on the majority of employers together with a program of minimum wages and maximum output per man per day. After the depression of 1893–94 the economy had picked up rapidly, and the printing industry had swirled into a mighty vortex of growth. The amount of advertising carried by the newspaper multiplied three and a half times between 1892 and 1914, and the number of newspapers published across the nation rose from 1650 to 2250 in the same period. By 1900 the total number of typesetters employed was the same as it had been before the Linotype machine had come into use, multiplying up to ten times the productivity of the old hand typesetters.

The ITU is the oldest national organizer of American labor (although New York printers had been organized since the Revolution), and no other union managed so quickly and so determinedly to wrest from management so much of its authority over those employed. The union, not the management, decided whether piecework or time payment was to be offered, how the work was to be handed out during the day to the various groups of workers, how many trainees were to be admitted to each chapel. But even while New York Governor Theodore Roosevelt was inspecting the priceless printed documents and historical treasurers at the Grand Central Palace, Big Six was in the midst of a struggle against the publishers of the *New York Sun*, which had begun publishing the previous August and continued until March, 1902. The local spent thirty-one months in bringing pressure—ultimately successful—against the employment of a team of compositors who had been imported by management from Philadelphia in answer to a Help Wanted advertisement. Big Six would not permit nonunion labor to enter its jurisdiction, and at the end of the fight management, $300,000 poorer, agreed to pay the union's rates to all workers, and the union agreed to admit the Philadelphians to its ranks. No nonunion labor would be permitted henceforth.

At the turn of the century the market for all forms of printed material was growing much faster than the productivity of printing workers, and the union's determination to control the new machinery led to a relatively peaceful acceptance of new technology by workers who, at that moment, had ceased to feel fundamentally threatened by it. In fact, because of it they experienced higher wages, shorter hours, and better physical conditions. The experiences of the eighties and nineties of the last century have entered the souls of all trade unions in the printing industry, and not only in America; the arrival of the Linotype machine and its attendant traumas is still exercising its influence over labor relations and attitudes to technological change in journalism all over the world.[2]

In many cases, both employers and printers are descendants of the men who fought out the problems of technological innovation nearly a century ago. The existing patterns of employment, now under pressure, are those that emerged as a result of the introduction of fast presses and automatic typesetting in an industry run for a mass market and financed through display advertising. Now, as then, dozens of different kinds of new equipment are being offered to publishers and printers who hesitate to buy one brand before making sure that something else isn't just about to arrive on the market capable of doing the same work faster.

Thus, the time was right for the development of automatic typesetting in the late 1800's, when newspaper publishers were benefiting from both a rapid cheapening of newsprint (down from 12 cents per pound in 1872 to 6 cents in 1882 and 3 cents in 1892) and a rapid increase in the market for the product, yet found their entire production held back because of the slowness with which type was being set. At the time of the Civil War they actually offered a series of rewards adding up to half a million dollars to anyone who could save a quarter or more of the work of hand-setting. By the end of the century there were 1500 registered patents for typesetting gadgetry, and a hundred different machines were actually made, although only a handful ever went into serious production.

The Empire Composing Machine was the first of these, appearing under the Burr imprint in 1872. It could work five times faster than the 800 ems per hour achieved by the fastest hand-setters, but it needed two men to work it, with a third to redistribute the type afterwards. Even when improved this model sold only a couple of hundred. Ten years later came the Thorne Simplex One-Man Typesetter, although this did require a second man to do the work of justifying the lines of type. The Thorne, too, managed to sell only a few hundred. The Paige machine, which Mark Twain said could do the work of six men except drink, swear, and go out on strike, cost a fortune, consisted of nearly 20,000 moving parts, and sent its owners into bankruptcy.

Ottmar Mergenthaler, a German immigrant who had settled in Baltimore, solved the remaining problems while searching for a quite different kind of machine. He was commissioned to produce a typewriter that would make automatic copies of legal transcripts, and his invention was very well publicized from the start. He worked on an utterly different principle from his competitors and tried not to cast type so much as assemble lines of matrices from which type could be cast. With the help of a typographer from Milwaukee he found a way to make cheap brass matrices that would redistribute themselves as soon as they had performed their task. A current of air sent the matrices into position in line, and it was this that gave the first machine its name of the Blower, although the name Linotype was coined by the *New York Tribune* editor who watched the first demonstration in 1886.[3]

Despite its success the machine was sold in very small numbers in the early years as Mergenthaler improved the design, section by section, and fought a bitter lawsuit against an early rival over patent rights. Within a decade, however, Mergenthaler was outselling all rival machines by eight times, although the Monotype Machine, invented just a year after the Linotype, had several advantages that kept it permanently in business. The Monotype's keyboard produced a paper tape, which was then used to drive the typesetting device; the machine was greatly favored by publishers who had to set a large number of charts and tables and had the great advantage of being correctable as it went along, rather than only at the end of a line.

Once the typographical workers had established their jurisdiction over the new machinery, the basic problems of innovation had been solved. Their claim did not arise primarily out of a dislike of unfamiliar machinery, nor even the temporary displacement of labor that this entailed. What they and all printers for five centuries have in effect achieved is complete group control over the functions of presswork and setting type, long before these tasks multiplied into a series of specialized mechanical skills. The seventeenth-century Anglo-Dutch printer, Joseph Moxon, has left us with a detailed account of the organization of printing in his time, including ten pages of description of "Ancient Customs," all clear evidence of the tightness and exclusivity of the craft of printing that had already prevailed for centuries before his time.[4] Indeed, the Stationers'

Company, which was given a state monopoly over the whole printing industry in the sixteenth century, had descended from a company of scriveners who had enjoyed comparable privileges even before the invention of moveable type. Print workers have always seen themselves as the aristocracy of skilled workers, and their wages have generally confirmed this sense of superiority, which is expressed in their collective authority over an important industry. "The Chappel cannot Err," writes Moxon, repeating an old printers' saw, "[and] when any Controversie is thus decided, it always ends in the Good of the Chappel."[5]

Despite their solidarity, printing workers have long felt a keen sense of the internal demarcations of skills within their industry. They have shared out the various specialisms among themselves and have attached to them degrees of skill and exclusiveness. Even Moxon noted that "Insomuch that for the more easie managing of Typographie, the Operators have found it necessary to devide it into several Trades, each of which (in the strictest sense) stand no nearer related to Typographie, than Carpentry or Masonry, etc. are to Architecture."[6] Some of the techniques well established in the seventeenth century have enjoyed a remarkable continuity, as has the pattern of unilateral self-regulation, which has ultimately descended from the method of royal privilege conferred upon a self-organizing group of workers whose hold over their circumstances of employment was strengthened through their democratic methods of governance.

The ideal that lay beneath this ancient and very powerful urge towards guild organization and, later, to trade unionism among print workers was the ideal of maintaining a stable social framework in which to work. Every man was supposed to pursue his trade as a right, and in former times both wages and prices in this and comparable trades were fixed by law. Thus the state and the workers' fraternity jointly controlled the flow of labor to correspond with demand at any moment. So firmly was this tradition established that it has survived on both sides of the Atlantic through a century of laissez-faire and private-enterprise capitalism—though more strongly in parts of Europe than in the United States.

Print workers, by the nature of their craft, were the first group of workers to be completely literate, and their organization into trade unions came earlier than for any other group of skilled workers. (We know that a Scale of Prices for piecework was fixed in London in 1785, and the hopelessly complicated Scale that persists today in the national press of Britain is a direct descendant of it). Printers imposed rules against the employment of children—and women, in certain categories of work; they fixed maximum hours and the numbers of apprentices to be admitted to any craft. In 1786 in London the proprietor of the newly founded *Times* had an advertisement rejected by the printers at the *Daily Advertiser* because he was attempting to hire apprentices beyond their stipulated limits.

Even the restrictive practices of the twentieth century are of ancient lineage. For instance, when printing plates or stereotypes were first introduced, advertising agencies started to cast their own material and provide the newspaper with advertisements in the form of an already made "mat," or block. It became quickly established that this practice, which would deprive print workers at a particular paper of work that would otherwise be theirs, would be subject to special payment known as "fat." In the United States this work is still actually set in type in certain newspapers by typesetters and then thrown away—sometimes long after the actual advertisement has appeared in the paper. The system was designed to maintain the level of work represented by a given enterprise unit within the printing industry. The printing workers refused to give up their jurisdiction over this work, feeling they had no reason to lose employment merely because the advertiser had found it convenient to provide his material in mat form. The survival of such practices has greatly complicated negotiations over the introduction of new technology in many newspapers and was an important issue at stake in the major disputes at the *Washington Post* in the early 1970's.

Another source of conflict at the present time that has its roots in the transition to new machinery a century ago is the series of relationships hallowed by time between groups of skilled and unskilled workers in the newspaper industry. When the first web-fed presses were introduced (a decade or so before Mergenthaler's Linotype), they replaced machines that had for many decades depended upon unskilled "feeders," who thrust sheets of paper into the machines. Gradually a series of unskilled grades of machine minders entered the business of newspaper production, working under the supervision of a skilled mechanic. The other processes of the newspaper, typesetting in particular, were carried out by men with traditional and high levels of skill, who protested against press work being put into the hands of men who had not been apprenticed to the skilled printing trade or awarded to the new semiprofessionalized unskilled grades.

In England the printers succeeded in their demand that the supervisors in the pressroom be members of their craft (though in the United States they failed to secure this), and in the course of time the pressroom became the scene of a permanent tension between unskilled process workers (in one union) and skilled supervisors (in another). The demarcation became a matter of historical pride, and any attempt today to make drastic alterations in the system of printing newspapers scratches these ancient sores. In America, too, a division exists between different unions organizing these different wings of the industry, although the level of union organization is not nearly as high as in Britain and the other countries of Europe. In the course of time the arrival of new equipment in London newspapers brought about a number of splits within the skilled union, and a series of specialist crafts went off to organize their wage bargaining in separate units. This process has occurred also in the United States, though in the last quarter century several of these not-so-ancient divisions have been mended. In England in 1945 there existed among the skilled grades within the national (i.e., "Fleet Street") newspapers the London Society of Compositors, the Printing Machine Managers Trade Society, the Typographical Association, the National Union of Press Telegraphists, the Association of Correctors of the Press, the National Association of Electrotypers and Stereotypers, and the Amalgamated Society of Lithographic Printers. All of these are now contained in the NGA (National Graphical Association), after a series of mergers took place in the 1960's, but there are at least fifteen other unions representing other skilled and unskilled occupations in Fleet Street, most of whom have now merged into two large unions. All of them bear witness to the processes that the new technology of the last hundred years has brought into the business of newspaper printing and distribution.

A very similar process of progressive fragmentation under the impact of new technology took place in the United States. The International Typographical Union, which contained most of the skilled grades of printing workers in the 1880's, lost a group as early as 1886 to the International Printing Pressmen and Assistants Union; then the engravers left at the turn of the century to form the International Photo-Engravers Union,[7] and also the International Stereotypers and Electrotypers Union. By the late 1950's there were fourteen clearly demarcated unions in the U.S. newspaper industry, including the Newspaper Guild, which organizes the journalists (as well as clerical, custodial, and other groups). Many of these started merging in the 1960's, and more mergers are planned as the present generation of new equipment sweeps away the technological basis of traditional divisions.

Entry into the printing trades tends to be influenced by ties of family and friendship in many countries, and this means that young people applying to become apprentices are already familiar with the customs and social attitudes belonging to the particular craft they intend to learn.

Many fathers bring their sons directly into the industry before they have acquired a knowledge of the world of work in general, and the system means that patterns of change occurring in other industries have relatively little spillover into newspapers. Indeed, it has been noticed that much of the opposition to the new computerized equipment stems from fathers who are trying "to do something for their sons" and guarantee them a dignified and well-paid career. The feeling is paralleled among the publishers of newspapers.

Printing is one of the industries in which training has remained in the form of apprentices, usually of rather long duration. It can take a decade or more, even today, for a New York apprentice to become a fully recognized journeyman, and the unions insist on four to five years of continuous instruction at the workbench, a process through which attitudes as well as physical skills are inculcated. The whole tradition of the printers is transmitted through the apprenticeship system, which is often associated with "rites de passage" and rituals alarming to outsiders. Strange and painful initiation ceremonies persist among printers in many countries and help to reinforce the belief or feeling that the jobs of those initiated have become a form of property, earned by dint of apprenticeship and acceptance by colleagues. The employer does not have the right to create or abolish jobs, only to create and change work. The jobs themselves have passed into the ownership of the union, wherever trade unionism has become firmly entrenched in the newspaper business. The print worker, as described in one American study,[8] considers himself as somewhere between the working class and middle class, and this self-perception of separateness influences the social as well as the working life of the printer. He tends to associate with other printers during his spare hours, a custom reinforced by the large amount of nighttime work they must do. In the great printing cities—London, Amsterdam, Frankfurt, New York, Vienna—there are pubs and clubs frequented almost entirely by printers, a fringe social world in which gossip about the state of the industry passes rapidly from person to person and group to group. The solidarity bred at work and leisure has helped to keep print workers conscious of their heritage of high wages and job security.

All forms of computerized technology threaten printers with the diminution of jobs and therefore, however strong their organization, with the inability to pass on a valuable property-right to sons, nephews, and other family connections. They are threatened with the reduction in skills necessary for remaining jobs, which is a blow to their pride as a group and as individuals who have invested a high proportion of their lives in obtaining the right as well as the skill necessary to perform the job. They are threatened too with the loss of their collective jurisdiction over type-setting, which is in large part being handed over to reporters and editors in modernized newsrooms in North America and elsewhere.

Technical change has brought about occupational schisms and re-joinings since the middle of the last century, but the acrimonious nature of relationships between unions is likely to increase, if anything, as the real technical basis of their separation declines and the crafts are left with job property-rights rather than skills as their main surviving bargaining weapons. The "family tree" in Figure 8 shows how just one of the British printing craft unions has evolved, painfully absorbing the traditions and exclusivities of dozens of defunct occupations. Wherever their power is established over an industry, print workers are going through a period of instransigence in many societies—Britain, France, and America conspicuous among them. Today the nonskilled tend to resent the separateness of the skilled, and both are wary of accepting the word of employers who have so frequently cried doom since 1960 while their profits have risen and much of the financial disaster they have predicted has failed to materialize. They are wary, too, of being blamed for newspaper failures in a period when several other factors as important as manning and wage levels are at least equally responsible for the financial and corporate problems of the industry.

One British study of industrial relations in the national newspaper industry has concluded that a system that amounts to "sub-contracting" has evolved between publishers and unions, comparable to employment systems in certain British and American ports, for example.[9] Here, in practice, managements exercise "little or no executive control in the production and maintenance departments." Middle management has shrunk to a technical role only, its other functions having passed to the chapels of the various unions. The publishers have thus come to purchase "effort" or "tasks" from different groups of workers, who proceed to undertake the work of hiring, function allocation, discipline, and rotation among themselves. A similar phenomenon has been noted in many American newspapers, though the multiplicity of forms of organization and the predominance until recently of family ownership has tended to conceal the principle hidden beneath the decades of accumulating negotiation.

This system has spread throughout the publishing and machine departments of newspapers, as groups of workers attempt to protect themselves from the effects of what amounts to casual employment. Negotiations must take place whenever management wishes to alter any of the working arrangements or production schedules. Although all chapels and managements conduct comprehensive negotiations, these are subject to alteration whenever there is a change in circumstance, which can be very often. Thus the industry has become subject to repeated and detailed haggling, and negotiations are made more complicated because of the backlog of past "comprehensive agreements" that have to be knitted into a maze of microsystems of work and principles of payment worked out to suit previous circumstances. However, it is the unions who decide the *unit* of work covered by a negotiation, and it has been in the interests of each group of workers to multiply the number of units and therefore increase the degree of job security conferred by each new agreement. Minor areas of jurisdiction multiply. Management has slowly ebbed away from the newspaper plants. In the United States renegotiations take place at the end of a formal contract of work, which normally lasts two years, and in the intervening period disputes rarely break out. But the underlying principles are remarkably similar, and complex pieces of microjurisdiction pile up for resolution at the end of contracts.

To the outside observer the labor relations of the newspaper industry in many countries can appear to be chaotic, not to say anarchic. From inside, however, they appear highly organized and consist of a vast pile of precisely even pedantically detailed enactments, conventions, and agreements over rates of pay and compensation for variations in the conditions envisaged by previous agreements. As one British former editor puts it,[10] it is circumstances rather than men who break agreements in the newspaper business, but it is in the interests of the many-layered system of worker representation to exploit changing circumstances and in the interests of employers, very frequently, to change the circumstances in which the work is being done. Newspaper publishers suffer from the fact that they are dependent on the workers from a particular area. They are not free, as other industrialists are, to move their plant to a more agreeable city if they find they cannot live happily with the employees available in the area around them. As a result, they have attempted quite often in the course of history to bypass uncongenial groups of workers or uncongenial circumstances by introducing machinery that reduces their dependence on them. The highly legalistic nature of newspaper labor relations is partly the result of well-organized sections of the work force insisting on jurisdictional agreements that provide inalienable rights over certain areas of work for certain groups of workers. When, for instance, in the late 1940's early forms of photocomposition seemed about to arrive on the scene, the vice-president of the ITU proposed a merger with the lithographers' union because he saw the immediate impact of the new techniques in terms of jurisdictional prob-

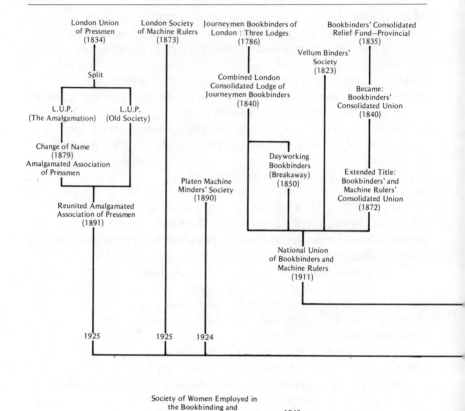

Figure 8   SOGAT family tree. The title of SOGAT originates from the 1966 merger with NATSOPA and was retained by the NUPBPW after the 'divorce' in 1970. A further merger took place in 1975 when the Scottish Graphical Association (7000) was absorbed in SOGAT.
Source: *SOGAT Journal*, February 1975.

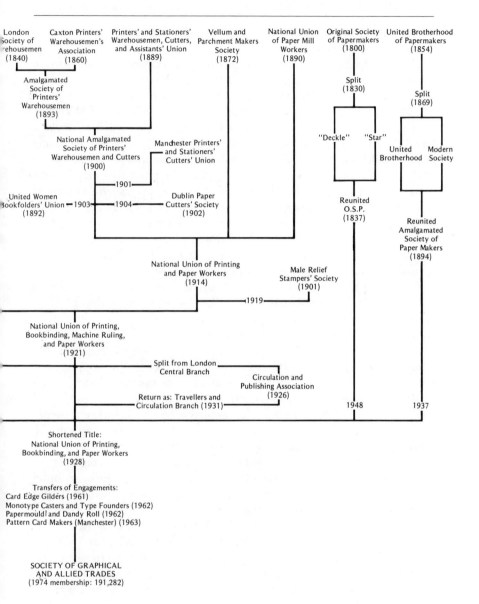

lems between typesetters and lithographers. In this case his colleagues turned the plan down.

The multiplication of demarcations or jurisdictions did not operate entirely to the disadvantage of the publishers, since each union within a plant was always on the lookout for ways in which it might obtain more overall political power vis-à-vis other unions. Publishers tended always to take care to ensure that contracts with important groups of workers had different expiration dates, so that the absence through dispute of one group would not necessarily bring the whole operation to a halt. From 1919 onwards prototypes and experiments in phototypesetting were quite common, and as long as a publisher had his photoengravers still at work, he could find ways to produce his paper on a VariTyper,[11] a TTS (teletypesetter), or, when pushed, on a common typewriter—if a pasted-up version could be photographed and turned into a plate. There were innumerable substitutes for hot metal long before the "offset revolution," ramshackle and unreliable though they often were.

The attitude of the ITU towards all the new techniques, such as teletypesetting and other early tape devices for speeding up the operation of composition equipment, was to cooperate with the introduction of equipment as long as their own men operated it. To this end they fought two major struggles in New York and Chicago against managements who armed themselves with squads of hastily recruited varitypists and fotosetters in order to keep their journals functioning. The Chicago battle was fought also in the teeth of the Taft-Hartley Act of 1947, which had the effect of permitting employers to hire nonunion printers and discriminate against all ITU members determined to carry out the traditional working agreements negotiated by their union. It was an antifeatherbedding law that would have opened the way for employers to offer work on new equipment to members of other unions or to those who were not unionized at all. The National Labor Relations Board would have been free to decide that a given group of workers constituted a separate bargaining unit and lay outside the jurisdiction of the ITU or some other craft union that lay claim to their areas of work, and in these cases the union would have been powerless to assert itself. In particular, the new teletypesetters could have been handed over to members of the Newspaper Guild, which mainly organized reporters, or to the Commercial Telegraphers Union or even the Office Workers Union or groups of nonunion typists. It was mainly to prevent this that the Chicago Typographical Union No. 16 voted to strike in November 1947 against the six daily papers of the city.[12]

At the same time, Big Six in New York was preparing for a city-wide struggle against 14 newspaper publishers as well as against the provisions of the Taft-Hartley Act; this fight was successfully mediated by Theodore Kheel, who was to figure in every industrial dispute in New York newspapers until the great struggle of 1978. The peace formula in New York was based upon reassurances that the established protective arrangements for typographical workers would be continued and that the union's jurisdiction over the new phototypesetting machinery would be accepted. Nonetheless, delicate negotiations dragged on for many months over such problems as the length of the working week, back pay, and the areas of newspaper work to which the varityper would be admitted. A strike of several weeks stopped the papers of New York, and finally only in August was peace restored and a new contract signed. The publishers, however, were forced by events into further pressure for modernized phototypesetting equipment. They had accepted the offset press, and once into "cold type" they were in urgent need of a non-hot-metal typesetting device.

Another threat to the jurisdiction of the ITU arose as a result of the use of the TTS, or teletypesetter, in news and feature agencies. While this type of equipment was acceptable within newspaper organizations when it functioned directly under the supervision of ITU members, it created a number of problems when used in outside offices. The King Features Agency, for example, had started to distribute its syndicated features already punched on tape that could be easily copied and circulated to subscribing publications. In the wire services, tape was being punched by members of the Commercial Telegraphers Union, which was affiliated with the AFL.

A number of disputes erupted around the country when publishers demanded unlimited use of outside tape and typographical staff insisted on limiting its use and on controlling the training and selection of all who used TTS equipment. It had become clear to both sides that a fully trained TTS operator could punch tape at a rate double that which was recognized by the ITU as a standard of competence on Linotype machines—375 lines per hour. The issue of control was further dramatized when the ITU found that taped features were being sent out to newspapers in dispute with its members and then triply complicated when the *Wall Street Journal* asked to negotiate an agreement to cover an electronic device that operated a Linotype keyboard *remotely*. This would have greatly simplified the problems of the *Journal* in producing a national newspaper in several different production locations across the country, all for distribution the same day. Although the publishers were aware of the advantages of being able to play the interests of one union against the other in this jurisdictional minefield, they were on the whole fearful of the repercussions of a dispute between two or three unions over these new techniques. One New York newspaper, the *Tribune*, had already broken ranks and made a separate agreement to have the stock market prices set by tape that was transmitted by wire direct from the Associated Press. The result was a comprehensive agreement giving the ITU jurisdiction over the operation of this entire generation of photo-composing equipment. The contract was signed late in 1955, but already half of the country's newspapers were using TTS equipment and 370 locals of the ITU were bargaining over the introduction of this form of equipment.[13]

The policy of the ITU of establishing complete control over the phasing in and operation of new techniques logically led it into undertaking its own training and even development work. Its early technology agreements all involved agreeing either to train its own members to work the new machines or to permit the employers to find and train substitutes. To keep its members working, therefore, the union had constantly to guarantee a flow of fully competent printers able to set type at speeds agreed to by management. It reduced the length of apprenticeship from six to four years in an effort to ease the inward flow of recruits to the industry, although in the most highly organized areas of the country (such as New York) it has continued to take ten or even twenty or more years for a man to be accepted as a full member of his craft. In 1962 the ITU opened its new headquarters and training center at Colorado Springs and installed one million dollars' worth of new equipment, constantly updating it and adding examples of the latest techniques of typesetting, photogravure, color, paste-up, and photographic techniques. For a long time it was able to stay abreast of developments and occasionally even invent improvements and modifications, to the delight of publishers. When the first Photon 200's came into service, typographical workers were taught to perform the photographic work and the new kinds of keyboard work. In 1957 the *New York Times* was the first to take on this machine, and union officials watched the first batch of men being trained to set display ads with this extremely complicated equipment, terrified that failure to learn the technique quickly on their part might persuade management to demand non-ITU men for future training programs. In this particular case, the Photon remained within the jurisdiction of the ITU.

Important advances were therefore being made jointly by publishers and unions in the field of new techniques, but there were many new problems and fears of new problems arising from the issues of productivity gained by adapting the new equipment. Clearly, tape typesetting had brought about a tremendous speedup in the process of actually setting type, but it increased the amount of maintenance work in newspaper offices because it involved the use of a greatly increased number of machines. It also involved additional work in supervision of machinery and a great deal of capital expenditure. A number of studies proceeded that made it clear that the equipment was of great value in certain limited conditions and could be extremely valuable where a newspaper, such as the *New York Times*, was required to set a large number of news stories in different production locations simultaneously (in the case of the *Times* for its European edition).

TTS and the Photon and Linofilm machines had whetted the appetite of publishers for a revolution in typesetting productivity without satisfying it. Meanwhile, a number of new companies were being encouraged to move into the business of printing machinery that had been a virtual duopoly of the Mergenthaler and Intertype concerns since the 1880's. Now IBM, Fairchild, and RCA all came into the field, bringing with them expertise in photographic and computer operations that had been built up through government development contracts in space and military work. The competition brought about a welter of new projects and models and left the trade unions in a dilemma. Should they continue their normal policy of cooperating with new technology on condition they were given total control over the manner of its introduction? Should they continue to slow down the arrival of new equipment? What other means could be adopted for safeguarding the jobs of their members? Until the computer arrived, all new techniques had been introduced on a rising market for labor, but now there were problems in the newspaper industry arising from the arrival of television, and it was by no means clear that the cheapening of printing methods would continue to lead to an overall increase in jobs.

The 114-day strike that blacked out the whole of the newspaper publishing of New York (nine papers in all) was basically fought to recover union power in the negotiating processes. All ten unions held a common front until the very end of the strike, something very rare in newspaper disputes in America where unions have regularly crossed the picket lines of other groups of workers. The strike secured an agreement for a general and joint expiration date for all union contracts, so that publishers in New York would henceforth be unable to pick up negotiations or pursue struggles with their unions one at a time. The final peace formula was worked out by mayor Wagner, although a public ballot of all printing workers had to be held before it was finally accepted by a majority of employees. The workers secured for themselves a wide array of fringe benefits, compensatory and pension payments, while the publishers achieved the greatly expanded right to use tape setting.

After the strike the weaker newspapers, unable to recover from the extremely costly dispute, never returned to publication as the others did on April 1, 1963. Within a few months the New York Mirror, second-largest circulating newspaper in the United States (800,000 daily and 1,000,000 on Sundays), suddenly announced its closure to its 1400 employees. Owned by the Hearst group, this paper sold its stock and goodwill to its main tabloid daily rival, the News, without ever attempting to reduce its production costs through the introduction of new technology or increase its income by raising its cover price from the very low one of 5 cents. It ascribed its failure entirely to television, which was forcing newspapers to keep the cost of display advertising too low for safety, and the paper's demise sent a chill through the hearts of publishers and printing workers throughout the country.

A double crisis resulted from this catastrophe. On the one hand, New York's printing profession was flooded with unemployed printers with little prospect of employment in the city. Big Six responded by stopping all pensioners' work and banning all incoming printing workers from other cities. Hundreds of unemployed printers were given cards enabling them to gain priority in employment elsewhere in the United States. A new spirit of resistance to new technology swept through the unions. At the same time, the publishers came to the conclusion that newspapers could be kept alive under the new conditions of competition with television only if composing room costs were lowered and productivity increased.[14]

In the early 1960's computers began to make their way into composing rooms, but mainly those of newspapers where unions were not recognized in any case, such as the Los Angeles Times and Oklahoma City Times. These papers announced the successful adoption of the modern techniques and encouraged other publishers to follow suit. In Florida two newspapers belonging to the Perry group brought in computerized typesetting equipment without any form of negotiation with their workers; the seventy typesetters struck, only to see their papers brought out on time every day by the management itself. In Toronto the Globe and Mail, the Daily Star, and the Telegram also went ahead after months of unsuccessful negotiation over the introduction of computer typesetting in July 1964; 900 workers walked out from the typesetting and mail room sections at once, but the newspapers continued to appear as the Newspaper

Guild and craft union members worked alongside management personnel. One of the three papers, the *Telegram*, later said that it had managed to produce editions of 60 and 70 pages with only 120 out of the 200 journeymen normally employed in the composing room. It was clear to all involved in the industry that a fundamental change had taken place. No longer would the policy of accepting new techniques in exchange for jurisdictional recognition work—though the ITU continued to pursue it. The economies obtainable were too tempting to management, and the strike threat, in many places, would no longer be sufficient to protect workers' jobs, still less the overall level of employment in the industry. Many publishers agreed to give their workers "jobs for life," i.e., let total employment drop only through natural attrition, rather than through overt redundancy, as in the case of the San Francisco papers in 1973,[15] but this only threatened the ITU with a gradual diminution of its size and strength across the nation.

Traditionally printers had always sought to limit the numbers admitted to training, seeking security by preserving the "mystery" of their craft and surrounding it with ancient terminology, strange words, and titles. Now they began to realize that it was impossible to hold onto this mystery, since anyone who could wield a brush and a paste pot could learn to lay out strips of type on a dummy and photograph the results. They watched their 500 union locals fall victim to a mosaic of little tragedies all over the country as publishers wrestled with new techniques in a combination of idealistic modernizing, technological machismo, and, often, a lust for union breaking. Total ITU membership has dropped from 114,141 in 1967 to 88,900 in 1977, and with the coming of techniques likely to abolish the past-up stage of newspaper production, this hoped-for plateau is liable to fall by another 20,000.[16] One important stage in the ITU's response to its current problems lies in the merging of several of the craft unions, whose divisions have long been made anachronistic in much of America.

Fairly soon, if current negotiations succeed, there will be three main groupings remaining: the ITU (joined with the Newspaper Guild), the Graphic Artists International (including the lithographers and engravers), and the International Printing and Graphic Communications Union (IPGCU), which includes the pressmen and is likely also to accept the bookbinders and stereotypers. Even while protracted negotiations over various union mergers are underway, members of one group are crossing the picket lines of others. For some this makes mergers seem impossible, for others essential. It is relatively simple for the mailers to merge, as is planned, with the typographical workers but much more difficult, though equally urgent, for the Guild to join with the same group. Reporters and print workers have different ways of life as well as different occupations, but the former, as we have seen, are taking over the functions of typesetters and need to work closely with them through the next stages of technological transition. Already the Guild has found it possible to merge with the truck drivers, so it should not be impossible for further links with blue-collar workers to be forged. The merging of unions and crafts is made all the more logical in an era of newspaper groups and chains, since joint negotiation among the papers owned by a single publishing house is perhaps the only long-term means for recovering lost negotiating power.

Unions are often more keen to keep their pension rights than the right to specific functions. Within large groups it should be possible in time for individuals to transfer across traditional lines of craft and professional demarcation, from pressman to makeup editor, from typesetter to ad salesman, but only after across-the-board negotiations have taken place among all the groups of workers concerned. Many newspaper managements have already undertaken retraining programs to help manual workers switch to white-collar jobs.

The need for interunion solidarity was the cornerstone of any policy designed to preserve the unions' power position vis-à-vis management in the era of computerization when functions would switch constantly from one group of workers to another. The first classic dispute over computer automation was fought out over the barely surviving *New York Post* in 1965, when the paper was still in the possession of Dorothy Schiff. The typographical union insisted that no computer be operated without their prior consent, which would entail a large proportion (50 percent) of all the savings won by the introduction of the computer being paid into the ITU's automation fund, to which Mrs. Schiff objected. She argued that her defection two years earlier from the otherwise united stand of New York publishers against the ITU had preserved the power of that union and deserved a degree of consideration in return. The union remained adamant and permitted a handful of its members to be trained to use the new machinery, as long as the computer was not made the basis of regular work prior to a settlement. Mrs. Schiff demanded in turn that the computer be used and that "savings" from its use be paid only when the newspaper itself became profitable again—to which the union offered its objection. Subsequently, the computer was switched off and the union rejoiced in its victory. Meanwhile, the *Times* and the *Tribune* had already agreed to pay the union automation fund 100 percent of all savings accruing from the introduction of direct tape typesetting from outside the newspaper (i.e., material from the wire services).[17]

The insistence on receiving direct cash payments to union funds as a result of savings from automation arose from the calamitous actuarial position of typographers across the nation. By the mid-1960's nearly 20 percent of ITU members were pensioners, which meant that one pensioner was being supported by every 4.5 members, below the 6 active members required to provide pension funds for a single retired member. Where in other professions early retirement would have been the answer (or a large part of the answer) to the problem of widespread redundancy due to drastic modernization, in the actuarial conditions of the typographers the reverse policy had to be encouraged. The average age of typographers was fifty, and had it not become normal for thousands of members to remain at work long after the age of sixty, the pension fund might have been unable to meet its commitments. There were nearly 11,000 members at the time of the entry of the first computers into the industry who were past retirement age—over 10 percent of the total membership—all of whom had been in the craft for a quarter century and were eligible for pensions. Contribution rates were constantly increased, and a proportion of the raise earned in every new contract was placed in the fund, but the demographic trend within the typographical craft was forcing the union towards a negotiating stand that insisted upon fringe benefits and direct payments into union funds in exchange for automation.

Big Six was in a particularly bad position, since its members had contributed to an additional pension fund supplementing the normal ITU pension. The employers also contributed to an additional fund, which paid a supplementary pension to all workers with over twenty years of service, but in New York the total proportion of members who were drawing pensions had increased by 50 percent since the first stages of automation in the mid-1950's. The union was emphatic in its refusal to permit employers to take the full financial benefits of their investment in new technology and even withheld its cooperation in reducing personnel through natural attrition. This was clearly going to be the basis of further disagreement and struggle as the computer revolution got into full swing.

Until the demise of the majority of New York newspapers, the city was virtually the printing capital of America, containing nearly a fifth of all the printing work in the United States and a fifth of all printing personnel. The deals worked out between Big Six and the New York employers stood as models for the rest of the industry—or the part of it that accepted unionism. Across large parts of the United States the computer's arrival signaled the departure of thousands of print workers, as well as much wage cutting and dismissal.

In New York, however, the jurisdictional power of the ten unions was virtually complete, an advantage that turned out to be two-edged when in 1966, despite the intervention of Mayor Lindsay, Robert Kennedy and a large group of prominent American citizens, several of the city's papers finally disappeared. An attempt was made by the owners of the *Herald–Tribune*, the *Journal-American*, and the *World-Telegram and Sun* to merge into a single unit, producing one morning, one afternoon, and one Sunday paper. The negotiations were undertaken by the prospective publishers of the *World Journal Tribune*, as it was to be called, in a piecemeal fashion, with every union subject to a different set of negotiations. Agreement was not reached for many months, and the negotiators were harassed by a 140-day strike, in the middle of which the Whitney family announced that the *Tribune* was unable to stay in business. The total number formerly employed on the three papers was in any case to have been halved in the new amalgamation from nearly 5000 to 2500, but the death of the Whitney paper meant that 500 more had to be dismissed. The new paper died after a few months, and the ITU local instituted its own program of attrition: all printers were banned from entering the city in search of work until the excess of printers became once again a dearth. With a high average age, it is relatively easy to "lose" a sudden glut of skilled men, since New York alone consumes typographical workers at two or three dozen per month. Nonetheless, it was a long time before New York printers recovered from the upheaval or were absorbed into the growing work force of the three remaining papers, the *Times*, the *News*, and the *Post*.

Throughout the country as a whole, however, the 1960's were a period of increasing numbers of newspaper titles. It was the metropolitan areas, with a plethora of ancient papers, that were the scene of carnage. In twenty-five cities mergers took place between two or three papers, and large displacements of printing personnel resulted. In San Francisco, for example, the *Examiner*, the *Chronicle*, and the *News-Call Bulletin* agreed to turn into a pair of morning and afternoon papers, plus one Sunday—all to be set in the composing room of the *Chronicle*, but technically under the ownership of rival publishers. In 1970 the Newspaper Preservation Act made legal such arrangements for joint printing and joint collecting of advertising revenue of rival newspapers in a given list of cities—which could be increased only after special application to the Justice Department antitrust division.

The only experience the unions had to fall back on in designing a policy to fit the period of changeover to computerized printing was that which their forefathers had gained before the turn of the century when Linotypes came into the newspaper offices. Thus they treated the new machine as another form of automation, rather than a fundamental change in the nature of the printing business. They demanded complete authority over any machine or process that impinged upon the preparation of type for printing and insisted on training a sufficient number of their members to operate any new machine. The training center at Colorado Springs started to train and retrain thousands of printers in a wide range of wholly new skills, many of which had little to do with printing in its traditional sense. Employers, however, became increasingly enthusiastic over the new technology when they saw it beginning to reap real financial benefits, and bitter battles were fought out paper by paper. Out of the ten printing unions it was only the ITU that managed to retain the right of prior veto over all new techniques of printing.

One unusual aspect of the attitude of typographical workers—not only in America—is that they tend to refuse to reduce their economic demands at times when their jobs are threatened. The classic reaction of groups of workers to new technologies that displace or reorganize manual work is often to let themselves slip slowly down the hierarchy of pay among comparable groups of workers. However, print workers have demanded and received a share of all benefits that accrue to publishers as a result of automation and have continued to win large, sometimes spectacularly large, wage increases during the period of attrition and transition to new techniques. In the U.S. the ITU and other unions were able to achieve this partly because of the vigorous positions they had taken up at earlier stages of history, thus bequeathing advantages won by one generation to the next. For instance, the ITU had won the right to unionize all printing foremen and render them accountable to the union hierarchy. Employers themselves were excluded from their own composing rooms.

Even with the most advanced machinery it was difficult for publishers in a city where the ITU was well-organized to bring out a newspaper during a strike (though this was relatively easy in cities where the ITU had not been recognized or had been successfully ousted in the past). In Chicago, where the employers used VariTypers and other equipment to bring out viable newspapers for nearly two years without a single ITU man in the composing rooms, they were finally obliged to bring back all their employees when the dispute was settled—entirely according to the rules of the union. Any newspaper that continued to depend upon newsstand sales could not move its central plant out of the city center. However, papers that were entirely home-delivered, such as the *Wall Street Journal* and the *Journal of Commerce* (which rely relatively little upon street sales), did find it possible to function outside the main city of distribution and move their plants to places with lower operating and printing costs.

To the print workers the lesson to be drawn from the newspaper fatalities of the 1960's was quite different from that generally propounded by management. The latter would take the view that featherbedding, or the insistence by workers that the paper hire more men than was necessary at higher rates per hour than it could afford, had led to the demise of old and much loved newspapers. To the union the lesson was that job security was very weak indeed for men employed by financially weak newspapers. The papers that died between 1963 and 1966 in New York, for example, had been losing circulation and advertising over a long period. The publishers concerned had made no moves to bring in new techniques that might have reduced their printing costs. They had concentrated instead on reducing the work force in the new merged paper. For the union, therefore, the logic of events led them to insist on higher levels of job security and compensation on papers that seemed to be financially ailing. In fact, in the course of time the union might have moved towards a blanket industry-wide or city-wide job-security system for all printers.

Even in New York at the beginning of the 1970's, despite the loss of numbers of newspapers, there were more people employed in printing works as a whole than in the past, and the employers on the whole were operating on satisfactory profit margins. The newspaper industry was highly profitable, unemployment levels among typographical workers and pressmen were manageable, and prospects for the future extremely good. Newspapers presented a happy contrast with the fate of other industries hit by sudden computerization. In fact, the ITU was beginning to worry that the continued use of traditional printing equipment, especially in the non-newspaper sections of the printing industry, would in time sap the profitability of the business and threaten the livelihoods of its members. The expansion of public demand for printed material seemed ultimately the only guarantee of a secure future for their members; and the greater the use of electronic methods the greater the demand was likely to be—perhaps even in sectors of the economy that had not previously supported the employment of print workers.

When the New York papers negotiated their 1974 contract with the composition room workers, they experienced a difficult and vexing round of bargaining, but at the end both sides thought that the age of computerization might be reached without either side having to give up its long-term minimum demands. Big Six retained its sovereignty over typesetting, with the prospect of direct input by reporters and ad-salespersons starting five years later, while management gained the opportunity to achieve lower total wage payments as a result of its investment in computerized equipment.

The seismic dispute with the pressmen of New York in 1978 (which frightened the industry in many parts of the U.S. and the world) was the logical corollary to the 1974 negotiations with the typesetters. Its starting point was over the details of a new contract, over manning levels and job security, rather than over new technology of any major issue of principle, and the Newspaper Guild and pressroom chose to take a firm stand, after management had seemed to get through the round of talks fairly easily with the other sections of the work force.

In hindsight, it seemed to all the participants a classic case of an avoidable conflict,[18] and in its aftermath it became clear that its long-term effect was to weaken the *News* and the *Post* and break the solidarity of the New York employers, one of whom (Rupert Murdoch of the *Post*) had defected from the fight before it was over, insisting later that the strike had not been worth it. The *Times*, on the other hand, took the view that the new contract would enable them to cut pressroom costs by a third before the end of the contract (in 1984), which was finally struck, while the unions argued that the maximum saving would be less than a fifth, which represents not much more than one percent of the *Times'* total operating budget ($300 million). Yet in the aftermath the *Times* got to work to reduce its payroll by offering payments of between $15,000 and $40,000 to pressmen willing to quit. After months of strike and protracted negotiations, however, it secured nothing that promised a manning level as low as that of the prosperous suburban papers with which it has to compete. Nothing, in principle, has changed. The *Newark Star-Ledger*, whose manning levels were eventually accepted as the ones to act as the future point of comparability with the Times', was itself attempting to lower its manning levels in the course of its next round of negotiations. The upshot of the strike, therefore, was that further disputes would break out at the *Times* and perhaps at the other New York papers until manning levels are agreed upon that satisfy the publishers that they can compete on an equal footing in suburban circulation areas.

The great strike left many lingering anxieties for the New York newspapers. The Gannett Company owns a group of eight afternoon papers in Westchester, just north of New York, and as soon as the dispute began (August 9, 1978), it decided to convert a combination early edition into a regular morning newspaper entitled *Today*, to be sold at the remarkably low price of 10 cents a copy. By using Gannett's skill and resources, *Today* quickly rose to a daily circulation of 50,000, Monday to Friday, and penetrated into the northern reaches of New York City itself. It is a very solid paper carrying a great deal of material from the Gannett News Service and also the AP, which supplies much of the city's news. *Today* is clearly not a major challenge to the established papers of the city at present, but it is a good example of the kind of seed that may be planted at the edges of major circulations when they are allowed to lie fallow through prolonged industrial action.[19]

The spectacle of the New York strike, however, nudged many papers in other cities (Louisville, for example) into making rapid automation agreements before contracts had expired. Outside New York, the atmosphere of the industry is much easier, and agreements can sometimes be reached without conflict when the issues themselves have been made clear. With each generation of new equipment, levels of employment are permitted to sink, and with lifetime job guarantees for those who remain, excess personnel can be paid off. In Louisville, twenty-one pressmen—just under a quarter of the total pressroom staff—were paid $35,000 each to go. There was no longer any unresolvable issue at stake.

In Washington both the *Star* and the *Post* reached agreements that seemed to augur a period of natural attrition of staff in areas subject to automation. At the *Star* a sharp drop in composing room and other staff was arranged in exchange for wage increases and a major effort to preserve the life of the paper, which, even after its take-over by Time Inc., continued to be in danger. The new management reopened contract negotiations some months before the due expiration date of existing arrangements in the autumn of 1978 and managed to obtain from nine of the eleven unions agreements that would reduce staff, permit the introduction of new equipment, and enable five new zoned editions to be produced. The pressmen and the Columbia Typographical Union resisted, and the management filed for bankruptcy in December, forcing a very reluctant concession from the two groups. Eight of the paper's 175 printers were to be retired with payments of $40,000 per head, and further staff reductions were to occur during the life-span of the new contract. The paper's new masters, only eight months after acquiring the paper, were clearly intending to keep its staff on a long-term knife-edge of suspense.

At the *Post* there were fears that management would bring in nonunion personnel if agreements could not be reached on some or all of the eleven contracts involved in the paper. (The longer it takes to reach agreement the more new processes can be brought in and the easier it is for management to keep a paper in existence during a period of dispute.) At the *Post*, however, the power of the Newspaper Guild has declined since the earlier dispute of 1975, when many reporters returned to work and the spirit of the reporters' organization was badly broken, and in such modern technical conditions as exist there, it is difficult today to stop publication if the reporters are there to file copy and input it to the computer.

In other parts of the world this shift of internal power from printing workers to reporters is not taking place at nearly the same pace.[20] In Europe very little direct input by journalists has been introduced, except for certain papers in Finland, and the subject is being approached in a more holistic manner. In only one British newspaper has direct input started, and there on a comparatively small scale. The *London Times* dispute, lasting a year from November 1978, emerged from a number of issues, one of them being the question of direct input. The National Graphical Association has refused even to discuss the possibility of journalists or clerical workers starting direct input on a token basis, although agreement was found possible on the use of editors' vdt's. In Western Europe new technology has been arriving step by step and does not present the same spectre of cataclysmic social change that it does in Britain. New techniques are subject to the joint scrutiny of management and workers, and there is joint planning on equipment introduction, on manning levels, timing, etc. in many countries. Where advanced systems have been installed (as in Holland), there is close supervision and monitoring by all sides of the industry in advance of further innovation. But perhaps the most important difference in Western Europe (from both the United States and Britain) is that new technology is not perceived by management as an urgently needed way of reducing *over*manning. Most publishers in Western Europe look forward to the new economies in staffing but do not suffer from the feeling that they are currently overstaffed in relation to the equipment now available and to the financial position of their industries. In Germany and Japan there have long been serious shortages of skilled typesetters.

In comparison with those of the United States, European publishers have been relaxed in their attitudes towards computerization.[21] Clerical workers, journalists, and graphical workers are all deeply and equally concerned about the new technology and its influence on gaining work or losing it, but these groups tend to negotiate separately with their employers. They have different sets of expectations as workers and quite different perspectives on the technology. They represent profesional, craft, unskilled, and white-collar groups who traditionally have belonged to different social classes with different levels of political consciousness. Employers on the whole have understood the problems that flow from this historically quite unusual factor in the process of negotiation and have attempted sometimes to deal with the groups separately, sometimes in a kind of contrived unison.

In the experience of European publishers, to negotiate with one or more sections while omitting others is simply to court trouble, since any group reaching an agreement in the absence of the others will find itself accused of treachery or, at least, of failure to understand the problems of the others. This is not surprising, considering the very wide divergences of social class and outlook covered by these workers who are so directly affected by the present stage in the automation of the press.

In Sweden journalists and typographers actually did come to an agreement (without the participation of the employers) over new technology—and decided that the traditional demarcations should continue. However, there were highly significant developments. An important concession was made at the *Dagens Nyheter* in Stockholm whereby tele-ad girls are permitted by the typographers to take down ads by telephone and transmit them directly via vdt's into the computer; journalists on the same paper are permitted to input via vdt's only for a tiny fraction of the total day's output. In Malmö the *Sydsvenska Dagbladet* has its tele-ad girls typing ads on paper and then inputting them through ocr's, a practice that has been going on since the start of the decade. Malmö's socialist paper *Arbetet* has very little classified advertising but permits its journalists to use vdt's for the bulk of their copy. Thus, even where unions representing the separate affected groups have come to some agreement, it is made to operate in quite different ways on different papers.

In February 1978 the Norwegian arbitration court came to a long-awaited decision on a dispute between journalist and graphical unions after the former had agreed to permit reporters to present manuscripts either in scannable form or direct to computer through vdt's. The graphical workers contested the legality of this agreement and won a major concession whereby journalists are allowed to send scannable copy but not to use vdt's themselves.

Over in Finland, however, a firm contract has been drawn up between the warring parties based upon two very clear principles: that no individual should become unemployed as a result of new equipment and that unnecessary duplication of work should be eliminated. Within this framework it has been possible to introduce vdt's into all sections of several newspapers, and in the *Helsingin Sanomat*, the country's largest newspaper, there are now vdt's being used for both reporting and classified advertising, and the tele-ad girls are permitted even to code the billing and filing date with the ads.

In Denmark a monumental strike took place in 1975 affecting one of the largest papers in the country, the *Berlingske Tidende*, in the aftermath of which the publishers and typographers agreed that journalists might use vdt's for their own work as individuals, but that no journalist may key in the original copy of a colleague. Editorial copy from free-lancers or others not employed by the paper may be input only by typographers, although wire service copy may be placed directly in the newspaper's computer storage system. The agreement also permits classified advertising taken by telephone to be typed directly into computer storage, but ads taken at the counter must be handed over to ordinary typographical workers. The journalists of Denmark, however, were less than happy to cooperate with an agreement made without their signature, and they continued negotiating for two more years until January 1977, when they agreed that their members operate vdt's for their own work. OCR's, which are beginning to enter the country's newspaper offices, were not mentioned in the agreement and were the subject of further talks that took another year. They finally agreed that OCR's might be used for appropriate work but that all retyping of manuscripts would be undertaken by skilled typesetters, not by journalists working, as it were, as unpaid copyists.

Netherlands newspapers have also managed to patch together a set of agreements whereby most of the range of new techniques may be introduced but are subject to individual house agreements in every newspaper. No employee may be forced to use a vdt against his will.

In Italy progress has taken the form of a similar outline agreement at national level that is built upon the principle of obligation to make the fullest use of new equipment. Every newspaper, however, must create its own internal contract satisfactory to all groups of workers required to operate a particular set of machines. In Milan the workers at one newspaper have claimed a special "boredom supplement" to their wages on the grounds that the new machinery reduces them to mere checkers and correctors of photosetting machines—a sign of things to come, perhaps, when more groups of workers come to realize that elimination of skilled traditional work can produce psychological problems, especially for the generation of workers that first moves over to the new equipment.

The most interesting of the new national concordats establishing a framework within which local agreements are to be made is that of Paris, where a large reduction in the number of workers is provided for, unlike the agreements previously mentioned. The Parisians have devised a plan for modernization embracing all forms of new equipment, including photogravure and new engraving techniques. However, two years after the signing of this treaty the only journalists' vdt's operating in Paris were those of the *International Herald–Tribune*, jointly owned by the *Washington Post* and the *New York Times*. Outside Paris vdt's are being used for editorial and advertising work, but only by skilled typesetters (apart from certain clerical workers who take classified ads by telephone).

In Germany, as in Britain, the first set of agreements were made between the formal negotiating parties and then turned down by the plant workers themselves. In January 1978 all sections of the industry, after well over a year of talks and several brief shutdowns of plants, signed a general framework pact. The clerical workers had stayed out of it, but the rest of the industry believed that a firm foundation had been laid whereby the whole German newspaper industry would be computerized within five years, which would bring about a considerable reduction in the work force. German publishers have been troubled for several years by the shortage of skilled typesetters, so there was little fear of actual redundancies, although compensation was arranged in the pact for any that might unavoidably arise. In February and March of 1978 a series of sporadic strikes took place at large publishing concerns selected by the typographical union. The employers replied with a massive lockout that shut down almost the entire daily newspaper industry, inducing the federal government to step in and mediate. The final agreement permits journalists to use vdt's only on their own stories, as in Denmark, and vdt's may also be used by the editors at the copy desk. The period of transition between old and new contracts of employment is to be eight years (instead of the five hoped for), during which time all layout and makeup work, all photocomposition and correction work, is at first to be performed by the traditional workers. At the end of the period, management may decide which group of workers is to use which machine. The German publishers were fortunate that the shortage of skilled typesetters and their relatively high average age (over 50) has made it possible for a completely modernized system to be phased in within a specific and calculable period of time. Even now, however, there is no agreement in Germany concerning the use of vdt's for advertising work, although it is felt that clerical workers will, in fact, be permitted to type on vdt's and place classified advertisements directly into the computer.

The newspaper industry is, in a sense, the dove sent from the ark of mechanical society to test the waters of computerization. It is the first of the traditional, major industries to start the process of complete transformation to computerized methods—a transformation that, as we have seen, changes the nature of the tasks of the information industries as well as their methods. The United States is possibly the only country in the world in which it is possible to discuss this massive change without dealing first with the human questions. Many American employers are, of course, deeply concerned about the welfare of their work force and especially about the impact upon their lives of the gigantic changes entailed by this transference of an industry from one mode to another, but American newspaper publishers often become rhapsodic when they think and speak about the new technology and fail to look at the phenomenon from the perspective of their employees.[22] They argue that the continued profitability of their industry is the only way to guarantee steady employment. They are supported to a great extent by official prognostications for the printing industry,[23] which is that printing is likely to grow, though slowly in the 1980's—that the total volume of printed materials will rise rapidly because of population growth and the trend towards the greater use of printed information in packaging, commerce, and in industry in general. However, most of the increase in actual employment brought about by this will tend to go to clerical, maintenance, and administrative workers and to certain specialist crafts (such as lithography), rather than to the general range of printing trades. Within the newspaper, of course, publishers expect typesetters virtually to disappear in the next decade or so and paste-up personnel a few years after that.

For the workers in the ancient craft of printing, the future seems very grim, despite the financial predictions. Monetary compensation is not enough when an ancient livelihood that entails its own complete view of the world and of the individual's identity appears to be disappearing. As one of the officials of the ITU put it in a speech in 1974, "Automation has its place in society. But ruthless, selfish, and irresponsible automation with the ultimate goal of total uncoupling of the human element is predictably going to draw even the aloof, ivory-tower advocate of such a system into the very vortex of this whirlpool of chaos he is helping to create."[24] It is, perhaps, impossible to expect those being sucked into a whirlpool to appreciate its beauty as a natural phenomenon.

III
THE NEW MEDIA

III

THE NEW MEDIA

7. NEWSPAPERS

& VIDEOTEX

We have seen how the new technologies used in newspaper production and distribution prefigure a set of changes that go beyond the mere publishing of newspapers. The computer and its attendant industries have found a market among newspaper publishers, and the latter have reached out towards the computer to help solve a whole range of current problems—which, in turn, have arisen from changes in demography, in the structure of cities, in the life-styles and needs of twentieth-century people. There is an interaction between these two industries, both of which are driven by social forces that they have helped to generate but that continue to create new demands and new patterns.

Prediction of social patterns has become an essential element in technological production—and vice versa. The problem is that when the two interact the results can sometimes promise more than common sense will warrant. Mere extrapolation of a tendency or a current need can lead to absurd conclusions and false panics.

The history of communication devices is littered with accounts of deluded hopes and predictions embarrassingly unfulfilled. The Victorians thought that the telephone would rapidly become an instrument of mass entertainment. Newspaper editors in the 1930's were confident that television could never become a medium of news. Computer experts in the 1950's believed that three or four computers would be the total number required to fulfill the needs of an entire society. Of course, there have been other sets of forecasts that have been fairly accurate in predicting the social importance and even the social role of various devices; these have tended to be predictions that combine good guesses about society's needs and developing tastes with good guesses concerning technical possibilities. There is a complex and interactive connection between social and technological trends that is virtually impossible to unravel, except by hindsight. At the same time, one has to acknowledge today that social prediction has itself become an important element in all forms of planning; industrialists invest in new techniques on a scale large enough to exercise widespread social impact only when an image of the future society's needs is clearly imprinted in their minds. Futurology and investment are, between them, self-fulfilling, but only when they move in the same direction hand in hand.

In outlining the scope of new media in the next decade or two, one has therefore to use both a mental brake and a mental accelerator. New technologies cannot normally run ahead faster than (or take directions different from) the naturally evolving needs of individuals and societies; but, at the same time, past experience teaches that new technologies *can* leap ahead much faster than can be foreseen if they come to satisfy a newly arisen social need. It is imagination rather than calculation that often makes the difference. The connections between social need and practical possibility are made by people who can see a society's needs more deeply than their competitors. The evolution of person-to-person wireless telephony into the medium of radio was enormously enhanced by the imaginative guesswork of an immigrant Morse code tapper. In 1919 David Sarnoff, barely out of his teens, saw the possibility of making a kind of wireless musical box by separating the speaking end from the reception end of a wireless telephone device that had been widely used during the First World War. This was not a technical discovery but the matching of a technical possibility with a gap in the provision of mass entertainment. Even so, it proved to be wrong, to the extent that Sarnoff at that moment thought the market would consist of people living in rural areas who were deprived of the chance of hearing music performed live in city concert halls. He had placed radio in the context of a perceived social problem of the time—the cultural and economic inequalities of town and country, which in any event was not the prime motive force in the development of radio.

The new experimental teletext services now spreading in many countries derive from the perceived possibility of multiplexing with the television signal, pieces of text that would subtitle television programs for the deaf. This simple but useful device for helping a deprived group is being transformed by manufacturers and broadcasters into a mass medium, the result of the interaction between engineers perceiving a social need and manufacturers with a need for a device to help boost the market for color-television receivers. The "invention" lay as much in social guess-work as in laboratory research; in some sense the latter was generated by the former.

We have been examining in some detail the role of the computer inside the existing newspaper industry and have seen something of the impact it exercises over employment, industrial structure, and profits. The trans-ference of information storage to computer is, however, also creating a new range of external media, so to speak, new devices to bring reading material into the home or office. As a result, a vast range of perplexing issues is opening up. Should we consider these new media merely as extensions of the newspaper form? Are they simply new publishers (and old) moving into a new form of competition with the newspaper? Are they a threat to the newspaper or to any other information medium? Are they news media at all, or rather some new kind of reference medium? Will they remain forever locked into specialist forms of information, thereby stripping the newspaper of some range of material but leaving the bulk of information paper-bound as in the last several centuries?

There are other questions to be faced as well. Who is responsible for these new media that all depend upon telecommunications carriers that are either designated as common carriers or as nationalized monopolies? Is it possible, therefore, to transfer to devices that send information direct to the home on video screens the whole panoply of ethical and regulatory paraphernalia—the rights of reporters, editors, and pub-lishers; doctrines of objectivity; editorial freedom; news values? Are all these terms now to become part of some antiquated information theol-ogy, displaced by a new set of ethics emerging from a rearranged set of tensions between governments, providers of information, carriers, and readers? What will happen to libel laws, codes of journalistic conduct, contempt rules, and copyright protection in a medium that through its sheer profusion of material is unpoliceable, as ungovernable technically as the telephone conversations of an entire society?

Every medium acquires its own associations, resonances, professional-isms—in effect, its own microculture—and our purpose will now be to see what can be learned from our present understanding of future devel-opments in electronic information about the social applications and spe-cial characteristics of the new, emerging media.

II

The decade of the 1980's will—*almost* without doubt—be the decade of the birth of the new text services delivered to the home by means of the common television receiver. As will become apparent from the account that follows concerning the problems as well as the advantages of these new media of communication, they are not likely to displace the traditional newspaper during that decade. However, they are certainly going to establish themselves in one form or another in one or another area of the information market during the eighties, and this means that the decade of the nineties is going to be one in which the traditional newspaper may face decline, extinction, or at least complete internal self-reappraisal. This writer would choose the third of that triad of possibilities, but our purpose is not to speculate so far ahead but to look at the paths now being laid down by a series of new electronic devices that have been evolving slowly and spasmodically since the end of the 1960's. What we can learn from studying them now is the way in which new information media interact with old ones, either driving them out of existence or driving them into new and more distinct social roles.

In 1976 a lexicographical chaos set in when the makers of each system of what we shall call "videotex" attempted to provide its own name as a label for the whole group of services and techniques. Between 1976 and 1979 it became almost impossible at times to discuss the new media across national boundaries because of the complexities of nomenclature. In Britain the BBC and its commercial competitor, the ITV group of companies, both inaugurated services that sent several hundred "pages" of material by way of the normal television signal directly into specially adapted home-TV receivers. They called these services Ceefax and ORACLE respectively, each hoping that perhaps one day the entire world would choose one or the other name for the medium as such. Gradually the word "teletext" came to be used as the generic term.

Towards the end of the decade the British Post Office introduced a text service that sent material stored in a central computer by way of existing telephone wires to the same domestic television receivers (appropriately adapted with special decoders); this it chose (and still chooses) to call "viewdata." Some people treated viewdata as a species of the genus teletext, but soon it became apparent that there were fundamental differences between services that were multiplexed with a television signal and services (with a much greater capacity) that went via the telephone. For one thing, the regulatory background was different: the former was a one-way medium, exactly like the television signal that it partnered, while the latter was an interactive medium, enabling the reader or user to send fairly simple messages back to the computer and the information provider. Viewdata and teletext then emerged as parallel (and potentially complementary) media rather than as direct competitors. In Britain it was thought that both terms would pass into the international lexicon of computer-based media. The word viewdata, however, cannot be translated easily into French or German, the first half of it being a specifically English word. Teletext was too similar to the Teletex system planned in Germany, which was adapted from the conventional telex system. It was also too close to the U.S. "teltex" system, also a text transmission device.

The ITU worked out in collaboration with the European Broadcasting Union (EBU) a number of problems of technical standardization, and the ITU Study Group came up with the term "videotex" as the generic name for the new text media, making careful distinction between interactive videotex (which the British continue to call viewdata) and broadcast videotex, which the British and others continue to call teletext. The British Post Office by 1979 had made great strides in the development of viewdata and had launched a public service under the trade name Prestel. It has refused to go back on its terminology, since its service is far more advanced than any other by several years. It remains to be seen, therefore, which term will win, and the interactive text services (which are now themselves divisible into several further categories) may come to be known as videotex or viewdata. Meanwhile, the world's best-known actual commercial service will continue to be known as Prestel, with other national services also using their own names, such as CAPTAINS (Japan); Antiope, Titan, Didon (all from France); Telidon (Canada); and Bildschirmtext (Germany). Some of these services are in a sense national "inventions," but others are adaptations or importations from Britain. It is still possible, therefore, that the British terms will spread or wither depending on the commerical success of individual national services. For our purposes we shall use videotex as the generic term together with teletext for the broadcast services plus, of course, all the individual national service names. Perhaps starting new text services was easier in the days of Gutenberg.

A teletext system is one that transmits alphanumeric material and simple graphics via a television signal. The normal television signal does not use all of the lines allocated to it (525 in the U.S., 625 in most of Europe and Japan) but leaves some of them as a "field blanking interval," to be used for special control messages to the transmitter. These lines can be used most of the time for additional material, which is sent "piggyback" on the television picture and can be accessed by the viewer if he has a special decoder attached to his set and a keypad for choosing the pages of material he needs. In the two earliest services of this kind, Ceefax, run by the BBC in London, and ORACLE (Optional) Reception of Announcements by Coded Line Electronics), which is run by the commercial television service of Britain, all the available material is cycled past the television set every twenty-five seconds, and the decoder, under instruction from the viewer, "frame-grabs" (i.e. "snatches" out of the electronic flow of material) a given moment. It takes up to twenty-five seconds to register on the screen in readable form.

In one area of Long Island the Reuters agency runs an experimental frame-grabbing news service to subscribers equipped with a special receiver, while on the Manhattan Cable it runs a different kind of text service in which the material passes across the screen in serial order, without interaction by the viewer. It is possible in these services to supply the reader with a relatively small number of pages for each line of the television picture reserved for the purpose. With a total store of 50 pages it is possible to supply a chosen frame in a maximum waiting time of ten seconds as the page numbers race past; with 100 pages the time doubles and with 200 it doubles again. A system could be devised with 800 or so pages constantly available, but the viewer would have to wait up to several minutes before the chosen frame of material arrived on his screen. The only possible interaction on the part of the viewer is the choosing of pages; he cannot pursue a private route through a complex meter of pages (the "logic-tree") or wander at will through the material.

Teletext thus has characteristics similar to television itself: the channels can be chosen or switched off, but the viewer—having made his selection—gets exactly the same product as his neighbor. Nevertheless, it is an extremely cheap system both for the operator and the receiver. The former has to collect a limited quantity of information and keep it up-to-date, paying for this by advertising or providing it as a free extra service with the normal television content; the latter pays for his decoder and no further payment is necessary, other than purchasing his annual television license or being prepared to read the accompanying advertisements.

Videotex systems can provide an infinite number of pages, the number dependent entirely on the computer storage capacity of the operator of the medium. The response time after the viewer selects a page is a fraction of a second; complex interaction will eventually be possible; and the user can be routed through long sequences of pages as he searches for the particular fact that he wants. However, there are certain "privacy" problems involved in videotex, especially for information providers who want to send certain categories of material only to a selected or self-selected group of users rather than to the general public. There are problems of cost as well, since evey page provided has to be paid for by the consumer or the provider must pay for the use of the telephone line throughout the period of contact with the central computer. It is possible for videotex systems to be sent via coaxial cables, if these are interactive, or through a combination of telephone and cable. With the British Post Office's Prestel (the first public service of this kind), the user can almost forget about the telephone involvement in the system; his keypad automatically connects him to the system through his telephone line.

Teletext and videotex are different in various ways from the on-line retrieval systems that have been functioning for a number of years. These tend to be specialist devices with specialist data bases that can be interrogated in sophisticated ways. The New York Times Information Bank, for example, or Lockheed's Dialog system for academic and medical abstracts or the Reuters Monitor service for currency exchange information are all geared to a relatively small number of clients (ranging from a few dozen to 2400, in the case of Reuters Monitor), and all are relatively expensive, costing up to $100 an hour.

There are many factors that promise to blur the edges of our definitions of these media. It is possible that the use of microprocessors in the receiving terminal could greatly increase the capacity of teletext systems. The French Antiope system (really a combination of videotex and teletext devices), operated by Telediffusion de France (TDF), which transmits all France's radio and television channels, is planning to allocate the whole of a fourth national TV channel to the transmission of text. Instead of merely using one line of the field-blanking interval, Antiope would use all the lines of a whole 625-line channel, thereby multiplying its capacity very greatly. France also tried out a separate videotex system called Titan. Today, however, all her new devices for generating alphnumeric symbols share the same national computer storage (Didon).

Germany, which is active in both forms of text media and firmly separates its broadcasting from the postal and telecommunications administration (unlike France, whose CCETT is a combined research and development organization), has decided to call teletext "videotext" and to call videotex "Bildschirmtext" (screen text). However, the German newspaper industry is not at all pleased with the development of such services outside its purview, and the association of newspaper publishers (BDZV) tends to describe both media as "Bildschirmzeitung" (screen newspaper), thereby implying that both are derogating unfairly from the privileges of the press and that both are placing an information mechanism that history (and the German federal constitution) long ago decided should not be a regulated medium into the state-regulated field of television and the telephone.[1]

The telecommunications operators in both Britain and Germany have been at pains to argue that their intention is only to provide the lines and storage for these systems and not to provide the content (apart from simple, uncontroversial public information). Indeed, the German videotex system will enable all information providers to store information in their *own* computers as well as in the central one, so that the public authority concerned (the Deutsche Bundespost) will not find itself involved in the policing of content. The British system is founded on a different principle: the Post Office provides *all* the storage facility (although large providers may in time be able to use their own) but will then operate no more control over content than it does over that of its telephone service. As will become apparent, there is considerable pressure in Britain and elsewhere in Europe for some form of regulation of information providers, even though a large proportion of the material in the system has been provided by existing newspaper groups who are used to functioning without content regulation or public supervision. The long-term question of whether to regard videotex as an adjunct of the press, as German publishers do in the very naming of the medium, is yet to be resolved. The new text media are electronic publishing systems, which, not being particularly geared to the provision of mere news, are likely to create quite new sources of material, available for all comers.

There is little doubt that a large number of further "inventions" will be proclaimed (and some acclaimed) during the 1980's. Quite often a new invention merely consists of the pursuit by one group of a line of development abandoned by another. The former will claim to have solved a set of problems that had hitherto defeated all other competitors, but in reality this is an area of development in which innovation is relatively simple and where the technology involved is highly flexible.

The Japanese, because of the complex nature of their written language, have opted for a system that will permit still pictures to be drawn and transmitted through their CAPTAIN (videotex-type) system, even though this will mean that access time to the user may be fifteen or even thirty seconds. The British Prestel developers, with quite different problems uppermost in their minds (namely, to get ahead with a service that will bring in fresh revenue from telephone subscribers as quickly as possible), turned aside from a method that would have permitted the transmitting of pictures. They did so at much greater investment cost, however, with a longer access time for the viewer, and with the knowledge that one day they would have to redesign their system to permit still pictures. Any additional mechanical method of writing is of extreme value to the Japanese, and worth the investment. For the British the opportunity offered by Prestel meant the expansion of the telephone network. The choices made by system designers, both in policy and engineering, are nearly always makeshift and reversible. It is social custom and institutional necessity that has tended to dominate the design of a medium, and that is as true of videotex as of Gutenberg's printing press.

A newspaperman watching Ceefax or ORACLE for the first time will be struck (or relieved) to realize that with headlines and spaces a full "page," or frame, can hold no more than 100 words; it normally contains no more than 75, even though the screen could technically hold 24 rows of 40 characters, upper- and lower-case, in a range of 8 colors. The entire 400 pages of Ceefax and ORACLE combined contain little more actual text than four sides of a broadsheet newspaper. Ceefex journalism, therefore, operates more in the tradition of the radio than the newspaper (offering small gobbets of information), since space and the attention span of a reader looking at a screen permit little else. Each page, however, can be automatically made to join with three additional automatically generated "cycling" pages—with no extra decision on the part of the viewer—so that a given story can be made to run to several hundred words. Since the BBC has two television channels (and therefore two hundred-page Ceefax magazines), it has decided to make the first channel give frequently updated news material while the second carries background, soft features, and information that requires weekly rather than hourly updating. The medium began expensively, in 1976, with decoders and keypads costing roughly $2000. It has been very slow to expand, but by the mid-1980's there could be several million domestic receivers equipped for Ceefax and ORACLE, and at this point the relationship between newspaper content and teletext information should become a subject for urgent discussion, although little of the material on such systems will actually cause newspapers to feel usurped. Afternoon papers might be hit in certain regions and countries where these are purchased as "second papers," and if hard-copy printouts for teletext become very cheap additions to the medium, rather than merely exhibition gadgetry as at present, newspapers could begin to feel a powerful competitive impact at the end of the decade.

As for advertising, the ORACLE system now offers two lines on each page of information. However, it could in time, become an important medium for various kinds of highly specialized low-volume classified advertising (e.g., executive jobs, resale of expensive cars and homes). With the Prestel system the viewer must learn a fairly simple technique. He logs into the system by punching the telephone number of the videotex computer on his keypad, which switches his telephone line through to his decoder and television receiver. This process can also be done automatically on the more advanced Prestel keypads. He then punches his own private number, and the set responds by answering with his name and a suitable greeting for the time of day. He is now connected, and every frame he chooses will be charged to his telephone account. He must keep his keypad out of the way of children (and other unauthorized persons), because he must pay the cost of a local telephone call (3 pence, or 6 cents, for two minutes in peak time, but for 12 minutes in the evenings and on weekends), plus a special charge of 5 cents per videotex minute, plus the cost of each page he selects (which may range from zero to one dollar). It is this last charge (minus a 5 percent collecting fee, which also covers Post Office insurance against unpaid bills) that goes to the information provider (IP), a private person or company who has rented the special equipment and computer storage necessary to set up in business as an information seller to the videotex clientele.

There are always three partners in a public text medium such as Prestel and its counterparts: first, the post office or telecommunications administration that has invested in the creation of the network and the computer storage and the various "ports" necessary to link the subscribers to the database; second, the information providers who have invested in the collection of information that they wish to sell, either for cash direct or through the sale of advertising; third, the receiver manufacturers who also have to make a major investment in plant and equipment. All three have simultaneously to recognize their mutual self–interest in the new medium. The content of the medium must be of a standard to attract an audience large enough to pay for the storage capacity and the network. If one of the three partners has doubts or if one wishes to go in a different line of development from the others, the new system will quickly break down. All three have to recognize a clear need in society that their new medium will uniquely satisfy. Otherwise, it will fall by the wayside like the Victorian Electrophone (which brought the sound from London theatres to telephone subscribers in the 1890's) or the Bell Telephone company's Picturephone of the 1960's.

There are many important institutional reasons why the British Post Office has invented the Prestel system. For one thing, it has none of the

constitutional or antitrust restrictions that affect North American telephone administrations. The British Post Office may operate the data
storage centers, rent out computer storage, and provide the links. In
Britain data-processing is not legally separate from communication, as in
the United States. The Post Office is able to link its own billing system
with the Prestel billing system, which gives it a powerful advantage over
any potential rival carrier who would find it an expensive business to set
up a parallel mass billing system comparable to that of the telephone.
Furthermore, Britain's television receivers are for the most part rented
rather than purchased, and this means that viewers wanting to go over to
videotex or teletext can simply turn in their set on the next rental day
and ask for one equipped with the extra service. Introducing new
receiver-based services is thus much easier in a society with a high level
of rented receivers than in one where new sets or adapters must be
purchased. (Persuading the *manufacturers* to invest in the new mass market is, however, a more difficult matter).

Finally, the British Post Office, like many European PTT's (but unlike
AT&T in the United States), charges for local calls according to time;
the system of a flat charge covering rental and local use was abandoned
soon after the World War II. It can therefore increase its revenue automatically whenever it can find a way of inducing subscribers to make
extra use of their telephones—the British being more reluctant users of
this service than the Americans, averaging only ten minutes a day. With
the total level of households subscribing to the telephone still at 60
percent (compared with 97 percent for television) new subscribers must
be tempted to the telephone so the Post Office can increase its off-peak
domestic revenue in order to pay for the cost of developing the network.

Eventually there will be coin box public terminals for use in shops,
libraries, schools, railroad stations, and airports. But a number of "free"
terminals will also be installed, programmed to transmit only those pages
for which the IP demands no charge. It is a kind of closed-user group in
reverse, available to advertisers and those information providers who use
Prestel to support sales of some other commodity. The manufacture of a
pay Prestel terminal is extremely complicated, since the machine will
have to calculate whether enough money has been inserted before the
pages are offered and demand more, if necessary. In Britain itself the
problem of rendering the public terminals vandal-proof will prove extremely difficult; they will probably have to be mounted behind bullet-
proof glass and equipped with sturdy touch keys resulting in a relatively
high price for the consumer.

Gradually the Prestel system will enlarge its range of services to the point at which it will become an all-purpose means for sending and receiving written information for private, individual, and general audiences. In the beginning, messages can be sent only according to set formulas ("I will arrive at x hours," "Meet me at the station at x hours," "I will get home at x hours," "Happy birthday," etc.), which the subscriber chooses simply by pressing the numbers on his numbers-only keypad. At the next stage, business subscribers will be equipped with larger pads containing alphabet signs as well as numbers through which ordinary correspondence can be sent and received. Flashing lights will indicate to the receiver that messages await him. Later, all of the U.K.'s 60,000 telex terminals will be connected to the system to transform the flexibility and convenience of this older Post Office text service. At the same time, it will be possible for Prestel subscribers to send out multiple messages through the telex links so that private wire services of information can be constructed.[2] There is a further potential for Prestel to operate in the conversational mode on a split screen, a device developed originally during a search for means to help the deaf communicate. It could permit simultaneous conversation between two people equipped with alphanumeric keypads. Prestel is also capable of providing a sophisticated calculating service to fill the gap between the pocket calculator and the complete computer; it can explain mortgages and interest-rates repayment periods, for instance, and advise on insurance, income tax and loan schemes. A variety of complex quizzes and games have been available since the first experimental months, and horoscopes and personality tests are provided featuring complicated skeins of questions and answers that are checked by the central computer, which can take account of all standard psychological types.

Each information provider on Prestel is responsible for his own database and frame design, which means that there is a great need for an expertise that is still scarce. The IP must catch the user's attention and explain himself as quickly and succinctly as possible, then attract him through a number of pages that route him towards the information he seeks; the more skilled IP's manage to provide scraps of interesting and helpful information as the routing pages pass. IP's can publish quick routes to frequently required pages. For example, it is not necessary to go all the way through an airline's timetable from the announcement of the company's name down a long series of route choices in search of the time of a night flight to Abu Dhabi. The user can simply punch a string of numbers that will get him through to the required page without reading ten or more routing pages. The storage system is like a maze through which the unititiated must wander in confusion unless he is firmly and clearly guided by a chosen tree of logic; to the experienced it seems more like a tunnel with a small light at the end of it.

The rules imposed by the Post Office upon the management of the data base by the private IP's are very simple. The name of the IP must appear in the top left-hand corner of the frame, but in the case of an IP working through one of the large "umbrella" providers, it is the latter whose name must appear, since it is the principal information provider in each case whom the Post Office considers legally responsible for the content. The price of every frame of information must appear in the top right-hand corner of the frame, and the number of the page must be placed in the center at the top of the frame. Apart from this, the design of the page is entirely the responsibility of the IP, and many have been pure experiments in layout and frame design, not all of which delight the eye. But a number of house styles are emerging, especially from the larger umbrella IP's who process up to 5000 frames of material on their own account or on behalf of smaller providers, and who have developed strong design preferences and have advanced the medium's development to a considerable degree. Two of them now provide courses in Prestel layout and are training hundreds of specialists in the medium.

Each IP provides the reader with a sufficient routing through his own data base, using two or even three lines of the frame to explain to the reader how to proceed to the next relevant page and how to return to an earlier page or to skip to information of potential interest. Naturally the IP in unwilling to direct the reader to data bases rivaling his own, and therefore complementary information may be difficult for the user to reach. Without the assistance of the IP, he will be obliged to take a far more circuitous route than necessary. This is, in a way, the logical corollary of free enterprise, but it may nonetheless lead to complaints. A newspaper is not obliged to direct its readers to rival newspapers, but a Prestel IP is *perceived* to be deceptive if he directs the reader away from information belonging to rival providers. It is here that the IP's ethical codes may in due course provide a satisfactory solution.

Putting information into the database requires the use of the large keyboard supplied by the Post Office; the first-generation keyboards are fairly crude, but those of the second generation offer much of the versatility of modern word processors, with small local memories to save long periods of connection to the central processing unit. An experienced keyboard operator, working with a preplanned frame pattern or set of patterns, can complete a page of 500 characters in a few minutes, but it can take up to half an hour to fill a page with diagrammatic or graphic material that requires experimentation on the screen. Some of the larger users are building their own software to transfer previously constructed databases over to viewdata in their entirety. British Airways, for example, and data STREAM and the Stock Exchange have prepared such systems for themselves.

When the service is fully developed, there will be a network of Prestel computer centers situated in all the major cities. Information will be switchable from city center to city center as well as from national to local centers. If there are 3 million subscribers by the mid-1980's (the most optimistic assessment), about 80 such centers will be necessary, each with 384 ports serving 100 subscribers. Some information will reach the subscriber from local storage, some from regional and some from national. Originally there was a plan for a star system, with regional centers fanning out from the national and local centers in each region, but this placed too great a pressure upon the transmission capacity, and so it has been decided to duplicate a very high proportion of the information stored at the local centers, thus increasing the amount of traffic generated by the updating of information but reducing that resulting from user requests. A mesh of transmission lines will gradually appear, but all transactions between user and system will be conducted locally, with all billing information and logging-in information held at the local centers and all messages held locally until requested.

Prestel has been built to hold a 96-unit character set suitable for the English language (52 upper- and lower-case letters, 10 numerals, 31 special characters, and 3 spares), but like the telephone it is essentially an international as much as a national device. The main set has been devised in such a way as to add 94 additional characters, which are used by sixteen other European languages. Although in some ways the simplest of the new media (all the programs were written in twenty-four man-years of programmer time), it is also the most ambitious—with its aim of providing, at a stroke, a whole society with a multi-access, interactive, all-purpose information system. It offers a complete new phase in the evolution of business enterprises and in the relationship between information and the user, and it offers a new tool for business administration, but is at the same time the largest on-line computer system ever designed. Nevertheless, the path between conception and reality is still strewn with rocks.

The manufacturers of broadcasting equipment in Britain have responded very cautiously indeed to the new range of equipment that various service providers expect them to produce. Videotex has perhaps been the medium they treat with the greatest caution, bordering on severe scepticism. They can see a quicker though still hazardous market for teletext, with its low-capacity no-charge service, but even here the market has disappointed them, since it has grown in thousands, not in tens of thousands, in the early years. Meanwhile, cassettes and video-discs have come onto the market, and it is clear that the same pioneering public will be loath to buy everything at once, even though each device adds to the range of possible applications of the same television screen.

The first overall feeling of manufacturers in Britain, which is, in effect, the first place in which the whole range of new electronic devices are being tried out publicly and simultaneously, is the sense of a shifting away from mere entertainment in the home towards more active systems and interactive relationships with the TV screen. Some manufacturers think that at this stage they should begin offering a modular design that would place a transducer, or television screen, in the center of an array of devices that could be added one at a time to the same basic unit. There would be plugs for off-air uses (including cassettes, discs, and games) plus teletext, printing, videotex connection via the telephone, etc.

The television industry is also inexperienced in selling equipment to the new kinds of markets created by Prestel among closed-user groups and in the commercial world. It has thus confined itself to very small orders from the semiconductor manufacturers, thereby losing the oppor-tunity of reduced unit prices. Meanwhile, the IP's have grouped them-selves for self-protection against their two partners in a kind of trade association, which is also trying to establish itself as a self-policing organ-ization for advertising and editorial standards, etc., in order to circum-vent the imposition of an outside controlling body. The Post Office has set up consultative committees to enable its partners to have easy access to one another for complaints. All of the partners in this new medium have problems of their own and distrust somewhat the ability of the others to understand them. This is almost inevitably the kind of problem likely to arise in multiform information systems of the future, and soci-eties with different constitutional configurations, such as the U.S., are likely to enter into this kind of medium in a rather different way. How-ever, the sheer size and nature of the Post Office commitment and that of the providers is of a scale large enough to ensure the survival of the Prestel service. Videotex will not arrive in a flash like the radio of the 1920's or the pocket calculator. It will have to find its aficionados and live with them for some time before it becomes a social necessity.

Videotex should also be seen as one of a number of international developments providing "computing for all." It consists of joining the average home to a sophisticated computer, and therefore partly belongs to the new wave of microprocessor-based domestic equipment. Ceefax,

ORACLE, and Prestel are all additions to the television receiver that contribute to a kind of home video center, further evidence of the fragmentation of the television audience that has begun in the late 1970's. Cheap hardcopy printout machines are being tried out—among the twenty-six different items of videotex-oriented equipment on the market—and Prestel, zealous in its hybridity, will develop also as a kind of home video-printing center in the course of time.

The Post Office, despite its telecommunications monopoly, does not attempt to exercise a monopoly over videotex-type systems as such, and so there could be many intraorganizational systems, in time, acquiring the necessary software package from the Post Office for specialist purposes. The Whitbreads brewery, for example, uses its system to operate an in-house communication network, using Post Office telephone lines but its own storage and terminal equipment. Eight different manufacturers make the necessary equipment, and common standards between teletext and videotex mean that many receivers now being manufactured supply the possibility of both media. It is also now possible (since the Post Office has decided to relax a previous rule that banned receivers adapted for videotex and teletext, but not for ordinary television), so that cheap text-only receivers for business users may be sold in Britain, and during the first years of the medium, business users may prove to be the main revenue providers.

To set up in business as a "publisher' or IP in videotex is extremely cheap by the standards of print publishing. The IP pays the equivalent of $8000 per year for the right to a three-digit directory number, plus $8 per year for every page rented (much less if he takes a five-year option). If he wants to operate one of the closed-user groups (CUG's), he pays an extra $8000, and for this he receives the right to a specially secure section of the data storage computer to which only other members of the group may have access (another facility likely to be of professional and business use). The IP also needs some editing equipment, including his input terminal, which can be rented for $800 from the Post Office, although a sophisticated, intelligent word–processor will cost anywhere up to $40,000. He will also need a staff trained in graphic as well as editorial skills. However, this equipment functions well below the staffing levels and costs of a newspaper or magazine and will equip the IP to sell information at prices determined by himself (with a permitted maximum charge of one dollar per frame) to the entire market. His operating costs are no different for an audience of one than for an audience of 10 million. His revenues will be collected for him, and he is insured against bad debts. Within months of the start of the videotex trial, and still months before the public service was inaugurated in 1979, 150 IP's had come forward. Not all of them paid the costs just listed. Many were content to share terminals and directory numbers or publish under the umbrella organizations that sprang up—equipped with relatively expensive three-digit numbers. An entire Prestel "universe" of IP's, consultants, and electronic publishers came into existence overnight, the whole of it functioning for the benefit of a few hundred subscribers equipped with the special receivers.

The problems of Prestel arise from its structure and organization. Nobody is quite certain who is really responsible for marketing the medium as such—the Post Office, the information providers, or the set manufacturers—and since the medium is far from established, all three have different or overlapping views of where the launch market really is. Until all can see this clearly, none of them is prepared to go all out and invest.

Is Prestel really a mass medium connected to people's homes? Is it an additional specialist tool of business? Is it an educational instrument, or a toy for wealthy people only? Each of the three partners to Prestel would have given different answers at different points in time, yet all three *have* to move together if the new medium is to find favor with any section of the public. The real long-term answer is probably that videotex services are not mass media in the traditional sense, but are addressed ideally to hundreds of small overlapping information markets, every one of which has to be separately attracted to the medium and provided with its own micro group of information providers. The problem is that the start-up period for the three major partners simply cannot be allowed to last for a very long period of time because their willingness to continue to invest often will diminish if the returns are not immediate. The problems of transition in electronic media, in which the receiving public has to make deliberate and individual investment (by acquiring receivers), are so great as to jeopardize the successful introduction of a given medium.

The Post Office has its own priorities in investing in storage and local computer centers, not necessarily wanting to place them where the information providers want them. One major provider, for example, wanted to concentrate activity in a single region at first, but this had no priority in the computer installation program, and so he was obliged to provide *regional* information for sale throughout the country.

Before launching the medium, the Post Office has assumed its total capacity at the outset ought to be 30,000 pages. Before the public service was ready, however, nearly 100,000 pages had been rented, and within a few months, by Autumn 1979, 165,000 were taken up. The *Economist* magazine said that Prestel was "a bicycle made for three. Unless the P.O., the set makers, and the IP's all pedal hard, the bicycle will not climb the hill of consumer resistance."

One of the problems entailed in managing a vast database without a single editorial authority (since the Post Office has decided to run the system and steer clear of all content control) is that the total store can look rather ragged and confusing to the subscriber. Competition may breed an oversupply in one subject and a dearth of information in another. Inexperienced providers can leave the viewer with a hopelessly complex morass of indexes to pass through vexed at having to pay for wasted telephone time as he stumbles along poorly signposted information routes. The subscriber thinks he is buying a kind of encyclopedia, but in reality he is getting a vast newspaper with no editor. Many IP's have gone into the business not realizing the differences between running a newspaper and a section of a rather novel database, while other providers with good information to sell in conventional media have entered the field with insufficient understanding of how to arrange Prestel pages, how the "journalism" of the medium works. A new newspaper starts out with a small number of daily or weekly purchasers and calculates how much money will have to be spent before the break-even point is reached.

The added problem with Prestel is that the cost to the consumer, in addition to acquisition of the receiver, is variable—quite different from radio, television, and the newspaper. It is quite likely that other societies starting videotex-type services will arrange for a single annual flat fee for each subscriber, for which an infinite or a stated but limited number of pages could be accessed. That, at least, would provide useful comparative data and indicate how new media of this type might best be established. Prestel, it is agreed by virtually all involved with it, will one day be an extremely important adjunct to the information media in British society—but the problem is how to incubate it, how to prepare a society to make use of its benefits.

Perhaps the greatest long-term doubt hanging over the medium is that of whether to have (and if not, how to prevent) governmental regulation. If, eventually, public pressure for "standards" in computer-based information becomes overwhelming, some kind of statutory body could easily arise to check on the accuracy of advertising, to ensure that medical and legal information services are provided only by qualified people, and to supervise the separation of information from advertising. European societies enjoy no "First Amendment" rights. If existing newspaper concerns become major suppliers of information to Prestel and other new systems (and especially if such activity becomes an important part of their overall activity as information collectors and distributors), then newspapers would find themselves at a kind of historic crossroads, halfway between the traditional freedom from control that goes with the printing press and a regulatory status comparable with that of broadcasting. There are many points from which the pressure could come: telephone administrations tend to favor clarity of regulation over the chaos of a totally free market system; home subscribers may not want their children to have easy access to material, say, of a sexual nature; telephone administrators may find themselves under (what they feel to be) intolerable pressure to interfere with certain categories of IP, or simply to admit IP's only if they fulfill certain conditions, or to admit to the full status of three-digit IP's only those who give certain guarantees and consent, in effect, to censor the material they accept for publication.

Whatever the basis of regulation, once it starts it will almost inevitably come up against additional pressure from would-be reformers of advertising, protectors of the public against inaccurate information, who will henceforth have a regulatory agency through which they can wield influence. It will be very difficult in the long run to keep these new services free from content regulation, even though the British Post Office, at the start of its Prestel service, decided to set itself against such regulation. It adopted the attitude of a newsprint supplier to the industry, deeming it Post Office business only to supply the raw material, not to ask what it is being used for. In the case of Prestel, the legal restrictions on content (libel, official secrets, contempt of court, and the other controls that apply to all information within Britain) are dealt with under a special clause in the contract signed by intending IP's. Under this agreement the IP accepts all legal responsibility for the material he places in the Post Office computer, while the Post Office reserves the right to exclude (temporarily) any material suspected of being a breach of the law. The Post Office lawyers then advise both parties as to whether the material is likely to lead to a prosecution.

Under British law the Post Office can be held partially liable as publisher of any legally offensive information, both in civil and criminal proceedings, but can greatly reduce the risks in law if it can be seen to take reasonable steps to withold the information until its legality has been tested. This in itself, of course, could prove to be the first stepping-stone towards a system of content regulation. It may take years before we know. However, an information system that contains some hundreds of thousands of pages (and under existing plans there is little to prevent Prestel from reaching the million-page level within two or three years of operation) may be virtually immune to content regulation through its sheer size. The expense and bureaucracy entailed in any systematized prior censorship of information would be prohibitive.

A compromise solution to the question of regulation could turn out to be a system of self-regulation by a committee appointed by the IP's themselves, whose recommendations would not be legally binding but which might, in practice, give the reader an adequate level of protection and enforce a clear distinction between information and advertising. Of course, when an IP places an advertisement in the bottom three lines of a frame, it is easy to identify the material for what it is, but many advertisements are, in fact, full pages of perfectly good information (company reports, for example, or advice from insurance companies), and it is impossible to separate them from other text in the reader's mind. One of the Prestel IP's who specialize in financial information publishes this noneditorial material but insists on labeling it "advertisement," often to the disapprobation of the individual information supplier who is indeed providing accurate and balanced data for the public, even though it has not passed through the normal editorial consideration of an outside newsroom.

The traditional separation between information and advertising is difficult to maintain, not for technical reasons but because the whole nature of information supplied in a text medium is altered in subtle ways. This represents a new stage in the history of information itself, since it makes possible the placing of information before the public by organizations that for the last century have depended upon the newspaper and the professional reporter as a kind of authorized intermediary. Today any company can book space on videotex and offer material to the public, and it would be unfair to prevent it. It also wouldn't be fair to force the provider to wear the label advertisement when his information could be as reliable as an airlines timetable or meteorological report—provided in total good faith. The dilemma will remain with us and it poses a profound challenge to accepted editorial concepts. Self-regulation by IP's will undoubtedly provide in due course an acceptable system, but it is not yet clear what rules will emerge. Much pressure is being currently directed at shielding the public against inaccurate or alarming medical information or misleading legal advice that might simply disappear at the instigation of the IP's themselves. The problem of creeping regulation is one that will dog computer-based information systems of all kinds until society has become thoroughly familiar with them. Only then shall we see whether the traditional Western attitudes toward relations between authority and the press survive into the age of the computer.

III

The case history of Prestel has been dealt with at some length because the system's early experience points up some of the future characteristics of most electronic distributors of information. The most important though perhaps obvious point about Prestel is that it is not a passive medium like television or the newspaper; it doesn't just happen but has to be induced. If the reader doesn't push the button, the page will not change. It is therefore an *individual* medium, though attempting, in the long run, to become a mass medium—a paradox, which might well mean that it is too far ahead of society's patterns to succeed. Secondly, it is a publishing medium, unlike the computerized information-retrieval systems that have been in existence for some time. The pages accessed are set out with all the editorial and design talent the IP can muster; they do not consist of specific units of information so much as pages and services published and offered by a given editorial mind. It is a system in which the reader looks up frames or pages, so he must therefore come to *think* in pages.[3]

Prestel is the first constantly updatable general-information medium, and it is clearly an excellent one for perishable information. It will tell you which theaters still have unsold tickets on a particular evening, whether there are any places left in the sleeping car to Rome, whether a given quantity of copper scrap is available in a particular city—and can give up-to-the-minute stock prices as well. The reader would have to spend more money to get such information the moment he needs it by any other means or would have to take more time to get it. But this kind of information is the most expensive to provide, in terms of man power, since every minute is, in a sense a new deadline. In due course it could be an advanced kind of interactive medium, but in its early years it will not permit instant banking or even armchair shopping.

One problem for the reader presents itself when he must go backwards through his choice of pages. His skill in pursuing the logic-trees is a key element in his ability to benefit from the medium. Three lines of every page tend to be used up in routing information: how to get to the next page in a given sector of the database, how to get back to the opening page of a particular IP, how to get back to the Prestel starting page and choose a new IP. This imposes a tremendous discipline upon the IP: first, to keep each page clear and succinct and second, to keep the reader moving intelligently through what might be a complex web of information or argument or a large mass of classified information from which one nugget must be effectively extracted. Some IP's see the tree as the wrong image for the system; it is rather a series of concentric circles around a theme at the center. A reader may initiate his interest in a subject at various points in the database layout but must still be led skillfully through the material in such a way as to understand it. One important lesson learned very early on was that readers hate to have to pay for index pages, and therefore the wise IP is one who tells the reader something of interest while he is going through the index pages of a given subject. This is a good browsing medium only if the reader is helped to cope with the computer's ways and kept interested as he goes from contents table to contents table.

In the course of time it is likely that competition will cause the merging of IP's with identical information and eventually the evolution of wholly new journalisitc forms. A gush of creativity could suddenly issue forth through viewdata and dazzle everyone, but it is likely that the successful ideas will be those that offer the reader simple pieces of hard information in a quickly assimilable form. One interesting characteristic of the medium with important political implications is that it is a "by-passing" medium. It is an excellent way to send messages across bureaucracies over the heads of middle management: within organizations the head office can reach junior staff and cut out red tape. Airlines can leap over the heads of travel agents; news agencies can get their news to the public without depending on the judgment of editors as to what they might like to read; journalists, indeed, could by-pass newspapers and sell their ideas direct to the reader.[4]

Many of the lessons derived here from a study of the early days of videotex will apply to other systems in other societies whichever teletext or videotex system they finally adopt. But certain other plans for new text media deserve to be described in some detail for the technical and social differences they entail and for the ways in which the press is likely to be involved with and affected by them. The first of these is Japan's. The Telegraph and Telephone Corporation (NTT) has created CAPTAINS (the Character and Pattern Telephone Access Information Network System) which is very similar to Prestel but designed to act as the forerunner of a Video Response System. VRS will offer animated and still pictures (with sound) to the home—the world's first composite household information system—some years after CAPTAINS has established itself. It is therefore seen as a transition medium to something much bigger and better than videotex as we now know it. In the years 1976 to 1978 the Japanese conducted a complex multimedia experiment in Tama New Town, in which media as diverse as facsimile newspapers and cable television were tried out, all in the same community. CAPTAINS was present in a rudimentary form, accessed via microfiche at a central point, and it has been selected for rapid development in the 1980's. A CAPTAIN System Development Association was set up in 1978, 3 billion yen were set aside by NTT, and 120 information providers volunteered to participate in a test of 1000 homes, 20 newspaper companies, 25 publishing companies, 10 travel agents, 10 stores, and 21 broadcasting companies and public associations.

Japanese studies of the patterns of use by ordinary consumers of the total volume of information circulating in society convinced the telecommunications planners that the next priority should be to counteract the one-way flow of mass communication media. In particular, it should be possible to use new processes to provide information for individuals, rather than mass audiences, and allow them to select what they wish to receive from the total flow. The researchers discovered that since 1969 public use of the new (sound only) telephone information services had been leaping upwards, nearly doubling every year, even though the telephone is not conducive to the provision of highly diversified information.

Nearly 3000 different telephone information services—sent by private IP's to the public—now exist in Japan. CAPTAINS emerged in the minds of planners as a way of filling the gap between one-way mass-audience communication and completely individual communication (telephone, telex, letter, telegram). The Japanese feel they have found the point of breakthrough between two stages in the evolution of the Information Society. They calculate that by the end of the 1980's the average household will use 1000 pages of CAPTAINS per month, equal to half an hour's use per day in the average home. This would involve an average household spending of 5000 yen per month (compared with the British Post Office's estimate of $100 per annum for the average Prestel user) at which point it will become economic to introduce the advanced VRS medium with its full-scale picture service. It will be possible to collect CAPTAINS material relatively cheaply overnight on a cassette tape recorder. Unlike Britain, Japan will have a statutory central editorial authority, but with a great deal of internal self-regulation among the providers. The Japanese have already experienced political difficulties over allegedly pornographic telephone information services, and the NTT is not leaving the issue merely to chance. The "regulators" have thus won their first battle.

Unlike the British Post Office, the NTT finds that a number of institutional and constitutional hurdles still have to be surmounted before the new medium can be launched into the world of Japanese information.

There are problems concerning the legal validity of the NTT monopoly if it moves into this territory, and other problems arise from broadcasting legislation and involve the status of information monopolies under Japanese law. The common-carrier status of the NTT in this field must be clarified as well as the overall legal status of IP's. In addition, issues of copyright and various provisions of the criminal law have to be dealt with. A great deal of groundwork has to be done, therefore, and this is likely to take several years, although it will not prevent the experimental and trial services being put into motion. All societies that have clear provisions in their national constitutions guaranteeing press liberty or liberty of information will—paradoxically—find a number of obstacles to the easy development of public information from computerized systems. The British, without a Bill of Rights or explicit constitutional freedoms or a separation of powers, and the French, with their highly centralized control of telecommunications, are both relatively free of such problems and are able to steer the relevant national institutions into these uncharted seas.

CAPTAINS is likely to be a tremendous boon to Japanese society, especially if it is attached at the receiving end to hard-copy printout equipment. The Japanese language has been extremely difficult to adapt to the common typewriter, and setting newspapers in a mixture of Chinese characters, arabic numerals, roman letters, and two indigenous syllabaries involves a much higher degree of skill than setting Western newspapers. Journalists in Japan submit their copy handwritten in pencil on special paper marked in rows of squares, and the compositors have the task of deciphering the sometimes hurriedly corrected text. Very few Japanese are capable of handling a typewriter. It takes about twenty years to train a first-class compositor who must be able to recognize up to 50,000 characters, although he uses about 4000 in daily setting work. (Indeed, it is the shortage of such skills that has encouraged the introduction of computerized typesetting in many parts of Japan.) A combination of the Kyodo News Agency's system for translating romanized script to kanji by means of CAPTAINS could have considerable impact on the whole development of Japanese culture—just as the typewriter has had for the alphabet-endowed cultures—since it could enable the Japanese to have a form of instant artificial writing that is generally available.

The computer promises, therefore, to remove one of the last remaining obstacles to modernization in Japan, without causing the destruction of its traditional writing system. It will, however, require a great deal more computer power to do this than comparable information systems in the West, as the simple storage of the capacity to generate 4000 characters (each composed of up to 33 brushstrokes) requires a memory of 700 Kbits (compared with 7 Kbits for Prestel). This is why CAPTAINS is rather different in design from the present systems in Europe where the character-generator equipment is contained inside each receiver. Instead, CAPTAINS will place the character generator in the system Center, which can cope with up to sixty callers at a time—each of them requesting text material by keypad and then waiting fifteen or thirty seconds for the Center to reply by sending a complete page of text down the line into the receiver. (In due course the number of callers that can be handled at one time will be multiplied.) Placing the character-generator at the Center means that each receiver need have only one tenth of the computer capacity that would otherwise be necessary with Japanese script. In the experimental era (which will last through the early 1980's) the domestic user will have a sixteen-button keypad. However, a fifty-button pad will arrive in the mid-1980's permitting very sophisticated forms of interaction with the Center, which will make possible a kind of home printing system.

Each frame or display can contain up to 120 characters, although the later refinements will make possible the use of up to 480 smaller characters in a single display. Because of its high capacity CAPTAINS is capable of generating a number of simple pictures, since a set of patterns made of mosaic elements has been built into the memory (see figure 9), and these may be composed at will into designs. Each display will have a fixed design or one that can be vertically scrolled upwards at constant speed until the end of a flow of text or sequence of pictures; the reader can push "stop" or "start" at any point in this process. The usual range of eight colors is possible as well as the ability to make any section of the text "blink."

Placing information into the CAPTAIN system is rather more difficult than with Prestel. The providers can physically send their copy to the Center or send it by facsimile, which will involve the use of an extra terminal at the information-sending base. Only the staff at the Center will be able to punch the material into the system, which necessitates the creation of a complete and perfect manuscript copy of every frame of text by every IP.

The main group of intending suppliers of information in Japan are, of course, the newspaper publishers, and the association of publishers (NSK) is heavily involved in the development of the system. The total storage of the public system will begin at about 1 million frames but will rapidly grow with a goal of 100 million in the planner's minds. The Japanese public has demonstrated since the 1950's a huge capacity

Figure 9

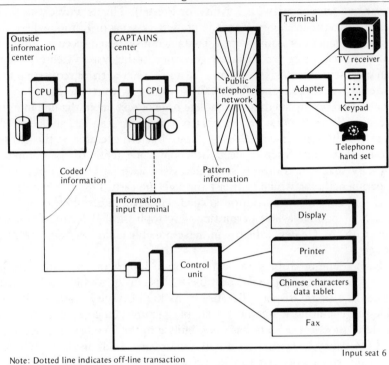

Note: Dotted line indicates off-line transaction

Input seat 6

to absorb information, and CAPTAINS will undoubtedly help to fill an important gap, which although present in all industrial societies is particularly large in Japan where the transmission and manipulation of text is extremely labor-intensive.

The interconnection of CAPTAINS with teletext-type services also presents something of a problem. Two such systems have been designed in Japan. The first belongs to Nippon Hoso Kyokai (NHK), the public broadcasting system, whose engineers have devised a method for disassembling ideographic images into dots, converting them into impulses, and superimposing them on the field-blanking interval, as with Ceefax, ORACLE, etc. Asahi broadcasting has developed another, similar system that scans the material vertically, as opposed to NHK's horizontal scanning method. Both can be superimposed over a TV picture. It is difficult, however, to find a way of rendering these systems compatible with CAPTAINS in the same receiver. When the services finally go public, the information offered will be coordinated between teletext-services and CAPTAINS, rather than offered competitively as in the United Kingdom's services.

We have concentrated on those text services that have been furthest developed at the end of the 1970's, but it is by no means certain that these will be the ones that prove the most durable in the long run. Appendix A provides a complete list of those extant or in planning stages, and any one of them could, for reasons quite unconnected with purely technical design, turn out to win the international scramble for media. At Rennes, in France, the Antiope system, developed by the Centre Commun d'Etudes de Télévision et de Télécommunications (CCETT), contains a host of capabilities absent in its rivals, and despite a relatively late start it is gaining ground among the European systems. Antiope (Acquisition Numérique et Télévisualisation d'Images Organisées en Pages d'Ecriture), the key to France's drive toward mass high–technology, is able to generate characters from any of the alphabets in use around the world, together with simple pictures and diagrams. It can be sent either multiplexed with a normal television picture, like Ceefax, ORACLE, etc., or can be generated through a radio signal or wire. Its ability to perform a large number of "tricks" is the result of a decision by CCETT engineers to provide it with a kind of electronic version of a typewriter's carriage-return device. This frees it from the need to send out a signal for every single space on the screen, whether used in a given frame or not, and thus multiplies its character versatility. This does mean that the signal is in danger of loss of clarity in mountainous areas or wherever the broadcast signal is difficult to receive. But where the signal is generated through wires, this potential deficiency does not arise, and thus the long-term potential of Antiope is very promising. Like CAPTAINS, Antiope contains a number of (sixty-four) semigraphic forms that can be composed into pictures. Like the other teletext systems it may be used for superimposition over a television signal, for subtitling for the deaf, for the flashing of urgent news.

France has decided that the closed and integrated structure of Prestel (and similar services in Holland, Finland, and elsewhere) is not suited to its requirements and has devised a structure that completely separates the information service from the network. Antiope began as a method for packet-switching through a broadcast signal, i.e., sending large quantities of information in digital form in short bursts along an ordinary broadcasting frequency. An experiment started in September 1976 by which this computer device—known as Didon—sent stock exchange information to ordinary adapted TV screens, in other words as a kind of teletext system. Didon is the heart of Antiope but its separate development means that all other problems associated with public-information systems are handled elsewhere. Antiope came about as a system of public information built upon a number of existing databases, which were regularly updated in real time—and the elements of this system were partly modeled on Prestel and compatible with it. In August 1977 an attempt was made at the Berlin Radio Fair to demonstrate that Antiope information could be sent both as a broadcast mode (via Didon) and in an interactive mode by way of the normal telephone network. A month later British, French, and German engineers managed to work out the basic standardization of *display*, which is used today by Antiope, Prestel, and the Bildschirmtext and videotext (with a final "t") systems of the Federal German Republic. The differences of transmission and of basic concept have not interfered with the construction of a European display system compatible with all 625-line adapted TV receivers.

The French system is a kind of hybrid. Broadcast videotex units will receive information from a number of public sources (the Bourse, the weather office, etc.) and from other authorized suppliers, including the normal television channels. This information may pass either into the national network or into a regional subdivision of it. Individual providers may operate within the system on the basis of a closed-user group (as in Prestel). But, equally well, the system may be used for interactive material sent from a very large number of subscribers, which is automatically switched by the telecommunications administration through the telephone network. The PTT takes total charge of the transmission system but has no control over the content, which is entirely in the hands of the providers and retrievers.

During the opening hours of the Paris Bourse—to take one interesting example of how this system might operate—a magazine of eighty-two pages is sent out, continuously updated with information on prices, through the Didon broadcast network. Outside those hours, the information is deemed to be of interest to a much narrower audience, who may wish to be highly selective of the information required. The data is therefore switched to the telephone network during these hours, at corresponding cost to the user. Antiope can also work together with facsimile services, and it will be used for a national telemail system when cheap hard-copy devices are available (i.e. it can send material to individual receivers in hard copy). Antiope can receive material from a subscriber in its character mode and then retransmit it to a hard-copy device owned by another subscriber, in facsimile mode. Unlike many other telemail services being pioneered in the 1980's, Antiope should be able to send pages of material—at four minutes per page—from an office to the home of a domestic subscriber, with interesting and imponderable results for the traditional postal services of France. The transmission authorities are planning to re-engineer one of their national television channels that has been transmitting in duplicate on 819 lines to the needs of broadcast videotex (teletext) and thus could make a whole channel (instead of merely a few redundant lines within a channel, as is the case with Ceefax and ORACLE) available for broadcasting text information.

In the early 1980's field trials are being held in various parts of France both for broadcast and interactive versions of the transmission system of Antiope. From the point of view of existing information suppliers (such as newspapers), Antiope's institutional arrangements have a great deal to offer: a mass audience at very low cost without the intervention of a broadcasting newsroom or editor. This corresponds very closely to what the German newspaper industry demanded of Bildschirmzeitung, but which is currently only obtainable elsewhere in Europe through the more cumbersome and expensive viewdata systems.

A very interesting constitutional dilemma has opened up in Germany over the introduction of public services of computerized text, although it has not greatly hampered the new media in their experimental phase. Until the problems have been resolved, no real development can take place, and German industry, as well as the information providers, finds itself somewhat hampered. However, the resolution of the issue, as will become clear, will present Germany with an additional series of problems affecting the entire regulation of radio, television, and telecommunications as a whole.

The federal government has no jurisdiction over broadcasting in Germany—radio, television, and associated issues being the responsibility of the eleven "Land" (state) governments. However, the Federal Ministry of Posts and Telecommunications is the licensing authority and the Bundespost (Post Office) operates the only legal carrier. It so happens that at present the political parties at Land level are particularly keen not to surrender any constitutional authority over the broadcasting system of the country, since there are powerful commercial interests (revolving around the Springer press concern) lobbying for the opening up of commercial television. Meanwhile, the German press is most anxious to ensure that no new printed medium is inaugurated under the control of Land or Federal authorities, and the newspaper publishers have themselves experimented with text systems, exhibiting their version of teletext along with that offered by the Bundespost at the 1977 Radio Fair in Berlin. The newspapers argue that a written text belongs to the genre "press" and is not subject to broadcasting regulation, whatever the mode of its transmission. The broadcasters argue that anything transmitted via radio waves is naturally and legally within their orbit and must therefore be regulated as broadcasting is regulated (i.e., under the authority of the Land parliaments. The conflict echoes an older one, going back to the formation of the modern German state, between broadcasters and print publishers.

The newspapers take their determination to the point of employing different terminology in their descriptions of the new media. They always refer to videotex and teletext as Bildschirmzeitung (screen newspaper), whether it is in the broadcast or interactive mode. Their version of the media would depend upon advertising, while the broadcasters' would be sent free of charge, an extra service disseminated in exchange for the payment of the normal radio and television license fee.[5] The Bundespost and the Länder (the provincial state administrations) use the term videotext (with a "t") for teletext services and Bildschirmtext for the interactive (Prestel-type) service.

The Bundespost has been operating advanced telephone information services for many years, and to this neither Länder nor newspapers have objected. Now the Bundespost argues that the development of public-information devices into visual form is merely an extension of a practice that has always continued without objections being raised. Länder and press might be able to compromise over the setting up of an organization that would operate the provision of a service but that would exercise no editorial authority over the content—and this would avoid the establishment of a Federal Ministry to run a service received on domestic television screens. But if the press were to make this concession and a special new transmission authority were created, the Länder would be in the awkward position of tacitly surrendering their monopoly over broadcasting transmission, thereby opening the door to the lobby for commerical broadcasting. In the interim, however, the German newspapers continue to argue that both media rightfully belong to the world of the press— although no one can really envisage newspapers ever being granted authority over a teletext system, tied as it is to a television signal. Germany's videotext system will almost certainly end up as an adjunct to the ARD and ZDF television networks, while the Bundespost, when the constitutional issue is resolved, will be able to move ahead with a service it hopes will bring large amounts of revenue from telephone users.[6]

Another society with a dual approach is Canada, where the Telidon system has been developed by the Communications Research Center of the Canadian Department of Communications, and Vista has been produced by Bell Canada in consortium with the publishers of the *Toronto Star* and the *Southam Press*. It is the former, a highly sophisticated version of Prestel, that is arousing the greatest interest, since it is compatible with every available form of transmission system—telephone line, coaxial cable, optic fiber, and broadcast signal. It is far more interactive than any of the other systems hitherto devised, but it is partially compatible with all of them in its display characteristics: Telidon receivers could display Antiope, Prestel, and CAPTAINS, etc., but these could not display all of the figures and forms offered by Telidon.[7]

Telidon uses an adapted television receiver plus a microcomputer and a keypad. The system requires a central computer and a network. Its users are offered the facility of common intercommunication, and with the use of a special keyboard terminal all forms of written and graphic communication are possible; the user can draw material on his screen with a light pen and transmit it to an interlocutor. Telidon has been constructed on the basis of very high resolution produced by a much larger terminal memory store than any rival system. While the other systems are built upon forms constructed in mosaic patterns, Telidon describes its basic forms as points, lines, arcs, rectangles, and polygons—building up pictures from a large repertoire of geometric elements. A Telidon monitor can register resolutions built upon 4096 x 4096 elements on a single display, compared with 240 x 320 for the average color receiver. It can therefore transmit photographs by describing them as a series of points. The Telidon terminal contains a built-in mini-computer, which offers a tremendous versatility, although all of the necessary equipment can be packed in a box the size of a telephone directory. It is estimated that it will eventually be sold as a $250 addition to the TV receiver.

Telidon offers the prospect of a kind of total domestic communciation system, including telebanking, education, and shopping. Its only drawback is simply that it is too far advanced for the average telecommunications network. When advanced transmission systems such as optic fibers become widely used, it will be possible for systems as complex as Telidon to perform to their full potential. It is this problem of transmission capacity that now bedevils the regulation of this new text device in Canada. Cable companies are arguing for the right to disseminate services of the Telidon variety, since their operation as telephone adjuncts would in due course leave cable to wither. However, if the cable companies were to develop text and graphic services, it would be tantamount to the development of rival common carrier networks to the telephone. So far, experimental licenses have been granted to cable companies, but the main constitutional question still remains to be faced.

At the end of the decade of the 1970's, an atmosphere of flurry has developed in the videotex and teletext worlds. Nation after nation is announcing its debut in one or another mode, and several countries, such as Canada, are involved in internally competitive systems (or experiments). It is not surprising that the newspaper industry is beginning to worry about the potential effect of a sudden spread of cheap computer-based information systems around the world. However, the problems of standardization between systems (without which no mass market in domestic equipment across national frontiers is likely to arrive) and problems of national regulation, which may remain unresolved for many years, mean that the existing systems may remain in the experimental phase for a very long time.

When the outstanding problems are listed, it becomes clear that the time scale of development is much longer than was once envisaged. First, it will be necessary for North American regulatory authorities to determine whether videotex will be treated as electronic data processing (EDP), which would place it outside the scope of U.S. and Canadian telephone companies and other common carriers, unless these operate as "value-added carriers." (These carriers simply purchase a transmission service from a telephone company, add processing services to the information they acquire, and sell the combined result to the public.) In the U.S. at present Telenet and Tymnet already operate specialist services in this value-added carrier role. Until this grey area of regulation is clarified, it will not be clear whether AT&T will be permitted to provide a UK-type national network for the mass domestic market. In the meantime GTE is purchasing Telenet and has also acquired the right to use the British Prestel system's software. One related set of problems pertains to the American view toward CATV as a whole. Will CATV operators be permitted to move into the field of videotex, using their localized transmission systems as the building blocks of a national network?

In the European context there is a problem of frequency provision for teletext services. It is possible, by adopting something of the French approach, that some countries could satisfy their needs for mass-information services without constructing new networks and without building a national system on the telephone network. Germany, as we have seen, is experiencing a number of constitutional variations of the "normal" tensions between existing information suppliers such as newspapers and the new potential IP's. All countries, in fact, have to sort out the same problem in one form or another and decide whether to keep all existing publishers—apart from registered broadcasters—away from the teletext services, even when these succeed in expanding their capacity to store and transmit. Many countries have yet to decide who should be permitted to operate the central information store: new or existing publishers, computer bureaus, or the carrier?

Hanging over the entire development of the medium is the problem of demand: is a mere long-term expectation of mass demand sufficient to persuade providers, receiver manufacturers, and the other parties in the medium to undertake the large investments necessary? It is arguable that the real image of the medium will not emerge in the public imagination until all the earlier regulatory and technical problems are resolved. Only then will it be possible to foresee the level of eventual demand and only then will it become wise to plan long-term investment in assembly lines, promotion, and the training of personnel. As with color television, cassettes, and other electronic devices, the manufacturing of this equipment is likely to be based upon international markets and suppliers. There could well be room in the international scene for a few new major companies to arise, especially in Europe where a determined effort might be made to reduce the volume of Japanese imports in the 1980's.

However, no international market can be established until problems of standardization of national systems are solved. Furthermore, until 1983 or 1984 no major initiative within the international bodies concerned will be made in dealing with the four remaining technical issues in which standardization has a number of political overtones. These relate, first, to the precise character set that is to be adopted for Latin-based alphabets, where accented letters and currency symbols have become locked into various international technical disagreements; second, to the techniques for the provision of graphics where there is a range of different approaches, the resolution of which involves an agreed trade-off between the quality of the graphics provided and the cost of providing the generating capability in terminal equipment; third, to problems of display format, where the 625-line systems of Europe offer 25 lines of 40 characters and the 525-line system of North America offers 20 lines of 32 characters, and fourth, to Code Extension techniques, or the way in which foreign alphabets and other special symbols are added to the repertoire of a system. In all these matters the problems of interface with the Japanese information devices are a further complicating factor, and one that has a special bearing on the attitudes of manufacturers.

It is this long set of sobering complexities that makes the time scale between enthusiastic pioneering of videotex, teletext, and their variants and the provision of mass public services an ever lengthening one. For newspaper publishers the 1980's will be an era in which participation in a new medium becomes possible, when staff can be trained and styles explored, but it is not likely to be an era in which fundamental changes occur in the whole configuration of the newspaper as a form. That will not be until the 1990's, perhaps late in the 1990's.[8]

IV

What one begins to see emerging from these extensions to the common television receiver is a kind of home-printed information apparatus, the latest in a long line of equipment that began with the home music apparatus, or phonograph, and continued with the home audio and visual information apparatus of radio and television. One might place the washing machine in this list of devices that all have in common the transference of a set of functions from public to private, from general to personal, from imposed service with narrow choice to individualized service with infinite choice. The new media all tend to suggest a process of domestication of living functions, the privatization of information. Some of the new experimental services open up another whole area of life to this process—the purchasing of goods, which remains an activity not yet altered by any new technology in the course of this century. We continue to acquire goods, for the most part, in public places rather than at home, but some of the new devices now being offered will give consumers the opportunity to review, select, and actually purchase goods from their homes.

It is in this respect that the QUBE system of Columbus, Ohio, requires some discussion, for it will offer a combination of home information, selected home entertainment, and the purchase of merchandise from the home (even though this has not yet figured in the public experiments in Columbus). QUBE is the most versatile of all existing cable systems, and its various capacities, while not exclusive to QUBE, are impossible to find in a single project or in such profusion elsewhere in the world.

The system is owned by Warner Cable, a subsidiary of Warner Communications, and is available to all 100,000 homes in its area on payment of $11 per month. Well over $10 million have been invested in what is clearly designed to be a pilot scheme for future mass development. Warner already had 13,000 homes subscribing to its normal cable system in Columbus, and QUBE is thus a refinement of a standard service.

There are thirty channels on the system: ten offer commercial television station signals from five local cities; ten offer (at extra cost) first-run and other movies, live performances of orchestras, ballet companies, etc., sports and other events, college courses, adult films, games and instruction in cooking, musical instrument playing, etc.; and the last ten channels are assigned to community activity—including local information on sports, news, consumer-interest material, children's programs, religious material, etc. See figure 10 for an example of QUBE program.) All of this is chosen and accessed from a three-button pad that chooses a main category and a further row of ten buttons to select a channel within each category. In addition, there are five response buttons, used for QUBE's interactive services and operated in conjunction with a microprocessor similar to that of a hand calculator; this device unscrambles the material in the second group of channels (for what extra charges are made) and enables viewers to "vote" in local programs. (All the viewers can be polled, and the reaction announced in ten seconds.)[9]

QUBE features an important facility for "narrowcasting," whereby a specified communicator (e.g., a pharmaceutical firm wanting to contact doctors, a university wanting to contact certain faculty members) can provide a list of homes to receive a specific program some hours ahead of time and then send the tape or live programming only to those on the list.

Because of the possibility of constant monitoring of all homes on the system, there are inevitable fears about the invasion of privacy and other, perhaps more urgent, fears concerning the overall cost. (Viewers can run up large bills for those programs that require extra payment without being fully aware of what is happening.) Live sports events cost $2.50 and first-run movies slightly more. Plans nonetheless exist for a second community in Ohio to be brought into a similar system and for an increase in the total amount of extra programming to forty-five hours a week. In the early 1980's another five cities should be added to the Warner experiment, and major advertisers are beginning to interest themselves in QUBE's possibilities. Local movie theaters are inevitably concerned about loss of business, although QUBE offers the film maker a completely new outlet for his work that could in the long run prove highly profitable.

One of the most interesting additional services incorporated in the design is a burglar and fire alarm as well as an "energy load leveling service" whereby the system will automatically lower the thermostat in subscribers' homes during working hours. (This might be how the subscriber could come to cover the cost of QUBE as a whole.)

Perhaps the most important characteristic of QUBE for students of information systems is the way in which it concentrates information of a particular kind into a single channel. The children's program has a whole channel to itself, and in the course of time different channels could become the exclusive domain of different "genres." This involves a kind of negation of the normal scheduling of a television channel, development that is already being pioneered by the home video cassette recorder, which permits selection of network programs at nonscheduled times. QUBE goes much further and permits the viewer to indulge only his own particular interests. In the long run, when local stores take channels of their own, subscribers will be able to make their normal purchases from their armchairs, choosing from a display of merchandise on their screens. It would be difficult to scan as many varieties of goods as is possible when standing in front of the shelf of a store, but the device reduces traveling time and inconvenience and permits the growth of organized home-delivery services, which have declined in most parts of the United States fairly steadily since World War II. QUBE, therefore, is a potential revolutionizer of entertainment habits and could play an important role in the privatization of many areas of social life—and, in a sense, of political life too—in its capacity to conduct instant scanning of viewers' opinions and choices. It monitors a community as it feeds them with information. For the traditional newspaper QUBE presents, in the long term, a serious challenge as well as a fresh opportunity. It would be relatively simple to add a videotex–type service or any other form of alphanumeric information through a single spare channel and produce an electronic newspaper, paid for according to usage.

Among QUBE's most attractive new services are its sensoring devices, which could become the basis of the system's commercial success, although they are not related to any of the information services that are QUBE's most conspicuous elements. QUBE offers its customers a black box that will warn the local police whenever anyone enters a pre-set room—a motion-sensing burglar alarm; it will also set a buzzer off if smoke activates a ceiling detector, which can be attached to the system. QUBE offers a "duress button" for calling the police and a medical emergency button for calling an ambulance. There is even a personal security medallion that will send off warnings automatically, if, for example, an elderly person wearing it slips in the street close to home. The computer, when alarmed, disgorges the individual's medical history for the ambulance crew. All of these alarm services work from a single black box packed with microprocessors, which is under constant questioning from the central QUBE processing unit. In effect, it is constantly being asked, "Is everything OK?" and takes action as soon as it gets a negative response. Altogether, these services will cost an extra $100 to install plus $12 per month.[10]

At the other end of the scale of services there is a channel dedicated to soft porn (Hard R, in QUBE management's language), which has to be specially requested by the subscriber and which has a special locking device that supposedly keeps it from the eyes of children. The difference between QUBE and other Home Box Office lines is that with QUBE a differential pricing system is possible for each selection (75 cents for a shorthand course, to $9 for a major football game), while Home Box Office charges a monthly fee for its services. QUBE normally allows a two-minute period to intervene between selection and the start of the service, in case the subscriber suddenly regrets his decision.

There are fairly primitive examples of interaction between subscriber and center, however. *Columbus Alive*, the nightly local program uses collective audience feedback as a basic technique for its shows. The host of a program can poll his audience constantly, asking their reaction to the subject under discussion and informing them instantly of the percentages of the results. After book review programs subscribers request a book that has been discussed, and after pressing their button, their name and address automatically go forward to the distributor. Services of this kind hover between information and advertisement and are known as infomercials (a short infomercial is called a Qubit). They are paid for by the provider and are not infrequently used by companies wanting a cheap and rapid form of market survey. Advertisers pilot different versions of television commercials this way; magazine publishers sample viewers' reactions to different possible magazine covers.

The QUBE system contains a vast amount of demographic data about the homes that subscribe to it which can be switched on at any moment; the market researcher can therefore receive demographic information of a sophistication never before thought possible—and all of it instantly on his desk. By 1980 interactivity will be developed to the point at which an electronic funds-transfer system can be built into QUBE. Subscribers will not only be able to buy products displayed on the screen but have their local bank accounts instantly billed and deducted for the goods before they are delivered; special security measures are being added to prevent or inhibit the misuse of this feature.

The next large city in line for a QUBE-type system is Pittsfield, Massachusetts, but other two-way cable systems will be coming to the Borough of Queens in New York (through the Knickerbocker Communication Corporation's cable franchise) and to Boston. Cable has been growing steadily but slowly in the United States since the first community antennas were established in the 1950's. It is thought by many cable operators that two-way cable might be the long-looked-for extra attraction that would encourage the public to raise the level of cabling from the 20 percent of all television households of 1978 to the 30 percent level necessary before cable can turn into an important mass device. The advent of satellite channels supplying cable installations with rich packages of material has transformed the prospects for cable as a whole. Warner decided to invest its $20 million in QUBE in the hope that a massive injection of material and services into one pocket of homes of above-average wealth would prove one way or the other whether cable was going to win the fight for existence.

In 1974 there were 3000 systems functioning in the U.S. The rate of growth has increased so that 4000 systems (serving 9200 communities) were functioning within another four years. Many more thousands of systems have been licensed but not installed, as companies continue to guess the market trend. Already, however, the cable business has reached the billion-dollar-a-year level. Teleprompter Corporation is the largest single operator, with its Manhattan franchise, and feeds its service to over 1 million subscribers in 110 systems; its cable earnings in 1978 were just below $20 million. Nonetheless, the cable has not yet reached the critical mass of viewers it requires to become a permanent and profitable feature of the country.

Unquestionably, the issue of privacy is the most vexing problem in the context of the QUBE experiment. Viewers are warned whenever they are about to indicate via their buttons a fact about themselves that will be recorded. Warner management has taken care to institute regular procedures to safeguard all data that their subscribers have supplied about themselves. QUBE could easily cause friction within as well as between families. It could reveal the fact that a subscriber who votes a straight "puritan" ticket in all the polling programs is, in fact, a secret heavy user of the porn channel. It could analyze over a time the accumulating information from a single family, revealing its internal tensions at many levels. It is a system that can wreak havoc through the creation of shame and by manipulating the fear of shame. It can monitor the spending habits and cultural tastes of individuals within a family. In the hands of the unscrupulous it could bring misery and terror into peoples' lives. The odd thing is that the privacy question is seldom raised by the subscribers themselves. It could be that the privacy issue is a slow time bomb awaiting detonation by some dramatic incident or cause célèbre, or that privacy is far less highly prized in our time than it was in the past.

Perhaps, also, people are beginning to feel sufficiently secure in their tastes and life-styles and no longer require a wall of secrecy around large areas of their lives.

However, with public support for the deregulation of services by the FCC continuing to grow, it will become easier for the unscrupulous to intrude. If the whole system of federal regulation that has functioned since the 1920's is ended, as may well occur, the only safeguards of secrecy left will be local laws, which are often weak and inconsistent. Of course, public sentiment and responsible management will remain powerful safeguards, but they cannot guarantee the security of information that may be damaging years after it has been inadvertently supplied. Only a society that has decided to relax the traditional social taboos against the exposure of personal details could allow such a change to take place. Perhaps the sacrifice of privacy will be the trade-off for the national dislike of bureaucracy.

Prestel, QUBE, and CAPTAINS are still only interesting pioneer services among the new media—not domestic necessities—and we are not likely to know which if any of them have the prospect of becoming so before the end of the 1980's. By that time we shall be living in a new "infosphere" in which the whole relationship we have with information (as individuals and societies) will most likely be altered. The habits of work and leisure that have been the basis of the existing media and their methods of financial support may be in the process of radical change at the end of that decade, and this fact must surely change the terms in which new media become plausible and old media seek out new roles or disappear.

V

The services we have discussed are fundamentally extensions of existing media or existing ways of transmitting material. They are all attachments, basically, to the common television receiver via telephone wires or special cables. At the same time as these pioneer services are being devised and while they are, in a sense, testing the social temperature to see whether new markets and new kinds of choices are likely to take, much broader and potentially more powerful technical possibilities are being explored. In fact, the growth of such phenomena as home alphanumeric information will depend upon the development of radically new ways of storing information, switching it from storage to user and transmitting it through wires or through the spectrum by digital techniques. By the time the pioneering services have proved their usefulness, these new methods of greatly enhancing their capacity and reducing their cost will be widely developed.

In 1970 it cost about one U.S. cent to "store" one bit or single character on a magnetic disc. Within five years the cost had dropped to a hundredth of a cent, and by 1980 it will have dropped by a further proportion, i.e., to one thousandth of the 1970 cost, despite the upsurge in general prices during that decade. There are prospects of further dramatic declines between 1980 and 1990. A holofiche, a clear oblong piece of plastic about as large as a human hand, can store 200 million bytes of information, enough for a couple of volumes of an encyclopedia. Magnetic bubble memories, which store bits of information in great quantities in tiny crystals of garnet stone and which have the advantage of keeping material stored even when they are not connected to any other computer or source of power, operate at extremely high speed, absorbing and offering information nearly a hundred times as rapidly as the magnetic discs normally used in computers. In addition, there are charge-coupled devices (ccd's) that store information as a series of electrical charges on a silicon chip, and still further developments are underway such as the 'ultrafiche,' which will compete for use in terms of cheapness of storage and speed of access in the new "intelligent terminals" of the future. These newer devices have a whole generation of older techniques still to compete with, such as magnetic discs and tapes and drums, which will all remain in service for some time to come.

Some computer experts have begun to feel that the process of miniaturization of microprocessors is reaching a plateau. Their view is based upon the belief that photolithography (the precision skill by which carefully prepared drawings are progressively reduced to the minute sizes of silicon wafers and which lies at the heart of the microprocessor revolution) is coming to an end of its current phase of rapid development.[11] In 1970 photolithographic expertise enabled resolutions in microns (or in millionths of a meter) to be achieved. At the end of the 1970's precision of 2.5 microns will be achievable, but nobody believes that in one further decade this will have been reduced again by the same amount as it has in the last decade—which would mean resolutions of 0.5 microns. However, a completely new technology might come to the aid of an "exhausted" photolithography, in which the circuit patterns on silicon wafers could be drawn with a computer-controlled beam. IBM has joined this particular line of development and it appears to base its future prospects in semiconductor technology on success in this endeavor.

Parallel with this research, efforts are being made to improve the means by which microprocessors are mounted and packaged into the circuit cards or circuit boards in such a way as to permit maintenance and repair work, cooling and interconnection. We are at the beginning of an exploration of new techniques for chip packaging through the multi-chip module and new ways of cooling and repairing the devices.

The growing capacity of memories in the most widely used computer series (the IBM 360's and 370's) has demonstrated through the 1960's and 1970's how rapidly the cost of main core storage (i.e., in the body of the central computer) is falling. The IBM 3850 can store 472 billion characters with an access wait of one third of a millionth of a second, with improvements to come. The costs of storage in 1977 have dropped to one fiftieth of what they were in 1966. But a swing is taking place between "shelf" storage of material on discs and on-line storage, which is now overtaking the former. This suggests that more and more organizations are using their computers for operational work, rather than periodic calculation activity. At the same time, the speed at which material can be read onto magnetic memories is increasing consistently with the rate of increase in storage space, thus guaranteeing that the data-access rate is keeping in step with storage data. Unfortunately techniques of improving "seek time" (the time it takes to scan magnetic discs to find the material requested) are not improving as fast, and wholly new technologies will have to be explored to break this bottleneck. The way through this will probably turn out to be either through the new bubble memories or charge-coupled devices, which will make the link between the relatively expensive main memories with their rapid access and the slower, larger magnetic storage systems. The dizzyingly rapid evolution of the electronic memory represents, however, only one major area of contemporary activity.

In the second major area of development, satellites, innovation has gone much further than the economic and political arrangements necessary for exploiting it, and we may now expect that satellites will be developed with much less sophistication in the next decades than the satellite designers themselves wish. Modern space craft have much greater power than their predecessors through more efficient storage batteries, and they can focus their beams far more narrowly on the earth's surface than in the past, thereby permitting longer space life and a greater range of services. Within the decade of the 1980's it will be possible for a great deal of rooftop-level communication via satellite to be introduced. Already the Japanese are using an antenna that can be manufactured for $100 each and is only twenty-four inches across. The new space shuttle operated by NASA can put satellites in orbit cheaply and efficiently, and plans exist for a space platform that could hold a number of satellites belonging to quite different nations and agencies, offering cheap satellite capacity to individual companies and small countries. Each such satellite could carry 100,000 voice circuits, equal to one hundred television channels. In addition, satellites will be able to transmit direct to the home.

However, all such development depends upon the small number of nations who are active in such technology obtaining the right to use adequate bandwidths from the international community. The Third World countries have much bargaining power, though little technical expertise in this field, and are likely to hold back the development of satellite capacity in the hope of holding onto their share of the world's limited stock of suitable bands until they are technically able to exploit them. Until these international questions are settled, the bands within the electromagnetic spectrum that are used for sending signals from earth to satellite and back again will become highly congested, despite great advances in the improved use of the signal power available. Nonetheless, during the eighties the important and indeed revolutionary function of the satellite—to reduce distance as a factor in the cost of sending messages—will begin to become apparent in the field of data and print communication as it already has in the telephone business.

One new transmission technology based upon satellites is the "moving finger," or electronic beam scan; this is a tiny microwave beam that would sweep across a landmass, rather like the electronic beam that sweeps across the television receiver. Given fully digitalized messages, this device could increase very considerably the overall channel capacity of a nation and permit the use of much smaller, less expensive ground stations.

The third basic area of development consists of various new systems of transmission. By far the most important in the next period of time will be optical fibers that send light signals through fibers as thin as human hairs, wrapped inside a cable. These will probably come to replace most of the existing copper wire that has been accumulating beneath the ground for over a century. They will probably also replace the coaxial cables that have been the basis of the breakthrough of the last ten years from narrow- to broad-band transmission. Glass fiber has been thoroughly tested by the military and is in commercial use for civilian purposes in Canada, the U.S., Japan, Britain, and Australia.[12] The main problem with the technique is that the fiber is subject to considerable attentuation of signal over long stretches, but it is now possible to re-boost the signal very efficiently over intervals of several miles.

The capacity of optic fibers is potentially colossal, and it changes the whole outlook for domestic and business use of telecommunications. A single strand of fiber will be able to carry half a billion bytes per second, but by combining a number of fibers in a single cable, it is possible to carry many two-way television signals simultaneously, or the equivalent in voice, still picture, or text material. Already all the necessary subsidiary technologies have been developed to turn optic fibers into social realities, such as methods of cabling, splicing methods, and repeaters for boosting signals over long distances, as well as advanced LED's (light-emitting diodes), which are the source of the new form of signal sent into the fiber.

In the United States the optic fiber is finding its way first into telephone connections within metropolitan areas, where there is a shortage of duct space underground. As the prices of this form of cable drop from $1 per meter in 1978 to 10 cents in 1981, it will begin to outpace most of the other forms of cabling used in various specialist networks (e.g., for video-transmission). It will gradually be used for long distance links, as is already being done experimentally in Britain. Bell Laboratories is planning an optic cable that can carry 4000 simultaneous voice channels, due for service in the mid-1980's for long-distance telephony. The worldwide optic fiber market reached takeoff in 1978 at a global sum of $33 million (excluding Japan); by 1983 it will reach $480 million, a compound growth rate of 70 percent.[13]

Optic fibers are a typical example of the new generation of devices being used in the telecommunications business; their cost is a result of research expenditure rather than raw materials. Glass is a cheap substance to produce, even in its most sophisticated forms, once development costs are written off or amortized in terms of large-scale production. (Before the end of the century it may well be possible for PTT's and other telecommunication administrations to derive useful capital from "remining" their vast quantities of copper buried beneath the ground and reselling it for scrap.) Optic fiber is also very versatile and can be used in conjunction with all existing transmission systems, so that it can be fitted into rapidly enlarging national networks, enabling gradual and sporadic growth that is consistent with the piecemeal growth in demand.[14]

At the same time that these new developments are taking place, however, all of the traditional methods of transmitting signals are undergoing upward revision of their potential as well. Microwave signaling, coaxial cables, ordinary cables, and even the common telephone double wire, when used in conjunction with advanced devices and switching systems, are capable of much higher performance than was ever thought possible. New equipment can treble the signal capacity of the microwave networks already in use. The latest versions of the coaxial cable can carry 132,000 channels. The wave-guide system, on the other hand, which entailed sending light signals through a tube, was very recently thought to be the trunk-carrying system of the future, but it has already fallen by the wayside, defunct before its time. Though this technique, too, might suddenly enjoy an unexpected revival (it has been the subject of much research in many parts of the world), it currently languishes as a result of the surge of interest in its more flexible sibling, the optic fiber.

One can see from this very brief account of the new transmission and data storage methods that communication within and between nations is being endowed with three revolutionary new qualities: given concomitant increases in demand (which alone can bring about the necessary reductions in prices), it will be possible to store electronic signals at a fraction of the cost and effort of the past; distance will have less and less bearing upon the price of sending messages—whether by telephone, television, facsimile, etc; and, finally, it will be extremely cheap to send material through telecommunications-based media compared with traditional paper-based media (although paper may remain an important subsidiary means for local collection and storage of the message once it has been sent). Around these important developments a host of new or cheapened services are being planned, too numerous to list in full. It is likely that the rate at which services are invented will increase as the new capacity reaches one society after the other. Each society will have its own inbuilt bias towards particular services, depending upon geography, social traditions, the originality of individual citizens, and the regulatory system for telecommunications within society.

This last factor will prove to be of particular importance in the early decades in which the new systems are established, since the decision as to which services to pioneer tends to depend upon what is *permitted* at a given moment by the regulatory authorities. Thus, Britain has embarked simultaneously upon teletext and videotex services ahead of its rivals, almost entirely as a result of the special problems of the British Post Office. France, on the other hand, has developed its own device, Antiope, along lines consistent with the whole information tradition in France, which is heavily biased towards centralism; one can see the historic patterns of development of French television and newspapers repeated almost unconsciously in the early evolution of these new services. Germany's plans are greatly influenced by the constitutional problems of the Federal Republic.

The United States regulates its telecommunications in completely different ways from all other countries within the Western bloc. It allows private organizations much greater freedom to involve themselves in the construction of common-carrier services; thus private companies are allowed to build point-to-point satellite services under superivison of the Federal Communications Commission, which would be impossible in most other societies. As a result, the building of a Satellite Business System (SBS) will almost certainly take place within the U.S. in the early 1980's. This will be of value to organizations that currently use very large amounts of telecommunications bandwidth. SBS will send out a constant avalanche of "bits" a combination of voice, data, facsimile, and other signals, including video, from one private earth station to another via its own satellite. Each client will purchase only as much bandwidth as he needs at a given moment, since the entire traffic will be conducted in "packets," or high-density digitalized information by computer. The SBS system plans to be able to undercut all the other common-carrier services with its combined packet-switched system covering the entire country. It even predicts that the cost of sending a page of text from one office to another (i.e., from one word processor to another) will be less than 10 cents, possibly as little as one cent—an extraordinary saving in office costs when compared with conventional postal, facsimile, telegram, and other existing systems. AT&T would thus have a direct competitor able to offer precisely the same service but using its own satellite, rather than AT&T's telephone network. In due course AT&T might be permitted to run its own satellite system; but the end is surely coming to that era in which it has enjoyed a virtual monopoly over telephone communication in America. Perhaps the most dramatic impact of SBS and its inevitable later rivals will be the mass development of electronic– or tele–mail, replacing most of the volume trade of conventional postal services with an electronic substitute. The ancient role of national postal systems will have to be reorganized if the private sector usurps this function—or the paying part of it. Already many large U.S. corporations run their own internal telemail systems, achieving considerable cost economies. The political, social, legal, and financial implications of this rapidly developing offshoot of satellite and computer technology lie outside our present purpose but will inevitably interact with the systems by which written information for a paying public is circulated in society.

VI

The new telecommunications devices of the late 1980's and 1990's will have a considerable impact on the newspaper itself, while creating the possibility of popular alternatives to it. The new memory devices can lead to the creation of the all-electronic news camera, which would eliminate the time-consuming business of film development. The photographer would capture the images he wants in these tiny storage devices and transmit the pictures direct to the newsroom, where they would be viewed on a vdt and sent on for use or stored again. Newspaper technology researchers are already developing such a camera but are still some years away from achieving it. The Associated Press, however, has already succeeded in converting conventional photographs into digital form for storage and projection on a vdt on which they can enhance the picture quality before transmitting it to their newspaper members. ccd's and bubbles will also make possible the fully electronic photo library in a newspaper morgue, where existing memories are still rather expensive for such uses.

Optic fibers will also have early uses in the newspaper industry after a little further development. The signals that pass through these fibers are virtually error-free, because the rapid light signal (working at a speed of 200 million flashes per second) is not subject to electrical interference; its use for facsimile transmission of pages of text is an obvious future newspaper device. At present, facsimile systems exist for transmitting pages at a rate of one every four minutes; the Frankfurt edition of the *Financial Times* is received by facsimile at a rate of a page in two minutes. With optic fibers a whole page would pass through in one second, an ideal means for sending pages back and forth from central newsrooms and to remote local printing plants in suburbs.

Perhaps the most important of the new transmission systems for the newspaper industry will be the new satellites, for with the satellite the newspaper will be able to regain the national advertising it has lost in recent years.[15] The newspaper industry requires—urgently, some would say—a low-cost advertising facsimile receiver that would send and receive from rooftop "dish" antennas both news and advertising. The advertiser would simply examine his proposed marketing area in terms of a newspaper industry map from which he would be able to select the necessary newspapers at a glance and book his space for the following day. His advertisement would be scanned instantly into the relevant newspaper computers, and he would be billed automatically according to prestated rates. All the geographical disadvantages of newspaper markets that were evident in the 1960's would be virtually eliminated at a stroke. With these new satellites newspapers will be able to fight back against television, although the latter will probably absorb a good deal more advertising after deregulation makes possible more competing national channels.

Like most countries the United States has enjoyed a preferential rate for the press on all of its telecommunications services. The 1934 Communications Act permitted AT&T and Western Union to lease private lines at different rates for press and non-press traffic, and for many years the wire services benefited from this effective subsidy. But after World War II the commercial rate was gradually reduced until the difference disappeared, and it was eventually formally abandoned. By this time the services had built up vast networks designed to circulate news to every hamlet newspaper, and they began to grumble as the rate slowly started to climb. In 1967 the annual bill paid to AT&T by the AP and UPI together amounted to less than $11 million. In 1976 it was still less than $12 million. In 1978 it went up to $17.2 million, with further rises inevitable. The loss of special press rates was overcome by the acquisition of additional equipment by the wire services, which enabled them to multiplex, or make multiple, simultaneous use of the same wires. The increases of 1978 cannot be overcome in the same way: the increase amounts to 45 percent and is based upon an alteration in the whole cost structure. Between small neighboring cities the rates are increasing very greatly, but between large, distant metropolitan centers the rates have gone down. AT&T was attempting to beat the new competition of private microwave common carriers that had been licensed by the FCC to operate the high-density routes, and the wire services were to be the victims of the new policy, since their requirements are for routes between their main offices and 8000 clients and for interconnecting the 200 news-collecting bureaus.[16]

It is not surprising that the AP and UPI have now turned to the satellite as a possible means of overcoming this victimization by accountancy and taking control of their own communication costs for the first time in their history. What they are devising is a receive-only network covering all of their clients and members who would purchase rooftop dishes. The services themselves would lease a satellite facility, probably from the Harris Corporation, with signals sent up from the *Daily News* building in New York and received back again by AP and UPI bureaus in the same city. The two services would remain separate competitive organizations and would admit other news services (Dow Jones, Reuters, Commodity News Service) to the system—which would not at first have the necessary bandwidth to cope with pictures as well as text.

The economics of the proposed system are typical of those of new telecommunications devices. Each paper would spend $5000 on its earth stations; the transponder (the device attached to the satellite which receives and sends signals), which would serve all of them, would cost $1 million a year to lease. The telephone bill would be cut by $12 million per year, but the agencies would pass much of this on to the clients who had bought earth stations. The main outstanding problem is the cost of the special investigations that the FCC is obliged to hold before it can license the receive-only dishes (it makes no distinction between these and normal earth stations with two-way capacity). The license for each dish is likely to cost more than the dish itself and take a considerable period of time, since all radio traffic in every area would have to be assessed.

In addition to these three major areas of development (new memory devices, optic fibers, and satellites), there are two further computer functions that are undergoing important, fundamental technical reappraisals necessary to help the performance of computers catch up with growing storage capacity. At present, methods for putting information into computers and then reading material when it emerges are rather crude, compared with the amount of material stored and the potential speed and flexibility of the processors themselves. The typewriter keyboard invented in the last century is still the standard inputting device, although a series of refinements have been added in recent years. The new services of pay-TV, viewdata, teletext, etc., have meant that unsophisticated methods of communicating with computers from the home have had to be devised, and a series of simple keypads are now on the market, able to signal fairly standard requirements to a computer, although nothing amounting to actual text material.

The Japanese access device for ordinary consumers to the new CAP-TAIN system will be a fifty-key pad, which is necessary if this system is to perform operations that are at all sophisticated, given the 4000 characters of the Japanese written language. On the other hand, the Qube experiment in Columbus, provides a pad no more complicated than a pocket calculator, through which it is possible to get a wide variety of services.

However, for all operations that involve putting text into a computer-based communication system, the typewriter keyboard is still the most reliable instrument—and will remain so until speech-recognition techniques can be more fully developed. Attempts at turning speech into computer language have been continuing for many years, and it will be necessary to have a multitude of cheap devices for recognizing languages and individual voices if the new generation of computer-based banking and translating services is ever to become generally available. Some are now predicting some kind of "voicewriter" at the end of the 1980's, a device that could be of tremedous importance in the development of all forms of computer input. (It would turn speech into printing and back again.) In Finland, the *Helsingin Sanomat* is already examining a prototype.

In the meantime there will be a gradual cheapening of a number of intermediate techniques for inputting text, including facsimile and optical character readers, which we have already seen within the new newspaper offices. In the Japanese CAPTAIN system, facsimile will probably be the standard method by which information providers file their material in the central processing unit; otherwise, all material that is handwritten to begin with will have to be painstakingly input through the Japanese optical typewriter with its thousands of characters, activated by the touch of a light pen.

The most flexible and versatile method for extracting information from a computer and displaying it is the familiar TV cathode-ray tube (CRT), although there are today additional devices which use sound and create hard-copy. The former are being introduced for such purposes as reading out telephone numbers to subscribers calling a computerized directory service, and hard-copy devices have been familiar in payroll and other computerized services for a long time.

Cheap pocket computers have familiarized the public with light-emitting diodes and liquid crystal systems for displaying information, and it is felt that these might develop in due course as rivals to the cathode-ray tube as means for displaying letters and numbers. However, a number of revolutionary new techniques are under development that would have an important bearing on the development of text distribution on the scale necessary for any medium to approximate the conventional newspaper.

The basic need is for a flat panel that can be hung on a wall or placed flat on a desk but that would function in a similar way to a CRT. It might be possible for a larger screen than a calculator or watch face to be constructed from a large number of connected LED's, which emit light at the pressure of electric current. Another possibility is the development of a current technique that involves placing a layer of liquid crystals between plates of glass. Already, a third technique has been used for display, plasma panels containing inert gas that produces brightness when electric charges are applied. There are still more experiments being conducted in electroluminescent materials, in various advanced magnetic films, and in ceramic materials. Pressure to develop a substitute for the CRT, which can be laid flat, is coming from manufacturers of newspaper technology, since complaints from journalists involved in direct input are likely to increase as more newspapers become computerized. There continue to be fears about health hazards in the constant use of CRT's, and even before these new display panels are placed in relatively expensive items such as television receivers, a healthy market would emerge around the world for substitutes for CRT's—even at high cost to business news-papers, airlines, etc. Eventually the real demand for new display panels will come with the demand for increased portability of communication devices; battery-powered computer terminals will require a means more flexible than the CRT and less subject to limitations of size. In the very long run, holography will probably become serviceable for cheap three-dimensional display systems, but nobody predicts domestic uses for such techniques until the closing years of the century.

The most promising new device with direct implications for the news-paper is ink-jet printing, which forces tiny droplets of ink to be sprayed into finely woven patterns. By 1978 it was possible to print by this means at ninety-two characters per second, as fast as an electric type-writer, but this should improve more than tenfold in the next few years, with the added possibility of an ability to perform in color. It will be some time, despite one or two encouraging experiments, before the speed necessary for publishing a newspaper will be developed through ink-jet printing. A new phenomena called electrophotography, however, offers a facility that might arrive sooner. Under computer control this method of laser-driven reproduction has reached 20,000 lines of copy per minute (a rate at which the Bible could be done in two and a half minutes). It can produce a good repertoire of typefaces and backgrounds, and unlike many other techniques under consideration, it produces a single copy at a time, making possible, perhaps, the tailored newspaper that is increasingly being discussed.

For more specialist forms of printing electromatic technology might prove very useful. It uses a paper coated with a black chemical com-pound and then with aluminum, which a stylus burns away leaving lines of dots behind. It is very cheap in hardware, although expensive in the materials it employs, so that it will prove useful for printing information of a specialized kind direct from a computer, but probably not for a mass-information system.

Such are the basic input and output technologies designed to provide the new services that will flow through the new networks. They offer the opportunity for many of the functions of individual life to be trans-ferred from manual and mechanical to computerized systems. Further-more, as we shall see, they offer an increasing intermixture of services that, in combination, suggest a rather different relationship between individual and society, one that might be thought of as a new type of citizenship.

One may easily extrapolate from the combined vision of these new technologies a kind of total world system, an ultimate network of transmission facilities, completed with a fully computerized switching system. It would permit a completely interactive system of communication both stationary and mobile. It would encompass all of the activities currently separately labeled as publishing, broadcasting, telephone, postal, banking, advertising, libraries, and, to some extent, government. The whole network would be linked with all manner of terminal and storage equipment, permitting an individual to send and retrieve at very low cost whatever he or she required at whatever moment. All messages could be stored before timed reception; all visual content could be received in three-dimensional form, all information now available in libraries could be obtained on convenient screens or hard copy. Such is the theoretical construct that can be built upon the known technical possibilities.

Computer engineers often use this vision of the future as a kind of mental Mecca towards which the face of their industry is permanently turned, and like Mecca the hope is to reach it well within the lifetime of those at work on it. When one sees how long it has taken for, say, color television to pass from the stage of invention (the 1920's) to the stage of industrialization (the 1960's) and then to the stage of complete availability in a reasonable number of countries (perhaps 1980), one wonders whether the ultimate system will arrive in time for the pioneers to see it. Any device based upon a network by definition must be more than partially built before it can exercise any real impact upon a way of life.

However, any "realistic" prediction about 1980 in 1965 would probably have fallen short of the mark.[17] There were no lasers then, computers still used large heaps of punched cards, and transistors were an innovation. Satellites were used for extraordinary feats of television transmission but were only just being tried out for the now familiar purposes of sending data and telephone conversations around the globe. Cable television was just about in existence as an adjunct of community antennas in bad reception areas, but fifteen years later it has hardly moved from that position in most countries—although North America and a few European nations may be reaching a high level of cabling (i.e., above 30 percent of the population) at the start of the 1980's.

Development is uneven, often outstripping all forecasts, often falling well behind even official predictions. It is not the technical dexterity that is lacking but the ability of given societies to absorb the institutional implications of certain forms of change. Cable television would have almost certainly arrived more rapidly if television in all of the countries outside of North America had not been so firmly controlled by governments and unified national broadcasting institutions. It is impossible to say that this has overall been a bad thing, although when a real broad-band, or multichannel, system of television does eventually come in to being in the market of the developed world, we shall probably wonder how long we managed to do without it. Existing institutions, existing investment, existing attitudes, and existing job interests of important skilled groups act as brakes upon certain forms of change in technology. Where a new technology can advance into an institutional vacuum, it can usually be introduced very rapidly (as with the computer). Radio in the 1920's was placed everywhere inside new institutions specially devised for it, and it spread universally within a decade. The telephone, how-ever, arrived in the last century as part of the postal administration in most societies and has taken a century to become a mass instrument.

Yet if one expresses the changes that have taken place in monetary or statistical terms, the extent of the change since 1960 can be seen to be very great indeed, far greater than was predictable at that time. It would have then cost 3 million or 4 million dollars to acquire computing capac-ity, which by 1980 has come to cost only a few hundred. Walter Baer of the Rand Corporation calculates that information processing and storage have fallen by a factor of three every two years for two decades, while the size of each unit of capacity has dropped to one thousandth—an evolution that has still not run its course, with a "microprocessor revolu-tion" still at hand.[18] When such developments have been predictable, their speed has always been considerably greater than estimated. In the eighties computer chips as large as a human finger nail will be built by large-scale integration methods (LSI), with more than 50,000 compo-nents, each able to perform 4 million commands per second. The quality of intelligence will be contained in common domestic items of equip-ment, from washing machines to ovens and telephones, at very little cost. Yet it would be unwise to predict a date by which time a given level of homes would contain these facilities. It is possible that in the 1980's, we shall continue to see time predictions overrun, but it is equally likely that the stabilizing factors—existing institutions, bureau-cracies, problems of compatibility, investment write-offs, job security—will cause reality to arrive much more slowly than technical possibility.

The overall speedup in the rate of change is a result of the way in which different functions are being interconnected in the course of the evaluation of advanced telecommunications. We have seen how easily a telephone plus a television set plus some computing capacity can create a completely new set of information media. There are other acts of techno-logical and institutional fusion and interconnection taking place at the same time. For example, telephone wires have been constructed to take analogue, or wave, signals while computers handle their traffic in digital form. It has been possible for many years to translate one kind of signal into the other and then back again to analogue when it is required in its original form (voice, music, picture).

The new microprocessors render the business of translation (normally via a method known as pulse code modulation, or PCM) very simple, and since digital signals can be packed into a much smaller telecommunications bandwidth and are more reliable to transmit in any case, it is becoming much more common for telecommunications systems to process all incoming signals into digital form and then back into their original form at the termination of their journey. It becomes extremely thrifty to take this process a stage further and enter the age of packet-switching, which has been referred to earlier; this technique entails sending a group of signals very quickly through a channel in digital form and interspersing them with quite different messages for different destinations. The two speakers in a telephone conversation do not, in fact, use the line continuously and are quite unconscious of the use of packet-switching, by which sections of their speech are collected, digitalized, and hurtled through the channel for decoding at the other end, while the same wire is being used for scores of other conversations, each duly routed between different pairs of speakers. This makes it extremely difficult to calculate the cost of any particular service since much of the traffic projected into the stream of bits in this way can consist of quite different categories of material. Pages of a newspaper may be interleaved with private telephone conversations, or a radio program. It also complicates the work of American regulatory agencies, since the function of processing data becomes inseparable from the business of transmission; indeed, the processing of data takes place automatically in every act of transmission. The legal problem entailed will have to be sorted out before very long.

The electronic office machinery that the new telecommunications highways make possible brings about a fusion between the typewriter, the telephone, the copier, and, in fact, tends to blur the distinction between printing and person-to-person written communication. The key to this transformation is the evolution of the word-processor to replace the typewriter. The combination of a keyboard with a microprocessor, a memory, a graphic display, and a printout device—all connected by a telephone network—means that a secretary can store drafts of correspondence, edit them, have them reviewed, and then transmit them direct to another comparable piece of equipment anywhere in the world. The functions of typing, filing, posting, computing, are merged into a single activity. One additional item of office equipment is the intelligent copier, which, as well as making multiple versions of the same text, will contain its own character-generator and supply of fonts, so that type can be redesigned—a piece of machinery whose function overlaps with that of the offset press with photocomposition.

Even in the late 1970's there exist private networks of linked word-processors (such as the Hewlett-Packard Corporation's network) that provide a cheap substitute for physical postal services within large organizations. To interconnect the terminals of different organizations will be a major breakthrough of the 1980's, but this will present problems for societies, especially in Europe, where national monopoly postal and tele-communications organizations exist. Nonetheless, the advent of word-processing will deal a heavy blow to existing physical postal services. By the mid-1980's the cost of telecommunicating a text the length of a brief business letter should be less than 50 cents, which, taken with other attendant savings in internal labor time, will be sufficient to attract large quantities of mail from the post.[19]

Another area where electronics can replace a physical acitivity is that of teleconferencing, widely developed by telecommunications authorities in Europe and North America (e.g., AT&T's Picturephone Meeting Service). With additonal recording devices, conferencing becomes a kind of visual extension of the business letter, participants being able to pack-age a video recording of themselves—together with pictures, diagrams, and graphs—and place it on record in the teleconferencing file of another organization. Alternatively, they can link themselves in two or three or multiple-sided video conferences, recording the interchange as they go along. (The videophone itself will be considered a front-runner for non-business use, however, until the closing years of the century.) Videocon-ferencing has already become a valuable technique, though not widely used outside the circles of ardent experimenters. A three-minute video connection coast-to-coast in the United States costs under $20; for a one-hour two-way discussion it costs about the same amount as a return air fare, although price-cutting among airlines may gradually steal the advantage back to physical transport.

Researchers at the British Post Office do not expect such services to get much beyond the stage of novelty until 1990, although a cheap substitute in the form of a sound-only link plus a facility for sending still pictures (by "slow-scan" techniques) in two directions could become a very useful business service in addition to the telephone. Here the extra cost is that of the slow-scan terminal, capable of dealing with a slowly emerging rather than instantaneous image. Inextricable from the vision of the "ultimate global network" is the ultimate home terminal connected with it. This is a device towards which all the existing novel items of equipment are tending: a cheap, small, multipurpose terminal for the consumer, through which facsimile, electronic mail, and automatic fund transfer would pass—a neat gadget that would also house the telephone, the television receiver (with all its additional services), word-processor, and video recorder. It would calculate and entertain, educate, amuse with games, and cost not more than $500 (with voice recognition an optional extra). It is a long way off, but in some sense it is inevitable as a means of interconnection of services, the spreading of "intelligence" to one terminal after another, and the fusion of different kinds of service proceeds.[20]

One important area of this vision of the future may well be reached in the 1980's via the "intelligent telephone" which could combine the electronic credit card with a number of information and message services. One part of the dream that will almost certainly *not* be reached is the home facsimile service for large quantities of printed material, the long-awaited substitute for newspaper delivery. The facsimile newspaper has been predicted since the 1930's and demonstrated experimentally in the U.S. half a century before its trials at Tama New Town in Japan. The facsimile newspaper may be important in special geographical conditions, and facsimile itself is becoming an important standard device within the production of newspapers, but bulk mass facsimile other than for documents is likely to remain rather expensive. It would not, in fact, even save the high cost of distributing large quantities of paper to millions of homes, since the printout paper for the ever larger newspapers of the Western world would have to be home-delivered, and the sheer size of the terminal equipment in the house would act as a deterrent to ordinary members of the public. Only a cheap, small machine that could recycle or erase its own paper and then operate at less than half a cent per page (the maximum cost of newspaper delivery in the U.S. in 1980) would begin to be commercially attractive.

Perhaps the most important preliminary to home distribution of printed material was created with the Betamax consumer boom that began in 1977 after more than a decade of protracted and postponed prediction. Both tape and disc have become viable as means of home delivery of video material, and the same techniques can be used for the storage of text as well as video entertainment material. At a dollar a disc the disc recorder may penetrate the market sooner than the more flexible but more expensive cassette or tape recorder, and estimates vary widely as to the extent of U.S. households likely to contain such devices before the mid-1980's. No one seems to predict that these will become mass media (which, again, means reaching more than 30 percent of homes) before 1985. At about this level, or even lower, the disc could become a useful substitute medium for the magazine publisher. Nonetheless, these will all play their part in retraining the public in the direction of self-entertainment through selection and away from the purely passive acceptance of homogenized material. It is not necessary for any single device or service to become a mass phenomenon for the traditional mass audience of the last century to start breaking up.

It is probable, however, that fragmentation of the audience will tend to concentrate at one end of the market or social spectrum: those who can afford the most information devices will create for themselves a considerably enhanced range of choice. In order to spread that choice further into society, an enormous increase in investment in domestic equipment must take place, and that will depend entirely on the overall development of Western economies. All of these devices—and the above account has dwelt only upon those that might have some bearing on the development of general information—involve a transference of investment from some central institution to the home, to individuals who have to be coaxed into placing their savings in the relevant hardware before the software can reach their eyes and ears.

In a sense, the whole evolution towards the ultimate network and the ultimate terminal is a culmination of processes that have been underway for a hundred years and more. Book publishing and newspaper publishing, the theater, and the circus, all involved a single central investment, with peripheral costs in promotion and distribution. It is relatively easy to change the forms of drama or opera or the content of a newspaper or publishing house because the investment is in one place and under one control. The worst that can happen is that a group of people lose their jobs. With all of the media that have developed in the twentieth century, the investment has spread outwards, and more people and institutions have been necessarily involved in any act of change. Film has brought the growth of an exhibition industry, a technical-processing industry, and an equipment-building industry; a change in style or content can affect all of these and produce great resistance from companies whose investment in the old item has not yet been written off. Human investment is capable of even greater acts of resistance to change. In the case of radio, a relatively cheap medium, the audience had to undertake the bulk of the investment themselves, and in television the audience's share of the total investment is even greater. Likewise with the phonograph.

With the electronic media, however, a further complication arose:

governments became involved in the cost and decision making and have remained involved in every subsequent act of change and development. The age of regulation began just as the age of censorship of the press came to an end, or at least to the end of its acceptability in liberal societies. Regulation is today taking something of a knock as a result of the decline of the audience for mass television, which seems to have reached its peak in many societies in the late 1970's. Since the spell of television was broken, and especially since cheap video became available and a certain amount of cabling had taken place, the role of governmental regulation has come to seem slightly suspect. In Washington the van Deerlin Committee recommended widespread deregulation, especially of radio where the old argument of spectrum scarcity no longer applied. The demand for a greater role for independent program makes in Germany, Canada, and Britain has been another aspect of the deregulatory movement in broadcasting.

Throughout Europe, closely monitored by the Council of Europe, cable installations and a variety of other forms of community broadcasting have been taken up in experimental form. Local radio stations have spread steadily in Britain, Canada, and elsewhere—all of them dedicated to the spirit of community rather than with a desire to create miniature versions of the national broadcasting system. A great schism has broken out in broadcasting structure where people demand to use the airwaves for themselves and cease merely to be audiences.

For more than a century now, ever since the primitive telegraph proved a reliable alternative to the carrier pigeon, telecommunications have been spreading around the world, substituting for physical forms of communication. But all telecommunications services are, ultimately if not immediately, regulated by government, whether they are simple telephones or complex satellite-borne data links. However, one response to the latest wave of telecommunications development has been a demand for deregulation, a demand spreading in many parts of the Western democracies. While the traditional telecommunications authorities (post offices, telephone and broadcasting administrations, and American-style common carriers) are being provided with new tasks and new problems, they are also being faced with new demands to relax their tutelage and supervision over existing services. Where telecommunications are becoming abundantly available (e.g., with radio signals or videotex or business telemail links), traditional forms of regulation are beginning to seem inappropriate or even irksome. However, from the Third World there come pressures towards new forms of regulation. UNESCO resolutions demand the "balancing" and "equalizing" of the skewed flow of information between developed and developing worlds. Furthermore, where the newspaper is concerned, we have the example of a non-regulated medium, which, in moving over to new telecommunications systems, is laying itself open to forms of regulation by government simply by reason of its decision to use data links, facsimile, interconnected word processors, and so on.

In the very long run, it would seem that regulation will become a physical impossibility. Quantities of material are simply growing too large for a public bureaucracy to scan and control, even if it wanted to. However, this is not so in the short run, and in the foreseeable future there is no way of preventing unscrupulous governments or powerful private corporations from eavesdropping, manipulating the flow of material, or otherwise intervening. As more and more communications functions are extended to the home or transferred to the home, there is a growing danger of more of the links between individual and society being mediated by information bureaucracies. As private captial and public bureaucracies move towards the establishment of and commercialization of the new media, they become more powerful, and their power becomes more difficult to dismantle, despite the modern tendency towards "deregulation," and increased competition.

It is largely for these reasons that the careful monitoring of the vision of the ultimate network needs to be undertaken in all societies. The dominant information values of our society for an easy and unrestricted flow of information from government to public and back again, have evolved alongside the struggle for a free press. It would be a painful contradiction if such levels—whether closely adhered to in practice or not—were to be defeated at the end of the twentieth century through a misunderstanding of the nature of advanced telecommunications.[21]

That is why the values associated with the newspaper medium are of crucial importance, more so, perhaps, than the physical survival of the medium in its traditional guise. We have already seen how the structure of the newspaper industry itself, in the U.S. in particular, belies the pluralistic ethic on which the newspaper was built in the last century. The vast industrialized groups, inevitable though they are in this phase in the evolution of Western economies, are not conducive to the maintenance of traditional press freedoms. They offer monopolies of local information and complex interconnections of content. They have a natural tendency to reinterpret the First Amendment freedoms in terms of corporate business freedoms. They also offer a certain stability and continuity to an industry that might otherwise have withered in the age of television, and so the negative aspects of the present structure of the industry should not be overemphasized. However, it becomes even more important, as society passes through the age of electronics, to find ways to reestablish and reguarantee the basic individual freedoms of expression and of information, and the strength for doing this is likely to come still from the world of the printed press, from its professions and traditions.

The new media will find their own codes in their own circumstances, but they will borrow heavily from the body of doctrine bequeathed to them by the press. How they will interact physically with the press depends on the various possible readings of the situation that confronts society in the 1980's in the field of electronics. It is unlikely that the printing of information on paper will suddenly or even gradually evaporate, but it is equally unlikely that the new media will allow the newspaper to continue its entire range of traditional activities. A shifting of functions is bound to take place as society charts its course through the maze of technical possibilities now opening up. What we will now examine, therefore, are some of the tracks that might be followed.

8. AN ELECTRONIC

ALEXANDRIA?

At the brink of a new era of communication devices, one inevitably has cause to stop and ask, Who wants them? How will the demand for them be generated? The public will have to buy their way into these new media, as they have already done in the case of radio and television, but which they have not had to do in the case of film, newspapers, magazines, and other printed forms. The balance of investment has already swung from center to periphery, from publishers to receiver, from producer to audience, in the electronic era, and the pendulum will swing farther yet in the same direction if printed information is to reach a sizable section of the readership by way of the new devices we have been discussing. Nor is it going to be as easy, even if all the economic and demographic preconditions exist in perfect form, for a series of new devices to be marketed en masse and simultaneously to societies already brimful of entertainment and information gadgetry.

Of one thing we may be certain, these new devices will not take off with the rapidity of the radio in the 1920's, for they supplement and replace, rather than provide a fundamentally new experience. The first broadcast took place in 1920, and by 1922 there were 220 radio stations in the U.S., with licenses available at $10 a time. There were 2.5 million sets in use within three years of the first mass-produced models, and the American public made this instrument the focus of their lives. So did many advertisers; by 1931 the American Tobacco Company was spending $20 million on a campaign for a single product, Lucky Strike. Few people expect the new cable services or even the free-of-charge teletext services to have such impact so quickly over so many. There are, to be sure, certain historic trends that make the new media inevitable but not in so dramatically short a period.

One important aspect of the initiation problem is the difficulty in aggregating sufficient investment in the early stages of a new medium to make the content appear attractive to the small pioneering audience. The unit costs of equipment in the first years of any device are necessarily high (thus holding back the rate of acquisition), while the smallness of the new audience for the medium means that total revenue is low. Yet the whole point of the transformation lies in the profusion of choice that the new media, as a group, will make possible. Long periods of inanition are therefore possible during which new media may be considered failures or simply badly organized.

Videotex is a good example of a medium that would provide an extra-ordinary choice of services at extremely low cost as soon as the potential audience is developed. It can improve its content (e.g., by adding a facility for color pictures or by introducing a direct shopping service) as soon as its public has passed a given profitability barrier—perhaps 10 percent of the population. To reach that point will be very difficult, while newspapers, radio, television, and postal services between them provide a very large proportion of the total benefits desired. However, it is the cross-subsidy from these traditional media that will probably help videotex and other services to cross the acceptability threshold. Nevertheless, the availability of investment from newspapers, film, magazines, postal authorities, and television companies for expansion into new electronic systems of delivery will have to await a change of perception on the part of the suppliers. One might therefore be led to expect a slow evolution, perhaps a bewildering period in which a great deal of money is or appears to be wasted and in which one device after another simply fails to spark public interest. Only then will the point of a very rapid upswing be reached.

In similar circumstances in the 1940's, American television benefited from the system that radio had originally created for grasping the full potential of the mass audience. It was Bill Paley of CBS who discovered how to perform the "network trick" when he offered all CBS affiliate stations the right to plug into the flow of material at no cost to them-selves; all they had to do was give CBS the option to transmit its adver-tising at any point in the affiliates' schedules. Thus, the networks won the right to sell time right across the nation; they could make contracts with advertisers with total certainty, while the station found that the bonanza of free network programming increased its audience in geometric progression. Once the deal between sponsors, networks, and stations was made, they remained interlocked in perpetuity, a vast reticulated mesh in which the audience was ineluctably shoaled.

The position of the daily newspaper within a monopoly market is very similar, where it is free to concentrate on the task of increasing its rate of household penetration without the presence of constant competition lowering advertising rates, forcing increases in pagination, and necessitating financially crippling circulation campaigns. The typical newspaper audience of today has been constructed on the opposite, but in a sense complementary, principle from that of the television networks. The newspaper is local, uncompetitive, reliant on small advertisers; the television network is widespread, highly competitive, dependent upon large national advertisers. Between them their hold over the public is almost foolproof, and breaking into their highly organized audiences will be the task of many decades, inevitable though it probably is. In the final analysis, it will be achieved only when newspaper corporations and television networks are politically and financially ready for it, that is, when they themselves can see the way to prosper from the change from homogeneous to heterogeneous audiences, from "free" to paid itemized information, from a narrow editorial centrality to a profusion of individual choice. Perhaps many fortunes will be made by successful nibblers at this audience—from cable companies, specialist magazines, pay-TV, telephone-attached information systems. A transformation with real social and political consequences will be possible only when the existing holders of the major blocs of audiences are ready to loosen their grip. In some societies new entrepreneurs might succeed in prizing their grip loose.

One must look to the overall trends in the growth of population and the number and location of households for anything that one might point to as firm evidence of social preparedness. If households continue to grow at a rate of 1.8 percent per year, then by 1990 the U.S. will have around 95 million of them, compared with 75 million in 1980. Lower fertility and death rates will continue to reduce the average size of households, and it will become even more common for two-member households to contain two wage earners, thereby greatly increasing the propensity of the public to acquire more goods of ever higher quality. What two people who live together but work during the day most often tend to demand is an environment that provides a sense of personal enhancement; they need to feel that their lives are worth living in themselves, not for some exterior purpose. They will want to live in cleaner, more spacious neighborhoods; they will want to possess objects of scarcity; they will want the sense of their own and their possessions' uniqueness.

Even if advertising continues to expand at a rate slightly above 3 percent a year, total advertising expenditure in the U.S. will increase from $40 billion to $60 billion between 1980 and 1990. Taking into account the increase in the number of households, the value of advertising per household will increase from $500 per year to $625, while consumer spending (assuming a parallel year-by-year increase through the decade) will increase from around $1.25 billion to $1.75 billion. It is not, however, the total amount of money available that is the key to the changes we are trying to guess at as much as the changes in the nature of markets for consumer goods. The median age of the population will be higher, with a higher proportion of working age; more will be educated, more will live in suburbs with space around them. If, as all forecasters expect, there is to be a greater emphasis on style and quality in the economy as a whole, one must expect this to relate to information and entertainment as much as to physical goods. Indeed, since the search of the generation is already for individualized life-styles, one might expect the information industries to be even more affected than the normal range of mass-production industries.

The Arthur D. Little studies of consumer behavior patterns, from which some of these assessments have been derived, point to two important though seemingly contrasting tendencies that flow from this vision of future market patterns. The first is a stronger market for those goods and services that save time and increase convenience (everything from catalog shopping to household labor-saving devices) while the second is an increase in time-consuming individualized activities (work turned into hobbies, hobbies becoming major preoccupations). Both of these trends fall directly into the line offered by the new electronic gadgetry. Catalog shopping is easily developed via telephone ordering to videotex or Qube-type devices for electronic shopping. The desire for further enhancement of domestic labor-saving devices is satisfied by home computers programmed for various household activities, which also offer home information systems of great sophistication. At the same time, these developments of economic fashion will tend to increase public propensity to rent rather than buy new equipment, an essential prerequisite for the rapid dissemination of the new technologies. The leasing habit is crucial to the new systems, as much as an increase in leisure time and in the drive towards fulfilling the sense of individuality.

There are additional factors that might help the new media enter the ordinary marketplace of household goods more easily. First, there will be throughout the 1980's a powerful growth in the business use of computer-based information systems; terminals and storage devices of many kinds are already pouring into the office blocks of large corporations, lawyer's offices, and educational institutions. Thousands of people will become more accustomed to the use of 'intelligent' typewriters, word processors replacing common typewriters, and other paraphernalia of the modern office. They will acquire experience in tapping into complex databases in order to extract business files, statistics, and salary information. Machines will be available in shops and stores and factories designed for nonspecialist users, and even though these might not contain the material normally carried in the newspaper, they will familiarize both providers and readers with the special conceptual problems and skills involved in these forms of communication. Local advertising and local news will probably remain completely outside computer-based information systems for a long time to come,[2] but people throughout the developed world will nonetheless frequently come into contact with vdt's and small computers in the course of their nondomestic lives. Real-estate agents will start to use viewdata-type services in Western Europe as travel agents already do in London. Customers will check the times of trains and planes, apply for holiday brochures, familiarize themselves with the techniques of burrowing through a database in search of simple information, and perhaps find the task pleasant in itself and the information more clearly implanted in their minds afterwards.[3]

Meanwhile, the high-income home will start to acquire a range of new appurtenances to normal household goods that contain microprocessors for discharging fairly simple tasks. Ovens and washing machines, radios, television receivers, and recorders will contain some of these new devices, helping the user to switch household gadgetry and heating systems on and off or higher and lower, to monitor usage, and to check bills and payments. Disc recorders and cassettes will become familiar items, although they will probably remain luxuries until the 1990's, and the full range of "intelligence" will be absent from the cheaper models. Whatever the overall lines of eventual development, it is most likely that by 1990 society will be prepared psychologically for a great leap forward into the exploitation of computer-based information in quite novel ways. The microprocessor revolution will have taken place in industry, and new communication systems will have substantially changed the organization of the average office. The next step to totally interactive information media will then begin to seem plausible. It might still be technically and economically remote, but the public may well have lost the sense of its being revolutionary, impossibly futuristic.

As the newspaper contemplates a new situation in which its readers are prepared to handle computer-based information, and the better-off among them can afford the new differential cost of home entertainment and information, publishers might well feel a sudden frisson of helplessness. If they have invested previously in some of the new systems, they may begin to feel the glimmer of relief of those who have successfully cast bread upon the waters. In the course of the decade they will, in any case, have begun to feel the repercussions of the expansion of television outlets in every home (through cable or over-the-air stations that are likely to arise in the years after the reform of the Communications Act of 1934), as national advertisers, previously caught up in the monopolistic tendency of the networks, withdraw their business from the printed press and spread themselves in the audio-visual media.

Around the year 1990, therefore, newspaper publishers will come to feel the effects of a series of trends that had been apparent but not real for fifteen years or more. They will begin to find that their readers are looking to the new information systems for some of the specialist and semispecialist material that newspapers have traditionally carried in their multiform package of goods. But they will also, really for the first time in the television era, notice the implications of a genuine drift of advertisers to television. However, they will be conscious that the newspaper is still the cheapest, most up-to-date, and most comprehensive package of information their readers have access to, even though some of its contents are under threat. The newspaper, even at its worst and most socially irresponsible, is a very rich store of information. It is only after this era of slow growth of computer-based information systems through the 1980's that the newspapers in their traditional form will meet a major external threat to their economic well-being. The 1970's, so this prediction goes, will turn out to have been the decade of internal reorganization of the product (new technology, the establishment of convenient local monopoly, new forms of consumer journalism, adjustment to the new conditions of expensive raw mateials and distribution costs). The 1980's is the decade of consolidation and further exploitation of the newly formed natural market for newspapers as a number of rival media begin to establish themselves. Newspaper chains are liable to grow in this period, gathering together for safety and profit in preparation for the cold blasts of the 1990's, when electronic systems may begin to overtake the traditional printed press, having proved themselves in a variety of special conditions.

It is possible that in a number of societies certain regions may find themselves particularly rapidly equipped with videotex-type services that may begin to eat into the classified advertising revenues of the local press. This is not considered a very likely area of rapid and widespread advance, since the first generation of such services will depend upon CRT screens with a small word-capacity, but it could begin to have an impact on newspapers in certain localities where, say, entertainment is an important source of classified advertising. (Entertainment happens to be one section of classified material that might go electronic faster than real estate, for example, and in special circumstances local newspapers might quickly feel the loss of it.) Of course, phenomena of this kind would not lead to a drop in circulation unless other factors (such as increased subscriptions, vastly increased newsprint prices, etc.) started to price newspapers out of their traditional market. One great blessing of the newspaper is that where it keeps its price very low it enjoys almost total inelasticity of demand. Everybody who can be induced to want it can afford to have it.

The new media will arrive in their first years of maturity armed with all the statistical and marketing expertise that the printed press has been building up during its difficult period. The study of the specialist demographic groups that newspapers have set out to serve better in the late 1970's will reach a level of perfection in time for the new electronic media to identify their own special layers of the market. The new media will also have benefited from the extensive research in the specialist fields that they will concentrate on in their first decade, and their rate of advance into these markets will itself have been greatly influenced by the ways in which traditional newspapers try to keep them out through competition. Of course, government may seek directly or indirectly to intervene (certainly in European societies) in order to protect existing interests against new ones. The first such action in the U.S. could perhaps be the refusal to permit AT&T to offer videotex services on the grounds that a common carrier may not simultaneously act as a processor of data for public service. On the other hand, the government might grant this permission and make AT&T the focal point of a vast new expansion into the role of national data storage and disseminator, like the telecommunications and postal authorities of Western Europe.

The one item central to this whole evolution is the small decoding unit that has to be attached to a television receiver in order to run it into a terminal for teletext or videotex services. This item has entered the market at a price of some hundreds of dollars, but this could, with progressive refinement and large-scale integration, fall to a nominal sum, rather like the pocket calculators of the 1970's. For this to happen, there will be a need for a very large research investment, of a size that might justify government intervention—certainly in the case of the larger European countries which are increasingly determined to grasp this new potential, and perhaps with NASA or PBS in the U.S. A decoder costing a few dollars would quickly transform downward the time scale in which these predictions are being offered, for it would almost guarantee the growth of a market for home database equipment at a rate equal to that by which television sets are replaced. The speed up in the growth of this market would, in turn, encourage the telecommunications organizations to increase the rate at which they adapt their systems to a variety of new refinements and gadgetry that would be necessary additions to the medium at the wide base of the pyramind of the mass market. But such a turn of events is not calculable nor foreseeable, and in 1980 nobody is planning for it.

One important change that will become more apparent in the newspaper of the immediate future will be the professionalization of its management. Newspaper editors have been complaining since the 1980's that they have passed into the hands of accountants, but the newspaper editor of the 1980's is more likely to complain—as he has done for several years—of having passed into the hands of Wall Street analysts. Many newspaper proprietors, even those, or especially those, who manage family newspapers and are trying to pass the business on to another generation, are finding that their businesses are forcing them to become ever more conscious of rates of profits and return on capital. Even papers like the *Washington Post* find that enormous energy has to be put into market management and the management of peripheral publications of high profitability in order for their stock quotation to remain as desirable to investors in the future as in the recent past. A kind of frenzy has moved into the newspaper business offices that formerly belonged exclusively to the newsrooms.

The structural decline in the number of newspapers sold per household has acted as a goad to managers, and the task of increasing household penetration (which is really the only way to increase profits at this time) has driven many newspapers "down market" in their approach to their readers or, at least, caused them to add material that caters to the marginal reader within the central zone of distribution. While the newspaper, as we have seen, has met this challenge also by entering heavily into the business of zoning and by sharpening the targeting of its own specialist audiences, it is also laying itself open to other, newer media that can concentrate exclusively on those small pockets of audience the paper may find it necessary or expedient to leave behind. Of course, the suburban newspapers, which are the fastest-growing sector of the business, can take such problems in their stride; it is the large old family-owned metropolitan paper that has to cope with all the problems simultaneously while trying to keep up with many of the new opportunities of distributing its material through new electronic means.

We have spoken rather loosely in this section of the new media considering them as an interconnected or mutually dependent gamut of gadgetry. In fact, they fall into three distinct branches: teletext systems (which use free-to-the-consumer television signals to reach the receiver), videotex systems (which combine the receiver with the ordinary telephone wire and require special payments according to usage), and home information centers (which use discs, tapes, and cassettes bought or rented from local suppliers, but which could cover a very wide range of entertainment and information nonetheless). These three groups of media will have separate and differentiated kinds of impact on existing paper-bound information and will develop at quite different paces in different sections of the market. The third may be the first to reach takeoff but the last to become a mass medium, since it will remain relatively expensive to the consumer; it will also be the least likely to harm the newspaper. Just as television through its coverage of sports helped sports journalism in the print media by increasing the whole scope of the sports industries, so home video equipment could bring about a rise in interest in descriptive material, critical and reviewing activity, advertising for hardware, etc.

The newspaper has, in the past, always succeeded in soaking up new business whenever something new arrived to capture the interest of some section of its public, and it could well do so again. It is the growth of the teletext, videotex and other public database services that in the long run will jeopardize the traditional form in which we receive daily news and general living information. But to assess the visibility of the newspaper as a form in the next stages of evolution of society, one must try to see how its particular way of organizing information is bound up with society and ask whether society is ready for that different relationship with the infosphere that the electronic mode seems to offer.

II

I sat up during the evening, reading by the light of the fire the scraps of newspapers in which some party had wrapped their luncheon; the prices current in New York and Boston, the advertisements, and the singular editorials which some person had thought fit to publish, not foreseeing under what critical conditions they would be read. I read these things at a vast advantage there, and it seemed to me that the advertisements, or what is called the business part of a paper, were greatly the best, the most useful, natural, and respectable. Almost all the opinions and sentiments expressed were so little considered, so shallow and flimsy, that I thought the very texture of the paper must be weaker in that part and tear the more easily. The advertisements and the prices current were most closely allied to nature, and were respectable in some measure as tide and meteorological tables are; but the reading matter, which I remember was most prized down below, unless it was some humble record of science, or an extract from some old classic, struck me as strangely whimsical, and crude, and one idea'd like a school-boy's theme, such as youths write and after burn. The opinions were of that kind that are doomed to wear a different aspect tomorrow, like last year's fashions; as if mankind were very green indeed and would be ashamed of themselves in a few years, when they had outgrown his verdant period.

—Henry D. Thoreau
A Week on the Concord and Merrimack Rivers
(Boston, 1867) p. 197.

If a newspaper is read outside the nexus of social habits to which it belongs, its contents quickly begin to appear contextless, unrooted. The newspaper is organized around the day of publication; this is the moment that gives meaning to everything it contains, even though this immediacy is often something of a trick concealing an amalgam of material that could have appeared on different days. It is not merely material gathered from different times that is rammed together into an apparently meaningful whole, however, but material coming from different sources. What the newspaper does is capture some of the thousands of information cycles of which a human society is composed and "fix" them into a framework of plausibility. It is the newspaper as a whole that appears to give these cycles a kind of guarantee and legitimize them, even though they may contain half-truths and errors. Each cycle and each item of information arises heterogeneously out of society and belongs again to society when the newspaper has finished with it. Stock prices might seem to "belong" to Dow Jones on the day of publication, but ten months or ten years later each price is historic fact belonging to society or to mankind in general, having outlived its ephemeral usefulness as a possible tool of business.

In fact, all information, before it is formally collected by an institution or individual, arises from nature and belongs to nature. The *fact* that China has invaded Vietnam is not the property of anyone, although the report of that fact may arrive at some other part of the globe as the result of great effort and a large monetary investment on the part of some person or organization. The same might be said of all elements of the newspaper: the review by Mr. X of a book by Ms. Y is the property of the former, subject to the will of the newspaper publisher, but the view held by Mr. X of Ms. Y's book before or after he has published an expression of it is merely a fact arising from society and belongs to no one, not even Mr. X. Only in special circumstances does his mind conceive of a piece of intellectual *property*. Information may be privately sold by one person to another, but it tends to be the secrecy rather than the information itself that is the real subject of the transaction.

Information arises from the nature of things in themselves, and the institutions, technologies, and organizational arrangements that help it travel through social space tend to impose their own natures and their own needs upon it. The newspaper is itself one such device, and its method of coding information into news—with its many subdivisions, features, advertising, and so forth—has played a tremendous part in establishing the relationships between individuals and their societies, in creating the iconography of modern social identity. The media attach values to the material they garner from the world.

The newspaper collects, stores, and transmits information, all of its decisions being designed to fit into perceived markets within a society. Some providers of information (advertisers and sometimes politicians or parties) pay for the right to send out their material through the medium, others are paid by the newspaper to yield their information to reporters and editors. Without the organized means of amassing and using the daily mound of materials, the information would slip back, as it were, into nature, into a state of ownerlessness. The commercial power of a newspaper depends on the habit of purchase by a circle of readers. This custom is an addiction, a social practice that fits into the rhythms of life, the patterns of mealtimes and traveling times, and it feeds its values into society by following the contours of the society it seeks to serve.

The inherited mechanical devices for reproducing newspapers for a mass audience symbolize, embody, encode, the relationships that the newspaper builds up between its contents and its readers, just as the computer-held information of today creates a different and more individual relationship with its readers. We live at that very moment in the evolution of information forms at which it is possible to see through the trick, as it were, to observe how a medium is resolvable, in theory at least, back into its component elements.

The aim of the newspaper, in the last century in particular, has been to create the impression—perhaps the illusion—that all information is the true business of all its readers. It offers them an implied universal citizenship by virtue of their acquaintanceship with the facts presented in its paper. As we have seen, it is now becoming much easier to supply them with a stream of the facts they elect to receive, rather than those that somebody else elects to give them, and this switch in the balance of sovereignty over the content of available information media has profound implications for the future of citizenship and for the evolution of the sphere of privacy, of identity.

The newspaper spearheaded the fight for freedom of expression (not of information), a freedom that was an essential prerequisite of a public information medium such as a mass newspaper of the newborn democracies. The printing press shifted sovereignty over the text to the editor, who became the collator and guarantor of the contents of the paper, the person who was deemed to represent the interests of his readers. The editor was the *readers'* editor, the newspaper was their link to the world of information and the world of power. Governments had attempted for several hundred years to assert the printer's sovereignty over the text and thus to substantiate their own higher sovereignty over the printer, often sharing the power between Church and State. That system was known as licensing—the control of information flow through the supervision of the industrial process by which publication occurred.

Censorship, in its current meaning, came later, when governments acknowledged the author's right to intellectual property and the rights of those the author delegated to hold it (such as the publisher), but they continued to assert their right to intervene in the interests of social order or political or religious orthodoxy. The struggle against censorship was an attempt to again shift sovereignty of the text and proclaim the right of the author and the editor over it. Freedom of expression was a right asserted essentially against the audience, against the society and those who chose to uphold any given version of social order. The right of expression was a right that was held to exist in nature or in society; it permitted an individual to impose his material upon those whom he could persuade to read it. All efforts to guarantee his work, to safeguard society against libels, inaccuracies, distortions, and thefts of information from private places are efforts to circumscribe or limit freedom of expression by interposing the right of society to be protected against the right of the author to express himself.

It is not difficult to see how the newspaper has shifted from being the embodiment of the struggle against censorship to the role of broker between readers and sources. When the newspaper was an editor's medium, it was the focal point in the struggle for press freedom. Now it is a manager's or publisher's medium, in the majority of the developed world, and its judgments are made not in the name of a body of citizens who happen to be readers but in the name of whole societies. The power of newspapers is thus much greater than it was, in a sense, but less willingly exercised. It is much harder for the *Washington Post* to bring down a President than it was for Fenno to rage against political enemies in eighteenth-century America. Investigative journalism has become important to the ability of the newspaper to operate politically, because pure information of a damaging kind may be legitimized in a powerful medium where damaging opinions by themselves may not be.

In the twentieth century we have constructed a series of electronic media that are similar in some ways to the early printing presses. They are devices whose sovereignty rests in society as a whole, and in no society has it been possible—though many have tried—to re-create the traditional norms of press freedom in the context of electronic media. Many approximations have been reached, at least in theory, but no one can restore to the microphone and the transmitter the same pattern of rights that seem to have been provided to the newspaper for a brief period in Western history. The electronic media occupy a position in the field of social forces that obliges them to take into account the susceptibilities of society as a whole on a variety of topics ranging from political controversy to advertising ethics to insurrectionary material to the spreading of violent behavior. Every blow struck for the protection of the information consumer is a blow against freedom of expression in its classic sense. It is clear, in the context of electronic media, that social freedoms in the field of information can be arrived at only at a point of resolution of various conflicting demands for sovereignty. Today the print media are slowly moving into the same electronic mode and are increasingly dependent upon telecommunications devices for their physical transportation to their audiences.

This is not to say that the eighteenth-century freedoms are outmoded or will be abandoned. New formulations of free expression will in time be achieved. But a deliberate swing of the pendulum has already taken place in the economy as a whole whereby producer sovereignty has been sacrificed to consumer sovereignty. It is unthinkable that information can escape the impact of the implications of this change. More than ever before, the reader rather than the speaker now dominates the *rights* within the information flow. In electronic systems it is the receiver who pays the cost of the equipment used in publication; it is the reader/viewer who watches the impact on children of the flow of images from the screen. It is the reader who decodes the bit stream and framegrabs the desired information searches through the index chain of CAPTAINS or Antiope or conducts a search of the New York Times Information Bank. All of these inventions are adaptations of technical potentials to physical social realities expressed as information markets.

This change in the locus of sovereignty over text, from author to receiver, is the key to the nature of the information society into which industrial society is now evolving. It may take a long time for such changes in essence to become physical changes that are visible in mores, institutions, and mass-disseminated technologies; nonetheless, in the long run, all those institutions born under the old conditions must adjust themselves to the new ones, including government, education, diplomacy, and academia. Industrial society has rested upon the accumulation of wealth by a few and their exploitation of it and the energies of others. It also has rested upon the accumulation of knowledge by a few and *its* exploitation in government, research, military and economic planning. Knowledge has been "owned" by the institutions and individuals who have created it, but in the electronic phase of knowledge storage and retrieval, information goes back to society or mankind in general. Power over knowledge remains with the institutions that control the systems by which it is transmitted and obtained, but information can move endlessly from place to place, from storage to storage, without being "copied" or "learned." The growing sovereignty of the audience over the selection of information occurs simultaneously with the rise of new controlling powers over databases. Thus, the triad of publisher, author, public, is transformed into a new triad of database controller, information collector/provider, reader. The formal designations may not change, but the altered technology changes the reality behind the labels.

It takes a very long time for realities to become facts. When Gutenberg overturned 1500 years of scribal practice, he set about performing the tasks of the scribes to the greater convenience of his customers who could henceforth purchase books more cheaply. But the new reality was a change in the nature of knowledge, in the whole function of the scribes. A change in the storage and dissemination processes of information must bring in its train a major shift in the realities of information power and in the relationship between all of society and all of the information to which it gives rise. There was once a great shift in the focus of knowledge that we have come to label the Renaissance, a hungering after the augmentation of knowledge, rather than the repetitive collation and recovery of knowledge. Scribal society with its image of the totality but inaccessibility of knowledge gave way to the reality of the infinite reproducibility and progressive corrigibility of all information, which led to the individual ownership of each successive accretion of knowledge.

As the scribe became intellectual, he moved from a relative humility in the face of a finite knowledge that he did not quite hold to a relative arrogance towards an infinitely flexible knowledge on which he could impose (temporarily) an individual will. A new, though still subterranean, pressure can be felt underlying the text in this era, the pressure of the new arrangement of sovereignty upon the librarian function. (It is not by accident that librarianship has been one of the first functions in society to be transformed in its professional practice and outlook by the introduction of on-line information systems.) The librarian makes information accessible to the consumer in an age in which the mere storage of information is becoming cheaper and cheaper. Indeed, there is some discussion in the world of new data of an enlarged system of storage, in which the charge for information is nil but in which revenue is collected for the task of inputting and amassing the material held. With the new very cheap memories it becomes sensible to permit the long-term storage of information free of charge and depend on its occasional use to pay the cost of retrieving it. Like a great attic or lumber room, knowledge could be held inactive in the long term until chanced upon and serendipitously disgorged.

The librarian chooses the codes in which to categorize information and arranges the key words through which information can be extracted. He now becomes a kind of author, and the author, in many ways, turns librarian. The librarian becomes, in a sense, the sentinel at the gateway of information and knowledge, and society may come to find itself demanding to see his credentials. What librarian ethic is the counterpart of the objectivity of a journalist or the scrupulousness of a judge? Who has made the computer-librarian lord and master over knowledge and how is his stewardship supervised and rendered accountable to society?

With the change in the nature of publication there comes a basic change in the "reality" of authorship. For a couple of hundred years now we have tended to mystify the author, to allow him to pretend that his work is semisacral, "original," the emanation of his spirit. The writer has held an exalted position in Western society since the invention of the printing press. His has been the scarce talent around which the process of publication takes place and which holds the audience together. It is his career through which the market for his material is built.

We have also come to honor the inventor and allowed the term to be applied to all manner of adapters and experimenters. The devices that have helped society move from one stage of producing to another have been marked by a succession of "inventions" whose eponymous authors are given the accolade, and very often the monetary profits, that have accrued from the device to which their ingenuity has led. (Modern researchers, perhaps, are seen more accurately as what they are, the collators of existing work who succeed in making one further crucial formulation of a problem.) Inventors are people who recognize a social need and adapt the available materials to meet it. Legal systems accord them priorities and privileges. The sacral element in invention flows from the feeling that the inventor has functioned outside a tradition rather than within it.

The computerization of memory causes us to perceive the nature of originality in different ways. The computer will not cause, nor change, nor bring about, but will help us to create an altered image of the author and inventor, a changed image that is growing out of the changed nature of the modern research publication processes. Within the creative process it is becoming clearer that the talent lies in the refining of past knowledge, in reformulation, in recirculation, in reordering the vast human storage of information that springs from the collective intellectual activity of the species, an unencompassable totality of versions and facts. The creative task lies in being able to manipulate this ever-expanding totality. It is a new perception of creativity that is now possible—a readjustment, not the elimination of the concept.

Perhaps it is wrong to speak of this attitude toward knowledge as new. In 1919 T.S. Eliot stressed the importance of this kind of relationship between the writers of the present and those of the past: "We dwell with satisfaction upon the poet's difference from his predecessors, especially his immediate predecessors; we endeavour to find something which can be isolated in order to be enjoyed. Whereas if we approach a poet without this prejudice we shall often find that not only the best, but the most individual parts of his work may be those in which the dead poets, his ancestors, assert their immortality most vigorously."[4]

It has become commonplace to speak of the information revolution as if it were a replay of the industrial revolution of the late eighteenth century, as if industrial society were about to undergo a new era of exponential growth in productive capacity as a result of a new kind of mechanization. But the concept of automation does not really fit the current stage, which is different in quality from previous periods of change in production. We have become used to the idea that technical change has its counterpart in a sensation of gathering pace in society, in a sense of social change all around us. The values of modern society have been colored by the phenomenon of massive industrial expansion, but it is possible that the transformation of the processes by which information is distributed will bring about a change in momentum.

Information is reaching smaller audiences. The massive marketing of entertainment and information is being broken down into specialized elements. Although the use of the computer in printing may seem to continue the lines of progressive statistical vastness, the values of society in its new information-rich stage may well begin to provide the sensation of a scaling down. The sense of exponential growth may give way to an age of gradualness, with the values of stability causing a flattening in the curve of development (which immunologist Jonas Salk calls Epoch B), in which the individual will need to take only what he needs and wants.[5] The artificial stimulation of wants, necessitated by the current phase of a consumer society, may pass into a period when values revolve around the discovery of relevant desires and tastes. The ethical adjustments of a societal change that creates new goals in the identification of needs rather than the maximization of desires are likely to produce further change in the same direction, and it would be easy to fall into the trap of treating "effects" in the sphere of values as direct results of particular machines or techniques. A technology, like a DNA molecule, possesses an encoded potential that cannot be known until it is released upon the environment (or the economy). Values evolve alongside man himself as part of his continuing dialogue with his natural and social environment. Technologies develop out of perceived needs and survive to open up new opportunities. They arise from the fight to survive, and they survive to take their place in the environment of man.

Survival today may be seen as the achievement of a balance between man and nature, rather than his continued effort to dominate it, and the values appropriate to any society sharing that growing perception must be impregnated with the desire to reach for what has been achieved and make use of it. The dead authors are what we know, says Eliot; they are essentially why we know more than they did. Our modern communications technology, in one sense, reverses the culture that was built in the age of the printing press, and presupposes an opening up of all knowledge, rather than a collecting of it in narrow institutions and specialist groups.

The interactive electronic mode of knowledge can be likened to an

Alexandria without walls, unified but universally accessible, keeping a better balance between what has been accumulated and what is to be added, emphasizing the sovereignty of mankind itself over the totality of its knowledge. There is an enormous difference between the potential of a technology and its uses; the latter are always approximate and make-shift, the former entails a scheme of values that are not necessarily accepted. Technology is only an interim statement of the relationship between man and nature, registering in the external world the stage that man has reached in his perception of the way of the universe, in his ability to manipulate the given in nature. Information is the raw material with which he does this, and communications media the bonds that today connect mankind to the changing environment of society as he searches.

CONCLUSION

This book has been an attempt to describe what is happening to the newspaper form in the context of late-twentieth-century society.

Before the arrival of radio and television, the newspaper enjoyed the same kind of social monopoly as the railroad did before the coming of the automobile and the airplane. It had acquired a special technology used by no other industry, and it dominated the sphere of information as the train dominated that of transportation. Countless industries and services depended upon the newspaper for their advertising, just as they did upon the train for the transporting of their products and personnel. With the arrival of radio and television, as with the new modes of transport, the incumbents faced the newcomers in a spirit of combativeness concealed as indifference. It took many decades for the railroad to discover the new roles and specialisms to which history was consigning it, and in some societies it appears that railroad has failed to identify them altogether and has since continued along a downward spiral.

The newspaper was confronted with a range of problems that challenged its entire self-definition in the 1960's and 1970's, when both of the electronic media became firmly entrenched in all the Western democratic societies. While the newspaper had previously seen its role as a highly competitive industry, it now started to become a monopolistic medium in most countries. Where it had been a party tool or a weapon of a political faction, it was now organized into large chains owned by powerful corporations anxious to play not too vexatious or conspicuous a role in the political sphere. Where the newspaper had been essentially a cheap medium to produce and distribute, it was now dependent upon expensive raw materials and, relative to other industries, was highly labor-intensive. Though it had worked hard to loosen any bonds linking its editorial control to government, it now often found itself dependent upon government aid in many countries.

At first, many predicted the demise of the medium altogether. Television gave the news instantaneously and visually to a wider audience; magazines provided more detailed information for those who really wanted it. In the 1970's however, despite several great financial and industrial crises, the newspaper emerged again, resplendent with a new and electronic technology, a new view of its social roles, and a number of new roles to play. In the United States, in particular, it became highly profitable. In Europe, Japan, and the U.S. it started to prepare itself for a wholly new phase of technical development that might in time free it from its traditional support—newsprint—or reorganize its contents among a number of parallel print media that were springing into existence. The generally heeded analysts no longer predict disaster, although clearly there is a very bumpy ride ahead.

The newspaper medium has been in this condition before. Every century or so this important carrier of social information has undergone a major technical transformation and has been reorganized financially and juridically; on each occasion it seemed as if the form in its traditional guise was on the verge of collapse, but quite quickly it became apparent that the process at hand was one of renewal rather than reversal.

If one glances back over the history of this medium as if it were recorded on a fast-moving film, one would witness a constant and progressive gathering of different types of information into a single form. The newspaper has grown bigger and bigger as a response to the increasing variety of tastes and interests within its audience. After three and a half centuries this process is reaching its culmination, and the next technological stages in newspaper history and in the history of communication devices in general must lead to the stripping away of some forms of information from the newspaper and to their transmission to readers in other ways. One can look at it a different way and argue that the dividing lines between different print media, ranging from the broadsheet to the newspaper, the weekly and monthly magazine, the paperback, the pamphlet, and the hard-cover book, are all shifting as a result of opportunities offered by new techniques and changing markets.

Until the seventeenth century each important or interesting event that reached the ears of a printer of news would be enshrined in a separate publication. The idea of placing a series of such "relations" in a single publication in order to multiply the market ("putting the occurences all together," as one early editor described it) was the beginning of the newspaper. It was a publishers' trick; it was a menu of information designed to satisfy a common denominator of taste and in order to spread the market still further by keeping prices down, it quickly acquired the habit of taking money from some of the *sources* of information, i.e., the advertisers, while extracting a coin or two from its readers. However, to keep this much larger machinery of publication together necessitated the second major characteristic of the medium after its variety—that is, regular, periodic publication. Whether it was daily or weekly or monthly was not important, as long as it could maintain its market by creating a habit of purchase that would in turn sustain the complex machinery of distribution that such markets demanded. And this, in turn, necessitated a third major element of the newspaper—the organization of the sources of information themselves in order to obtain a constant flow of suitable material.

Over the centuries the newspaper enlarged its audience by adding layer upon layer of additional material to its miscellaneous store while further expanding and complicating its machinery of distribution and of information collection. In the nineteenth century a new technology of printing had to be created to keep this growing machine functioning, culminating in the stereotype plate, which facilitated the locking of dozens of different pieces of information into a single "blanket" sheet of paper. Now the very technology of its printing indicated what the newspaper had become: a large miscellaneous farrago of information ordered in such a way as to maintain the habits of its now very large audience. The late-nineteenth-century stereotype plate and Linotype machine for the quick composition of type have brought the newspaper of today within an inch or two of its own culmination as a form. It has become almost too heavy for its readers to lift (in parts of America), too expensive to carry to their homes, holding ten times as much information as any single reader normally cares to read, and consuming cripplingly expensive quantities of its basic raw material—newsprint. In the late twentieth century it has begun a slow dismantling of itself, stripping away functions from the mixture and transferring them to other media, dividing itself into specialist supplements (resulting in the negation of the *idea* of the newspaper in a way) that provide extra sections for given geographic zones of its readership. All these new tasks and functions will undoubtedly "save" the newspaper and maintain its financial viability, but they will also spell the end of an era in the evolution of the newspaper form.

The newspaper cannot retain its monopoly of printed general information much longer; it has already lost its monopoly of news to radio and television. New teletext or videotex systems will gradually take on some of the newspaper's traditional tasks, while the newspaper concentrates on developing its new and rather more specialist functions that it has been identifying in the last decade or so. It is now dedicating itself more to "life-styles"—to supplements and special sections for housewives, teenagers, businessmen—and here too it will start to raise further questions about its very nature. For if a large section of the audience buys it for its special features, why should they buy simultaneously a hefty load of material that they do not require? Why should they buy it every day when their interests in a particular field are satisfied only once or twice a week? Here one may observe the newspaper very slowly losing its second defining characteristic—a periodicity entirely dependent upon the habit of the customer. What is happening to the newspaper as it undergoes these internal and external changes is a process that can be thought of as a kind of Hegelian self-negation. What the newspaper is turning into is something that is, in its essentials, the oppostie of what it set out to be.

One speaks of these processes in the present continuous or the future, although what is intended is a rather more speculative tense, a kind of future extrapolational, which falls short of being a prediction but expresses an implied inevitability within a certain range of circumstances. Such uncertainties are, however, of importance. The whole notion of citizenship in this century has been predicated upon the assumption that a certain modicum of contemporary knowledge is universally distributed. The newspaper carries with it the aura of a kind of citizenship committed to duties as well as rights. A society that simply did not contain a medium approximating the universality of the newspaper would be a society composed of consumers, not citizens. Information systems carry their own symbolic value in addition to their actual function.

The new media coming into existence in our own time have the tendency to individualize information, to make the acquisition of knowledge a matter of private choice. So far, throughout the twentieth century, we have enjoyed information systems (in radio and television as well as print) that have provided their material to large blocks of society and in so doing have "massified" the function of citizenship itself. The new computer-based technologies, now rapidly developing in most industrialized countries, offer the individual the chance to escape from general audiences into tiny groups selecting information according to atomized and itemized choices. At the same time, the satellite is helping to abolish distance as a factor in cost, and so an individual can choose to draw his private stock of knowledge more easily and cheaply from the total stock assembled by mankind. At least that is the perspective, and the meanings and emotions that the very idea sets off are important subjects for discussion. Where Gutenberg introduced the world of medieval knowledge to a continent, the mass press and television have shrunk the audience to that of the nation-state. Today a fascinating cultural reversal is underway: the individual is being offered, to an ever greater extent, individual access to a totality of information. But the processes by which his access is mediated need to be examined and criticized, which is why our topic is a *subject* and not a futurological scare.

New technologies of information are inextricably connected with new systems of government. In fact, they are nearly always used by government and change the nature of government before they are turned loose in society. Writing itself had an enormous impact on the growth of empire, the evolution of monarchical systems of government, and the establishment of clerical bureaucracies. The switch from stone to papyrus in ancient Egypt, as Harold Innis shows,[1] changed the nature of organized religion and brought new gods and new doctrines into being. It is arguably more revealing to use communication systems than production techniques as the boundary marks of history. In an industrial civilization such as ours, it has become customary to mark the development of mankind in terms of the wheel, the steam engine, and atomic energy. In a "postindustrial society," "knowledge economy," or "information economy" (to use the terms employed by Daniel Bell,[2] Fritz Machlup,[3] and Marc Porat,[4] respectively) it becomes perhaps more valid to use communication techniques as the boundary symbols of past eras. Certainly techniques of cognition are as dynamic factors in human civilization as techniques for hewing wood and drawing water. The British Empire was sustained as much by cheap pulp paper as by the gunboat. As we come to see our own society as a series of information cycles dependent upon the transmission and storage of knowledge, we shall come to emphasize the role of specific tools of information when attempting to define the great social changes of the past. Each change in the dominant medium implies a change in the dominant modes of cognition and effectively prevents each civilization from attaining an automatic understanding of others. The artifacts of one civilization seem mysterious, exotic, and remote from the moral considerations of one's own time because they are the evidence of a part of mankind that operated through different mental tools. Yet to discern the areas in which change is likely to occur within our own society as a result of changes in the dominant information medium does inevitably entail examination of the past. A certain perspective is necessary; parallels must be drawn.

The development of printing in the fifteenth century was inextricable from the whole social and cultural process known as the Renaissance. Gutenberg's printing press was partly a product of the new thinking, partly its instigator. It is easy to see certain patterns also evident in our own time, when new ideas about the nature of information are arising precisely at a moment when new methods for creating and disseminating the written word are being adopted. The Japanese have given wide currency to the "Information Society," and the phrase has now become popular in the United States. The French have added a new set of words to their vocabulary to indicate different aspects of this same phenomenon; they speak of the "informatisation" of society, the process by which new systems of information are being slotted into new roles; sometimes they use the terms "informatique," "telematique," and even "typotique" to refer to the electronic extensions of traditional print media into the new technologies of the 1980's.

Certainly we are moving into a period where entirely new devices are being marketed for disseminating the printed word and where at the same time traditional systems of printing are being transformed by the use of the computer and the reorganization of the industrial aspects of the newspaper. But inevitably the first uses to which new machines are put are traditional ones; the new printing technology is brought into use to resolve inefficiencies and dislocations that have occurred in the mechanical systems inherited from the Victorians. However, even at the moment of their installation it is possible to see ways in which this new technology can serve altogether new functions and change the environment of information in fundamental ways. The new printing presses of the fifteenth and sixteenth centuries were brought in to ease the pressure of demand on the European system of manuscript copying, but they then changed the way in which ideas circulated and facilitated new *national* cultures based upon the printed word.[6]

The switch from stone inscription to papyrus and handwriting signaled new patterns of thought and social organization. The switch from a scribal society to a printing one changed the whole focus of knowledge in the West and created new locations for information in society. The transition from paper to telecommunications systems can hardly prove to be less important, necessitating the development of new skills and new equipment, a new kind of text and a new method of text storage. As with the other great parallel transformation of history, the change is becoming evident in government before its impact reaches society in general. The defense and intelligence communities in the United States have already undergone a thorough changeover, and well over half of all documents relating to intelligence work are now transmitted, filed, and indexed electronically, passing through specialized networks without generating paper copy. The text is generated in video terminals and passed into data storage, to be retrieved and read by those concerned on other video terminals. Even in this and other comparable microsystems a host of moral, organizational, and economic problems are raised by the phenomenon of paperlessness. Technical librarianship is one of the next fields likely to undergo substantial transformation, and from there the change of system cannot but spread outwards throughout the education system to society as a whole.[7] Banking and monetary systems are meanwhile undergoing parallel and simultaneous transformation, and the work of conceptualizing mass systems of electronic funds transfer (creating a moneyless society?) is well underway. When governmental and financial communities adopt a new technology, they inevitably drag the rest of society between them, however inconceivable it may still be to nonspecialists that they should acquire this totally novel information skill and conduct the basic transactions of civil life via computer.

Today a major break with the past is clearly at hand, and with it will come, as has been argued in these pages, an important shift in the way we treat information, the way we collect and store it, the way we classify, censor, and circulate it. People will regard the process known as education in a quite different light in a society in which human memory will be needed for different purposes than in the past; we shall think of librarians, journalists, editors, and publishers as different creatures from those of today, since they will be involved in different mutual relationships, using a different technology.

In a sense the only choice which history does not make for us is that between optimism and pessimism. Whether we have "big" or "little" government, whether we become a gregarious or a lonely society, individualistic or regimented, is largely a result of the way we choose to use the technology. What the new electronic storage systems for information, interlinked globally, could come to offer is a renewed sense of the unity and accessibility of knowledge. The pursuit of a "New Alexandria" lay behind the tremendously rapid dissemination of printing technology in the late fifteenth century. Today, again, a new kind of Alexandria, without walls, has become possible (as an ideal, at least), an electronic system by which the totality of wisdom—or, at least, knowledge—can be shared, compared, aggregated.

Our society is poised between two different kinds of text, and we can see something of the culture and compulsions of both. Radio and television, in a sense, have provided a foretaste of the new electronic culture, in that they are based upon collective and institutional rather than individualistic authorship, upon social controls made on behalf of consumers rather than upon pure intellectual freedoms of individual expression. In some ways radio and television are late examples of the old mechanical culture: they aggregate their audiences and are then obliged by society to legitimize their authority over communication. In other ways they are the first of the new culture offering *systems* and continuous strands of information and entertainment, a complete flow of material designed to offer a series of parallel choices.

A system of information that grasps the attention of a large proportion of society at one moment finds itself obliged to address the perspectives and values of the most politically powerful segment of the audience; legitimizing the content of the medium takes precedence over the rights and freedoms that were so important in the heyday of the newspaper.

The broadcasting industry and broadcasting regulators have both found it very difficult to transfer the privileges and duties of the First Amendment from print to broadcasting; the freedoms that the U.S. Constitution provided for editors have largely been seized upon as the rights of media businesses. The successive reinterpretations of the First Amendment have not displaced the traditional freedoms but have overlaid them with new *commercial* freedoms and revealed new commercial constraints that society feels it needs to impose upon publishers. The further society moves from the printed to the electronic age, the more complicated does the problem of publishing freedom become, the more society as a group of consumers demands restraint of those sending out information and entertainment.[8]

This changeover also expresses important challenges to the philosophical underpinning of the activity of reporting and collecting information. Victorian "objectivity" is giving way to the relativism of the electronic age. Words have lost their hard edges in the age of the audio-visual. A world of facts is dissolving into a factless world overloaded with information, dominated by images. The provision of information has become the privilege of great feudalities, vast corporations that collect and disseminate material through a multiplicity of media; but at the same time the very abundance has made the reciever, the consumer, more powerful in the process of communication. The greater the profusion and the wider the choice, the more dangerous is the fact that very few control it; but that danger is set against the greater freedom of the reader and viewer. The computer removes the necessity of highly developed skills from the area of storage of information (thereby reducing the expense) and transfers it to the retrieval of information. Turning information into knowledge is the creative skill of the age, for it involves discovering ways to burrow into the abundance rather than augment it, to illuminate rather than search.

APPENDIX

APPENDIX

COUNTRY	SYSTEM	...WHICH MEANS	TYPE	SOURCE	OPERATORS
Australia	wired teletext		videotex	Telecom Australia, 518 Little Bourke Street, Melbourne, Victoria 3000	
Australia	broadcast teletext		teletext	Australian Broadcasting Commision (ABC), 145 Elizabeth Street, Box 487, Sydney 2001	
Canada	Telidon	"at a distance" + "I saw/perceived/know" (Greek)	videotex	Department of Communications, 150 Metcalfe Street, Ottawa KIA OC8	Department of Communications
Canada	Vista		videotex	Bell Canada, 1050 Beaver Hall Hill, Montreal, Quebec H3C 3G4	Bell Canada; IPs: Torstar Corporation (owner of Toronto Star) and Southam Press
Finland	Telset	.	videotex	Ministry of Posts and Telecommunications, PO Box 528, SF 00101 Helsinki 10	The Ministry, with Sanoma Publishing and Oy Nokia
France	Tictac	Terminal Integré Comportant un Téléviseur et l'Appel au Clavier	videotex	Centre National d'Etudes Télécommunications (CNET), 8 Avenue Jean Jaures, 92130 Issy-les-Moulineaux	Ministère des Postes et Telecommunications
France	Titan		videotex	Centre Commun d'Etudes de Télévision et Télécommunications (CCETT), 2 Rue de la Mabilais, BP 1266, 35013 Rennes Cedex	Télédiffusion de France, 21-27 Rue Barbec7/es, 92120 Montrouge

329

COUNTRY	SYSTEM	. . .WHICH MEANS	TYPE	SOURCE	OPERATORS
France	Didon		teletext	CCETT	
France	Antiope	Acquisition Numerique et Télévisualisation d'Images Organisées en Pages d'Ecriture	teletext	CCETT	
Germany, FR	Bildschirmtext	"videoscreen texts"	videotext	Bundespost, Adenaueralle 81, 5300 Bonn 1	Bundespost
Germany, FR	Videotext		teletext	ARD, 8 Munchen 40, Leopoldstrasse 10	
Germany, FR	Videotext		teletext	ZDF, 6500 Mainz Postfach 40 40	
Germany, FR	Bildschirmzeitung	"screen newspaper"	teletext	BDZV, 53 Bonn-Bad Godesberg, Riemenschneiderstrasse 10	
Japan	CAPTAIN	Character and Pattern Telephone Access Information Network	videotex	Ministry of Posts and Tele-communications 1-3-2 Kasumigaseki, Chiyoda-ku, Tokyo 100	Ministry, and Nippon Telegraph and Telephone (NTT)
Sweden	Text-TV		videotex	Sveriges Radio S-10510 Stockholm	
UK	Prestel (originally Viewdata)		videotex	Post Office, Prestel Headquarters Telephone House, Temple Avenue, London EC4	Post Office, Prestel
UK	Ceefax	"see . . . facts"	teletext	BBC, Portland Place, London W1	

330

COUNTRY	SYSTEM	...WHICH MEANS	TYPE	SOURCE	OPERATORS
UK	ORACLE	Optional Reception of Announcements by Coded Line Electronics	teletext	IBA, 70 Brompton Road, London SW3	ITCA, Knighton House, 52-66 Mortimer Street, London W1
USA	Qube		videotex	Warner Cable, a subsidiary of Warner Communications, 75 Rockefeller Plaza, New York NY 10019	Qube, Columbus, Ohio
USA	Closed Captioning		teletext	Public Broadcasting Service, 475 L'Enfant Plaza, S.W., Washington, DC 20024	
USA	teletext		teletext	Bonneville International Corporation, 36 South State Street, Suite 2100, Salt Lake	KSL-TV, 145 Social Hall Avenue Utah 84111

SOURCE: InterMedia, IIC, London, Vol. 7, No. 3, May 1979.

NOTES

PART ONE

1. Plato, *Collected Works* (Princeton: Phaedrus, 1961), pp. 520–21.
2. Frances Yates, *The Art of Memory* (New York: Penguin, 1966), p. 20.
3. Plato, op. cit.
4. Harold A. Innis, *Empire and Communications (Toronto: University of Toronto Press, 1972) pp. 10–11.*
5. Quoted by V. Gordon Childe, *Man Makes Himself* (1936), p. 12.
6. Lucien Fèbre and Henri-Jean Martin, *Coming of the Book: 1450–1800,* trans. David Gerard (London: New Left Books, 1976).
7. Ibid (see Marcel Thomas, "Manuscripts," pp. 15–28)
8. Quoted by Louis le Roy (1575) J. B. Ross and M. M. McLaughlin *The Portable Renaissance Reader,* (New York: 1958) p. 98.
9. Elisabeth I. Eisentstein, "The Advent of Printing and the Problem of the Renaissance," *Past and Present,* No. 45 (1969), pp. 19–89.
10. See introduction by Herbert David and Harry Carter in *Mechanic Exercises on the Whole Art of Printing (1683–4)* Joseph Moxon (New York: Dover Publications, 1960).
11. See Elizabeth Eisenstein, The Printing Press as an Agent of Change, (Cambridge University Press, 1979) Vol. 1 pp. 429–33.
12. See Margot Lindemann, "Deutsche Presse bis 1815," *Colloquium Verlag,* (Berlin, 1969).
13. F. S. Siebert, *Freedom of the Press in England,* 1476–1776 (Urbana: University of Illinois Press, 1965).
14. See Wilfred A. Beeching, *Century of the Typewriter,* (London: Heinemann, 1974), pp. 28–37, for quotes about women.
15. Asa Briggs, "The Pleasure Telephone : A Chapter in the Pre-history of the Media in Ithiel de Sola Pool," *The Social Impact of the Telephone* (Cambridge, Mass: MIT Press, 1977), pp. 40–65.
16. Ivar Ivre, "Mass Media: The Cost to the Consumer," *Intermedia,* Vol. 6, No 5 (September 1978), p. 20.

PART TWO, Chapter One

1. Frank Joseph, *The Beginnings of the English Newspaper* (New York: Oxford University Press; Cambridge: Harvard University Press, 1961), Ch. 1. Rene Mazedier, *Histoire de la presse parisienne,* (Paris: Editions du Pavoir, 1945).
2. Rev. George Crabbe, "The Newspaper," *Life and Works,* Vol. 2 (1834), p. 118.
3. C. Bellanger et al, *Histoire Générale de la Presse Francaise,* Vol. 1 (Paris: Presses Universitaires de France, 1969) passim.

4. Stanley Morison, *The English Newspaper*, (Cambridge: At the University Press, 1932), 60.

5. Charles H. Dennis, *Victor Lawson, His time and His work* (Chicago, University of Chicago Press, 1935), p. 45. James Melvin Lee, *History of American Journalism* (Boston: Houghton Mifflin, 1917), p. 359.

6. S. Kobré, *The Development of American Journalism*, (Dubuque, Iowa: William C. Browne, 1972).

7. Oswald Spengler, *Decline of the West*.

8. Walter Bagehot, *Physics and Politics*,(London, 1872).

9. Charles Pebody, *English Journalism and the Men who Have Made it*, (London: Cassell, Petter, Galpin, 1872), p. 5.

10. Irene Collins, *The Government and the Newspaper Press in France, 1814–81* (New York: Oxford University Press, 1959.)

11. J. Robertson Scott, C. H., *The Story of the Pall Mall Gazette* (New York: Oxford University Press, 1950), p. 138 of its first editor, Frederick Greenwood, and of its founder, George Murray Smith.

12. Anthony Smith, *Subsidies and the Press in Europe*, Political and Economic Planning (London: 1976) passim.

13. R. D. Blumenfeld, *The Press in My Time* (London: Heinemann, 1933), p. 12.

14. Statistics from Christopher H. Sterling and Timothy R. Haight, *The Mass Media: Aspen Institute Guide to Communication Industry Trends* (New York: Praeger, 1978), pp. 3–4.

15. Gerald Alperstein, "New Statistical Probe into the Decline of Daily Newspaper Household Penetration," (Paper delivered at the Annual Convention of the Association for Education in Journalism at Wisconsin, August 1977).

16. Leo Bogart, "The Future of the Metropolitan Daily," *Journal of Communication*, Vol. 25, No. 2 Spring 1975 pp. 30–41.

17. See Roper Research Associates, *A Ten-Year View of Public Attitudes Toward Television and Other Mass Media, 1959–1968*, Television Information Office (New York: 1970).

18. Ben H. Bagdikian, *The Information Machines: Their Impact on Men and the Media* (New York: Harper & Row, 1971), p. 60 (Figures provided by Newsprint Information Committee).

19. John Robinson and Philip Converse, "Social Change as Reflected in the Use of Time in: Angus Campbell and Philip Converse," *The Human Meaning of Social Change*, (New York: Russel Sage, 1972).

20. John P. Robinson, *Daily News Habits of the American Public*, ANPA News Research Center Study No. 15 (Washington: September 22, 1978).

21. Roper Reseach Associates, *Trends in Public Attitudes Toward Television and Other Media, 1969–1974*, the Television Information Office (New York, 1975).

22. Leo Bogart, "How the Public Gets its News," (An address before the Associated Press Managing Editors at New Orleans, October 29, 1977). *Seven*

Days in March: Major news stories in the Press and on TV, Newspaper Advertising Bureau, (New York, 1978).

23. *It's News to Me: Personal Reactions to the News*, Newspaper Advertising Bureau (New York, 1978).

24. See John B. Oakes, "Concentrations of Press Power," *Nieman Reports* (Autumn 1978), pp. 26–31.

Chapter 2

1. But see Antoine de Tarle, "The Press and the State in France," in *Newspapers and Democracy*, (Cambridge: MIT Press, 1980).

2. Christopher H. Sterling and Timothy R. Haight, *The Mass Media: Aspen Institute Guide to Communication Industry Trends* (New York: Praeger 1978). James N. Rosse, Bruce M. Owen and James Dertouzos, "Trends in the Daily Newspaper Industry, 1923–73, *Studies in Industry Economics*, No. 57, (Palo Alto: Stanford University, May 1975).

3. See Ben Bagdikian, "Newspaper Mergers—The Chains Tighten Their Hold," *Columbia Journalism Review* (March/April 1977). Ben Bagdikian, "The Media Conglomeration, Concentration," *AFL-CIO American Federationist* (March 1979).

4. Senator Udall has for several years been promoting an inheritance-tax reform that would help slow down the process by which families feel obliged to sell. The first version of the Udall Bill would permit the owner of an independent newspaper to start up a trust fund with up to half of a newspaper's pretax earnings; this trust would then not count as part of the owner's estate at the time of his death but would be used to pay his estate duties. Duties would also be payable over a fifteen-year period (plus interest) in installments.

5. Information in this section is derived from "Editorial Standardization in the Nation's Press," a Department of State briefing memorandum (July 12, 1978).

6. See article on death of Samuel Newhouse, *New York Times* (August 30, 1979).

7. "After a Rush of Take-Overs," *U.S. News World Report* (January 24, 1977), p. 54–56. The Big Money Hunts for Independent Newspapers," *Business Week* (February 21, 1977) pp. 56–62. Alvin P. Sanoff, "America's Press: Too Much Power for Too Few?" *U.S. News and World Report* (August 15, 1977) pp. 27–33. *Editor and Publisher* (July 9, 1977).

8. *John Morton Newspaper Research Newsletter* (Washington D.C.: Colin, Hochstin & Co., April 18, 1977 and on frequent other occasions).

9. See *Editor & Publisher* (May 7, 1977), pp. 7–8.

10. See Tony J. McIntosh, "Why the Government Can't Stop Press Mergers," *Columbia Journalism Review*, pp. 48–50.

11. See the *Courier-Journal* Centennial Edition, 1868–1968.

12. *John Morton Newspaper Research Newsletter* (March 29, 1977).

13. Lars Furhoff, *Dagspressens ekonomiska villkor (Economic Conditions of the Daily Press)* Stockholm: SOU (1965), p. 22.

Dagspressens situation (The Situation of the Daily Press), Stockholm: SOU (1968), p. 48.

(SOU = Government of Sweden Official Reports)

S. Jonsson, *Annonser och tidningskonkurrens* (Advertisements and Newspaper Competition), Institute of Economic History (Gothenberg, 1977).

For a full discussion, see Karl Erik Gustafsson, "The Circulation Spiral and the Principle of Household Coverage," *Scandinavian Economic History Review*, Vol. 26 No. 1 (1978).

14. James N. Rosse, *"Economic Limits of Press Responsibility,"* Studies in Industry Economics, No. 56 (Stanford University, 1975).

15. John Consoli article in *Editor & Publisher* (June 10, 1978).

16. See David Halberstamm, *The Powers That Be* (New York: Alfred J. Knopf, 1979), p. 292.

17. For a comprehensive list, see W. H. Masters, "Media Monopolies: Busting Up a Cozy Marriage," *More* magazine (October 1977) p. 13.

18. Rinker Buck, "Watertown N.Y.: Suitable Grounds for Divorce," *More* magazine (October 1977), pp. 14–20.

19. See Walter S. Baer, Henry Geller, Joseph A. Grundfest and Karen B. Possner, *Concentration of Mass Media Ownership: Assessing the State of Current Knowledge*, Rand Corporation publication R-1584-NSF (1974).

Guido Stempel III, *Effects of Performance of a Cross-Media Monopoly*, Journalism Monographs, No. 29, Association for Education in Journalism (June 1973).

William T. Gormley, Jr., *The Effects of Newspaper-Television Cross-Ownership on News Homogeneity*, Institute for Research in Social Science at the University of North Carolina (Chapel Hill, 1976).

Michael O. Wirth and James A. Wollert, "Public Interest Program Performance of Multi-Media-Owned TV Stations," *Journalism Quarterly*, Vol. 53 (Summer 1976), pp. 223–30.

20. James A. Anderson, "The Alliance of Broadcast Stations and Newspapers: The Problem of Information Control," *Journal of Broadcasting*, Vol. 16 (Winter 1971–72), pp. 51–64.

21. Stephen R. Barnett, "Cross-Ownership of Mass Media in the Same City" (A report to the Markle Foundation, September 1974).

22. ANPA figures.

23. Monroe Mendelsohn Research, Inc., New York, 1978.

24. GAMIS (Graphic Arts Marketing Information Service), Arlington, Virginia, 1977.

25. Newspaper Advertising Bureau figures, New York.

26. U.S. Bureau of Statistics.

27. *ANPA Newspaper Facts*, 1979.

28. Stephen R. Fajen, "More for Your Money from the Media," *Harvard Business Review* (September/October 1978), pp. 113–21.
29. *John Morton Newspaper Research Newsletter* (August 29, 1979).
30. *U.K. Press Gazette* (May 28, 1979), p. 48.
31. *New York Times* Sunday edition (December 24, 1978).
32. James Hoge of the *Sun-Times* to the author.
33. Leo Bogart, *Columbia Journalism Review*.

Chapter 3

1. Quoted in ANPA RI Bulletin No: 1148 (April 15, 1974).
2. Cecil B. Kelly, Jr., *The* Palm Beach Post-Times *Utilizes DLC-1000 Laser Typesetting,* ANPA RI Bulletin No: 1273 (November 11, 1977).
3. ANPA RI Bulletin No. 1286 (March 22, 1978).
4. This account has been prepared with the use of internal documents and design specifications supplied by the *Los Angeles Times.*
5. Kenneth R. Todd, *Computerized Circulation at the* Indianapolis Star and News, ANPA RI Bulletin. No. 1299, (October 4, 1975).
6. *Editor & Publisher* (June 3, 1978), p. 11.
7. Electronic Library/Morgue Retrieval Systems, ANPA RI Bulletin No. 1281 (December 12, 1977).
8. Hugh Folk, "The Impact of Computers in Book and Journal Publications," *The Economics of Library Automation,* ed. J.L. Divilbiss (proceedings of the 1976 Clinic in Library Applications of Data Processing, (Champaign-Urbana: University of Illinois, 1977).
9. Richard De Gennar, "Escalating Journal Prices: Time to Fight Back, " *American Libraries* Vol. 8, pp. 69–74 (February 1977).
10. Bernard M. Fry and Herbert S. White, *Publishers and Libraries: A Study of Scholarly and Research Journals* (Lexington, M955: Lexington Books, 1976).

Daniel Gore, *Farewell to Alexandria: Solutions to Space, Growth and Performance Problems of Libraries* (Westport, Conn.: Greenwood Press, 1976).

J. C. R. Licklider, *Libraries of the Future* (Cambridge, Mass.: MIT Press, 1965).

F. W. Lancaster, *Towards Paperless Information Systems* (New York: Academic Press, 1978).

Edward K. Yasaki, "Toward the Automated Office," *Datamation,* Vol. 21:59–62, (February 1975) pp. 59–62.
11. F. Wilfrid Lancaster, "Whither Libraries? Wither libraries," *College and Research Libraries* (September 1978) pp. 345–57.
12. Akiru Yamamoto et al., eds., *Yomiuri TV Information Industry Research Group: Japan's Information Industry* (Tokyo: The Simul Press, 1975).
13. Information from The Japanese Press, NSK (Tokyo: 1977) and The Japanese Press, NSK (Tokyo: 1978).
14. NSK News Bulletin Vol. 1, No. 2 (Tokyo: August 1978) p. 2.
15. ANPA RI Bulletin, No. 1307 (December 7, 1978).

Chapter 4

1. For a longer account of this phenomenon, see David Halberstamm's *The Powers That Be*, op.cit., p.67.

2. William H. Jones, "Papers Chase Segmented Readership," *Washington Post* (May 7, 1978).

Gayle Thompson, "Geographic Zoning of Newspapers, a Special Review," (Paper for ASNE Committee on New Technology, 1978).

Robert E. Hartley, "Special Interest Sectors" (Paper for ASNE Committee on New Technology, 1978).

3. ANPA RI Bulletin No. 1276 (December 12, 1977).

4. See Lee Loevinger, "Some Legal Problems of Metropolitan Newspaper Competition" (Presented to the Southern Newspaper Publishers Association [SNPA] Business and Administrative Committee session in Atlanta, June 1977).

5. See a paper by George N. Gill, Vice-President of the *Courier-Journal*, presented to IFRA at Nice, France, October 26, 1977.

6. Fred Loskamp, "On-line Inserter a Success at the *Washington Star*," ANPA RI Bulletin No. 1299 (October 4, 1978).

Chapter 5

1. Rudyard Kipling, *The Light that Failed* (London 1891), p. 18.

2. W. A. Swanberg, *Citizen Hearst* (New York: Charles Scribner's Sons, 1961), pp. 101–115.

3. W. T. Stead, "A Journalist on Journalism," in A Journalist on Journalism, ed. Edwin H. Stout (London: John Haddon & Co., 1892).

4. Lincoln Steffens, *Autobiography* (New York: Harcourt Brace Yovonovich, 1931), p. 179.

5. See Michael Schudson, *Discovering the News—A Social History of American Newspapers* (New York: Basic Books, 1978) pp. 61–120, for a brilliant analysis of these themes.

6. See Robert E. Park, *The Crowd and the Public & Other Essays*, (Chicago: University of Chicago Press, 1972).

7. Walter Lippmann, *The Public Opinion* (New York: Harcourt Brace Jovanovich, 1922).

8. Sir Norman Angell, *The Press and the Organization of Society* (London: The Labour Publishing Company, 1923).

9. Herbert J. Gans, *Deciding What's News* (New York: Pantheon Books, 1979) Ch. 2, passim.

10. Walter Lippmann, *The Phantom Public* (New York, Harcourt Brace Jovanovich, 1925).

11. Quoted by Schudson, op. cit., p. 123.

12. Park, op. cit., pp. 86–87.

13. Sir Norman Angell, *The Public Mind* (London: Noel Douglas Publishers, 1923), p. 12.

14. See the essay "MacArthur Day in Chicago" in *Politics and Television*, Kurt Lang and Gladys Engel Lang (Chicago: Quadrangle Books, 1968, 1970), pp. 136–77.

15. Tom Wolfe, *The New Journalism* (New York: Picador, 1975), p. 25.

16. Ibid., p. 35.

17. H. L. Mencken, "Prejudices—a selection," *Journalism in America* (New York: Vintage Books, 1955), pp. 216–17

18. See David Halberstamm, *The Powers That Be*, op. cit., p. 697.

19. *UK Press Gazette* (August 28, 1978).

20. Daniel Boorstin, *The Image: Or What Happened to the American Dream?* (New York: Harper and Row, 1961), p. 61.

21. See William A. Dorman and Elisan Omeed, "Reporting Iran the Shah's Way," *Columbia Journalism Review*, (Jan./Feb. 1979), p. 27.

22. Norman H. Nie, Sidney Verba, and John R. Petrocik, *The Changing American Voter* (Cambridge: Harvard University Press, 1976), p. 278.

23. See John L. Hulteng, *The Opinion Function: Editorial and Interpretative Writing for the News Media* (New York, Harper & Row, 1973).

24. J. K. Hvistendahl, "The Reporter as Activist: A Fourth Revolution in Journalism," *Quill* (February 1970), pp. 8–11.

25. Michael Herr, *Dispatches* (New York, Alfred J. Knopf, 1979).

26. Gaye Tuchman, "Objectivity as Strategic Ritual: An examination of Newsmen's Notions of Objectivity," *American Journal of Sociology*, No. 77 (1972), pp. 660–80.

27. Paul H. Weaver, "Newspapers News and TV News," *TV as a Social Force—New Approaches to TV Criticism* (New York: Praeger, 1975) pp. 81–99.

28. Sterling and Haight, op.cit., Table 520-A, p. 288.

29. Turner Catledge, *My Life and the Times* (New York: Harper & Row, 1971), p. xii.

30. Leon V. Sigal, *Reporters and Officials: The Organization and Politics of Newsmaking* (Lexington, Mass: D. C. Heath, 1973).

Chapter 6

1. Harry Kelber and Carl Schlesinger, *Union Printers and Controlled Automation* (New York: Free Press, 1967), pp. 24–25.

2. See A. H. Raskin, "A reporter at Large," first of two articles on the 1978 New York newspaper strike, *New Yorker* (January 22, 1979).

3. Willi Mengel, *Ottmar Mergenthaler and the Printing Revolution*, (New York: 1954).

4. Joseph Moxon, *Mechanic Exercises on the Whole Art of Printing*, op. cit.

5. Ibid., p. 323.

6. Ibid., p. 12.

7. See the account by Ben H. Bagdikian, *The Information Machines: Their Impact on Men and the Media* (New York: Harper & Row, 1971), pp. 124–26.

8. S. M. Lipset, M. A. Tow and J. S. Coleman, *Union Democracy* (New York: The Free Press, 1956).

9. Keith Sisson, *Industrial Relations in Fleet Street* (Oxford: Basil Blackwell, 1975) Ch. 12.

10. Simon Jenkins, *Newspapers, the Power and the Money* (London, Faber & Faber, 1979). pp. 107–20.

11. The Varityper, invented in 1932, was a typewriter that had been adapted for newspaper work.

12. Kelber and Schlesinger, op. cit., pp. 30–40.

13. Ibid. pp. 50–54.

14. Kelber and Schlesinger's account has been used, together with Gay Talese, *The Kingdom and the Power: The Story of the Men who Influence the Institution that Influences the World—the New York Times* (New York: World Publsihing Co. 1969), pp. 302–16.

15. Ernest C. Hynds, *American Newspapers in the 1970's: Studies in Media Management* (New York: Hastings House, 1975) p. 255.

16. *Typographical Journal*, Annual Reports Edition (March 1978) p. 82.

17. See A. H. Raskin, "The Great Manhattan Newspaper Duel," *Saturday Review*, XLVIII (May 8, 1965).

18. See A. H. Raskin's account in the *New Yorker* (January 22 and January 29, 1979).

19. *Columbia Journalism Review* (March/April), 1979.

20. See *Industrial Relations in the National Newspaper Industry*, a report by the Advisory Conciliation and Arbitration Service to the Royal Commission on the Press, Research Series 1, Appendix 2, Cmnd. 6680 (London: HMSO, December 1976).

21. See article by Alf Schiottz-Christensen, publisher of the *Aalborg Stifstidende* of Denmark, in *Editor & Publisher* (June 1978).

22. See Rex Winsbury, *New Technology and the Press—A Study of Experience in the United States*, Working Paper No. 1, for the Acton Society Press Group and the Royal Commission on the Press (London: HMSO, October 1975).

23. *Employment Outlook in Printing and Publishing*, (Washington D. C.: Bulletin 1875-4 U.S. Department of Labor, Bureau of Labor Statistics, 1976).

24. Speech given by Horst Reschke of the ITU at the University of Denver, November 14, 1974.

Chapter 7

1. Claus Detjen, "*The Conflict over 'Bildschirmzeitung,' or Electronic News*," Journalismus No. 12, Düsseldorf: Droste Verlag, 1978).

2. *Viewdata and Its Potential Impact, Interim Report—the U.K. Experience*, (London: Butler, Cox and Partners, 1978).

3. I am indebted to Richard Hooper, Managing Director of Mills & Allen Communications Ltd., London, for several of the reflections in this section.

4. See "Viewdata—Everyman's Database" (paper by Rex Winsbury and Martin Lane of Fintel Ltd., London, 1979)

5. Dietrich Ratzke, ed., "*Electronic News: Tele-reading to Replace the Tele-vision*" (Berlin: Colloquium Verlag, 1977).

6. Dietrich Ratzke, "*Network of Power—The New Media*" (Frankfurt: Societäts-Verlag, 1975).

7. H. G. Brown, C.D. O'Brien, W. Sawchuk and J. R. Storey, *A General Description of Telidon—A Canadian Propsal for Videotex Systems*, Dept. of Communications, CRC Technical Note No. 697-E (Canada: 1978).

8. Much of the information in this section has been derived from a special edition of *InterMedia*, a magazine published by the International Institute of Communications, London, Vol. 7, No. 3 (May 1979). passim.

9. John F. Jansson, "QUBE in Columbus" (paper for circulation within ASNE, 1978)

10. John Wicklein, "Wired City, U.S.A.—the Charms and Dangers of Two-way TV," *Atlantic Monthly* (February 1979), pp. 35–42.

11. See Iann Barron and Ray Curnow, *The Future with Microelectronics: Forecasting the Effects of Information Technology* (New York: Nichols Publishing Co., 1979) pp. 68–92.

12. John F. Jansson, "Two-way Cable TV in Japan" (A paper for an ASNE Study Group, January 6, 1978).

13. *Electronics Weekly* (April 25, 1979).

14. Izumi Tadoroko, *New Towns and an Advanced Cable TV System—the Background and Achievements of a Japanese Experimental Project*, Studies of Broadcasting, No. 14, NHK (Tokyo, 1978).

15. See William D. Rinehart, *The ABC of New Communications Technology*, ANPA RI Bulletin, No. 1266 (August 19, 1977).

16. James F. Darr and David L. Bowen, *AP and UPI Wire Service News Distribution*, ANPA RI Bulletin, No. 1266 (August 19, 1977).

17. James Martin, *Telecommunications and the Computer*, 2nd ed. (Englewood Cliffs, N.J.: Prentice Hall, 1976).

James Martin, *Future Developments in Telecommunications*, 2nd ed. (Englewood Cliffs, N.J.: Prentice Hall, 1977).

Douglass D. Crombie, ed., *Lower Barriers to Telecommunications Growth*, (Washington D.C.: Office of Telecommunications, U.S. Dept. of Commerce, 1976).

18. Walter S. Baer, "Communication Technology in the 1980's" in *Communications for Tomorrow—Policy Perspectives in the 1980's*, ed. Glen O. Robinson (Aspen New York: Praeger, 1978). pp. 61–123. A number of the points made in this section are derived from this very useful study.

19. Raymond R. Panko, "The Outlook for Computer Mail," *Telecommunications Policy* Vol. 1, No. 3 (June 1977) pp. 243–53.

20. *Scientific American*, special issue on microelectronics (September 1977) A. Barna and Dan I. Porat, *Introduction to Microcomputers and Microprocessors* (New York: John Wiley & Sons, 1976).

21. See A. R. Megarry, "The Information Society," (An unpublished paper delivered by the Vice-President of the Torstar Corporation Ltd. to the Science Council of Canada, February 9, 1978). *Telecommunications and Society, 1976–1991* (Prepared for the Office of Telecommunications Policy, Washington D.C. by Arthur D. Little Inc., Cambridge, Mass., June 1976).

Chapter 8

1. Erik Barnouw, *A Tower in Babel* (New York: Oxford University Press, 1968) pp. 237–38.

2. In some local videotex and teletext experiments, however, classified advertising is playing an important role. It is not, however, thought likely that in their early years these media will make significant inroads into the main areas of such advertising.

3. Source of projected figures: *The Impact of Electronic Systems on News Publishing 1977–92* (an Arthur D. Little multiclient study, Final Draft Report, December 6–7, 1978).

4. T. S. Eliot, "Tradition and the Individual Talent," in *Collected Essays*, (London: Faber & Faber, 1958).

5. See Jonas Salk, *How Like an Angel: Biology and the Nature of Man* (London: David and Charles, 1972) for an examination of this argument.

Conclusion

1. Harold A Innis, *Empire and Communications* (Toronto: University of Toronto Press, 1972), pp. 6–11.

2. Daniel Bell, *The Coming of Post-Industrial Society* (New York: Basic Books, 1973).

3. Fritz Machlup, *The Production and Distribution of Knowledge in the United States* (Princeton: Princeton University Press, 1962).

4. Marc Uri Porat, "Global Implications of the Information Society," *Journal of Communication* Vol. 28:1 (Winter 1978) pp. 70–80.

Marc Uri Porat, *The Information Economy: Definition and Measurement*, Vols. 1–9, U.S. Government Printing Office (Washington D.C., July 1977).

5. Simon Nora and Alain Minc: "L'Informatisation de la société," *Documentation française (January 1978)*.

6. Elizabeth Eisenstein, "Some Conjectures about the Impact of Printing on Western Society and Thought: A Preliminary Report," *Journal of Modern History*, Vol. No. 40, 1 (1968) pp. 1–57.

7. F. Wilfred Lancaster, "Whither Libraries? or wither libraries," *College and Research Libraries*, (September 1978), pp. 345–57.

8. Fred W. Friendly, *The Good Guys, the Bad Guys and the First Amendment*, (New York, Random House, 1976).

GLOSSARY

Alphanumeric (or alphameric) Capable of printing or otherwise using both letters and numbers

Bandwidth The range within a band of wavelengths, frequencies, or energies

Bit The physical representation (as in a computer tape or memory) of a bit by an electrical impulse, a magnetized spot, or a hole whose presence or absence indicates data

Bitstream The total flow of digitalized information through a network

Blanket The rubber sheet in an offset press that receives the inked impression from the plate and transfers it to the surface being printed

Broadband Capable of operation with uniform efficiency over a wide band of frequencies

Bubble memory A memory system in which vast quantities of information are stored in tiny crystals of garnet. It differs from other memory systems in that it retains the information even if it is disconnected from its power source.

Byte A group of adjacent binery digits (often shorter than a word) that a computer processes as a unit

Cassette A light–tight magazine for holding sensitized film or plates for use in a camera

Cathode–ray tube The electronic tube used by high–speed photocomposition machines for transmitting the letter image (consisting of dots or lines) onto film, photopaper, microfilm, or offset plate

Chapel   An association of print workers

Chase   A rectangular iron or steel frame in which pages of type, slugs, or plates are locked up

Chip   Mini–computer circuitry printed out on a tiny piece of silicon

Chromolithograph   A picture printed by chromolithography

Chromolithography   Lithography that is adapted to printing in inks of various colors

Coaxial cable   An insulated cable used to transmit telegraph, telephone, and television signals of high frequency

Cold type   A method of printing that produces a photographic image, as opposed to (hot) metal letterpress type

Common carrier   A public service company

Cursor   A part of a mathematical instrument that moves back and forth on another part

Database   Any filing system or collection of information

Di–litho   Technique for printing directly onto paper from an offset plate which is mounted on the saddle of a letterpress

Dish   An often paraboloid microwave antenna that is usually highly directive in wave reflection

Electrophotography   Photography in which images are produced by electrical means

Facsimile   The process of transmitting and reproducing (as printed matter or still pictures), originally by facsimile telegraph but now chiefly by a system of radio communication

Field   A particular area (such as a column or a punched card) in which one type of information is regularly recorded

Font   The assortment of type of a particular size and style (including caps, small caps, punctuation marks, common symbols and accents) used in a printing press

Frame–grab   British term for scrolling. Enables the user of a vdt to locate and select a particular piece of information by cycling the body of data across the screen

Front–end system   A computerized system which files and stores all information fed into it and sends it to the typesetting machine with all typesetting commands after the information has been edited

H–and–J   Hyphenate and justify

Holography   The process of making or using a hologram, which is a three–dimensional picture produced in the form of an interference pattern on a photographic film or plate

Intelligent   Able to perform some of the functions of a computer

K–bit   A unit of computer storage capacity equal to 1024 bytes

Keypad   A pad with buttons used to request any kind of information (e.g., a pushbutton telephone)

Letterpress   A type of printing process in which the surface of metal type is inked and paper pressed against it to form an impression

Light pen   A hand–held photosensitive device that is connected to a computer and used with a cathode–ray tube for adding, deleting, or altering information

Linecaster   A machine that produces type in the form of metal slugs

Linotype   A typesetting machine that sets solid lines (or slugs) of metal type from circulating matrices

Lithography   The process of printing from a plane surface (i.e., a smooth stone or a metal plate) on which the image to be printed is ink–receptive and the blank area is ink–repellent

Logic–tree   An indexing system for the information stored in a database

Man–year   The work of one person in a year composed of a standard number of working days of standard length

Matrix (matrices)   In hot metal composition, the mold in which letters are cast; in cold type composition, the image of characters on film

Microfiche   A sheet of microfilm

Microwave   A very short electromagnetic wave

Morgue   A collection of reference works and files (such as newspaper clippings and photos) in a magazine or newspaper office

Multiplex   To send messages or signals by a system in which they are simultaneously transmitted on the same circuit or the same channel

Newsprint   A cheap machine–finished paper used mainly for newspapers

Off–line   Not being in continuous direct communication with a computer, or operating independently of a computer

Offset   A printing process whereby a design or page is photographically reproduced on a thin metal plate, which is curved to fit the revolving cylinders of the printing press

On–line   Being under the direct control of or in continuous direct communication with a computer

Packet–switching   Transmitting digitalized information at high speed so that the same transmission system, either wire or frequency, can be used by different messages at the same time. The data is sent in highly concentrated "packets" of bits.

Pay–TV   Individual television programs or special television services paid for by the viewer. They can be distributed by normal broadcast frequencies, direct from a satellite, or through coaxial or other cable systems.

Photocomposition   The composition of text by means of characters photographed on a film that serves as a basis for making (by photoengraving or photo–offset) a letterpress printing surface when developed.

Photoengraving   A metal relief plate prepared by etching a photographically produced image on the metal with acid, or the process by which this is made

Phototypesetting   See Photocomposition

Preprint   A printing issued in advance of book or periodical publication; especially, a portion of a larger work issued before publication of the whole

Rim editor   The copy editor who sits on the inside of a horseshoe–shaped copy desk

Saddle   Device put on the roller to which the plate is screwed before printing commences

Silicon wafer *See* Chip

Slot Editor   The copyreader who sits on the outer edge of a horseshoe–shaped copy desk

Stereotype   A metal printing plate cast from a paper matrix that is made from a page of type

Telemail Any system by which an item can be sent to a specified addressee by electronic means

Teletext The medium for distributing alphanumeric information through a radio or television frequency

Teletypesetter A machine that sets telegraphic news as it comes off the wire on either Linotype or Intertype machines

Time–sharing Simultaneous use of a central computer by different users at remote locations

Transducer A device that converts something (such as energy or a message) into another form

Transponder A radio or radar set that—upon receiving a signal (usually in the form of a coded series of pulses)— emits a radio signal of its own (which may also be coded)

Turtle A two–wheeled truck for making up and transporting a newspaper page prior to stereotyping

VariTyper A machine used for composing text matter (often in justified lines) that is like a typewriter but has changeable type

Vdt Video display terminal. The most common device for displaying computer–stored material

Videodisc A machine for playing audio–visual material from a plastic disc resembling a phonograph record

Videophone A telephone that transmits video as well as audio signals so that users can see each other

Viewdata British term for the domestic information system created by adding the transmission system of the common telephone to the display face of the common television. "Videotext" is the new internationally–designated term.

Voicewriter A device still under experimentation that converts spoken language into printed text by electronic means

Wave–guide system A system that makes use of a metal pipe or cylinder that propagates electromagnetic waves in radio and television transmission

Web–fed press A press that is fed paper from a continuous roll

Word processor A system that takes raw information and puts it in a formated form

ABBREVIATIONS

ADI   American Documentation Institute

AFL   American Federation of Labor

ANNECS   Automated Nikkei News Editing and Composing System

ANPA   American Newspaper Publishers' Association

ANTIOPE   Acquisition numérique et Télévisualisation d'Images organisées en Pages d'Ecriture

BDZV   Bundesverband Deutscher Zeitungsverleger

CATV   Community Antenna Television

CCD   Charge-coupling device

CCETT   Centre commun d'Etudes de Télévision et de Télécommunications

CEEFAX   See facts

CPU   Central Processing Unit

CRT   Cathode ray tube

CTS   Computerized type system

CUG   Closed user group

EBU   European Broadcasting Union

EDP   Electronic data processing

FPPS   Full page phototypesetting system

GTE   General Telephone & Electronics

IFRA   The RA at the end stands for Research Association. The I at the beginning is the first initial of INCA, which is the International Newspaper Color Association. The F is the first initial of FIEJ, which is the Fédération Internationale des Editeurs de Journeaux et Publications. Thus, IFRA is the INCA-FIEJ Research Association, sometimes known as the Newspaper Industries' Research Association (which does not provide the acronym).

IP Information provider

ITU International Telecommunications Union

ITV Independent Television

LDP Liberal Democratic Party of Japan

LED Light-emitting diode

LSI Large-scale integration

MEDLARS Medical Literature Analysis and Retrieval System

NELSON New Editing and Layout System of Newspapers

NHK Nippon Hoso Kyokai

NSK Nihon Shinbun Kyokai ·

NTT Nippon Telegraph and Telephone Public Corporation

OCR Optical character reader

ORACLE Optical Reception of Announcements by Coded Line Electronics

PCM Pulse-code modulation

PTT Postes Télégraphes, Téléphones (generic term for national postal and telecommunications administrations)

SBS Satellite Business Systems

TDF Télédiffusion de France

TTS Tele-typesetter

VDT Video display terminal

VRS Video Response System

INDEX

351

Not since the invention of moveable type has there been an innovation with so great a potential to revolutionize communications as computerization. *Goodbye Gutenberg*, developed in conjunction with a BBC program also broadcast in the United States on PBS, is the first analysis of the new realities of newspaper publishing.

Unlike other books recently written about the newspaper industry (Gay Talese's *The Kingdom and the Power*, David Halberstam's *The Powers that Be*), *Goodbye Gutenberg* ranges well beyond the people and politics of a glamourous industry. In choosing this broader perspective, Anthony Smith opens up a world of newspaper publishing of far greater substance, whose problems are part of the twentieth-century knowledge revolution.

Though its merits are still being bitterly debated in some quarters (*The Times* of London was shut down for nearly a year because of this very issue), computerization has in less than a decade turned an ailing newspaper industry into a healthy one. It has created a new role for the newspaper, enabling it to meet the challenge of radio and TV. It has the potential, Anthony Smith maintains, to alter the very quantity, nature, and texture of information.

"Writing and printing each in its time, symbolized and facilitated a great psychic transformation of mankind," Smith writes. "Today computer-assisted communication is bringing about a third great transition." The newspaper is the first of the traditional print media to undergo this new transition.

Some of the effects of computerization